Stanley A. Schultz and
Marguerite J. Schultz

The Tarantula Keeper's Guide

With 104 Photographs

Illustrations by Stanley A. Schultz

BARRON'S

Photo Credits
All photos by Stanley A. Schultz and Marguerite J. Schultz except photo on page 86 by Doug Maddison.

Note and Warning

This book deals with the care and husbandry of tarantulas. Even though many appear to be merely large, gentle spiders, they are still venomous animals, and enthusiasts keeping them as pets must acknowledge this fact. Even if the pet is well known to be gentle and harmless, the enthusiast must assume that the potential for a serious reaction always exists, and must be prepared to take appropriate action.

In addition, many of these animals are known to have urticating or irritating bristles. Even if the pet's bristles are known to be relatively benign and inoffensive the enthusiast must assume that, upon exposure to them, the potential exists for a serious reaction. Of particularly grave consequence is the trauma caused by the bristles in the human eye.

In any case, anyone suffering a reaction to the bristles or bitten by a pet is strongly counseled to seek immediate medical attention by a physician or emergency clinic. The responsibility for failure to do so must be borne totally by the person involved.

All through this book appear instructions and warnings concerning the care and husbandry of tarantulas, the conduct and behavior of their keepers, the use of various substances, mechanisms and appurtenances, and the recounting of the knowledge and expertise of the authors and others who have kept tarantulas for many years. The reader and enthusiast is strongly admonished to heed those instructions and warnings.

Tarantulas have been kept as pets for only a few decades. There is much that is still not known about them. That theme is stated repeatedly throughout the book. The keeper of a pet tarantula must acknowledge that these creatures are still wild animals and must treat them as such. Keeping any animal as a pet requires a great deal of responsibility. Keeping a wild animal as a pet absolutely commands that responsibility.

If for any reason, a pet tarantula can no longer be kept or adequately maintained, the keeper is strongly urged to give it to either another competent enthusiast or a responsible pet shop. **UNDER NO CIRCUMSTANCES IS THE TARANTULA TO BE TURNED LOOSE INTO THE WILD!**

All inquiries should be addressed to:
Barron's Educational Series, Inc.
250 Wireless Boulevard
Hauppauge, New York 11788
http://www.barronseduc.com

International Standard Book No. 0-7641-0076-9

Library of Congress Catalog Card No. 97-36904

Library of Congress Cataloging-in-Publication Data
Schultz, Stanley A.
    The tarantula keeper's guide / Stanley A. Schultz,
Marguerite J. Schultz.
       p.   cm.
    Includes bibliographical references (p. 274) and index.
    ISBN 0-7641-0076-9
    1. Tarantulas as pets. 2. Tarantulas. I. Schultz,
Marguerite J. II. Title.
    SF459.T37S38   1998
    639'.7—dc21   97-36904
                           CIP

Printed in China

Contents

Prologue

Prepare Yourself

You are about to embark upon a long and winding journey. You will go to places that you cannot now even imagine. You will become familiar with a group of creatures more alien than any you can imagine, and you will come to know them almost as well as you know the family dog. In the process of learning about these creatures, you will come to learn an immense amount about yourself as well.

Best of all, this is real, not a figment of someone's overactive imagination. You will return from this journey a much wiser person. You will never look at the world the same way again.

Preface

What the reader now holds is an interim report of the state of the art of keeping tarantulas as pets. Surely someone, probably one of this book's readers, will write another book extending and elaborating on the knowledge and techniques described here.

This is good. Although these huge spiders are known from only a few fossils just a few tens of millions of years old, it is probable that they have existed far longer than that. Their precursors predate the dinosaurs by many million years and were among the first animals to venture onto the land. They deserve that attention and credit.

This edition is dedicated to these giants of the spider world and to the people who have worked long and hard to learn more about them.

This book is written for several reasons.

1. The first edition contained several fundamental errors that could not be corrected before going to press. This second edition is written in an attempt to set those errors straight.

2. Much new and useful information is now available, and is presented here.

3. This book is intended as a guide for the first-time tarantula keeper, to supply all important basics of caring for the newfound pet.

4. This book is intended to also meet the demands of the veteran, and, therefore, it must hold much advanced information such as details of tarantula biology and information about breeding them.

5. This book is intended to beget more of those mad spider people, for they are the best hope for the survival of these spiders.

Because of all these, the book tends to be rather more intense than most people would want. Fear not. The end result of more than a third of a billion years of evolution can't be expected to be simple. These are amazingly complex creatures, and, therefore, any meaningful treatment of them is also bound to be complex. For the novice, being able to quote all this information from rote isn't necessary to be able to take good care of a pet. But if it is needed, the information is here, ready whenever the cover is opened.

The more advanced, technical information presented here is a starting point for the experienced aficionado. These people are encouraged to follow the gospel for now, then elaborate or experiment when a need or potential benefit arises. Thus, progress is made in understanding and caring for these enigmatic creatures.

The original edition of this *guide* had a sole author. This edition now has two. Stan has now officially been joined as coauthor by his wife, Marguerite. Thus, she will now receive the credit that is due her for all the years that she has labored in the pursuit of knowledge about these creatures.

The authors would like to acknowledge the help and support of everyone who contributed to this book. Alas, there is not enough space, for they are legion! A few of those people are:

Shane Berger
Gio Bianchini
Barbara and Karen Bigley
Franca Bonari
Greg Bracken
Jason Brooks
Bryant Capiz
Steve Chandler
Ian Dunn
Mr. and Mrs. Willie Edwards
Margaret and Kevin Elsdon
Wendy Folk
Mike and Colleen Fostaty
Martha Gonzales-Cardona
Mark and Rhonda Hart
Ralph Henning
Bonnie and Todd Hlady
Wes and Cory Hunt
Takuya Inoue
Carie Kerr
K. David and Cathy Kerr
Robert Kerr, Sr.
Sandrine Launois
Don and Nancy Lounds
Ben Luyendyk
Doug Maddison
Pierrino Mascariño
Laura Neilsen
Tom Nelson
Jeff Newbury
Margaret Olive
Steven F. Perry
Ernesto Rodriguez
Marty Schafer
Michael Schafer
Crystal and Greg Schoeler
Devon Seitz
Scott Shore
Calvin Slimmon
Christian Straus
Barney Tomberlin
Andrew Van Velzen
Jim Williams
Roger Williams
Byron Wise

There are a few whose help was crucial to completion and success of this book. We list them here for special recognition.

Dr. Robert Gale Breene III, of the American Tarantula Society, must be given special thanks for critiquing the manuscript. Without his review this book would have been just another mediocre book on tarantulas instead of the reference that it is.

Dr. Wei Xiang Dong is to be highly commended for his patience and expertise in the preparation and photography of the scanning electron micrographs. Without his uncanny ability to manipulate and cajole the often recalcitrant machines, these remarkable photographs could not have been made.

Rob Kerr, Jr., has helped immeasurably with the care and maintenance of the spiders in the authors' collection. For that, he deserves a special thanks.

Miep O'Brien deserves special mention for her help with the dictionaries.

Rick C. West must be gratefully thanked for his help with many of the technical details of this edition.

Last, but by far not the least, we must recognize Dr. John E. Remmers for all he has done, directly and indirectly to make this book the very best possible.

The authors appreciate comments and questions by readers. Any readers who wish to communicate are encouraged to contact us through either the publisher or the American Tarantula Society (see page 248).

Calgary, Alberta, Canada
July 4, 1997

Introduction

The Mythical, Mystical Tarantula

There is something mysterious about tarantulas. They startle people. They are creatures of the night, magically appearing and then disappearing into the dark again. They have long, hairy legs and appear huge and forbidding. But foremost, they are spiders!

Because of this, it is natural that superstitious folk should credit them with all sorts of sinister properties. And where fact does not exist, myth runs rampant. As a result, tarantula lore is a very fertile field.

The very name *tarantula* is a double misnomer. There is a spider, belonging to a very distantly related group, that became notorious during the fifteenth century. This spider, named for the Italian town of Taranto (Tarantum to people of the Renaissance), is credited with causing a strange disease called Tarantism (Gertsch 1979). By legend, the bite of this spider was blamed for the disease, and anyone having been bitten was obliged, as the only cure, to engage in a frenzied, feverish dance, a tarantella.

Now, several centuries later, and in more moderate times, authorities suspect that the tarantella was merely an excuse for some limited revelry in a time when fun was ruthlessly suppressed.

As a result of the superstition concerning tarantism, any large spider was suspect and much feared by the peasantry. As Renaissance explorers probed the far reaches the world, they would return with fearsome tales of giant spiders, *tarantulas,* through the tropics, subtropics, and warmer temperate zones. Gradually, English-speaking people, especially North Americans, applied this name to a group of much larger and more spectacular spiders than the one from Europe, forgetting almost entirely about Taranto and tarantism. This myth of large, dangerous spiders still persists even today. Interestingly, Europeans often refer to our tarantulas as *mygale* or *Vogelspinnen* (singular: *Vogelspinne*) saving the term *tarantula* for the original spider.

The name *Mygale* is also a mistake. It was first used by a prominent naturalist, Baron Georges Cuvier, to name a kind of shrew, a small mammal that resembles a mouse. However, another prominent biologist, Baron Charles Walckenaer, created it independently in 1797 to describe those huge, hairy spiders that were caught in the tropics. Thus, the entire group of spiders became known as Mygalomorphae. But, because the name had been used previously for the mammals, it was invalid as a name for the spiders. We are, however, still saddled with mygalomorph spiders, even in the scientific literature.

In the early eighteenth century, an aristocratic Swiss lady by the name of

Engraving of a tarantula eating a bird.

Madame Maria Sibylla Mérian took a Caribbean cruise to (among other places) Suriname, in South America. In this period, the Caribbean Islands and South America were exceedingly primitive and uncivilized. A trip such as hers was fraught with much danger. Aristocratic ladies did not go running off to such wild, barbarous places. Their obligation was in the home with their husband and family, or attending proper social functions.

Madame Mérian published several accounts of her travels, the last appearing in 1771 (Mérian 1771). Her excursion gained her profuse notoriety and her reports considerable rebuke. She suffered particularly vicious verbal abuse because she had the unmitigated audacity to publish a woodcut of a tarantula eating a small bird. For the zoologists of the day, this was unthinkable heresy. Spiders, according to prevalent scientific belief, most definitely did *not* eat vertebrates! As a result, she was publicly denounced. Not until 1910 did anyone of scientific authority actually confirm that under some circumstances at least, some tarantulas do eat birds (Bates 1910). Madame Mérian was vindicated, and a radical, new concept was bestowed upon us.

Even then the circumstances under which they may eat birds, whether the birds were live, dead, or in between, or what portion of their diet birds represent, is still much debated. See page 75 for a more thorough discussion of the feeding habits of tarantulas.

This is the origin of the names *bird-eater* and *bird spider* in English, and *Vogelspinne* in German. Unfortunately, these names have given people the impression that tarantulas must be fed birds, a wholly untrue and preposterous concept to be sure.

Additional illustrations from old texts are reproduced here as examples of the fascination that science and the laity had with these incredible spiders. To this day, tabloid newspapers, pet dealers and circus side shows alike attempt to amaze prospective patrons with their bird-eating spiders.

To make matters even more complicated, there is another animal, distantly related to spiders, and appearing at least as fearsome, that arachnologists have placed in a genus named *Tarantula,* but is neither a spider nor possesses a

> **A** discussion of the methods for naming tarantulas, and their many idiosyncrasies, is covered in Chapter 2: The Name of the Tarantula.

venom. (The term *genus* will be discussed more thoroughly on page 62.)

For now we will simply state that what we mean by the term *tarantula* is a collection of eight hundred or more kinds of extremely large, hairy spiders that usually live in burrows, and leave a more precise definition for Chapter 2: The Name of the Tarantula.

The laity often confuses tarantulas with the widow spiders and the malmignatte of southern Europe, thus enhancing the myth. Even worse, there are a few kinds of tarantulas and some of their close allies that really are dangerous (Bucherl 1968; Maratic 1967), thus adding fuel to the fire.

Tarantulas have also received a lot of bad press in the movies. Many movies and television programs starring such noted actors as Sean Connery, The Three Stooges, Harrison Ford, and William Shatner, have featured tarantulas as menaces to civilization or humanity. *The Tarantula That Ate Tokyo* is a long-standing joke among horror-movie devotees. The fact is that these movies play with the ignorance and fears passed on for generations by unenlightened people. Nobody would pay to see the movie *The Beagle That Ate Boston* since everybody knows what a beagle really is. Few know tarantulas as well.

Almost every property attributed to tarantulas by these movies is in direct contradiction to reality. Although such movies may be recommended as entertainment, they must also be recommended as detailed accounts of what tarantulas are not.

But, it doesn't stop there. The great German composer, F. W. Nietzsche, in *Also Sprach Zarathustra,* uses the line "Tarantulas are ye unto me, and secretly revengeful ones" as a reference to disloyalty or untrustworthiness. The mental-

Engraving of a tarantula eating a bird.

ity of a tarantula is such that the concepts of revenge and loyalty are totally alien, and therefore meaningless. Once accustomed to handling (not too difficult a task with many kinds), they are at least as trustworthy as the family dog.

The following two stories, recounted by William Baerg, illustrate the magnitude of the ignorance and superstition of rural folk regarding tarantulas. The first story concerns a prevalent disease of horses in Mexico.

> "The tarantula climbs over the hoof, cuts off the hair in a narrow strip surrounding the leg. If allowed to do this undisturbed, no damage results. (In another version the damage comes incidental to the cutting of the hair.) If disturbed, the tarantula bites and this is followed by the loss of the hoof. It is

Engraving of a tarantula eating a bird.

believed that the spiders use the hair thus acquired in the construction of a nest. According to other variations of the legend the loss of the hoof is caused by the urine of the spider, *mierda de araña,* also by the *excreta de araña*" (Baerg 1938).

In truth, the condition is probably brought on by allowing casual scratches on the horses' legs to become soiled with mud contaminated with urine, feces, and a bacterium, *Bacillis necrophorus,* during wet weather. This bacterium is known to infect minor cuts and scratches in these circumstances, causing a condition similar to that described by legend.

Indeed, many common people in rural Mexico call the tarantula *hierba,* meaning weed, and *mata-caballo,* meaning horse killer (Baerg 1929).

This second little story illustrates the magnitude of ignorance and hysteria possible even in the rural United States of 1929.

"The high degree of fear exhibited towards this innocent creature is well illustrated in a story that recently appeared in one of our daily newspa-pers. A man driving along in a Ford touring car suddenly realized that a huge tarantula had somehow gotten into the car. Without attempting to stop the car, he leaped out over the door. The car ran over an embankment and was wrecked, but the man consid-ered himself lucky to be alive and unharmed" (Baerg 1929).

The following list of tall stories about tarantulas, and told with straight faces, is offered for the reader's entertainment and enlightenment.

"I almost died from that tarantula's bite!" Tarantula bites are relatively rare. When tarantula keepers are bitten it is usually because the attack was pro-voked, or the keeper attempted to han-dle a tarantula improperly. Even if a tarantula does bite, it seldom injects venom (a so-called dry bite). And, even if venom is injected, the effect is hardly worth mentioning. Nearly all serious spi-der bites recorded in North America are either by one of the widows (*Latrodectus* species), the Recluses (*Loxosceles* species), or in the Pacific Northwest, a European import, the Hobo Spider *(Tegenaria agrestis).* In fact, there are probably fewer than one hundred dan-gerous kinds of spiders (including taran-tulas) worldwide, and fewer than a dozen of these are tarantulas or their brethren.

To illustrate the point, please con-sider these questions. How many of your family members have been made ill or have died of a spider's bite? How many of these were tarantula bites? How many of your neighbors? When was the last time the local newspaper reported a death due to a spider? Was it a taran-tula? Considering the number of tarantu-las sold in pet shops, if they were really that dangerous, would you not expect *some* mention of the fact?

Out of ignorance, and with the help of horror movies, the laity persists in confusing tarantulas with dangerous kinds of spiders even though there is little resemblance. Tarantula bites will be discussed more thoroughly on page 142.

"That tarantula jumped twenty feet (six meters)." This is one of the more prevalent myths that one finds among the laity. As will be explained more fully later in this book, most tarantulas are physically incapable of launching themselves more than a few centimeters. Even if long distance jumps were possible, their body walls would not be able to absorb the impact as they landed. They would splat like rotten tomatoes! One impetuous leap would end it all.

There are a very few significant exceptions to the no-jump rule, however. In the New World tropics, India and neighboring islands, and in Africa, there are a few kinds of tarantulas (not necessarily related to each other) that live entirely in trees, bushes, and tall grasses (so-called arboreal tarantulas). Some will even take up residence under the eaves and in thatched and clay tile roofs of buildings. The total number of these kinds is probably less than fifty, however, so that they comprise a decided minority among tarantulas. Because these tarantulas ordinarily live far above ground, and indeed seldom come to ground, they have developed habit patterns which allow them to jump and often glide with great ease and relative safety. It is important to note, however, that they cannot jump upwards any more than any other tarantula. To reach any altitude beyond a few centimeters, they must climb first, then jump and glide to a new position some distance away.

"I swear, that tarantula was a yard (ninety centimeters) across!" As of this writing, the largest tarantula of official record, *Theraphosa blondi*, only spanned twenty-five centimeters (ten inches, Gertsch 1979), was a male, and therefore, had much longer legs and a lighter body than its corresponding female. Even then, it was truly formidable to be sure! Recently, these authors have heard anecdotal reports of other kinds that exceed that size. *Lasiodora parahybana* and *Pseudotheraphosa apophysis* are now believed to reach leg spans of thirty-three centimeters (thirteen inches). We anxiously await formal articles reporting these enormous spiders in the scientific journals.

Because of the limitations of their construction, it is doubtful that any tarantula will be found that is significantly larger. In the excitement of the moment, an objective size appraisal cannot be expected from the casual observer who is startled by a huge spider. This is especially true for those who endure a deep-seated fear of them. Spider stories, like fish stories, tend to grow with time and with the gullibility of the audience.

"The tarantula bit him while he sat on the latrine!" Although the terrestrial tarantulas are capable of climbing, they certainly aren't comfortable at it. They are just too heavy to efficiently scale vertical surfaces, much less hang from the underside of a latrine seat. Furthermore, latrines and privies are among the most inhospitable places imaginable for tarantulas to be found, for their lifestyles are such that there is nothing in such a habitat to attract them and everything to repel them. If a tarantula is ever found in a latrine, it is there entirely by accident. A more thorough discussion of bites and biting will be presented on page 142.

A few tarantulas are arboreal and, in areas where they are common, may be found under roof overhangs and may even blunder into a latrine. However, they are typically not aggressively vicious (although some will bite if touched) and probably would not account for this myth. Wandering male tarantulas of some kinds will occasionally seek refuge from predators in buildings or by climbing up into bushes or low shrubs during broad daylight. It is conceivable that one might stray into a latrine, but again, this would be rare. As before, the probability of being bitten by one of them is so small as to be irrelevant.

Typical latrine bites, and those in other outbuildings as well, are characteristic of the bites of the widow spiders. Not only are these far more common in such situations, but the symptoms match far better (Parrish 1959).

"The female tarantula always eats her consort after mating." This is probably a direct consequence of a similar myth regarding the widow spiders. In reality, in both groups of spiders, the male is seldom eaten. In fact, in most spiders, widows and tarantulas included, the male may remain in the vicinity and mate with the same female several times!

"The stevedore was attacked by the tarantula as it crept out of the bananas." There was a time when fruit and vegetables from the tropics were transported virtually as they were plucked from the tree or vine. In this cargo, many animals were also transported as stowaways. When the ships arrived in port to unload, exotic crea-

tures were a frequent source of terror to the dock and warehouse workers. This was quite justifiable. The snake might be a fer-de-lance, the spider a *Phoneutria fera*. Both are dangerous. The workers seldom took the time to distinguish between the fer-de-lance and a harmless boa constrictor, between *P. fera* and a harmless tarantula. All were ruthlessly killed. Subsequently, these people then felt compelled to pass the tales of their bravery and close escape on to any who would listen. The stories spread, the embellishments multiplied.

Modern methods of harvesting, packing, and shipping have largely eliminated this problem. The stories, however, continue, no doubt fueled by the very rare stowaways that manage to survive the voyage.

It wasn't until the twentieth century that some people really began to understand the tarantula. We are still pitifully ignorant about many aspects of their lives and lifestyles as we approach the beginning of the twenty-first century. It is sincerely hoped that this book will help.

Will the Real Tarantula Please Stand Up?

The real tarantula is a melange of surprises. Forget all those absurd stories. The real tarantula is far more bizarre, far more fantastic.

Tarantulas have their roots buried in the mists of time. We simply don't know in what strange primeval forests, swamps, or veldts they originated. They arose from a stock of animals that split from the more familiar branches of the animal kingdom more than half a billion years ago. We have only a few haunting clues to trace their evolution.

Their forebears evolved along a path that, though delicately intertwined with the rest of life on Earth, has remained distinctly different and unique. Their anatomies are outlandishly unconventional, their physiologies unexpectedly complex, their lifestyles bizarre in the extreme. They chose to do it *their* way, and they have succeeded admirably.

As with most other spiders, most tarantulas aren't especially aggressive, dangerous, or dreadful. In fact, many of them will become docile enough to allow themselves to be picked up and handled freely by children. And, once picked up properly, many of the remainder will submit to being held, once in the hand. The enthusiast is urged to read the subsection "Handling," in Chapter 5: The Pet Tarantula before attempting this, however.

They produce virtually no noise, no odor, no mess. They do not come home with a litter of young every few months, shed hair on the sofa, track mud into the parlor, or leave dead mice on your back stoop. They exist in a very special sort of world, accepting life for what it is, expecting little more than a few crickets a month.

Therein lies the real mystery. So astoundingly different when first encountered, these creatures seem so familiar once we overcome our initial astonishment and apprehnsion. What are they, really?

It is hoped that as this book is read, that question will be answered and their real value appreciated.

Once and for all then:

Tarantulas do not ravish fair maidens!

Tarantulas do not cause tarantism!

Tarantulas do not embalm people or towns!

And lastly,

Tarantulas did not eat Tokyo!

Tarantulas are the fall guys. Misnamed, falsely accused, slandered, and convicted without a trial, these giants of the spider world still persist, oblivious to it all, waiting at the mouths of their burrows for only another beetle.

Fortunately, we are learning. There is still hope.

PART ONE
The Scientific Tarantula

While these huge spiders have been known by primitive people for tens of millennia, our science has recognized them for little more than two hundred and fifty years. Only now, after all these centuries, are we beginning to understand the basics of tarantula biology.

Chapter One
The Physical Tarantula

Anatomy and Physiology

Tarantulas belong to a vast group of very successful animals called arthropods. Of the approximately ten to thirty million kinds of animals on Earth (this estimate varies widely with the authority), more than ninety percent may be arthropods. No other group of animals on Earth boasts more kinds. Few boast more individuals.

Although no arthropods really seem conventional by our standards, one subdivision of that group, the arachnids, have developed such outlandish shapes, bizarre lifestyles, unorthodox physiologies, and exotic modes of reproduction that they seem to have evolved on an alien planet. The arachnids are arguably the most preposterous of a group of already outrageous organisms. The spiders, a further subdivision of that group, are no exception.

The truth is that they did evolve on this planet, as did we; and ultimately, lost far back in the mists of time, we probably share a common ancestor. Almost two-thirds of a billion years ago our family tree split. The arachnids, "doing their own thing," took an evolutionary branch going in one direction, and our more immediate ancestors took a branch in another.

We tend to look at them from a very self-centered perspective, not necessarily a valid point of view. The question is really which line of evolution is more bizarre, ours or the spiders'?

External Features

Exoskeleton. As with most other arthropods, tarantulas possess a thick hide or shell called an exoskeleton. The exoskeleton has been around for considerably longer than half a billion years, possibly longer. Its underlying principle is undeniably the most successful and widely used structural system ever developed on this planet. It is the most fundamental characteristic of the entire group of arthropods, and it influences virtually every aspect of their lives.

Among its many functions are that it defines the arthropod's shape, and the shape of each of its external appendages and organs down to the minutest detail. It serves as points of attachment for the majority of the arthropod's muscles. It impedes water loss in terrestrial animals like spiders. It serves as armor, preventing mechanical injury to the delicate internal organs. It serves as a barrier to infectious agents, e.g. bacteria and fungi. The exoskeleton's extensions (bristles, setae, trichobothria, see page 18 for a discussion) are sensory structures, sensing a wide variety of things around the animal. Frequently, its color and adornments serve as identifying markers or warning labels for the animal.

This exoskeleton, for the most part, comes in the form of a box made of a set of interlocking plates, or a set of jointed tubes. Less commonly, it may be a leathery bag held taut by internal pressure. Superficially, the exoskeleton resembles a medieval knight's suit of armor with each plate having a unique shape, position, function, and name.

The exoskeleton has a complex layered construction with many folds, ridges, and indentations to provide strength, allow for the attachment of muscles, and allow for the movement of appendages. Its exterior is usually bedecked with a truly bewildering array of sense organs and defensive bristles. It may be transparent, pigmented, or bear iridescent areas that allow for literally more colors than the rainbow.

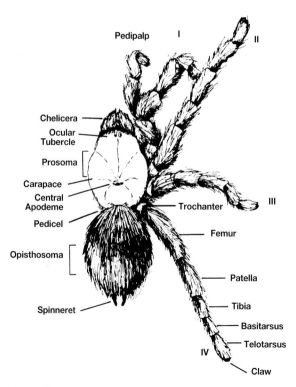

Tarantula anatomy, dorsal aspect.

The exoskeleton is composed of many different substances. Among the more important is chitin. Chemically, chitin is a nitrogenous polysaccharide. Polysaccharides are huge, complex supermolecules made of interconnected strings or matrices of sugar molecules. Associated with chitin is a protein called sclerotin. Like chitin, sclerotin is actually a supermolecule made by cross-bonding simpler protein molecules into a vast matrix. These cross-linkages supply the exoskeleton with its hardness.

Another very important component of the tarantula's exoskeleton is a waxy coating on the outside. This layer of wax retards water loss, preventing desiccation.

The Body. Tarantulas have no head, thorax, or abdomen in the same sense as humans. Their bodies are divided into two obvious parts, the forward prosoma and the rearward opisthosoma. These are connected by a narrow hourglass constriction called the pedicel (sometimes also called the peduncle or petiolus), which is actually a part of the opisthosoma. A little practice at pronouncing them will make even the novice sound like a professional.

Many arachnologists consider the prosoma to actually be a fused head and thorax (cephalothorax) and the opisthosoma to be an abdomen. However, this suggests the same body plan and organ arrangement as found in man and other vertebrates. As we shall see shortly, this is not so. The organization of the tarantula's internal organs does not follow the conventions assumed by these labels; therefore, to sidestep the debate, we use the terms prosoma and opisthosoma instead.

The dorsal (on the back) plate of the prosoma is called a carapace (tergum or dorsal tergum in some books). In the center, the carapace usually bears a little pit or dent. Although this area appears as a depression on the exterior, it points down like a little stalactite or icicle on the inside. It is called the central apodeme (also dorsal groove, median fovea, thoracic groove, or tergal apodeme). More will be said about apodemes on page 34. This spot is where the carapace is deeply infolded to allow a firm place for muscle attachment. The entire carapace is thickened, heavily trussed and arched to sustain the force of those contracting muscles.

Often, the central apodeme and the carapace are decorated with radiating lines or grooves which may be of a contrasting color. The central apodeme itself may appear as an oblong pit with no obvious curve, or curved with the tips pointing somewhat forward or backward. And, in at least two groups of tarantulas, the genera *Ceratogyrus* and *Sphaerobothria,* the pit is replaced by a small growth that resembles a horn.

The character of the central apodeme is used by some authorities as a means of differentiating between the kinds of tarantulas. Unfortunately, there is some confusion about the exact terminology used to describe it, and the enthusiast can easily be mislead or confused. Because this may be an important identifying characteristic, we will dwell a moment on it.

If the central apodeme shows no obvious curve it is called transverse by most authorities, and if the ends curve forward it may be called either crescentic or procurved. However, if the ends curve backward it may be termed either recurved or procurved, depending on the authority. This conflict of definitions is not easily resolvable. The reader must examine the remainder of the ref-

Puzzled by scientific names? Read Chapter 2: The Name of the Tarantula and Appendix A: Tarantula Species as Pets for explanations and a cross-reference between scientific names and common names.

erence closely to deduce the meaning. Generally, if a definition is lacking and the authority speaks of both crescentic and procurved apodemes, we may presume that, in this instance, crescentic means bending forward, and procurved means bending backward. If, however, the authority uses both procurved and recurved, we should assume that the intention is for procurved to mean ends pointing forward and recurved to mean ends pointing backward. This is yet another instance where these animals have confused even the experts.

Although the present authors are in no position to read semantics or definitions to greater authorities, for the record it should be pointed out that the dictionary definitions are procurved: ends pointing forward; recurved: ends pointing backward.

Ceratogyrus dolichocephalus.

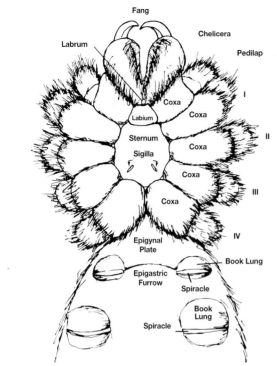

Labrum
Fang
Chelicera
Pedilap
Coxa
Coxa
I
Labium
Sternum
Coxa
II
Sigilla
Coxa
Coxa
III
Coxa
IV
Epigynal
Plate
Book Lung
Epigastric
Furrow
Spiracle
Book
Lung
Spiracle

Tarantula anatomy, ventral aspect.

The shield on the underside of the tarantula, on the opposite side as the carapace (on the chest, so to speak) is called the sternum. There are little, oval, bare spots called sigilli (singular: sigillum) on the sternum near the bases of the legs. Their purpose, if one exists, is a complete mystery.

Both the carapace and the sternum are bounded by the basal segments of the legs, called coxae (singular: coxa). All of these parts are joined by pliable membranes called the pleurae (singular: pleura) that allow the legs to move.

The opisthosoma is usually globose (bulging, round) in well-fed and watered individuals, and is covered with a thin, flexible, leathery exoskeleton. It is clothed with a dense layer of bristles

that will be discussed on page 18. The opisthosoma possesses only one obvious plate on the venter (bottom surface) toward the front, the epigynum, the epigyne, or epigynal plate. It is bounded by the pedicel toward the front, the forward pair of book lungs on the sides, and a groove at its rear margin. Farther back are another pair of book lungs, two pairs of spinnerets, and the anus. All of these will be discussed in length as we proceed.

Appendages. Tarantulas have eight pairs of appendages on their bodies. The very first pair on the front end are chelicerae (singular: chelicera). Although these might be homologous with the mandibles or jaws of insects and crustaceans, they now serve a somewhat different purpose.

Eons ago, on spiders' precursors, these were probably leglike or pincerlike appendages used for manipulating food. On our modern scorpions, for instance, they are still small pincerlike appendages. However, as spiders evolved, these became modified to resemble a single, heavy, finger joint with a clawlike fang hinged to the end, somewhat reminiscent of a cat's toe and claw. These fangs are stout, curved, hypodermic needles with passageways leading back up into the chelicerae to the venom glands. In present-day spiders, they are highly efficient weapons, used for subduing and (for some kinds) masticating (chewing) prey.

Even so, the tarantula uses its chelicerae and fangs for a variety of other purposes, as well. In their nuptial embrace, most tarantula kinds use the female's fangs as handlebars for stabilization. Later, the female will use them for holding and manipulating the eggsac. If a tarantula struggles to escape a presumed predator it may

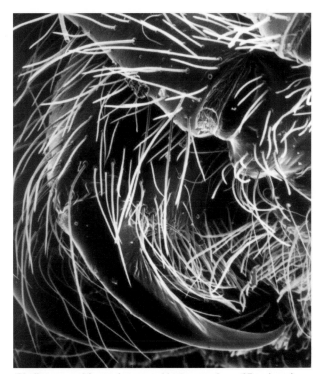

Chelicerae and fang of a second instar exuvium of Brachypelma albopilosum. *Baby tarantulas have significantly fewer bristles than their adult counterparts, allowing a clear view of many of the details of their exoskeleton not visible in the adult. The straight line distance from the base to the tip of the fag is approximately 0.6 millimeter (0.024 inches).*

resort to using its fangs as additional graspers as it attempts to crawl from harm's way. Indeed, the authors have had a tarantula (*Aphonopelma* species, see page 155) that was so severely crippled after a disastrous molt that its legs were useless for walking. It resorted to pulling itself along with its fangs! (Molting will be explained on page 22, and more will be said of this individual on page 155.

Older books and scientific papers sometimes refer to the chelicerae as falces (singular: falx), mandibles or jaws, and a fang as an unguis (plural: ungues).

Tarantulas do not have antennae. Instead, as the chelicerae evolved into weapons, the next pair of appendages assumed their tactile duties and added a few extra for good measure. These next appendages are called the pedipalps. Spiders' pedipalps and insects' antennae are another case of analogy rather than homology, however, and should not be confused with each other.

Although they resemble legs, the pedipalps have only one claw at the tip rather than two, and they appear to have one less segment (*article* in some books). As we shall see shortly, the latter is not really true.

The pedipalps act as feelers, probing and guiding as the animal moves or eats. In mature male spiders they have an additional purpose. They are secondary sexual organs. More about this will be said on pages 43, 80, and 203.

Enlargement of the fang tip of a second instar exuvium of Brachypelma albopilosum *to show the pore leading to the venom duct. The pore is approximately twenty microns (0.0008 inches) in diameter.*

lae, patellas), tibia (tibiae, tibias), tarsus (tarsi) and pretarsus and claw (Snodgrass 1967). Some authorities, particularly in the nineteenth century, use the term palp or palpus (palps or palpi) to mean pedipalp. Likewise, maxilla (maxillae, maxillas) is sometimes used to indicate the pedipalpal coxa.

The next four pairs of appendages are the walking legs. Tarantulas have four pairs of legs (total of eight) just like all other spiders. But, because the legs and pedipalps resemble each other very closely, tarantulas appear to have five pairs of legs. The legs are numbered from front to rear, one to four, usually with Roman numerals. They appear to have eight segments rather than seven. This is because one segment, the tarsus, is superficially divided into two false or pseudosegments. (This is disputed by some arachnologists, however.) They are called pseudosegments because they are not separated by a true joint, do not have their own driving muscles, and are not independently movable. Starting from the prosoma and moving outward, the segments are called coxa, trochanter, femur, patella, tibia, tarsus (basitarsus + telotarsus), and pretarsus and claw (Snodgrass 1967).

Historically, there has been much confusion about the naming of these segments, with various authors using alternate names. One source of confusion arises from the fact that there are different numbers of segments in the legs of many arthropods (e.g., trilobites, horseshoe crabs, crustaceans, insects, centipedes, and the chelicerates, including the arachnids). Not only does the count vary with the kind of animal, it sometimes varies with different leg pairs on the same animal, and even with different growth stages on a given animal.

The bases of the pedipalps may be toothed or ridged to aid in masticating (chewing) food. The bristles on them are used for straining the larger particles from their liquid food. Each pedipalp is composed of six tubular segments separated by pliable, leathery hinges (the pleural membranes), plus a seventh (also attached with a pleural membrane) that is more like an end plate bearing two pads of bristles and the claw. Starting from the prosoma, these segments are named coxa (coxae, coxas), trochanter (trochanters), femur (femora, femurs), patella (patel-

Arthropod anatomists try to name the body parts with uniform names between all these groups. This derives from an underlying presumption that all arthropods arose from a common ancestor, a presumption that is now strongly suspected of being untrue (Meglitsch 1972, Barnes 1980). The anatomist may unjustifiably be attempting to make arachnids in general, and spiders in particular, fit a stereotype that doesn't apply. To accomplish this, the names must be juggled to account for the differences. When the segments are named from the body outward, new names must either be added to account for any additional segments, or deleted to make the names match any analogous segments in each group of arthropods. Not even the experts agree on the character of this juggling, and the reader is cautioned against being confused by it.

The end of leg I showing the scopula pads and the paired claws on the pretarsus.

By way of example, in one scheme for naming the leg segments, metatarsus is used to mean basitarsus, tarsus is used for telotarsus (the same for patella, tibia, metatarsus, tarsus, and so on), and the pretarsus and claw is not recognized as a segment (Foelix 1982). In another system, protarsus is used in place of basitarsus and tarsus is used for telotarsus. And Pocock (1900), one of the world's most distinguished classical arachnologists, states, "In the palpus (the small front leg), the protarsus is absent." When the experts are unable to come to a consensus, what is the student to do? Answer: Be aware that a great deal of confusion existed in the past and still exists today. Then, employ some intuition when interpreting books and articles, even those written by the experts.

Many tarantulas have peculiar lined markings on the patellae and tibiae that have been likened to epaulets. On several kinds (e.g., *Aphonopelma seemanni*) they are colored to contrast markedly with the rest of the animal. The authors are unaware if these markings hold any fundamental significance to tarantulas. Do they mark the attachment points of muscles? Do they aid the female in recognizing the male? Are they merely decorative? Do they have any purpose?

Aphonopelma seemanni. *Several color forms exist, from light beige through chestnut to striking black and white.*

All of the appendages discussed so far have been attached to the tarantula's prosoma. The last two pairs of appendages are the only ones attached to the opisthosoma. These are the silk-spinning spinnerets. The discussion of silk will be deferred to page 46. However, the spinnerets require some comment here.

Fossilized spiders and their precursors are very rare. Because of this, we do not have a clear understanding of how the spinnerets or the silk-spinning facility evolved. (And a lot of other things as well, it must be stressed.) Many arachnologists hypothesize that the spinnerets were originally leglike appendages the same as chelicerae and fangs. However, these evolved into something other than manipulative organs. In fact, Marples (1967) offers the hypothesis that there were originally two sets of four spinnerets each, a total of eight.

It is presumed that secretory glands were associated with these appendages, and that these glands eventually evolved into silk glands. Most living segmented worms possess nephridia, primitive excretory glands. Typically, these occur in pairs, one pair per body segment, and each pair commonly opens on a neighboring body segment near to, or actually in the joint where the appendages attach to the body. It is perhaps not too difficult to imagine that in the dim reaches of prehistory there once existed a group of primitive creatures, too evolved to be called segmented worms, but too primitive to properly be called arachnids, in which certain sets of these organs began to suppress their excretory function. Instead, after untold generations, these glands enhanced the secretion of other substances that eventually became silk. It would have been a relatively simple matter for these openings to migrate, generation after generation, down the length of the associated appendage, especially considering the number of generations involved. At least one biologist has conjectured that these primitive creatures may have developed this silk-spinning facility to line and stabilize their marine burrows (R. G. Breene, personal communication).

With the passing of countless generations, it is also not too far-fetched to imagine that only the last four pairs of appendages evolved in this manner in one subgroup of these protoarachnids. These were in reality, the protospiders. The rest, as they say, is history.

Many professional arachnologists hold this hypothesis about the origin of the silk glands and spinnerets, or one similar to it. However, because fossil evidence is so meager, no such hypothesis has been substantiated, leaving professional arachnologists to worry endlessly over it.

Tarantulas' silk glands and associated structures are not particularly sophisticated compared to other spiders that can often spin more than one kind of silk, and that have elaborate structures for forming and manipulating silk (Apstein 1889).

Of the four pairs of spinnerets on the most primitive spiders, only the last two pairs are still present in tarantulas (Marples 1967). The anterior pair is very short and appears only as a pair of indistinct pads. The posterior pair, however, is much longer and resembles a pair of very delicate fingers. All four produce silk from silk glands that occupy a large portion of a tarantula's opisthosoma.

Bristles. Tarantulas appear to be literally carpeted with hair. Indeed, tarantulas and their kin are often called the hairy mygalomorphs. However, we must remember that these are actually non-growing bristles rather than continually growing hair in the mammalian sense. They have a completely different origin and structure.

Here, the term *bristle* is used to indicate all these hairlike structures in a generic sense, reserving the term hair for only mammalian hair. It must be noted that some arachnologists disagree with our use of the term *bristle* to refer to these structures in a generic sense, using the terms *spine, hair,* and *setae* in the sense that we use bristle. We use the term here for want of a better, all-inclusive term. When reading other texts on the subject, the enthusiast is forewarned to check the precise definition of these carefully to avoid confusion.

In the following discussion, because of their strong macroscopic resemblance to each other, we consider the various types of bristles to all be more or less variations of a basic structure or organ. This is almost certainly not true. The fact is that the origins and evolution of a spider's bristles is almost completely unknown. For purposes of a technical presentation, the reader is cautioned against accepting this summary without further qualification. See Barnes (1980) and Foelix (1982) for more comprehensive treatments.

There are many different types of tarantula bristles. Some of them can be categorized as defense (the urticating bristles, others as sensory (setae or filiform bristles, and trichobothria, singular: seta and trichobothrium, see page 35). Another type of bristle is used by some tarantulas for sound production (see page 21). And the scopulae, pads of bristles on the pretarsi, telotarsi, and basitarsi of the pedipalps and legs, are important for climbing and prey capture (see page 22). Some bristles seem to

Type I urticating bristles from Brachypelma emilia. *These are approximately 0.3 millimeter (0.012 inches) long.*

have no purpose except to cover the spider.

The defense bristles, on the top rear (or on the sides in some kinds) of the opisthosoma of many New World tarantulas, are loosely attached and bedecked with varying patterns of backward-pointing barbs. They are nonliving and noninnervated. At least four distinct types are recognized. In all but one type, the unattached end is sharply pointed and functions as a harpoon. These bristles come loose with very little effort, and the tarantula uses its hind legs to brush them into a cloud that wafts into the air around it. When these bristles penetrate skin or mucous membranes, they cause much irritation. Arachnologists call them urticating bristles. In at least one type, there is a short segment toward the rear containing forward-pointing barbs that ensure that the bristles will only penetrate far enough to cause the greatest irritation and then remain in place.

A predator, a mouse for instance, that is assaulting a tarantula that possesses

Type III urticating bristles from Brachypelma emilia. *The longest bristle in this illustration is approximately 0.75 millimeter (0.03 inches) long.*

urticating bristles, is indeed courting disaster. These bristles actually represent a deadly form of defense. As the mouse approaches the tarantula, the tarantula uses its rear legs to kick up a cloud of these bristles. As soon as the mouse enters that cloud, all areas of exposed skin, its eyes, and its nasal passages begin to itch or sting. At that point, the mouse becomes much more interested in escaping the bristles than eating the tarantula. If the mouse continues to advance and inhales some of these bristles, its throat and respiratory passages almost immediately react by swelling and pouring out large volumes of mucus (Cook et al. 1972). As the struggling mouse drowns in its own body fluids or strangles on its swollen mucous membranes, the tarantula makes good its escape. It is even conceivable, though not yet confirmed, that the tarantula could attack the disabled mouse and eat it!

Museum workers are all too familiar with the irritation produced when alco-

hol from specimen bottles holding tarantulas is splashed on unprotected skin. It is not clear if the urticating properties of these bristles are due to a chemical or a physical irritation alone, or a combination of both. Most arachnologists hold the opinion that the irritation is primarily physical, not chemical, in much the same manner as that caused by fiberglass. However, Fabio et al. (1995) report an IgE (Immunoglobulin E) reaction to prick and intradermal tests of the extracts from the bristles of some unidentified Brazilian tarantulas, strongly suggesting a chemical activity in addition to the physical one. The issue is far from decided, and much more research is needed.

For a time, some of the itching powder once sold in novelty shops was, in reality, the urticating bristles of tarantulas.

Several years ago, the authors encountered an article (long since misplaced) in a popular tabloid that reported on these urticating bristles. The researcher who was purported to be studying them and the tarantulas they came from, was dressed in a full environment suit reminiscent of a space suit. The byline strongly admonished everyone to avoid tarantulas at all costs. Anyone who ever got near one of the horrid creatures was urged to wear protection similar to that shown in their article. Furthermore, the article inferred that anyone having a tarantula as a pet was courting certain disaster because of the horrible dermatitis that would result if the bristles contacted unprotected skin, or a possible violent respiratory reaction if they were inhaled.

Most humans are only mildly allergic to the urticating bristles. The associated rash seldom lasts more than half a day, but it can be spectacular as well as most uncomfortable. Sensitive individuals need not worry unless the rash persists for more than twenty-four hours, or progresses beyond the simple rash condition. Very few people suffer a more severe dermatitis, popularly known as hives, on exposure to the bristles. In this case, a physician's attention is strongly urged.

A two or two and one-half percent hydrocortisone creme or salve works very well for alleviating most of the symptoms almost immediately. In most countries, a doctor's prescription is required for this medication, but it is relatively benign and prescriptions for it are not normally difficult to gain. Keeping some of the creme or salve in the medicine chest for instances when keepers or guests develop symptoms is probably a good idea for the enthusiast. Calamine lotion, another remedy, is all but useless in this application.

Absolutely the worst consequences are obtained if the bristles make contact with a person's eyes. The resulting lesion causes severe damage to the cornea and other eye parts, and requires immediate attention from an ophthalmologist (Chang et al. 1991; Hered et al. 1988). First-aid treatment is to restrain the patient to prevent rubbing the eye, then irrigating the eye with copious amounts of clear water. The patient should be taken immediately to an emergency clinic, then referred to an ophthalmologist.

Ordinarily the patient recovers completely after several months of treatment. Although there is seldom apparent, permanent damage to the eye, the condition is exceedingly painful, and there is the ever-present threat of permanent eye damage or infection. The people afflicted with this condition lose time from work or school and suffer much worry and stress not knowing if they will ever have full use of the eye again. Long-term treatment is also very expensive.

Prevention is by far the best course to take and is absurdly simple and easy. Don't touch your eyes or face after handling a tarantula, or any of the appointments in its cage, until you have washed your hands.

Contrary to the "authoritative report" in the tabloid, these authors are unaware of any respiratory complications in humans brought on by contact with the urticating bristles. So much for the credibility of the media!

Curiously, most New World tarantulas possess urticating bristles and are comparatively docile. By contrast, all Old World tarantulas lack urticating bristles, and many, if not most, tend to be pugnacious or possess a potent venom or both. This is hypothesized as evidence of two different strategies for defense and self-preservation. The correlation between geographic origin, urticating bristles, and aggressiveness is too nebulous to be used as a clue to the origin of any given tarantula, however.

Many tarantulas have highly modified bristles (plumose bristles) on the outer surfaces of their chelicerae that rub against other spikelike bristles on the maxillary processes on the opposing faces of the pedipalps' coxae. Similar bristles sometimes exist between the coxae and trochanters of the pedipalps and forelegs. At least one group, subfamily Selenogyrinae (Smith 1990) has these bristles on the opposing faces of their chelicerae. These are called stridulating organs.

Tarantulas scrape these bristles together to produce a hissing or buzzing sound, called stridulation, as a warning signal to potential assailants in

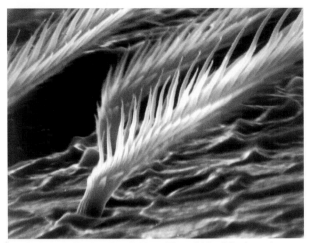

A bristle from Haplopelma lividum. *The width of the base is approximately four microns (0.00016 inches).*

the same manner as a snake's hiss or rattlesnake's rattle. In the larger species the sound can be quite loud. More will be said about stridulation on page 90.

The last bristles to be discussed are those on the pretarsi, telotarsi, and

Eye field of Brachypelma smithi. *The longest bristle in the center field is approximately 0.6 millimeter (0.0.24 inches) long. The large, round objects among the bristles are the eyes.*

basitarsi of the pedipalps and legs. These are grouped into pads called scopulae (singular: scopula) and allow a tarantula to walk up a glass aquarium wall with surprising ease. In the proper light, many tarantulas' scopulae are beautifully blue-green iridescent.

The mechanism that allows the tarantula to climb smooth glass is still not well understood. It seems to depend on adhesion mediated by a thin layer of water vapor on the climbing surface. In fact, this adhesion is so powerful that a tarantula weighing fifty grams is capable of climbing the glass walls of an aquarium to reach and push aside an unsecured lid, and escape. Be amazed, and forewarned!

The scopulae are a very important part of tarantula anatomy and physiology. Their adhesive capability is one of the principle mechanisms by which a tarantula can seize its prey. The arboreal species rely on it most heavily to allow movement through the forest canopy.

Tarantulas possess many other types of bristles and the forms they take may differ markedly from species to species. Many of them are a complete enigma. The accompanying scanning electron micrographs illustrate a few. As the magnification is increased, finer and finer detail can be discerned. Their complexity and beauty is as astonishingly wonderful as their purpose or function is obscure.

Ecdysis. The major disadvantage of a suit of armor is that once it's made, it can never change its size. How does a tarantula grow? Eons ago, arthropods' precursors solved this problem by periodically discarding the old, constraining exoskeleton in favor of a new one of more appropriate dimensions.

This poses a second problem. The only thing that contains and supports the arthropod is its exoskeleton. Without it, the owner could not retain its physical integrity and would be reduced to an oozing blob of formless tissue. How then does it manage to retain its form and functionality while it regrows the new exoskeleton? A system had to be developed to allow the production of a new, larger exoskeleton before the old one was discarded. This was solved by growing the new one inside the old before discarding the old skin.

So now we encounter a third difficulty. How does one produce a new, larger exoskeleton *inside* the older, smaller one?

The solution requires the production of a new, slightly wrinkled, soft exoskeleton just inside the old, shedding the old one, expanding the new one while it is still pliable, then causing it to harden.

Professional arachnologists divide this process into four phases, calling them either intermolt, proecdysis, ecdysis, and postecdysis or metecdysis; or intermolt, premolt, molt, and postmolt, respectively. Both nomenclatural schemes are used in the current literature (e.g., Barnes 1980; Foelix 1982; Meglitsch 1972).

Although it is spoken of as though it occurred in these distinct phases, it is really a smooth, uninterrupted cycle with only very indistinct demarcations. The entire process normally requires a year in adult tarantulas.

During most of the year, a tarantula is in intermolt, the suspended, passive phase. However, at characteristic times of the year, possibly different for each kind, the production of a sequence of specific hormones triggers the resumption of the molting cycle. Although these hormone-controlled mechanisms are well known for insects and crus-

Enlargement of the eye field of Brachypelma smithi. *The larger bristles are approximately eight microns (0.0003 inches) wide.*

taceans (Burdette 1974), little research has been done on spiders in general or tarantulas in particular.

During premolt, requiring several days to several weeks, a new exoskeleton is grown just inside the old. Along

Further enlargement of the eye field of Brachypelma smithi *showing the incredibly fine structure of the bristles. Each hairlike branchlet protruding from the body of the bristle is only three microns (0.0001 inches) long.*

Tarantula in intermolt. The bare patch is still light colored.
Brachypelma smithi.

with this new exoskeleton, an entirely new set of bristles is produced. Thus, if the tarantula were going bald because of the loss of any of its bristles, they would be replaced at the next molt.

Those New World tarantulas that shed their urticating bristles frequently

Tarantula in premolt. The bare patch has turned dark because of the new bristles forming beneath the old skin.

develop a bald patch on the rear, dorsal surface of their opisthosoma. The color of this bald area is an important harbinger of an impending molt. For most of the year, during intermolt, this skin is tan or light brown in color because the skin is nearly transparent and the body tissues beneath are light colored. As the new exoskeleton reaches completion, usually a week or two before molt, the newly forming bristles beneath the old skin become pigmented, causing the bald area to turn very dark in color.

None of this is apparent on Old World tarantulas because they do not possess urticating bristles and do not normally develop a bald area.

At about the same time, a liquid (exuvial fluid) is secreted between the old and new exoskeletons, and enzymes digest away one layer of the exoskeleton, the endocuticle. This process is called apolysis.

The end of premolt and the beginning of molt is signaled when the tarantula rolls over to lie upside down or on its back, so to speak. On occasion, a molting tarantula will not roll over, but will merely molt in an upright position or lying on its side. We haven't a clue as to why. Many tarantulas, especially newly caught imports, may spin a bowl-shaped web, the molting mat, and climb into it preparatory to actually molting.

During molt, with the tarantula upside down, the carapace loosens around its front and sides and is forced slowly out of the way. The tarantula, in its new, still pliable exoskeleton, miraculously works its way out of the opening with a nearly imperceptible pumping action. Molt may take as little as twenty minutes, or as long as two or three days. However, tarantulas that take too much time molting, especially the very aged ones, usually have great difficulty completing the process. See page 151 for a discussion of molting problems.

After it is finished molting, the tarantula may lie upside down several hours just resting, but it will eventually turn right side up. These authors and most other enthusiasts have witnessed this process many times, and still stand in awe of it. It is akin to a new birth, a marvel to behold.

In the next phase, postmolt, the new exoskeleton swells, possibly as a result of swallowed air, possibly because hemolymph (the tarantulas's equivalent of blood) is pumped forward under pressure from the opisthosoma into the prosoma. This may be possible because the exoskeleton on the opisthosoma never hardens, but remains very pliable, only becoming tougher. The new exoskeleton, which was slightly wrinkled inside the old one, expands to a size somewhat larger than the old one as it stretches and the wrinkles smooth out. These incredible animals have been using permanent-press clothes for more than a third of a billion years!

For the next several days the exoskeleton hardens as the chitin and sclerotin experience a sort of tanning process whereby the individual molecules become cross-linked. The concentration of cross-links determines the strength and hardness of the resulting part of the exoskeleton. During this time, the tarantula will lie completely flat with its legs stretched as far as possible to take full advantage of its temporary plasticity to gain as much additional size as possible.

The lining of the mouth, pharynx, and pumping stomach are also shed, and the tarantula will not eat until these are also thoroughly hardened. This may

Molting tarantula. Having rolled onto its back, it begins to free itself from the old exoskeleton.

require a week or more. While the progression from postmolt to intermolt is actually a smooth transition, and no hard and fast indicators define the exact instant of changeover, for our purposes it is signaled when food is again accepted.

Molting tarantula. It is laboring out of the old exoskeleton.

Molting tarantula. Having completely escaped the old exoskeleton, it lies still for a while, marshaling its strength.

Although the tarantula may be active during premolt, it is very vulnerable to predation and injury. Research has shown that the nerve endings for many of the sensory structures remain connected through the new bristles into the old. Thus, most of the tarantula's sen-

The freshly molted tarantula, vibrant and new.

sory abilities retain some functionality in spite of the extra thickness of exoskeleton, almost up to the time of molting. However, touch and sight, as well as senses analogous to smell and taste, might still be drastically impaired, and the tarantula could not sense predators effectively. At the same time, the old exoskeleton would tend to interfere with motion much the same as too many layers of clothing would, slowing the animal's reaction time and reducing its ability to flee or defend itself.

The new exoskeleton, still inside the old, must bare the burden of retaining the animal's hemolymph (see page 37), and is very fragile at this stage. If it should be accidentally damaged, the hemolymph could clot between the old and new exoskeletons, making the molt difficult or impossible (see page 151 for further discussion).

During molt, the animal is utterly helpless. There is no firm connection between the old exoskeleton and the driving muscles. Therefore, movement is exceedingly difficult. The legs are at some stage of being partially withdrawn. Therefore, the joints in the new exoskeleton no longer coincide with those in the old, making bending of the legs nearly impossible. The new exoskeleton is still far too soft and pliable to support any meaningful activity, and flight or defense is virtually impossible. During these few hours, the tarantula is totally at the mercy of the Fates.

During postmolt, a tarantula's sensory structures may be in vibrant renewed contact with the world, but the new exoskeleton is still far too soft to allow for any effective defense, being too easily pierced or ruptured.

These are among the most critical periods in the animal's life. The molting process holds much risk. The animal is very fragile and unable to defend itself or flee while actively molting or recovering. Also, if there are any complications during the molting process, the animal may remain trapped in its old exoskeleton to die a slow, lingering death (see page 151). During all these vulnerable phases, the wild tarantula seals itself in its burrow as a means of protection. In captivity it must rely totally on the wisdom and care of its keeper. **Do not touch or handle a tarantula during or after a molt, until it begins to accept food.**

Tarantulas are extremely fragile during these phases, and any contact or movement not made by them is likely to injure or kill them. In the direst of emergencies, if it is necessary to move the tarantula, use a piece of thin cardboard as a stretcher or litter by carefully sliding it under the tarantula's body. After moving to the new position, do not remove the cardboard unless absolutely necessary. Leave it under the tarantula until the spider moves itself.

The Exuvium. The old skin has been called a *molt, shed, cast,* and *exuvium.*

A small point of clarification: arachnologists use the singular *exuvium* and the plural *exuvia,* while those dictionaries that include the term insist that the singular is *exuvia* and the plural *exuviae.* Presumably, this is the result of confusion about the gender of the original Latin word. While the enthusiasts use "shed skin" most frequently, professional arachnologists prefer *exuvium/ exuvia;* we shall use the two terms interchangeably.

It is highly recommended that the enthusiast make every effort to retrieve the shed skin before it has an opportunity to dry. It may then be carefully arranged, using toothpicks or other thin probes, and supported with pins or

The molted lining of the esophagus and pumping stomach.

small cardboard props. Particular attention should be paid to properly expanding the opisthosoma. The authors try to stuff the still moist, pliable opisthosomal skin with a small ball of cotton.

Upon drying, the external supports can be removed and the exuvium placed in a protective container or case. Such mounts make impressive displays in shadow boxes. But, be extremely careful. Such dried sheds are light and crisp, and exceptionally fragile. They can only be handled with extreme caution. In a display case, these authors recommend that they be firmly glued in place using model cement.

The internal anatomy and amount of detail that can be seen with a small magnifying glass is astonishing. More will be said of this after we examine tarantula anatomy more thoroughly.

Instars, Embryology, and Development. In many arthropods (e.g., crustaceans and insects) the form and lifestyle of immature individuals changes with each molt as their growth and development proceeds, and each stage has specific characteristics not present or applicable to those preceding it. In these creatures, the number of molts between hatching and sexual maturity or completion of growth is often fixed. In an effort to uniquely characterize each interval in the arthropod's life cycle, biologists have adopted the practice of referring to each step as an *instar*. Sometimes biologists use the terms *stage* or *stadium* to mean approximately the same as instar. An instar is defined as the stage or state of development between molts (Barnes 1980) or an intermolt stage in the development of an arthropod (Lincoln and Boxshall 1987). Many arachnologists use instar to refer to the creature itself in a particular phase of development.

Tarantulas do not change their appearance or lifestyle during their postembryonic development as dramatically as do insects and some other arthropods. In fact, this scarcity of identifying characteristics to distinguish the precise instar beyond the first two or three has led to much confusion, even among professional arachnologists.

Partially because of a wide variety of varying opinions, and partially because of the difficulty of making direct translations between foreign languages, an abundance of multiple names have been used for each stage in a spider's embryonic development (Breene 1996), causing heated debates at all conferences and symposia where the subject is brought up. There was even disagreement about when to consider an embryonic spider as hatching, with some arachnologists questioning whether the term *hatch* should be used with spiders at all.

In 1987, M. F. Downes proposed a standardized terminology for describing the various stages in the embryology and development of a spider (Downes 1987). Most arachnologists now accept his system as the standard.

Using Downes's system, we call the structure laid by the female an egg. This egg is a mass of nutritive substances (yolk and others) with a nucleus, enclosed in a membrane deposited by the mother as a sort of factory-installed packaging called the *chorion*. At this stage, an egg resembles a yellow to cream-colored, milky bead or small ball. If the egg is fertilized and the embryo develops, it will eventually shed the chorion. This is the act of hatching or *eclosion*. Because the chorion is not produced by the developing embryo, it is generally considered to not be the future spider's skin or exoskeleton. Therefore, this shedding of the chorion is not considered to be ecdysis or a molt and the chorion is not considered to be an exuvium.

After shedding the chorion, the developing spider is called a *postembryo*. At this stage, it appears very much like a mite glued to the egg (a description used by R. G. Breene and others). While it may be able to move its appendages, it is not able to crawl around. It is living entirely on the nutrition stored in the egg.

Eventually it will molt its skin to reach the first instar. Because this cast-off skin is an exoskeleton made by the developing embryo/spiderling, the process is called ecdysis or molting, and the cast-off skin is called an exuvium.

The term spiderling is not an officially sanctioned term for any particular stage in a spider's development. Enthusiasts ordinarily use the term to indicate the developing spider from the first instar through at least the fourth.

Most tarantula spiderlings look like real spiders from the first instar onward. In some species the spiderling may be able to crawl around in this instar, in others not. Most species of spider subsist solely on the stored yolk at this stage, but it is suspected that a few tarantulas begin active feeding during this instar.

Over the next two instars, most, if not all, spiderlings become mobile, finish consuming all of the stored yolk on which to subsist, and begin their lives as predacious carnivores. However, beyond here, the instar question begins to become muddied.

In tarantulas, the total number of instars is inconstant, depending on the species, the state of nutrition, temperature, sex, the individual, and perhaps other variables. That molt at which tarantulas reach sexual maturity is called the *ultimate molt*, and the following instar is the adult or *ultimate instar*. The molt and instar immediately before the ultimate one are called the *penultimate molt* and *instar*, and the one before that is the *prepenultimate molt* and *instar*. However, the molts and instars between numbers two or three and the prepenultimate have no special designation. If it is possible to determine the exact number, they may be numbered, but unless the tarantula is captive bred and the enthusiast religious about recording molts, such a designation is tenuous at best.

After reaching maturity, subsequent molts and their corresponding instars are called first, second, third, and so on, *postultimate molts* and *instars*. Ordinarily, male tarantulas never reach a postultimate molt or instar (but see pages 88 and 153). However, female tarantulas commonly experience several to dozens of postultimate molts.

A dead tarantula. Contrast its pose to that of the molting tarantula.

Implications of Ecdysis. What follows here is a *potpourri* of important facts and considerations that the enthusiast must keep in mind when dealing with pet tarantulas.

Take careful note. A tarantula that is lying on its back is probably molting, *not* dying. Dying tarantulas almost never keel over, as the saying goes. They remain upright with their legs folded under them.

A tarantula that is bald is not necessarily old. Neither has it gone a long time since its last molt. This characteristic can neither be used as a gauge of age nor an indication of how much time has passed since the last molt. Baldness in a tarantula is merely an indication that it has seen cause to cast off a significant proportion of those urticating bristles since its last molt, which could be two weeks or two years ago; and the tarantula could be three years old or thirty.

Frequently, a long-term captive tarantula will not spin a molting cradle. This is not a sign of sickness or old age.

Occasionally a tarantula will molt in an upright position.
Aphonopelma chalcodes.

Is the lack of such a cradle an artifact of their captivity? Do wild tarantulas often fail to produce one in their burrows?

Occasionally, a tarantula will shed while merely laying on its side, or while remaining fully upright. This is no great cause for concern as long as the old skin comes off completely.

Tarantulas that are confined in very cramped quarters frequently have difficulty molting, most often resulting in deformed legs. This is most evident with tarantulas shipped through the pet industry in small condiment cups. Once these deformed tarantulas have the opportunity to shed in roomier quarters,

> If you should see a tarantula in a dealer's or pet shop's stock that is deformed because it molted in confined quarters, try to negotiate a better price. The dealer will be able to free himself of an otherwise unmarketable animal, and you may acquire a nice tarantula at a bargain price.

they return to their normal shape and function. How do they molt in the confines of their burrows? Why don't wild tarantulas display these deformities after molting in such cramped quarters? We simply don't know, but the enthusiast, with carefully thought out caging, might be able to discover and even photograph the answers to these questions.

In captivity, baby tarantulas molt quite frequently. One individual of the tarantula native to Arkansas (putatively *Aphonopelma hentzi*) molted four times the first year, two each for the next seven years, and one molt each year for the remaining three years. By the seventh year, the tarantula was almost full grown and the black patch of urticating bristles had expanded to cover the entire opisthosoma (Baerg 1938). Some other kinds of tarantulas, kept at elevated temperatures and given unlimited food may molt as often as once a month.

As old age approaches, the female will miss occasional molts. However, some adult female tarantulas (e.g., *Brachypelma emilia*) frequently fail to molt every year as a matter of course, rather than extreme old age.

The individual of *B. emilia* that the authors called Duchess only shed every year for the first three years after being acquired as an adult in the summer of 1972. After that, she shifted to a pattern of shedding every second year. Finally, she shed once in the spring of 1983, again in the spring of 1986 (three years), then lastly in the spring of 1989 (three years, again). She died in February 1991.

Although North American (northern hemisphere) tarantulas normally molt between March and September, southern hemisphere tarantulas often display a molting cycle that is shifted six months out of phase.

Newly imported southern hemisphere tarantulas that the authors add to their collection may shed September through December the first year of captivity, gradually shifting to molting between March and July as with the native northern hemisphere types. They are kept in a room in which the lighting is controlled by a timer, with sixteen hours on and eight hours off, all year long. No outside light reaches the tarantulas. The temperature tends to fluctuate somewhat in a diurnal (day/night) cycle, and in a seasonal rhythm, synchronized with the outdoor temperature. It is amusing to speculate that the circadian clocks of these tarantulas are reset by the minor fluctuations in ambient temperature to match the local seasons. The enterprising enthusiast with a flair for gadgetry might set up an experiment to test this.

How can you tell when a molt is imminent? For both New and Old World tarantulas, one of the first signs is that the individual will stop eating. Younger spiderlings will fast for only a few days before molting, older adults may not eat for weeks before shedding. One of the extremes is represented by *Theraphosa blondi* which may not eat for one to three months before and after a molt. Long-term fasting is no guarantee of an approaching molt, but if the season is correct, it's a strong indicator.

As the fateful day approaches, the opisthosoma may seem fuller than normal, appearing ready to burst. In some kinds of tarantulas, most notably *Aphonopelma seemanni,* the skin on the opisthosoma may develop a peculiar wrinkled appearance as though it had come loose, which may indeed be the case. At the same time, the opistho-

Brachypelma emilia. *This is the tarantula that the authors called Duchess.*

soma may appear to pull away from the prosoma a little with the pedicel appearing to stretch somewhat.

The legs may change proportion slightly, as well. In some kinds of tarantulas, they may appear to lengthen slightly, in others they may appear to thicken. All of these signs are rather subtle and require an intimate familiarity with the tarantula's normal appearance during intermolt.

We have already discussed the sign of an impending molt for those New World tarantulas that shed their urticating bristles.

Loss of Limb. The appendages of arthropods are constructed much like pipes with more or less rigid walls. If a portion of such an appendage is severely damaged or lost, would it not be advantageous to be able to turn off a valve a little closer to the body to prevent body fluids from leaking out? If the limb were supplied with a weakened place just outside the valve, it could even be broken off or lost preferentially at this more convenient place. Indeed, if the injured limb posed a threat to the animal, the owner might even be provoked into removing it at the special point for the sake of survival. For instance, if it were held by a tenacious predator, a voracious mate, or caught in an abortive molt, might it not be better to lose the limb than to forfeit life?

Indeed, this basic principle probably has been used by arthropods for eons as a method for dealing with damaged or entangled limbs, and is called *autotomy*. Crustaceans, for example, have a special chitinous edge and muscle arrangement at a particular place *inside* their legs. If the limb is injured severely enough, a nervous reflex flexes that special muscle and causes the limb to be sheared off.

Not all arthropods are capable of casting off a limb, nor all arachnids. Autotomy seems either to have evolved separately in each group or has been lost by many over the eons. Spiders are one of the groups that possess the facility. They have a joint between the coxa and the trochanter that has a peculiar arrangement. The coxa has a sturdy, collarlike ring around its distal end (away from the body) that serves to reinforce it. A pliable, hingelike membrane connects the trochanter to this coxal ring, but this hinge is somewhat narrowed between the two segments, a little like the spaces between the links in a chain of sausages. It is also weaker than any of the other hinges.

Coincidentally, only one muscle passes through this joint. All others arising from inside the tarantula attach to thickened areas (sclerites) in the joint membrane that remain attached to the coxa.

If enough force is applied on the femur, this coxa-trochanter hinge is the part that tears first, and the entire leg from that point outward is cast off. The muscles that are attached to the sclerites contract from pain, pulling in the edges of the joint membrane to reduce the size of the opening. Ultimately, only an empty socket remains.

If tugged forcefully by a predator, or in the case of difficulty withdrawing a leg from the old exoskeleton during a molt, the leg can separate from the tarantula's body. In the case of a severely injured leg, the tarantula may strain to reach around and grasp it with the fangs, pedipalps, or other legs in an effort to remove it. It is usually successful.

However, legs are not shed arbitrarily. The loss of a limb is a last resort effort to escape an otherwise hopeless situation. It represents a great loss for the owner. In the vast majority of cases, the owner will try not to lose the limb. And, even if the limb is partially injured, the owner may not remove it. For instance, in the case of a damaged segment near the end of the leg (e.g., telotarsus), the tip may simply wither

This Phormictopus cancerides *has lost legs II and IV on its right side.*

and dry. This may have significant consequences during the next molt. Difficulties encountered during molting are discussed on page 151.

On the occasion of the loss of a limb, and if the owner is not distracted or too weak, it may eat the lost limb with as much relish as though it were any fat beetle caught under normal circumstances (Baerg 1938; Bonnet 1930; and personal observations of these authors). This serves at least two purposes. First, it effectively disposes of the limb. Thus, no dead meat is allowed to attract predators, or promote an unsanitary condition. Second, eating the lost limb helps to recover lost protein, electrolytes, and fluids. As unpalatable as the act may seem, it's still good food.

Regeneration. Not only can an injured limb be lost, but during successive molts, the lost limb gradually regenerates! Apparently, this fact had been suspected, but never demonstrated before 1926 when reported by Baerg. That such a basic fact of their biology should have gone unreported for so long is an indication of how unsuspecting eighteenth- and nineteenth-century researchers were of the complexity of tarantula biology and how enigmatic tarantulas really are.

The initial size of the regenerated limb is determined by the length of time between its loss and the next molt. The greater this period of time, the larger it will be. Even though the regenerating limb can be quite small at first, it is still fully formed from the very beginning. It grows with each succeeding molt to become full sized in two to four years.

Legs are not the only appendages capable of regeneration. It is not unusual for a tarantula to break off the tip of a fang if it strikes a rock while

The same **Phormictopus cancerides** *three years later with fully regenerated legs.*

pouncing on prey. The fang's tip will remain blunt but will not necessarily inhibit the animal's feeding. During the next molt, the fang's tip will regenerate. Spinnerets may be removed by predators, but will also regenerate with several molts.

At this point, a word should be said about pain in tarantulas. Their anatomies and physiologies are so different that we would be tempted to declare that they do not feel pain in the same sense that we do, thus giving us a means of assuaging our consciences when we do something that hurts them. The fact is that they *do* react noticeably to any injury that we assume causes pain, and this has been reported by several researchers. Even in the special case of autotomy, they apparently feel something akin to pain. Until the coxal ring has completely sealed and a scab formed, the tarantula seems hypersensitive. It may pace its cage restlessly or overreact to almost all external stimuli.

Even though tarantulas are vastly different from us in many respects, they must still be treated as any other living organism by causing them as little pain or discomfort as possible.

Internal Structure

Endoskeleton. For many years it was thought that spiders possessed no internal skeleton. However, that is now known to be untrue. Although they do not possess an endoskeleton in the same sense that vertebrates do, they do possess an assemblage of other structures that fulfil many of the same functions, and many authorities use the term *endoskeleton* to designate them (Barnes 1980; Foelix 1982). It is important to understand that a tarantula's endoskeleton is somewhat analogous but certainly not homologous to a vertebrate's endoskeleton. (See page 15 for a discussion of homology and analogy.) The name is only used for want of a better one.

There are several structures in spiders which, though they have different embryonic origins, are usually considered under the global topic of endoskeleton. Two of the more important ones are apodemes and entosterna.

Apodemes (also called entapophyses) and apophyses (singular: apophysis) are infoldings of the exoskeleton. The structure is called an apodeme if it is hollow, an apophysis if it is not. We have already mentioned the central apodeme, see page 13. There are many other apodemes in a tarantula's body. They serve as important connecting structures between the tarantula's muscles and its exoskeleton.

The muscles' cells connect to individual cells in the tendon. These, in turn, connect to the apodemes as secure attachment points. The transition between tendon and apodeme is often gradual and poorly delimited, and the apodemes are often long, narrow, hollow threads passing some distance through the tarantula's body. This has some surprising consequences that will be discussed with the muscle system and movement on page 45.

There are also several structures in spiders that arise from a completely different embryonic tissue than the exoskeleton and apodemes, and cannot be considered part of them. These are the entosterna (singular: entosternum). They supply additional, internal attachments for muscles, and are composed of a substance very much like cartilage, not chitin or sclerotin. The largest is the prosomal endosternite. This is a bowl or horseshoe-shaped structure that lies in the prosoma immediately above the brain with the open end oriented forward.

Nervous System. The tarantula's nervous system is composed of a radiating array of nerve fibers originating from a brain that lies on the floor of the prosoma, in their chests, so to speak. It is quite large, approximately as long and as wide as the sternum shield. It exists in two portions, an upper, forward section called the supraesophageal ganglion, and a lower, rearward section called the subesophageal ganglion.

The supraesophageal ganglion tends to be compact and round, receives information from the optic nerves and other sensory nerves, and seems to have roughly the same function as our forebrain. It serves a central, integrative, and cognitive function.

The subesophageal ganglion is star-shaped and appears to have a more basic motor function, controlling reflexes and automatic functions. Thus, this part seems to also have a function somewhat similar to our hind brain.

In addition, the brain has several glandular bodies closely associated with it that are roughly analogous to our hypothalamus, secreting regulatory hormones. This superficial resemblance in brain organization is one of the few parallels between tarantula and human anatomy, but it is purely coincidental, merely an example of parallel evolution.

All of these parts are more or less fused into a thick disk shape that is perforated by the inlet of the pumping stomach (discussed below). The spider's brain resembles a fat, star-shaped doughnut.

From the points of the subesophageal ganglion's star, heavy nerve cords connect to the organs and appendages in the prosoma, and one major nerve cord passes through the pedicel into the opisthosoma. Thus, the brain is a concentrated, centralized seat of authority in tarantulas, in contrast to the rather diffuse system of nerve cords and ganglia in most other arthropods.

On the top of the prosoma, toward the front, is a small elevation resembling a cupola or turret. This is called an ocular tubercle and holds the eight simple eyes or ocelli (singular: ocellus). These are connected to the brain by optic nerves.

Although several other groups of spiders seem to be able to form images and derive useful information from their eyes, it is not known to what extent tarantulas possess that capability.

For the burrow-dwelling kinds, it is of dubious value. They spend most of their lives in dark burrows, usually coming out only at dusk. Even then, their eyes are situated inside a circle of legs; they see mostly their own knees! However, wild tarantulas, or those not accustomed to handling, do react to motions around them. They will turn to face an approaching hand or take flight from an approaching animal.

A notable exception are the arboreal varieties, many of which seem to have rather good vision. Much more work must be done to assess how well they really see. Can they see color? Can they distinguish patterns? Can they recognize prey? Can they perceive and estimate distances? This would obviously be very important to an animal that jumps from branch to branch.

We have already discussed the urticating bristles on page 18. Most of the remaining bristles on a tarantula's body are sensory bristles. Indeed, virtually every large bristle on the tarantula's body is innervated. Their bodies are almost literally carpeted with sensory structures.

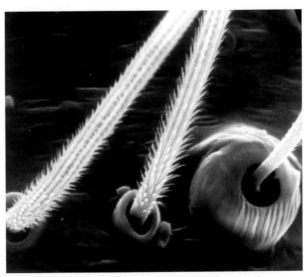

Tactile bristles on a second instar exuvium of Brachypelma albopilosum. *The left-hand bristle is a trichobothrium, the center one is a filifrom bristle. The largest socket on the right holds another bristle of unknown type. The left-hand bristle is approximately eight microns (0.0003 inches) in diameter.*

The trichobothria and other large setae are very sensitive tactile organs. These are seated in cuplike bases that resemble small craters in the exoskeleton. Each of these craters has several nerve endings (usually three) associated with it to detect the slightest deformations produced by the bristle if it is disturbed. The trichobothria are known to be so sensitive that they can pick up vibrations from a fly as far away as a meter (about a yard).

Virtually all arachnids possess strange organs called *slit sensillae,* and tarantulas are no exception. These appear as narrow slits in the exoskeleton, bordered by thick ridges. While many are solitary, most occur in parallel groups. It is thought that these sense the amount of stress that is born by a particular area of the exoskeleton, thus allowing the animal to monitor the amount of pressure it is exerting or how much weight it is supporting with a given appendage.

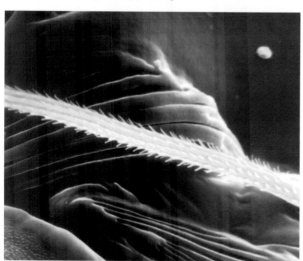

Slit sensillae on a second instar exuvium of Brachypelma albopilosum. *The bristle transecting the field is approximately eight microns (0.0003 inches) in diameter.*

Tarantulas seem to have an excellent chemosensitive sense. This corresponds roughly to a combined sense of taste and smell in mammals. At least two structures have been identified as chemoreceptors, tarsal organs, and chemoreceptive setae. The chemosensitive setae have nerve cells threading through a passageway to their tips, where the very end is exposed to the open air. While these are found over most of the tarantula's body, they are most common on the tarantula's pedipalps and front legs.

There are many enigmatic, microscopic structures situated among all those bristles whose function we can only guess. Although some serious research has been done on the sensory structures of spiders (Den Otter 1974), there is still much that we do not know.

How well do tarantulas really see? Can tarantulas distinguish colors? Shapes? How good are their senses of touch? Can they hear? If so, what and how much? How do they know which direction is up? Can they feel heat or cold? Do they have senses that we aren't aware of? What roles do any of these play in their day-to-day lives? The magnitude of our ignorance is staggering.

Circulatory System. As you might expect by now, the heart, arteries, veins, and blood (the *circulatory system*) of tarantulas are radically different from ours.

In vertebrates (including humans), the blood is completely enclosed within the circulatory system. The arteries and veins are sealed to the heart at one end, and are bridged by the capillaries at the other. The arteries divide repeatedly, becoming finer and finer until they eventually become capillaries. These capillaries, after a short distance, begin to coalesce to become minute veinlets.

These then continue to join to become major conduits, the veins, back to the heart. If blood ever escapes this closed system, a bruise is produced at the breach as the red blood cells escape into the spaces in our tissues. The important points are that, in vertebrates, blood seldom leaves the pipe work, and if it does, it causes a pathological condition.

By contrast, a spider's circulatory system is open. In tarantulas, the arteries may branch several times, but eventually merely open into spaces within the tissues. The hemolymph then seeps through spaces within these tissues until it finds its way back to the heart.

An important implication here is that the blood and body fluids of the tarantula are the same fluid, called hemolymph. In vertebrates (humans included), blood fluids are called blood plasma or simply plasma; and the fluids in the tissues (outside the artery/capillary/vein system) are chemically different and called interstitial fluid, lymph, or lymphatic fluid.

The oxygen-carrying pigment in spider hemolymph is hemocyanin and uses copper in its binding site (Ghiretti-Magaldi and Tamino 1977; Linzen et al. 1977; Loewe et al. 1977). This is in contrast to the hemoglobin in vertebrates (including humans) that uses iron. In vertebrates, all hemoglobin is held in red blood corpuscles (erythrocytes). Not so in tarantulas where the hemocyanin is dissolved directly in the hemolymph.

There are at least four types of cells (hemocytes) that wander through the spider's circulatory system and tissues, that appear somewhat similar to various white corpuscles in our own blood. We presume that they engulf invading organisms as a deterrent to infection or disease, but no one has yet verified this conjecture. Antibody formation is another important function that some mammalian white blood cells (e.g., lymphocytes) perform. At this time, no information is available to indicate whether or not a spider's hemocytes perform a similar function.

In sufficient amounts and under normal lighting, well-oxygenated hemolymph has a grey-blue tint, not red as in hemoglobin. Tarantula hemolymph feels slippery and slightly sticky, very much like our own blood. Like vertebrate blood, spider hemolymph fluoresces under ultraviolet light.

Of particular interest, the hemolymph of spiders and scorpions is quite toxic when injected into laboratory mice (Savory 1964). It appears that no one has yet tried to determine the identity of the toxin or how it works.

The spider's (and therefore, the tarantula's) heart is long and tubular, and lies along the top center of the opisthosoma, in its rear, not its chest, as it were. It can be seen as a dark dorsal stripe under the bald patch in New World tarantulas. The heart is enclosed in a pericardium, a tubular chamber that holds the heart and acts as a staging area preparatory to cycling the hemolymph through the circulatory system again. The tarantula's heart has four pairs of openings, called ostia (singular: ostium), along its length that act as valves. Hemolymph is drawn into the heart through these ostia to prepare for the next contraction.

Spider hearts are of special interest for a number of reasons. The tarantula's heart is suspended in the pericardium by elastic ligaments. When the heart contracts (systole) these ligaments are stretched. As the heart relaxes, these ligaments pull the heart back to its original volume.

As the heart contracts, a slight negative pressure is generated in the surrounding pericardium. This draws hemolymph into the pericardium from the opisthosoma. When the heart relaxes (diastole) and returns to its original volume, a slight negative pressure is generated inside it. This pulls hemolymph, that has been slowly draining into the pericardium, through the ostia into the heart in preparation for the next beat. Compare this to our hearts where the pericardium firmly adheres to the heart with no open spaces, and where blood is collected in special chambers (the auricles) made of heart muscle.

The differences don't end there, though. In the human heart, the basic heartbeat is produced by a distinct center of muscle tissue called the pacemaker. The contraction then spreads as a wave through the heart tissue as a whole. Although there is some nerve fibre modulation of our heartbeat, the pulse travels through, and is coordinated by the characteristics of the heart muscle itself. Vertebrate hearts are said to beat myogenically. *Myo* connotes *muscle,* and *genic* implies *start* or *beginning,* referring to the method used to start the heartbeat.

Spider hearts are neurogenic, not myogenic. The spider's heart possesses a fine strand of nerve fibre along its dorsal (upper) surface that not only initiates the heartbeat, but also coordinates its contraction. Its pacemaker is a set of nerve cells.

As the spider's heart beats, it pumps hemolymph *three* ways, sideways and rearward, as well as forward. Small arteries leave the heart from its sides and feed the tissues in the front and sides of the opisthosoma. The hemolymph that is pumped rearward leaves the heart through a posterior aorta and bathes most of the organs in the rear of the opisthosoma. The hemolymph that is pumped forward travels by means of an anterior aorta through the pedicel into the prosoma. It is distributed by arterial branches and released into cavities and spaces in the tissues and organs. From there it oozes through a network of spaces in the tissues (lacunae), and eventually passes back through the pedicel into the opisthosoma where it is directed past the book lungs (discussed next) by the orientation of the tissues and internal organs. There it releases its carbon dioxide and picks up a fresh supply of oxygen.

After the hemolymph percolates through the book lungs, it eventually returns to the heart, where it is collected in the pericardium to be recycled once more.

Respiratory System. By now it should come as no surprise that spiders have developed a different way to breathe, too.

Spiders, as a group, may breathe by means of either tracheae, book lungs or both. Tracheae (singular: trachea) are a system of tubes that carry air all through the spider's body. We need not worry about them here, however, because tarantulas and their kin do not have tracheae.

Tarantulas do have book lungs, however. There are four of them, and they resemble pockets on the bottom side of their opisthosomas, like the back pockets on a pair of blue jeans. The slitlike openings are called lung slits (also spiracles, stomata, and stigmata). If a tarantula is picked up and turned over, at least the rear pair can be seen. Often, in well-fed individuals, the forward pair is tucked under and hidden by the coxae of the last pair of legs. They are also quite obvious as four white patches inside the shed skin from the opisthosoma. Internally, they contain sheetlike folds of thin membrane, the lamellae (singular: lamella, also called leaflets or pages), that resemble the pages of a partially open book, hence the name. Hemolymph circulates inside these sheets, exchanging carbon dioxide for oxygen with the air that separates them. The lamellae are prevented from collapsing against each other by a multitude of tiny struts or columns. Book lungs are suspected of having their origins in apodemes (see page 34).

There has been much speculation about the presence or absence of breathing movements in tarantulas. Do they actively breathe, inhaling and exhaling as we do? Proponents point to perceived respiratory movements and to sets of muscles closely associated with the book lungs. Opponents have held that spiders simply didn't make breathing movements, period. Historically, experiments to investigate the matter have been contradictory or inconclusive. Recently, however, the results of a set of experiments were reported (Paul et al. 1987) that seem to lay the argument to rest once and for all. There are, indeed, very small movements in the walls of the book lungs, largely coordinated with the heartbeat and variations in hemolymph pressure. However, the amount of air circulated by these movements accounts for only a minute fraction of the total amount required for adequate gas exchange. Therefore, tarantulas do not inhale and exhale. They rely almost totally on diffusion of oxygen into their book lungs and carbon dioxide out.

Now that the puzzle has been solved, we may give a deep sigh of relief, even if they can't.

Digestive System. Spiders have no jaws. In their place, they possess stout, powerful chelicerae and fangs, and robust coxae on their pedipalps, often bearing spinous or toothlike processes.

The mouth lies between the pedipalps' coxae and immediately above a small plate called the labium, or lower lip. The labium appears to be a small forward extension of the sternum. Above the mouth, between the bases of the chelicerae, is another tiny plate called the labrum or upper lip. Do not be misled, however. Neither of these structures are very mobile, nor seems to function as our lips do. It was merely easier for the arachnologists of yore to give them familiar names than to create original, more appropriate ones.

From the mouth, a narrow tube, the pharynx, extends inward and upward a short distance. As the tube approaches the forward/bottom surface of the brain, it bends abruptly horizontally and passes through the brain. (Remember the perforation, as in the hole of a doughnut?) This horizontal portion of the tube is called the esophagus.

The esophagus connects to a boxlike, muscular organ called a pumping stomach. The pumping stomach, in turn, connects downward to the true stomach by means of a short extension. This true stomach lies between the pumping stomach and the brain in the prosoma. Fingerlike projections, gastric diverticula (singular: diverticulum), extend from the true stomach into the bases of the legs.

The true stomach empties into a relatively straight intestine that passes through the pedicel into the opisthosoma. In the opisthosoma, a cluster of stringlike organs, the Malpighian tubules, connect to the intestine. These serve many of the same functions as

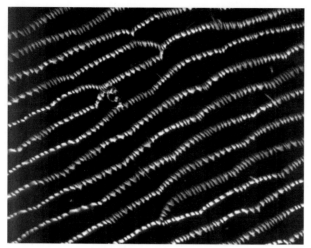

Part of the palate plate of Brachypelma emilia. *The distance between the rows of teeth is four to six microns (0.00016 inches to 0.00024 inches).*

our kidneys. A large outpocketing, a blind sac called the stercoral pocket, connects to the intestine a short distance before the anus. The anus opens immediately above the spinnerets.

Teeth on the palate plate of Brachypelma emilia. *The largest teeth are two microns (0.0008 inches) long. The hypothesis is that these teeth are the filtering mechanism.*

Tarantulas rely on their stout, powerful chelicerae and fangs, and robust pedipalpal coxae to masticate (chew) their prey. By contrast, most other spiders pierce their prey and suck the juices out through the small hole.

In spite of the tarantula's great size, only liquid food is consumed. Coarse particles are filtered out at the mouth by the various bristles on the bases of the chelicerae and pedipalpal coxae. Smaller particles, those as small as one micron (one one-thousandth of a millimeter) in diameter are filtered out by a filtering mechanism in their pharynxes, the palate plate. For comparison, most mammalian cells and most bacteria are larger than one micron in diameter. Spiders, and indeed most other arachnids, sip only liquids, never eating solid food.

As they eat, tarantulas regurgitate digestive fluids while masticating their prey. All of this is diluted by fluid from the coxal glands. The resulting, partially digested, liquid concoction is drawn up through the mouth, over the palate plate in the pharynx and through the esophagus by means of the pumping stomach in much the same way that humans use the backs of their throats when sipping a drink through a soda straw.

The pumping stomach is operated by powerful muscles, most of which are attached to the endosternite and the carapace. It passes the juices from the esophagus back and downward into the true stomach, for further digestion and partial absorption. More digestion and absorption takes place in the intestine. Toward the rear of the intestine, waste products are added from the Malpighian tubules to whatever remains of the digested fluids. The resulting mixture is stored in the stercoral pocket. This excrement is then periodically voided through the anus.

The Malpighian tubules are a good example of parallel evolution. Spider Malpighian tubules develop from a different fundamental embryonic tissue than those of insects. Because they resemble insects' Malpighian tubules, because they occur in about the same part of the digestive tract, and because they perform much the same function, they were given the same name. To be precise, they are analogues (having similar appearances and functions but having different origins), not homologues (having similar origins functions, and appearances).

An alternate nomenclature for parts of the digestive system is rostrum in place of labrum, sucking stomach for pumping stomach, proximal midgut for the true stomach, gastric caecum for gastric diverticulum, median midgut for the intestine, cloacal chamber or cloaca for stercoral pocket, and hindgut for the short tube between the stercoral pocket and the anus. Again, this duplicate nomenclature derives from an attempt to make these animals fit into a pattern based on a totally divergent groups of arthropods, instead of a system intended solely for their own unique case.

We have still one more aspect of spider digestion to discuss, the curious subject of the coxal glands. A description of these belongs in two places at once, digestion and excretion. Thus, this discussion is inserted between the two headings.

Most arthropods possess coxal glands that are direct homologues of more primitive excretory organs called nephridia, found in less advanced invertebrates. Tarantulas are no exception. They have two pairs located in the prosoma and emptying through pores along the posterior (rear) sides of the bases of the animals' first and third coxae, whence the name. For many years arachnologists have fretted about their purpose. Many held the opinion that they had no purpose, being vestiges of the more primitive nephridia that were no longer required. Other experts were not so certain. (Nephridia are discussed again on page 46.)

Recently, however, Butt and Taylor (1991) have determined that coxal glands do have a function. It seems that they secrete a salt solution that passes along the fold in the pleural membranes between the coxae and the sternum, toward the mouth. This fluid seems to have at least two purposes. First, it serves to maintain the fluidity of the food solution that the tarantula must drink, much like our saliva. Second, it may help to maintain the tarantula's salt balance by loading extra salt into the discarded food pellet. In a weird sort of way, the spider salivates through its armpits!

The final, well-blended pellet that remains after a meal is composed largely of the prey's indigestible body parts (e.g., its exoskeleton), the last few products of digestion that the tarantula couldn't extract, and excess salts. In the hobby, these are sometimes termed the tarantula's *spit ball,* the professional arachnologist refers to it as the *food bolus*.

In the large collection of tarantulas that the authors have amassed through the years (almost one thousand at this writing), feeding time is accompanied by a heavy, characteristic, sugary odor. What causes the odor? The digestive fluids from the tarantulas or the digested fluids of their food?

Excretory System. A major problem of all animals is the removal of the end products of metabolism before they build up to dangerous levels. Digestible substances are composed mainly of carbon, hydrogen, oxygen, and nitrogen with traces of several other elements. During metabolism, the bulk of the carbon is converted to carbon dioxide and leaves through the lungs or gills. Hydrogen is converted into water and is indistinguishable from the liquid water that may be consumed as part of the food or drunk from a water dish. The oxygen held in these substances may be incorporated into subsequent compounds or excreted as carbon dioxide.

The major element that has always been difficult to cope with, however, is nitrogen. When combined with hydrogen, it becomes ammonia, an exceedingly toxic compound. Aquatic animals can eliminate nitrogen as ammonia or some other extremely soluble compound by merely allowing it to dissolve directly into the water around them. There is usually abundant water, and little energy is required to guarantee adequate excretion.

Terrestrial animals are not in such favorable circumstances, however. Unless other strategies are used, nitrogen compounds rapidly rise to lethal concentrations in their bodies. Several

strategies have been developed as protection from nitrogenous waste poisoning. The most common is to convert the nitrogen into something less toxic than ammonia. If this alternate waste product is also relatively insoluble, an even greater buildup can be tolerated inside the animal as a compact solid or liquid. If the animal has the facility for isolating it from its physiology, the nitrogenous waste becomes even less dangerous. Lastly, the ideal waste product should be easily excretable with little or no loss of precious water, salts, or energy.

Arachnids in general, and spiders in particular, have developed techniques for accomplishing all of these. And (surprise, surprise!) they have done so in unique ways.

First is the problem of producing relatively nontoxic substances. Although spiders do excrete small amounts of other nitrogenous wastes (e.g., adenine, hypoxanthine, and uric acid), their principle waste product is guanine. This condition is unique with arachnids (Anderson 1966; Rao and Gopalakrishnareddy 1962), in direct contrast with the rest of the animal kingdom, which almost never excretes guanine as a waste product. To be sure, other animals produce guanine. Guanine is the principle substance responsible for the reflective retinas in cats and deer, for instance. Spiders, however, use it as a waste product, whereas cats and deer do not. Because guanine is totally insoluble, it does not interact with the spider's physiology and is, therefore, effectively nontoxic.

Second, because it's insoluble, it occurs as a concentrated solid, making storage much more efficient. Guanine occupies relatively less space, compared to urea for instance, and there is a much smaller demand to eliminate it.

Next, because it is a solid, it can be sequestered in harmless places. Some intestinal cells (guanocytes, no less) are capable of storing impressive quantities of guanine. Although they never actually remove guanine physically from the spider's body, they effectively get it out of the way, allowing the spider to get on with its metabolism without the material resource and energy losses normally associated with excretion.

Lastly, by concentrating the waste in solid form, the spiders can eliminate it with little waste of precious water, salts, or energy. Most guanine is secreted by the Malpighian tubules, stored in the stercoral pocket, and excreted with the remnants of digestion. Thus, arachnids in general, and spiders in particular, have used all four strategies to avoid nitrogen poisoning; and they have done so in an eminently efficient way.

An interesting ramification of all this is that tarantulas have no kidneys, do not produce urine, and therefore, don't urinate, at least in the sense that we usually use the word. Do they, then, guanate?

Reproductive System. The sex life of tarantulas is truly astonishing but will be discussed later on. For now we will confine ourselves to a description of their machinery.

Spider's gonads, ovaries in the female and testes in the male, are located inside the opisthosoma. The single genital opening (gonopore) is located on the ventral surface of the opisthosoma along a groove, called the epigastric furrow, that runs crosswise between the forward pair of book lungs. This groove defines the rearward margin of the epigynal plate. In older scientific writings, the epigastric furrow may be called the generative fold.

In the female, the two paired ovaries connect to a common oviduct that

A male Brachypelma smithi, *detailing the embolus and bulb on the pedipalp.*

leads to the gonopore. Immediately inside the gonopore are one or two out-pocketings called seminal receptacles or spermathecae (singular: spermatheca). During copulation (mating), the male deposits his sperm in the spermathecae where they remain alive until they are used to fertilize the eggs weeks or months later.

In the male, the paired testes are convoluted tubes that merge into a common duct. This, in turn, empties to the outside world through the gonopore. Associated with the gonopore are glands, called epiandrous glands, that are thought to either produce some of the semen that carries the sperm, or contribute silk to sperm web construction (Melchers 1964). Sperm webs are discussed on page 80.

The male has no penis or anything homologous to one. His copulatory appendages are the secondary sexual organs on the ends of his pedipalps. In the adult male, the terminal segment (pretarsus and claw) has metamorphosed from the relatively simple shape of the immature male's into a complex, intricately adapted organ used to introduce sperm into the female. This end segment is reminiscent of an exotic wine bottle with a bulbous body and a twisted neck. The body is called the bulb or reservoir, and the neck is called an embolus (plural: emboli). In turn, the pedipalpal tarsus has changed in shape to become a short, stout segment. The embolus and bulb are attached to it with a limber articulation that allows free motion in several planes. This modified tarsus is often called a cymbium (plural: cymbia). The cymbium, in turn, is attached to the end of the tibia with another limber joint.

The tibia bears a custom-fitted groove (called the alveolus) that matches the shape of the embolus and bulb. With the aid of the extra freedom of movement allowed by the cymbium's joints, the emoblus and bulb can be folded back into the alveolus when not being used. But, when the embolus and bulb are loaded with sperm and used to transfer the sperm to a female, they are unfolded so that they are fully exposed and held at a right angle to the rest of the pedipalp.

Musculature and Movement. Tarantulas have a multitude of muscles. The prosoma is almost two-thirds filled with them and each leg has more than thirty.

Most of the muscles in the prosoma are attached to the center of the carapace, at the central apodeme. These muscles have a multitude of functions. Some expand and contract the sucking stomach. Others move the chelicerae. Still others move the basal segments of the pedipalps and legs.

The muscles and segments in the legs of spiders pose an unusual problem. The insects and crustaceans (other vast wings of the Arthropoda) use a counterpoised system of hinge joints and muscles to extend and retract the segments of the legs. The fulcrum is part way down the cross section of the hinge, allowing extensions of the exoskeleton to protrude beyond it. Thus, muscles can pull on either the main body of the distal leg joint to bring it closer or pull on the extension to extend it.

In spiders, the muscles and joints in the coxae and trochanters raise, lower, and swing the legs forward and backward. But the muscles between the femur and the patella, and between the tibia and the basitarsi are quite different. The fulcrum of the hinge is on the upper edge of each joint. There are no extensions of the exoskeleton protruding beyond the fulcrum to allow a counterpoised pull. Thus, the muscles only pull the more distal segments toward the body and can never extend them. The musculature and hinges at these joints will only allow retraction.

"What then extends the appendages?" you demand.

Would you believe hydraulic pressure? That's right. Arachnids did it again. Their way! An hydraulic system for limb extension is unexpected among arthropods. The only other major groups of living organisms that use hydraulic pressure for body movement and limb extension are much more primitive. They are the roundworms and their allies (Aschelminthes, including Nemathelminthes, Rotifera and other less well-known groups), the segmented worms (Annelida), and the echinoderms (Echinodermata, starfish, and sea urchins).

The principle is not used by spiders in quite the same way as these other groups, however. Spiders' bodies are more or less hard capsules that cannot change shape appreciably without damage. With one exception, the same is true of their appendages. That exception is the flexible hinge that separates each pair of segments. The pressure of the hemolymph is used to inflate the partially collapsed hinges at these joints in order to extend them (Ellis 1944; Manton 1958; Parry and Brown 1959; Anderson and Prestwich 1975).

Around the periphery of the prosoma there exists a sheet of muscle tissue that connects the carapace to the coxal bases, the *musculi laterales*. When a spider must move its legs, it contracts this sheet of muscle. This has the effect of squeezing the prosoma and increasing the hemolymph pressure inside. Stewart and Martin (1974) measured this pressure in *Aphonopelma hentzi* at a maximum of 480 millimeters of mercury during a struggle. By comparison, normal human blood pressure is about 130 millimeters of mercury at rest and reaches 220 millimeters of mercury during heavy exercise.

This pressure is transferred through the legs' segments to the hinges and serves to expand or inflate them. By releasing the retractor muscles at the appropriate joints, the spider allows the leg to extend. Note carefully that little or no stretching has occurred in the hinges. They act more as bellows than as rubber balloons.

All this presents two very serious design limitations. First, although the hinges must be strong enough to withstand this pressure, they must also remain pliable enough to allow free movement. For an arthropod as massive as a tarantula (by terrestrial standards), this trade-off is crucial. The pressure required to lift their bodies more than a few centimeters would surely blow out all their joints. Further, if they became too large and massive, they simply couldn't move. The authors had a huge female tarantula, Duchess *(Brachypelma emilia),* that weighed more than fifty grams (1.8 ounces). She became so large that she was incapable of righting herself when turned upside down on a smooth surface.

Thus, all stories to the contrary notwithstanding, tarantulas cannot launch themselves more than a very short distance, perhaps the length of their leg spans, without actually touching *terra firma*. And they probably would not be able to get much larger than the *Theraphosa blondi* with the twenty-five centimeter leg span found at Montagne la Gabrielle, French Guiana in 1925. Do not be misled, however. They can dart surprisingly fast for their mass.

The other serious design limitation concerns the spider's endurance. Spiders tend to be sprinters, not marathon runners (Paul 1992). Why? Because they must hold their breath while running! The muscles for locomotion are in the prosoma, but their book lungs are isolated in the opisthosoma. The high pressure in the prosoma interferes with the circulation of hemolymph from the book lungs. Therefore, hemolymph in the prosoma becomes depleted of oxygen and heavily laden with carbon dioxide as they run (Anderson and Prestwich 1985). If pushed to the limit, spiders will resort to relatively inefficient anaerobic respiration (Prestwich 1983). However, the metabolic cost is dear, and soon they "hit the wall" in the same way as do human marathoners. Spiders in general, and the relatively massive tarantulas in particular, must at least slow down, if not stop altogether, to catch their breath.

Another very peculiar characteristic of spiders' musculature involves the

Burrow of Aphonopelma moderatum. *The silken veil indicates that the occupant is home but not accepting guests.*

1. Silk is used to line the lair. Indeed, some arboreal tarantulas (e.g., *Avicularia* species) make their entire nests of silk in the clefts in tree bark. These are virtually arboreal burrows!
2. Among terrestrial tarantulas, silk is used to cover the burrow's entrance with a fine veil when the tarantula doesn't wish to be disturbed.
3. Silk is used for draglines to help a roving tarantula find its way back to its burrow.
4. Milk is often used to lightly cover each parcel of soil that the tarantula expels as it enlarges its burrow.
5. Silk is used by many to construct a feeding web (place mat) when feeding in a cage. Do wild tarantulas also make such a feeding web in their burrows? Or, is this really only an abortive veil?
6. Silk is used to make a cradle when molting.
7. Silk is used as a temporary depository for sperm when the male is preparing for his search for females.
8. The male tarantula most often recognizes the presence of the female by the chemical qualities (we hesitate to say smell) of the silk at her burrow entrance.
9. Last, but certainly not least, silk is used by the female to make an eggsac, a purse for holding the developing eggs.

The source of silk, the spinnerets, is discussed on page 18.

manner in which the muscles are connected to the leg segments, including the pretarsi and claws. The muscles connect with tendon or tendon cells that, in turn, connect with long, tubular apodemes that are actually extensions of the exoskeleton. These apodemes extend some distance up the interior of the legs, and most surprisingly, their internal surfaces are shed with the old skin when the spider molts. These bizarre creatures shed the insides of their tendons!

Silk. Silk is the essence of spiders. Although it is true that other arthropods also spin silk, not all kinds of any given group will. Those that spin silk do so only during restricted phases of their life span and usually only for one or two specific purposes (e.g., by moth caterpillars for a cocoon). *All* spiders spin silk *all* their lives for an impressive variety of purposes. Tarantulas are no exception. Tarantulas use silk for many purposes.

The one purpose that tarantulas rarely or never use their silk for is the production of snares or traps as do many of the Araneomorphae, the so-called true spiders. In some kinds of tarantulas, however, silktrip lines are spun, radiating from the burrow's entrance, to alert the tarantula of an approaching meal or predator. This lack of snares or traps has been blamed on tarantulas being more primitive spiders. This, however, is not a valid argument. These creatures have had just as much opportunity to develop silk snares as the true spiders. However, because tarantulas tend to be much heavier bodied than the true spiders, as well as principally terrestrial or even subterranean, the manufacture of delicate surface or arboreal traps is simply not a practical solution to the problems of prey capture.

Chemically, this remarkable material is composed principally of proteins. It is produced by the silk glands on demand and is extruded through microscopic spigots in the spinnerets. As it leaves these spinnerets it is stretched, and this stretching reconforms the protein molecules to solidify the strand and generate its miraculous strength. It is important to note that the transition from liquid to solid is not a phenomenon of drying because spider silk will solidify under water as well as in air (for example with the European water spider *Argyroneta aquatica* [Clerck 1758], Family Argyronetidae).

Of the various properties of spider silk, its strength is legendary. Indeed, many primitive cultures around the world have used it for fish nets (for very small fish), and fine string when many strands are wound together. When compared with strands of steel of equal diameter, some spider silk is stronger. This high tensile strength, in addition to the extremely fine diameter, made it a fine candidate for gun and bomber sights during the Second World War. Spider silk will also stretch about twice as much as nylon before it finally breaks.

Lastly, in spite of the fact that it is almost pure protein, spider silk deteriorates very slowly. In the wild, it may hang in a bush for weeks after its creator has departed. In our homes, cobwebs will last almost indefinitely, unless swept away by the fastidious housekeeper. And in a cage, tarantula silk may persist for a year or more with little sign of degradation. Bacteria and fungi grow on it with great difficulty, and in nature few other animals eat it in spite of the obvious food value. Why so? We don't know.

The production of this silk can represent a considerable expenditure of both energy and protein. If all of this silk were to be discarded after its use, it could amount to a great loss. Most spiders eat at least a portion of their silken constructions after their usefulness is past. Tarantulas, however, do so to a much lesser degree than most other spiders.

It is tempting to say that this is evidence that they are a more primitive spider that has not developed the instinct as completely as the more advanced spiders. But, an equally plausible explanation is that the expenditure of energy and protein for their limited silk production is much smaller when compared by body weight. As a result, the mandate to conserve is not quite so compelling, and they can afford to be a bit wasteful.

Although tarantulas may consume the feeding web that they construct while eating their prey in the artificial environment of a cage, they do not ordinarily eat most of their silken constructions. These must be removed by the keeper from time to time.

But, what happens to all the silk that tarantulas spin in the wild? For many tropical kinds, the silken constructions are large and persistent. But for the tarantulas in the American southwest, little is obvious around a burrow's entrance, and very little silk is found inside the burrows. Do these tarantulas not spin much silk? Or, do they eat most of their old silk? If so, why is there such a difference between their silk-eating habits in the wild compared to those in captivity?

Metabolism and Thermoregulation. Tarantulas are poikilothermic. That is, they produce virtually none of their own body heat. Their body temperature tends to vary with that of their surroundings. Compare this with the more familiar animals like dogs, birds, and humans that are homoiothermic, producing physiological heat internally to maintain a constant body temperature. Homoiotherms maintain a constant, high body temperature in spite of the surrounding temperature.

For tropical kinds of tarantulas, the ambient temperature is relatively stable all year. However, for those tarantulas that live in more temperate climates, the ambient temperature may fluctuate through a wide range in the course of a few days to the full year. As an example, those tarantulas living in the region around Pueblo, Colorado (USA) may experience daytime temperatures in excess of 37°C (98°F) in August. That same evening, the temperature may drop to 15°C (59°F). And, in January or February, air temperatures will often go below freezing. During cold weather these tarantulas plug the openings of their burrows with soil and debris, and go into a state of torpor.

Some have referred to this torpid state as diapause, but this may be incorrect. Diapause requires a physiological preparation (e.g., deposition of fat), usually prepares an organism for a long period of unsuitable conditions, and is under hormonal control, mediated by temperature or photoperiod. The term is usually reserved to describe the suspension of growth or development in eggs, larval, or immature arthropods, seldom with adults. No one has yet examined torpid tarantulas to determine if the mechanism of their inactivity is merely immobility due to cold, a hormonal mechanism, or something else entirely. Neither do we know whether the state is different in immatures and adults, or if it is different with different species.

This torpor is most definitely not hibernation. Hibernation implies active physiological thermoregulation, even at temperatures near freezing (as with ground squirrels). Tarantulas are poikilothermic, and do nothing to control their temperatures while in a state of torpor. They are merely sealing themselves into a burrow while they are unable to defend or maintain themselves.

Although arachnids are poikilothermic, it is a mistake to believe that their body temperature is *always* the same as their surroundings. Tree-dwelling tarantulas probably bask in the rising sun to quickly raise their body temperatures above the ambient temperature. Burrow-dwelling tarantulas move up and down the lengths of their burrows to adjust their body temperatures as close to optimal as possible (Minch 1977, 1978). Although physiological thermoregulation isn't possible, behavioral thermoregulation is practiced by these remarkable creatures.

Most arachnids have been found to have unusually low metabolic rates, even at temperatures we consider normal (Anderson 1970; Anderson and Prestwich 1982). Tarantulas are no exception. These were measured at about thirty-five percent below the values predicted as normal for other poikilotherms of similar size (Anderson 1970).

Several reasons have been advanced to explain this. Perhaps as some of the first land animals, 400 million years ago, the arachnids developed lower metabolic rates to compensate for the unpredictability and harshness of the environment. Presumably, this is a characteristic that has been maintained through all those eons. Although this may well be true, it is hard to believe that a group of animals that has diversified so much in other respects has not been able to accelerate their metabolic rate, and thereby increase their competitiveness as well. Perhaps it simply wasn't necessary for some other reason.

They may have developed such a low metabolic rate as part of that tendency to diversify. It is possible that their low metabolic rate is a survival adjustment that does indeed give arachnids the competitive edge over both their predators and prey. The basic, primal demands of nearly all animals are to secure territory in which to live, secure a food supply, and then to reproduce. (Often, but not always, the first two imperatives are coincident.) We normally rate efficiency as the amount of food, territory, or offspring acquired or produced. However, by "doing their own thing," arachnids may have evolved a quite different yardstick with which to measure efficiency. Instead of securing a larger food supply, they developed a metabolism that allows them to thrive on much less food.

Most are reclusive, existing in relatively confined areas and requiring little space to function. Some varieties hardly move at all. Many live their entire lives within a few meters of their place of birth. They have little need for a high metabolic rate.

Now, let's do a little simple math. Because we will be making some rather broad assumptions, this discussion shouldn't be taken too literally. The principle is valid, the details are only crude approximations.

A tarantula has a metabolic rate one-third less than the average cold-blooded animal of the same size, a lizard for instance. That means that it operates at two-thirds the lizard's metabolic rate. We may assume that, on average, this lizard operates at a rate of about one-eighth to one-tenth that of a similarly sized homoiotherm, a mouse for instance. We'll choose one-eighth as the ratio to use. That means that a tarantula operates at roughly one-twelfth (two-thirds times one-eighth) the metabolic rate of a mouse.

If we assume that the average human weighs about seventy-five kilograms (165 pounds) and the average tarantula fifty grams (slightly less than two ounces) we see that there is a fifteen-hundred-to-one size ratio.

If we assume that mice and humans have about the same metabolic rate (Not true! But remember, this is only a crude approximation), we may multiply the size ratio by the metabolic rate ratio (one-twelfth times one-fifteen-hundredth). The result suggests that a pet tarantula may survive quite nicely on *one-eighteen-thousandth* the food that its owner does. If we each consume two kilograms (nearly four and a half pounds) of food and drink a day (at least in the Western countries), we eat sixty thousand grams of food a month. The average tarantula should survive quite nicely on 60,000 divided by 18,000, or three and one-third grams of food a month! Indeed, the adult tarantulas in the authors' collection remain in very good condition, even becoming obese, on six to eight crickets a month. By actual measurement, six adult crickets weigh about three grams. Crickets as food are discussed on page 127.

The fresh exuvium of Brachypelma emilia. *How much of the anatomy can you identify?*

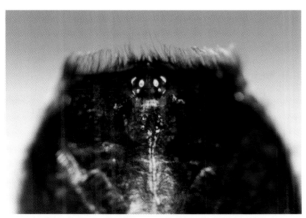

The eye field from inside the molted carapace. These are not holes in the integument, merely small transparent ports.

The Exuvium, Revisited

Now that we have discussed tarantula anatomy and physiology, it is time to reexamine the exuvium (the shed skin) in greater detail.

Look at the carapace. If it is held up to a bright light, eight eyes glowing like a tiny constellation of stars should be obvious. These are not real holes in the tarantula's skin, just transparent portholes.

At the same time, note the way that the central apodeme extends from the carapace down into the tarantula's body as a place for muscle attachment. From the outside it appears to be a small pit. From the inside it resembles a substantial icicle or stalactite.

Now, look at the floor of the prosoma. Notice the passageways left by the chelicerae, pedipalps, and legs. One can only marvel at the tarantula's ability to extract itself from them.

Along with the outer body surface, the linings of many passageways leading to the outside are also shed. If an exuvium is examined in good light, the lining to the pharynx, esophagus, and pumping stomach may be obvious as they protrude upward from the area between the chelicerae bases. Also obvious is the position of the mouth at the place where the pharynx is attached to the inside of the exuvium. The mouth is at that exact point, positioned immediately above the labium, and hidden in the bristles of the pedipalpal coxae.

On an especially good shed from an exceptionally large tarantula, the linings to the coxal gland ducts can also be seen as fine hair-like projections arising from the posterior (rear) sides of the third pair of coxae. On an extraordinary shed, another pair might also be found on the posterior sides of the first pair of coxae.

Taking a large, shed skin that is not otherwise salvageable for display, use a fine pair of scissors or a razor blade to carefully make a lengthwise slit through the basitarsi, telotarsi, and pretarsi of one of the legs. Several fine, stiff, white strings attached to the inside of the exoskeleton will be visible extending some distance up into the tarantula's leg toward the prosoma. These are the internal linings of the tarantula's tendons.

The book lungs are very obvious inside the opisthosoma. Look for the four relatively large, whitish areas. On larger individuals or with a dissecting microscope, the lamellae will be discernable. What is seen here, are the book lungs from the inside or hemolymph side of the tarantula, not the outside or air side.

Careful inspection will reveal the inside of the epigastric furrow, crossing the bottom surface of the opisthosoma between the rear edges of the forward book lungs. Look carefully at this furrow. If it is not apparent, or appears only as an insignificant wrinkle, the exuvium is from an immature male (see acompanying figure). However, if the epigastric furrow protrudes up into the body cavity as a distinct wall or leaf, and especially if there are one or two small swellings or fingerlike protrusions along its forward margin (the spermathecae), the tarantula is a female (see acompanying figure). In females, the spermathecae become apparent at a very early age, following the sixth or seventh molt. Unfortunately, this inspection cannot tell us whether the female is mature or not.

Also, from the inside, the position of the four spinnerets and the anus are quite obvious at the tarantula's rear.

Remarks

At the beginning of this chapter, we asked the question "Which are more bizarre, spiders or us?" This is a trick

Inside a female's exuvium. Note the four white book lungs and the leaflike extension of the epigastric furrow between the forward pair.

question, for the spiders would declare that we were, and we (of course) remain convinced that they are.

Inside an immature male's exuvium. Although a wrinkle of skin runs between the forward book lungs, there is no leaflike extension of the epigastric furrow.

So be it. We are humans, reading a book about tarantulas, not the reverse. We are allowed some prejudice here. Therefore, we shall (with some reservations) declare that it is the arachnids who excel at bizarreness. *They* are the ones who have developed outlandish shapes, curious anatomies, exotic modes of reproduction, peculiar biochemistries, and unconventional physiologies.

As a subgroup of these fantastic animals, the spiders are no exception. Their anatomy is more bizarre than any of us could possibly have imagined. They have a total of eight pairs of appendages, whereas we are only used to two. They have no jaws, but possess highly specialized and efficient weapons in their place. They have no distinct heads, but carry their brains where we might ordinarily expect a heart. Their stomachs (both of them!) are also there, instead of in an abdomen. Although their heart and lungs are toward their rear, the male's copulatory organs are up front, on the ends of feelers. Their skeletons are both inside and outside, their excretory organs bear almost no analogy to ours whatsoever, and their metabolic rates are so low that we could arguably call them "the living dead!"

This strangeness has caused much consternation and confusion among the experts, as evidenced by the duplicity of names for their body parts. It would appear that spiders have purposely conspired to mislead the student, causing much grief during final exams! If these differences cause grief among students, they inspire a fascination, even awe, among amateur and professional arachnophiles like us.

Upside down, inside out, and backwards, tarantulas seem as alien as any animal could be, and their excessive size commands instant attention. It is no wonder they are such prime subjects for myths, old wives' tales, and horror movies. And yet, the magnitude and scope of these differences are what make the tarantulas, these giants of the spider world, so completely fascinating to us.

Viva la difference!

Chapter Two
The Name of the Tarantula

One of the very first questions asked about tarantulas in a pet shop is "What kind is it?" It would seem that this would be the easiest question to answer. Unfortunately, it is one of the most difficult. To gain an appreciation of why, and some understanding of the difficulty, we must digress for a few pages.

The Big Picture

There are two ways that tarantulas are named, the common name and the scientific name. Neither method is simple, easy, or entirely satisfactory.

The Common Name

This unofficial method relies on a string of people, beginning perhaps with a villager in Thailand or Columbia, continuing through a series of collectors, exporters, importers, and dealers, and ending with the enthusiast. Somewhere along the line, the tarantula is given a common name. That name may accompany it until it is finally sold to the pet fancier, or it can be changed during its journey, perhaps several times. For instance, someone may decide, usually for economic reasons, that the current name isn't a very good one, and will change it to something more glamorous. Or, a dealer will simply forget the original name and make up a new one. The same kind of tarantula, caught in two separate places only a few hundred kilometers apart may come to have two completely different common names, whereas quite different tarantulas may have the same common name. Thus, the name given by the pet shop cannot be completely trusted. The authority is anything but trustworthy, and the name has no official standing. It must be viewed with the greatest skepticism.

Having said that, it is important to note that many kinds of tarantulas have been available to the pet hobby long enough and in large enough numbers so that their common and scientific names, discussed next, are more or less standardized and universally accepted.

The Gospel According to Linné

So, what is the "official" name? The story now becomes very complicated. What we present here is only a superficial explanation. The enthusiast who wishes a more rigorous treatment of the subject should speak with a biologist at a college or university, or seek books on the subject in a college or university library under the key word *taxonomy*.

In the Beginning There Was the Plan. In 1758 a Swedish botanist by the name of Karl von Linné (also called Carolus Linnaeus, and several other

> **A**ppendix A: Tarantula Species as Pets (page 261) is a cross-reference between common names and scientific names for many of the tarantulas available to the hobby.

variations. See page 63 for a discussion of Latinizing names.) published a system for naming every plant and animal that he knew (Linné 1758). At first, Linné intended his system to merely serve as a hypothetical means for organizing these creatures. Linné was convinced, as were his contemporaries, that God had created all organisms on Earth during the first six days of creation. His system was not intended to reflect any actual relationship between the various kinds of organisms. All kinds had only one real relationship. They were created by God. All that concerned Linné was establishing an ordered system for keeping track of them as they were discovered, of creating a glorified file card system that would be logical and easy to use. Its greatest immediate utility was in museums, where the ever-burgeoning collections desperately needed some unifying system for keeping track of the specimens.

But, naming every known plant and animal on Earth has proven to be much more difficult than could ever have been imagined by Linné. With the passing of two and one-half centuries, this basic system has been expanded, altered, and refined as our knowledge of biology advanced. If he were to return today, Linné would probably be able to recognize the rudiments of it, but that would be all. We will examine only the most important confounding influences.

Changing the Rules. About a century after Linné published his file card system, biologists went through a very fundamental change of philosophy prompting a corresponding fundamental restructuring of the system. Whenever the rules change in the middle of a game, chaos reigns.

In 1859, Charles Darwin published *On the Origin of Species* (Darwin 1859), the first successful explanation of a theory of evolution. Today, more than 135 years later, it is generally agreed to be a natural law, and virtually all biologists ascribe to it as the means by which we have acquired as many different kinds of organisms as we have. Note that, contrary to popular belief, Charles Darwin did not invent the theory of evolution. There were others who had the same idea, Jean Baptiste Lemarck fifty years earlier, for instance. Darwin's major achievement was taking the basic concept, collecting data, correcting a lot of the original shortcomings, and proposing a realistic, testable mechanism by which it worked.

Darwin's Law was almost immediately incorporated into Linné's nomenclatural system. This caused an instantaneous upheaval in the way animals and plants were named. Rule number one had changed. God may, or may not, have created all plants and animals on Earth, but now, all these creatures had some definable relationship to each other. In order for the system to work, these relationships had to be determined. Each organism must fit into an elaborate family tree, and the system must reflect that relationship.

Thus, the names that we give these creatures are not only used for organizing them in a list, like names in a telephone directory, but must also reflect the creatures' interrelationships, their phylogenetic relationship, like the family names in a human genealogy. To accomplish this, biologists have organized all living and extinct organisms into a cascade of succeedingly smaller and smaller, more and more intimately related groups, level by level. Thus, the twin sciences of taxonomy and systematics were born.

This first upheaval changed Linné's single-line, file-card system into a multidimensional tree structure, many times more complex than first intended. We will examine this tree a little more fully, later.

The Teeming Hordes. Another major confounding influence is the sheer number of kinds of organisms and museum specimens that are being dealt with. The current estimate of the number of distinct living species of plants, animals, and other more obscure living organisms varies with authority, but is probably well in excess of ten *million* species! Merely counting them at one per second, twenty-four hours a day would require almost *four* months! And these are only the living kinds. There are untold millions more extinct ones, most of which haven't been discovered or catalogued as yet. In fact, it has been estimated that 90 percent of the kinds of organisms that have ever lived in Earth's five-billion-year history are now extinct. Thus, the total number of kinds of living organisms ever to live on planet Earth may exceed one *billion*.

From the seventeenth century onward, with the rise of colonialism and outright military opportunism, the discovery and collection of new plants and animals accelerated at a rate that was truly staggering. Biologists simply could not keep up with the pace. Buried in the basements and on obscure back shelves in the world's museums are untold numbers of bottles of specimens preserved in spirits, as ethyl alcohol was frequently called. Each contains dozens or hundreds of insects, spiders, and other arthropods that haven't been examined since they were first collected. Dutifully, every few years, museum personnel replace the evaporated alcohol; but no one, not even the resident arachnologist, knows what mysteries or marvels the bottles contain. There simply aren't enough research dollars or hours in a lifetime to allow even a cursory examination of these specimens. In these bottles are new, important range records and habitat data for known species, males of species for which only the females are known, females of species for which only the males are known, specimens of species for which the original types have been lost or are hopelessly damaged, and hundreds, perhaps thousands, of totally new, undescribed species.

One Big Mess. Understandably, in the resulting attempt to cope with the deluge of new specimens, mistakes were made in the taxonomy of both the plant and animal kingdoms. Among tarantulas, different names were often assigned to opposite sexes of the same species, or to individuals of the same species from different localities. Unsubstantiated, perfunctory guesses were made of the identity of specimens. Often, the literature was not adequately reviewed or the specimen not compared to existing museum specimens, sometimes even from the same museum.

In all fairness, it is also very easy to innocently misidentify a specimen. It is very difficult to find truly definitive characters to use in identifying tarantulas and their brethren, and many of the earlier, written descriptions are poor at best. Even if an arachnologist conscientiously reviewed the literature, a specimen could be easily misidentified if that identification had to be based on a written description or drawing alone.

The question might be asked "Were specimens ever kept for future reference so that we might redescribe them properly?" The answer is a qualified "yes." Such specimens are called *type specimens* or merely *types* and are sheltered

Table I
Phyla in the kingdom Animalia

Acanthocephela	Annelida	**ARTHROPODA**
Aschelminthes	Brachiopoda	Chaetognatha
Chordata	Coelenterata	Ctenophora
Echinodermata	Echiuroidea	Ectoprocta
Entoprocta	Gnathostomulida	Hemichordata
Mesozoa	Mollusca	Nemertinea
Pentastomida	Phoronidea	Platyhelminthes
Pogonophora	Porifera	Priapuloidea
Protozoa	Sipunculoidea	Tardigrada

in major museums around the world. But, because of wars, accidents, natural calamities, acts of God, imperfect preservation, and just plain carelessness, many of the original specimens have been hopelessly damaged, lost, or destroyed. Unless these are recovered or replaced, we lack the reference specimens for many species. Distressingly often, we may have nothing more than a drawing or a poorly written description on which to base a determination, and no good means of redescribing the species more rigorously.

Regardless of the reasons, the results are the same. We now have a terrible mess on our hands. Every major museum holds untold numbers of specimens of tarantulas that may be misidentified, not identified, improperly catalogued or lost in storage; and, in the foreseeable future, there is little probability that anyone will be able to sort out the problem.

Most of the tarantulas commonly sold in pet shops are well known enough to science for the scientific name to be certain. However, for the less common ones, and for those that are newly imported, there is no really good way to know which species is being considered. An educated guess might be made, to be sure, and that guess has a fair chance of being correct. But who would be willing to stake a lifelong reputation as a research scientist on a name derived in this way? Unfortunately, neither research scientists, enthusiasts, nor casual pet keepers have much choice.

There is some progress, however. Over the last 250 years many attempts have been made to categorize tarantulas. Most notable are Ausserer (1872), Simon (1892, 1903), Pocock (1895, 1897), Petrunkevitch (1928, 1939), Exline and Petrunkevitch (1939), and more recently, Smith (1985, 1992, 1995), Raven (1985 and 1986) and Platnick (1989). Hopefully, with each attempt we are getting closer to the truth.

There is an interesting sidelight to this story, and a portent of things to come. Darwin's theory of evolution is now undergoing a critical reevaluation by paleontologists and biologists due to the fossil evidence found in the Burgess Shale near Field, British Columbia, Canada, and other, less well-noted fossil deposits around the world. In addition to Darwin's basic "over-reproduction/survival of the fittest" model, sceintists are now proposing a "punctuated equilibrium" model as a more comprehensive explanation of the way in which life

Table II
Subphyla in the phylum Arthropoda

CHELICERATA	Crustacea	Atelocerata
(Horseshoe crabs, sea spiders, arachnids)	(Lobsters, water fleas, pill and sow bugs, etc.)	(Insects, centipedes, millipedes, etc.)

evolves. In this new model, Darwinian evolution acts on a more limited, local level. The reader is referred to Gould (1989) for a more comprehensive treatment of this subject.

The ramifications of this have yet to trickle down through the twin sciences of taxonomy and systematics. One thing is certain: At least at the upper levels of the taxonomic hierarchy, important changes are inevitable, and yet another major source of confusion looms on the horizon.

Taxonomy and Classification

The Family Tree

So, what *is* the name of the tarantula? What follows is a quasiscientific description of the system for naming all animals in general, and tarantulas in particular. Some license has been taken to simplify the scheme for this book. Those interested in a more rigorous treatment of arachnid, spider, and tarantula systematics and taxonomy are encouraged to read Raven (1985), Coddington and Levi (1991), Breene (1996), and seek college-level books or a course on the subject.

For our purposes, we can adopt the admittedly simpleminded point of view that any living thing that is not a plant, is an animal. (This ignores such organisms as viruses, bacteria, and fungi as a means of streamlining this discussion.) All such animals are then lumped into one huge category, the animal kingdom (kingdom Animalia). This animal kingdom comprises at least ten million species of living organisms, with this estimate varying widely depending on the authority. In addition, there are untold millions of extinct species.

The animal kingdom is divided and subdivided through a complex of levels and sublevels in a descending hierarchy. Each such division and subdivision (and, therefore, group of plants or animals) is called a taxon (plural: taxa). For the record, the principle levels in this hierarchy are kingdom, phylum, class, order, family, genus, and species. As we shall see shortly, it is also possible for any of these major steps or levels to be subdivided into minor ones.

A gravid female tick on a dog. This is the ventral aspect displaying the four pairs of legs.

Table III
Classes in the subphylum Chelicerata

Pycnogonida	Sea spiders
Merostomata	Sea scorpions (extinct) and horseshoe crabs
ARACHNIDA	Spiders, scorpions, mites, ticks, and others.

One phylum in the animal kingdom is composed of all animals having an exoskeleton impregnated with chitin and sclerotin, and with more or less rigid, jointed appendages (Table 1). This phylum is called Arthropoda. It is far and away the largest and most successful group of animals on our planet (Meglitsch 1972, Barnes 1980).

Occasionally, a taxonomic group is so large, or displays a collection of characteristics so dissimilar that it cannot easily be broken into the basic levels of the system. Sometimes an extra level or two must be added to make things fit properly. This is the case with the phylum Arthropoda. There appears to be a clear division of this group into three subgroups. One such group is composed entirely of the organisms which we call crustaceans, subphylum

A windscorpion (order Solifugae) from western Texas. These creatures are fierce predators and exceedingly difficult to maintain in captivity.

Crustacea, and includes lobsters, pillbugs, and a host of other strange creatures, almost as bizarre as the spiders.

Another vast group, the Atelocerata, includes the insects, centipedes, and millipedes and their brethren. This is by far the largest single group of arthropods.

The last group, of paramount importance to us, is the Chelicerata which includes horseshoe crabs, spiders and their brethren, and sea spiders. While the previous two groups have distinct antennae and mandibles or jaws, the chelicerates do not.

Antennae are called *feelers* in the vernacular. They are appendages arising from the head of organisms like crabs and locusts, and are usually used as sensory structures. However, the crustaceans are notorious for subverting them to a multitude of other duties, some quite surprising. The chelicerates do not have antennae, and probably never did.

Typically, jaws are single segmented appendages that move against each other, ordinarily to chew food. In some organisms these are highly modified and hardly look like real jaws (e.g., mosquitoes), but their true nature can be deduced because the creatures bearing them are obviously closely related to other, similar organisms that do have real jaws (e.g., other gnats and flies).

In primitive chelicerates, the corresponding appendages usually have several joints that act like small pincers. Superficially, they resemble the claws of crustaceans (e.g., crabs and lobsters), but arise from a different part of the embryo during development, and upon close inspection are constructed quite differently. Lobster and crab claws are really highly modified legs, and are associated with the middle part of their bodies. Chelicerae are attached much farther forward, being clearly associated with the mouth.

The practice of lumping chelicerates, crustaceans, and atelocerates into a common phylum is under question by some taxonomists (Barnes 1980). There is much suspicion and some evidence that each group arose from ancestors that diverged much further back in prehistory than was previously thought. Many of their similarities would then be the result of parallel evolution rather than a close relationship.

Those chelicerates that possess only one pair of chelicerae, one pair of pedipalps, and four pairs of walking legs, are called arachnids, class Arachnida (Savory 1977) (Table III). These are some of the most bizarre creatures on earth.

The arachnids are then further divided into yet smaller subdivisions called orders, one of which is the order Araneae, the spiders (Table IV). Spiders are characterized by possessing two-segmented chelicerae containing venom glands, a single carapace covering the prosoma, a narrow pedicel separating the prosoma and opisthosoma.

The spiders are broken into two suborders (Table V). One, the Mesothelae, is composed of quite primitive spiders whose living representatives are found only in eastern Asia. They are important because they are apparently living fossils, missing links between our modern spiders (tarantulas included) and those much more primitive ones that haunted the coal age swamps and forests 380

South African rock scorpion, Hadogenes *species. These will tame enough to be handled by those who are brave. The sting is mild, but the pinchers are very strong.*

million years ago. The most important differentiating characteristic of the Mesothelae is that they possess clearly segmented opisthosomas.

A giant vinegaroon (order Uropygi) from Arizona, Mastigoproctus giganteus. *"So ugly, it makes your teeth hurt." Excellent pets.*

Table IV
Orders in the class Arachnida

Acari	Mites and ticks (also called Acarina)
Amblypygi	Tailless whipscorpions, genus *Tarantula* belongs here.
ARANEAE	Spiders (also called Araneida)
Opiliones	Harvestmen, daddylonglegs (also called Phalangida)
Palpigrada	Microwhipscorpions
Pseudoscorpiones	Pseudoscorpions
Ricinulei	Hooded tickspiders (formerly called Podogona)
Schizomida	Shorttailed whipscorpions
Scorpiones	Scorpions
Solifugae	Windscorpions (in North America), sunscorpions, sunspiders (elsewhere)
Uropygi	Whipscorpions, vinegaroons

The other division interests us much more, however. Here is an example where an additional level in the hierarchy was considered necessary, and the suborder Opisthothelae was divided into two subordinate divisions called Infraorders. Subgroups are discussed on page 58.

The division between these infraorders is based on the attachment, or articulation, of their chelicerae. If these appendages are attached beneath the spider's face, so to speak, and if the fangs work more or less toward each other, like old-fashioned ice tongs, the animals are considered to be true spiders, infraorder Araneomorphae (e.g., *Argiope* species). If, on the other hand, the chelicerae are attached to the front of the face and work more or less parallel to each other, like our index and middle fingers, they are considered to be the not-so-true spiders called mygalomorphs, infraorder Mygalomorphae. (See Table VI.)

Table V
Suborders in the order Araneae

Mesothelae	Rare, primitive spiders (also called Liphistiomorphae). Contains only one Family: Liphistiidae.
OPISTHOTHELAE	Virtually all living and many extinct spiders (except the Mesothelae).

Table VI
Infraorders in the suborder Opisthothelae

Araneomorphae	Most common spiders (also called Labidognatha)
MYGALOMORPHAE	Tarantulas and tarantulalike spiders (also called Orthognatha)

Table VII
Families in the infraorder Mygalomorphae

Actinopodidae	Mouse spiders
Antrodiaetidae	Folding door spiders
Atypidae	Purseweb spiders
Barychelidae	Brushfooted trapdoor spiders
Ctenizidae	Trapdoor spiders
Cyrtaucheniidae	No common name
Dipluridae	Funnelweb spiders
Hexathelidae	Australian funnelweb spiders (the deadly *Atrax robusta* (O. P. Cambridge) and its relatives belongs here)
Idiopidae	Armored trapdoor spiders
Mecicobothriidae	No common name
Microstigmatidae	No common name
Migidae	Tree trapdoor spiders
Nemesiidae	Tubetrapdoor, wishbone spiders
Paratropididae	Baldlegged spiders
THERAPHOSIDAE	Tarantulas

The name *Orthognatha* is used in place of Mygalomorphae in older texts.

The mygalomorphs in turn, are composed of several families (Table VII), one of which is the family Theraphosidae. Now, here is where we begin to have serious trouble. Almost from the day of its inception, arachnologists agreed that the precise definitions of the families and subfamilies of the entire suborder Opisthothelae were erroneous, but no one had a very good idea of how they should be redescribed and reorganized. In 1985, Dr. R. J. Raven published a revision of the taxonomy of tarantulas and their near relatives. In this paper, he reorganized all of the taxa of the Mygalomorphae, down to subfamilies and genera. That reorganization is followed very closely here, reflecting only a few changes made since Raven's paper was published. The reader must bear in mind that this organization is not accepted by all arachnologists, and additional refinements are constantly being made. Examples of this are the *Brachypelma/Euathlus* and *Aphonopelma/Delopelma/Dugesiella/Eurypelma/Rhechostica* groups, discussed in Appendix A.

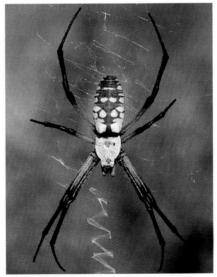

Genus Argiope *(suborder Araneomorphae, family Araneidae). An orbweaver from Texas.*

Table VIII
Subfamilies in the family Theraphosidae

Aviculariinae	Eumenophorinae
Harpactirinae	Ischnocolinae
Ornithoctoninae	Selenocosmiinae
Selenogyrinae	Theraphosinae
Thrigmopoeinae	

The spiders that concern us here are the Theraphosidae. We call them tarantulas. Over the centuries, professional arachnologists have also called this family of spiders Mygalidae after the original genus, *Mygale,* and Aviculariidae. Both names have since fallen into disfavor.

The family Theraphosidae is further split into subfamilies. Currently, nine are recognized (Table VIII). However, there are several genera and species whose relationships are still unclear. Raven was unable to place them in appropriate subfamilies, and some of them may eventually be incorporated into entirely new subfamilies. A revision is in progress even as this text goes to press, and the next iteration of this classification scheme will undoubtedly hold more subfamilies with the existing genera (and a few new ones, as well) redistributed between them.

*P*eer Review: The procedure whereby a scientific article, written by one scientist or group of scientists, is read and critiqued by other scientists who have some expertise in the same field. In theory, the authors are then obliged to correct any errors found, or answer any criticisms made about content or structure before the paper is published.

These subfamilies are then divided into smaller, more intimately related groups called genera (singular: genus) such as *Aphonopelma, Avicularia, Poecilotheria*. In each of these genera there are one or more species. The genus name with the species name (specific epithet) is considered the true name for the animal, e.g., *Aphonopelma hentzi* (Gerard 1854) and *Avicularia avicularia* (L. 1758). The genus name is always capitalized, and both the genus and species names are always italicized, or underlined if italics aren't possible. If there is a third name in italics, a subspecies is indicated (e.g., *Avicularia avicularia variegata* (F.O.P.-Cambridge 1896). In older books and papers, the scientific name may be printed in emboldened type or in small capitals rather than italics, but this practice has now been abandoned.

If the last word is not italicized (but may be abbreviated or in parentheses), it is the name of the person who first described that species, the original authority. In all scientific publications as well as many enthusiast books, the year in which the species was first described by the original authority is also given, at least at first mention. If so, this should follow the authority's name, within the parentheses, if present.

Nondefinition of a Species. What is a species? That depends partly on what type of organism is being considered, and by the people who are considering it. The fact is that there is no universally accepted, all-encompassing definition of a species.

Not that creating such a definition hasn't been attempted. One of the better-known attempts defines a species as a population of interbreeding organisms, whose offspring resemble the parents. But, what does one do with an organism in which no sexual reproduction occurs (e.g., some kinds of fungi, insects, and protozoans)? What does one do with races of fertile hybrids between what are apparently different kinds of organisms? Lastly, what does one do if only one dead specimen is available? (It is definitely neither breeding nor a population.)

Setting aside all the academic rhetoric, and from a purely functional perspective, a species is any kind of organism that someone (Almost anyone—you, for instance.) thinks is different enough from all other apparently related kinds of organisms to warrant a different name. The name must follow the basic rules for naming living organisms; but beyond that, all that is required is that a description of the new species be published in some book, journal, or magazine. There is an ideal format followed by the experts in the field, but nowhere is it written that everybody must follow it exactly, and many do not. Neither does the publication have to be a recognized scientific journal; the *New York Times* will work just fine. The description does not have to be peer-reviewed, either.

Ultimately, the description will be considered by the recognized authorities in the field. If the description is so poor that it is obviously inadequate, the experts will reject it. If it is too good to be rejected out of hand, but still quite poor, it will be roundly criticized, and perhaps redescribed later by one of them. If the description has only partial support, it may be submitted to the International Commission of Zoological Nomenclature of the International Congress of Zoology for a ruling. (This is true for tarantulas and other animal-like organisms only. Non-animal-like organisms are considered by other organiza-

tions.) If the name and description meets the requirements of the *Rules of Zoological Nomenclature,* the species with its name stands. If not, it is no longer considered a valid name or species, and is generally ignored except by encyclopedic scientific papers that attempt to list all known attempts at naming a species, or group of species.

A Little History in a Classical Vein. This nomenclatural system was established in the middle of the eighteenth century, during the *neoclassical period* when anything and everything Greek or Roman was revered, almost to the point of being worshipped. Every educated person had to be able to read ancient Greek or Latin, if not speak it fluently, and they often Latinized their names for publication (e.g., Linnaeus for Linné). Virtually every public and many private buildings were constructed to appear as though they had just escaped the Acropolis or the Roman Forum (e.g., Napoléon de Bonaparte's Arc de Triumph in Paris, France and the Lincoln Memorial in Washington, D.C.). All male statuary was nude with a laurel wreath about the head (e.g., a larger-than-life, nude statue of Napoléon in Apsley House, London, England. He does wear a fig leaf!). And most important here, scientific names were required to be couched in Latin or Latinized Greek, or at the very least, were Latinized personal names.

Over the intervening centuries, we have managed to outgrow nude statues in the Caesarian style, and buildings that look like mausoleums, but we are still bridled with scientific names in Latin. An elaborate explanation is usually given that the use of Latin, a dead language, ensures that the meanings of the names will never be lost because dead languages no longer evolve or change.

Table IX

Classification of a common tarantula

Kingdom	Animalia
Phylum	Arthropoda
Subphylum	Chelicerata
Class	Arachnida
Order	Araneae
Suborder	Opisthothelae
Infraorder	Mygalomorphae
Family	Theraphosidae
Subfamily	Theraphosinae
Genus	*Aphonopelma*
Species	*hentzi*
Authority, year	(Gerard, 1854)

Proponents of the system fail to mention that the overwhelming majority of dead languages have been long forgotten, as well. Although most biologists pay lip service to this logic, they often freely admit that it is only an inconvenient relic of the past, a nuisance at best.

Strictly speaking, the species' descriptions are also to be published in Latin for the same reason. The fact of the matter is that, at the end of the twentieth century, very few people, and especially biologists, know how to read or write Latin. Scientific descriptions of species are now generally published in any of the major scientific languages, English, French, and German being the most common. Because many tarantulas are native to countries where Spanish or Portuguese is the principle language, many species descriptions of tarantulas are also published in these languages as well. Slowly, Latin is truly becoming a dead language.

This has a mixed blessing. The good news is that one must no longer be fluent in an otherwise useless, archaic, nearly extinct language to understand a modern species description. The bad news is that one must now be reasonably fluent in four or five modern languages!

Linné was a very busy man indeed. Using this system, he named many thousands of different organisms (4,236 animals alone, Storer and Usinger 1957) more than anyone else in history. In scientific literature, his name appears so often as an authority that the scientific community has agreed to use only his last initial, L., to save time, space, and print. This distinction is accorded very few people in history.

When Dr. Raven revised the taxonomy of tarantulas and their near relatives, he determined that several subfamilies of tarantulas were not valid, and that many genera were duplicates (synonyms) of others. In such cases, the oldest name takes precedence. Thus, many tarantula species have recently experienced a name change. Even worse, in several instances, the original names were subsequently reinstated. This can pose an overwhelming obstacle if the enthusiast attempts to track a particular species through the literature. In an effort to ease this problem, Appendix A: Tarantula Species as Pets supplies a few of the former genus names in parentheses after the currently accepted genus name, wherever applicable. Thus, *Aphonopelma hentzi* (Gerard 1854) is listed as *Aphonopelma (Rhechostica/ Dugesiella) hentzi* (Gerard 1854), indicating that the two names in parentheses have also recently been used for it. The enthusiast is forewarned that this convention is not commonly adopted by taxonomists, but is used here for purposes of clarity.

The Name of the Game

The full classification of a common North American tarantula might appear like Table IX.

Of course, we don't recite this entire list every time we wish to discuss this animal. In the interest of saving time, effort, and print, we assume that the reader has some familiarity with the general scheme of classification or knows enough to be able to look it up in the appropriate reference book.

At the beginning of a scientific paper, the class or order and family names may be given to help locate the reader among the bewildering legions of living organisms. At the same time, the authority's name is also given. Thereafter, only the scientific name or its abbreviation (e.g., *A. hentzi*) need be used. Although this custom should also be used in non-scientific papers, it is often ignored.

The spider from which our tarantulas borrowed their name is classified among the true spiders (Araneomorphae) and is a wolf spider (family Lycosidae), perhaps even *Lycosa tarantula* (Rossi 1790) although that hasn't been confirmed. The widow spiders and their cousins are also true spiders in the family Theridiidae. The most notorious one is the southern black widow, *Latrodectus mactans* (Fabricius 1755).

Now, a word of caution. In this book, we are equating the term *tarantula* with the family Theraphosidae. This usage is not universally followed. The term *tarantula* is reserved as the official common name for theraphosid spiders, and only for theraphosid spiders, by the American Arachnological Society's Committee on Common Names of Arachnids, and is official only in North America, and only after April 1995 when *Common Names of Arachnids* (Breene 1995) was first published. However, written works published before 1995 often use *tarantula* to refer to many of theraphosid tarantulas' near relatives as well. In addition, scientists outside

The southern black widow, Latrodectus mactans *(suborder Araneomorphae, family Theridiidae).*

North America sometimes use the term in its more general sense. Lastly, many of the laity, enthusiasts included, who do not live in North America, or have never heard of *Common Names of Arachnids,* or simply do not care to be constrained by official common names, sometimes use *tarantula* to mean other things besides theraphosid spiders. See pages 66 and 261 for additional comments.

Professional arachnologists, at least in North America, accept the common name *tarantula* (lower case *t* and normally not italicized) to mean only members of the family Theraphosidae, and the scientific name *Tarantula* (upper case *T* and normally italicized) to mean only one genus of arachnids that aren't even spiders (Table III). The laity would call these tailless whipscorpions.

There are some theraphosids that the laity might not consider as tarantulas, and there are some spiders from closely allied families that might be considered to be tarantulas, and some people would apply the name to *any* large spider. The moral of this story is clear. When someone begins to talk about *tarantulas,* if there is any doubt or confusion, ask for a precise definition of the term.

Identification

Here is where all that grand organization falls apart. The mygalomorphs, theraphosids included, are a very difficult group to differentiate, describe, categorize, name, and identify.

Tarantulas have many different characteristics to help us define their species, but offer no indication of which are important and which are trivial. And, we have little fossil evidence to show us which characteristics are important in defining the various species' relationships. Furthermore, most of those characteristics that we can recognize are rather obscure.

At this time, the state of the art can best be called chaotic. Although Raven's treatment of the group is probably much more accurate than any before him, the major part of the job remains to be done, redescription and recategorization of the species.

Smith (1985, 1990, 1995) has undertaken this daunting task, but as of July 1997 has only completed part of his goal. As of this writing, there is no definitive work that neatly describes all of the known tarantulas. The only ways that we have of identifying a valuable specimen or a treasured pet are:

1. Compare it to very technical, written descriptions. These are often in foreign languages or in obscure scientific journals that we must laboriously unearth in major university libraries. A distressingly large proportion of those descriptions are wholly inadequate.
2. Try to find lists or keys to the fauna of the area in which the tarantula was collected (if this is known or suspected), and hope that the key or list is correct. These are very technical and usually written in a foreign language as well.
3. Compare it to named specimens in collections at major museums, assuming that the type specimens exist, assuming that we are allowed near the collections, and presuming we knew what we were doing in the first place.
4. Send exuvia or preserved specimens to recognized authorities for identification, then often wait months to find that they can't identify them because the material was inadequate, reference specimens were unavailable, or the expert simply had not the time.
5. Make a guess at the name, often based on rumor or a supposition by someone else who is perhaps equally ignorant.
6. Consult enthusiast or semitechnical publications. However, be forewarned that many illustrations in some of the most popular pet industry books, even those from presumably reputable publishers, are mislabelled. Even under the best of circumstances, picture keying (as it is called) is extremely unreliable.

Named, Renamed, Re-renamed, and Confused

The Committee on Common Names of Arachnids of the American Arachnological Society has endeavored to develop and maintain a list of official common names for all common arachnids. This list correlates them with corresponding scientific names in a one-to-one fashion, and is patterned after a similar list developed and used by the American Entomological Society for a century or more for insects. There are well-defined rules that govern the way in which common names can be created and applied. One of these rules insists that no name can be longer than three words. (The name of a country, e.g., Costa Rica, included in the spider's name is treated as only one word even though it may be composed of several words.) Another insists that once a common name is established, it cannot be changed except under a very few, well-defined sets of circumstances.

The intent of this list is to establish common names which do not change when the scientific name changes. It is intended to reconcile the confusion caused by the tangle of arcane rules and confounding changes to scientific names, with the wholly illogical, whimsical, and undisciplined way that common names are applied. The American Tarantula Society (see page 248) maintains and publishes an up-to-date list of the approved common names correlated with the corresponding scientific names. The names for tarantulas are published monthly in their *Forum Magazine,* as well. The master list of all arachnids with common names (including some mites) is published as a separate booklet (Breene 1995).

Although the intent is admirable, the result is less than perfect for several reasons. First, many exporters, importers, and dealers are completely unaware that the list exists. And, many of those who do, don't care, objecting to this perceived incursion on their freedom. Their principle goal is to sell the tarantulas, and they are willing to use whatever poetic license is necessary to accomplish the feat. As a result, we will continue to be barraged by new, creative

Appendix A: Tarantula Species as Pets (page 261) is a cross-reference between common names and scientific names for many of the tarantulas available to the hobby.

appellations in spite of all the two societies' best efforts.

Secondly, the creation of such a list has now given the amateur yet another set of names to learn, plus the cross correlations to the list of scientific names, plus cross correlations to maverick names that have been used in the past, those that are still being used despite all efforts to the contrary, and those that are yet to be composed by creative dealers and enthusiasts. The list has not alleviated our labor, but rather made it even more complex.

Thirdly, it is a North American list, based on the commonly used North American names, attempting to impose North American nomenclature on the remainder of the world, injecting political overtones to the debate. European enthusiasts, in particular, have taken issue with this heavy handed approach by insisting that their nomenclature is at least as valid, if not more so in many cases.

Lastly, many of the names on the list are forced, artificial constructs with long, unwieldy appellations box-carred together (e.g., Costa Rican chestnutzebra tarantula, Egyptian basementbrown tarantula). There is little or no poetry or meter to most of them. They are difficult to remember, and sometimes, difficult to pronounce. Thus, this list finds itself in the position of having many of the faults of the scientific system for nomenclature. Its single saving grace is that it is much more stable than the scientific system.

The best of all possible worlds might be for the scientists to change the rules of nomenclature to prevent the endless changing of scientific names and renaming of species. A new system might divorce the name from the phylogenetic tree once and for all with a new, more efficient method devised to keep track of the presumed relationships. Once a name is assigned, it might not be changed, come Hell or high water! Collaterally, the hobby might adopt the scientific name as the one and only official name, refusing to acknowledge alternate, common names. But alas, this is not a perfect world. Often, enthusiasts are as obstinately uncontrollable as the wind, and scientists can often be as distant and unreasonable as government bureaucrats!

Remarks

Although Raven, Platnick, and Smith's efforts are truly laudable, they are still incomplete, and the science and the hobby are left with only fragmentary, often contradictory and widely strewn portions of the information that they seek.

At this point, perhaps the single greatest need is for other arachnologists to help in sorting out the mess. The field is wide open and waiting for anyone with the interest and qualifications to accept the challenge. Although such researchers will not become over-abundantly wealthy, perhaps even having to take second jobs in order to pay the rent, they will discover fame and much gratitude from those of us who wander around with flashlights, seeking dark, eight-legged shapes in the still, desert night.

Chapter Three
Natural History

Distribution

Tarantulas are found in a broad belt around our planet in a truly diverse array of habitats.

In North America, they are found west of the Mississippi River and at least as far north as Sacramento, California, and Pueblo, Colorado. The two occurrences recorded from Florida were probably either stowaways on ships, castaways on driftwood, or escaped pets.

In 1996 a small colony of *Brachypelma vagans* was discovered in an orange grove in the state of Florida (USA), and subsequently exterminated by the Florida Department of Agriculture and Consumer Services. Although no information is available about its source, it is presumed that it arose from one or more escaped individuals from an enthusiast's collection or from the pet industry.

There is some controversy about allowing such invading species to survive, and this particular instance caused much consternation and discussion among tarantula enthusiasts. On the one hand, foreign, invading species most frequently pose a serious threat to competing native species. This arises at least partly because the invaders have no checks on their population growth.

On the other hand, the introduction and presence of such large predacious arthropods in an agricultural district (itself a form of uncontrolled foreign invasion) would seem to actually be a benefit. The debate over this instance will continue for some time.

Tarantulas are found all through Central and South America nearly all the way to Tiera del Fuego. In fact, the limits of the range of the most southern South American species is not well known.

Four species are rare in southern Spain, one in Sicily. The lone individual recorded from London, England, was certainly a stowaway on a ship. Theraphosid tarantulas occur nowhere else in Europe, except in collector's homes. European explorers were largely ignorant of these giant spiders until the Renaissance or later. No wonder their amazement!

Tarantulas are found in the Middle East and one species is found on Cyprus, but their northern limits in western Asia are uncertain. None have been found in the Ukraine or Russia.

Brachypelma vagans.

They are found throughout southern Asia, with the Himalayas probably being the northern limits of their range. They are found on all of the major islands and many of the minor ones of the Indian Ocean and Southeast Asia, including Ceylon, Indonesia, and the Philippines. None, however, are found in Japan.

Africa is replete with tarantulas. Only the severest deserts are without them. Some of the world's largest species, and perhaps the world's more dangerous species, are found there as well.

Theraphosid tarantulas are found in Australia, although other closely related families are more common (e.g., Migidae). A few tarantulas are found on some of the islands of the South Pacific (Roewer 1963).

Lifestyle

Habitat

Wild tarantulas are found in a wide range of habitats: terrestrially in desert, prairies, and scrub forest, terrestrially and arboreally in rain or moist forests. None, however, are aquatic or marine.

Most terrestrial tarantulas prefer relatively high, dry situations, though not necessarily desert. They will almost surely not be found in a swamp or marsh, or in an area that floods frequently. Significant exceptions to this last rule are tarantulas that live in those monsoon and rain or moist forests that are flooded for several months every year.

Terrestrial tarantulas prefer soil that is firm and solid, capable of maintaining a dependable burrow. They will live in sand only if it is well packed and stable. Thus, few are found on sand dunes, or in very loose soil.

Because of their lengthy generation time and prolonged life spans, tarantulas will seldom be found where the earth has been cultivated in recent history. Cultivation kills the former inhabitants and loosens the soil, preventing construction of acceptable burrows and colonization by any pioneering individuals. Agricultural pesticides destroy the food chain and poison the tarantulas. Once the soil has been disturbed, it must settle and pack well enough for efficient burrow construction, and any pesticides must deteriorate to tolerable levels. Depending on circumstances, either of these processes may require years.

Desert species are capable of tolerating very dry conditions better than most tarantulas, but only with the aid of burrows that protect them from desiccation and extremes of temperature. Predation and disease may be reduced compared to moister habitats, but so is the food supply.

Plains, prairies, veldts, savannas, and scrub-brush country represent an intergrade between extremes. Many species that live in neighboring desert areas have also invaded these habitats, and the reverse, as well. Moisture and food are more plentiful, but so are predators.

The rain or moist forests are the other extreme. To cope with the persistent downpours and periodic flooding, rain or moist forest species have developed at least three strategies. They either assume a vagabond's existence, ready to retreat to higher ground at the first hint of a deluge, or they build their burrows in well-elevated areas, often on hillsides, banks, or cliffs. Several groups of tarantulas have fled permanently into the trees.

The tree dwellers (the arboreal tarantulas) escape terrestrial predators and seasonal flooding. They may be exposed to a much more varied food supply and escape from a predator may be as simple as jumping to the next branch or tree. Because they live in the trees, they are exposed to breezes and, therefore, may escape some of the stifling humidity of the jungle floor, a humidity that promotes a growth of parasites, infections, and infestations.

The price that these arboreal tarantulas pay is dear, however. They relinquish the ability to dig a burrow wherever convenient, being forced to exploit whatever cover they can find, clefts in tree bark, bunched leaves, or a bromeliad, for instance. They must use silk to build and maintain a bivouac, representing a sizable expenditure in personal resources. High in the trees, they may be easy prey for the many animals that live there with them. And lastly, they must develop an anatomy and habit patterns that protects them from falling except under the most controlled circumstances.

Do not wax idyllic about life in the rainforest. It is still, after all, a jungle where things kill and eat other things, never gently, often gruesomely.

Humble Abode

The arboreal species frequently build elaborate nests of silk with several entrances. These are situated in the crotches of branches, among the bases of epiphytic plants, or in clefts of bark. Occasionally, bunched leaves and even tall grasses are used (Charpentier 1992). The nests may be bedecked with pieces of lichen or moss, pieces of exuvia, and discarded food boluses (see page 41). They often fortify the silk walls with their own urticating bristles.

The burrows of the terrestrial species may be dug under stones or grass hummocks (Smith 1990), but occur just as commonly in the open, distributed more or less at random. The domiciles of most North American species are unbranched, nearly vertical burrows, thirty centimeters to almost two meters (one to six feet) deep and up to six centimeters (two and one-half inches) in diameter, with these dimensions varying with the species and size of the individual tarantula. The diameter of the burrow may enlarge somewhat just inside the mouth to suggest a chamber, though a definite atrium is seldom found. The bottom end of the burrow usually expands slightly into a small chamber that serves as the tarantula's *sanctum sanctorum*. This bottom chamber may be dug at an angle to the axis of the main shaft, presumably to allow a more horizontal floor (personal observations of these authors).

By way of exception, some African species (e.g., *Harpactirella* and *Ischnocolus* species) are remarkable for the elaborate, branched burrows that they construct (Smith 1990). These sometimes possess multiple, parallel vertical shafts, connecting cross tunnels, side chambers, and trapdoors to seal off the side passageways.

In the neighborhood of Phoenix, Arizona, *Aphonopelma paloma* (Prentice 1992), North America's smallest tarantula, creates a tortuously contorted burrow in desert soil that has few obstructions that would merit such a twisting lair.

If the ground is rocky, the burrow may be twisted and contorted with such embellishments as atria or terminal chambers being unattainable luxuries. If the burrow is located on a hillside, the shaft may descend on an angle, even horizontally, instead of being vertical.

In some areas of the upper Rio Grande Valley of western Texas, tarantulas will make their homes in a network of anastomosing cracks that permeate the terrain. These cracks are permanent features of the landscape, expanding and contracting from year to year depending

Puzzled by scientific names? Read Chapter 2: The Name of the Tarantula and Appendix A: Tarantula Species as Pets for explanations and a cross-reference between scientific names and common names.

on the abundance of rainfall. In particularly dry years, they may expand to a width of five centimeters (two inches) or more, one and one-half meters (five feet) or more deep, and have individual segments with a horizontal length of half a meter (twenty inches) or more. These segments form a maze with the potential of a nearly endless length. A tarantula may widen a small portion of the crack slightly at a strategic point to allow for an entrance, and reinforce the mouth with a layer of silk. The vertical shaft will merely be a widened course downward through the crack. There may be no discernable bottom end, the burrow merely fading into the remainder of the crack. The authors have learned not to waste their time trying to capture a tarantula from such a situation. The tarantula merely retreats into the labyrinth when disturbed, and the collector can spend the next century pouring water down the hole, digging up the crack, and cursing the heat!

Baerg (1922) suggested that some tarantulas may have taken residence in abandoned rodent burrows, a point of view strongly supported by these authors. In at least one unidentified species of *Aphonopelma* from Texas and another from the Mojave desert of California, the authors found burrows that had apparently been appropriated from small rodents, then remodelled to suit the tarantula's preferences. The outward portion of the burrow was six or seven centimeters (two and one-half inches) in diameter and started at an angle of less than forty-five degrees from the horizontal, and continued on for an indefinite length. About twenty centimeters (eight inches) inside the mouth, another shaft of smaller diameter turned sharply downward to approximately vertical and extended to a depth in excess of one and one-half meters (five feet). (The authors were unable to excavate the full depth of the burrow owing to advancing darkness.) The soil was composed principally of highly compacted, coarse sand with little clay or loam, allowing the tarantula to easily excavate an extensive burrow.

Small leaves, remains of eaten prey, and the remnants of cast skins are frequently found on the floors of the burrows. The burrows may be lined with silk, but more commonly are not. We do not know the reason for the variation.

What motivates a tarantula to choose a particular spot to start a burrow? How often are they likely to move to new burrows? How many burrows does a tarantula dig during its lifetime? Do tarantulas ever engage in contests over possession of the same burrow? Do tarantulas ever

Aphonopelma species. *A large brown tarantula from Eagle Pass, Texas.*

pirate burrows from each other? How frequently do tarantulas move into empty, preexisting burrows? No answers are available to any of these questions, as yet.

Life in the Colonies

Immature and female burrowing tarantulas may be found singly or in loose aggregations called colonies. This is not to imply purposeful gregariousness as practiced by termites and ants. Most tarantulas would readily cannibalize each other if given the opportunity. Either they have such limited senses that they simply are unaware that other clan members are near, or they are such timid, retiring creatures that they rarely travel far enough to interact with their neighbors. They seldom stroll more than a few centimeters from their burrows; and when they do, they may lay down draglines of silk to help them find their way back (Minch 1978).

In some arid localities (e.g., the Mojave desert in southern California), life is too harsh to allow extensive colonies, but sporadic aggregations of as many as a dozen tarantulas can be found adjacent to, but above, water courses that flood during rains (personal observations of these authors). In chaparral and prairies (e.g., western Texas), the colonies' locations and sizes seem to be influenced greatly by the number and locations of grazing animals (personal observations of these authors). In other localities, the existence and locations of the colonies seem to be dictated by the presence of islands of firm but relatively soft soil in an area which is mostly rock, gravel, or shifting sands. Breene (1996) reports the unexpected and unexplained presence of large colonies of *Aphonopelma anax* in golf courses and lawns in southern Texas.

The Mojave desert at sunset. As parched, barren, and severe as this habitat is, there are tarantula burrows along the banks of the washes at the base of the distant hills.

If a female tarantula that has strayed from her original homestead should wander into an area otherwise unpopulated by tarantulas, she may start a burrow and remain there for the remainder of her life. If she is bred by an itinerant male, the offspring probably will not wander far from the mother's burrow before setting up their own homesteads. From then on, the only limitations to the size of the colony is availability of food and water and competition between the colony's members for space to construct a burrow.

How do the initiating members (the first colonists) get there in the beginning? As spiderlings, immatures, or adults? By random wandering, or by migration in some specific direction?

The Roomies

Many organisms will cohabit with a tarantula in its burrow. This is only to be expected when the interlopers are as minute and inconsequential as springtails, termites, fire brats, and silverfish (class Insecta, orders Collembola,

The chaparral of western Texas. Classic desert tarantula habitat.

How do these meek little frogs escape being eaten by the tarantula? Is there a chemical trick to fool the tarantula? Is it behavioral? The benefits to the frog are obvious, but does the tarantula gain anything from this association? If so, what? H. A. Dundee (Tulane University) hypothesized that they may protect the tarantula from marauding ants (Breene 1996). How so?

Worldwide, are there any other animals, barring those that are nearly microscopic, that also cohabit with tarantulas in the wild? If so, what are their tricks for avoiding becoming the main course for dinner? What, if anything, do they offer the tarantula in return?

Life as a Nomad

Some of the species from warmer climates are nomads, presumably because they don't require the protection from harsh climatic conditions. Marshall (1996) suggests that some *Phormictopus* species and possibly *Phrixotrichus spatulata* or *P. cala* fall into this group. They may occupy temporary burrows appropriated or excavated under fallen logs or rocks (sometimes called scrapes, Hancock and Hancock 1992), especially when molting or tending an eggsac. If they wander too far in search of food and lose their way or if they are flooded from their burrows by a downpour, they merely move to another burrow, perhaps eating the original inhabitant. They are subject to greater predation, but they also find food and mates more readily.

The vagabond tarantula's biology has not been studied in depth or reported in detail in the literature. We really don't know how many or which species follow this life-style, and to what extent. Until some budding arachnologist spends a year or two camping in Amazonia, Irian Jaya, or the Atacama,

Isoptera, and Thysanura, respectively), and even some minute spiders. For these creatures, any protection from the heat of the sun and exposure to predators is welcomed, regardless of how unconventional. However, it is difficult to understand how an indiscriminate carnivore like a tarantula would willingly allow cohabitation by such a highly edible creature as a small frog. Yet this is precisely the case.

Cocroft and Hambler (1989) report a little frog, *Chiasmocleis ventrimaculata,* living with *Xenesthis immanis.* This is particularly surprising because frogs and other small vertebrates are suspected of constituting a large part of many tropical tarantulas' diets.

In the American southwest, the Great Plains Narrow-mouthed Frog, *Gastrophryne olivacea,* is rather famous for occasionally sharing tarantulas' burrows (Hunt 1980, Breene 1996). On several occasions, these authors have been surprised when one of these interesting little amphibians was flushed out of the burrow along with the tarantula.

and publishes detailed reports, we can only wonder about these amazing, mysterious creatures.

Foods and Feeding

The Menu. In nature, tarantulas will eat almost anything that moves and is small enough to overpower. Thus, they have been known to eat small rodents, small lizards and snakes (Caras 1974), small birds (hence the name *bird spider* and *birdeater;* Mérian 1771; Palisot de Beauvois 1805; Bates 1910), insects and spiders, even other tarantulas! Tarantula-keeping enthusiasts are now finding that their pets will sometimes take dead, nonmoving food. It is now strongly suspected that wild tarantulas that are hungry may do so as well.

Little is known about the amount that wild tarantulas eat. Because of their low metabolic rate, they do not require as much food as we might at first guess. In the artificial environment of a cage, an average-size adult tarantula will do quite nicely on six or eight crickets a month. In fact, many of the authors' pets may be accused of being obese on such fare! (Refer to the discussion of metabolism on page 48. Crickets as food are discussed on page 127.)

Boom and Bust. In the wild, the food supply may vary unpredictably. For instance, in the western Texas chaparral, carabid, tenebrionid, and scarabaeid beetles are abundant during times of adequate rainfall. However, during times of extreme drought these populations diminish drastically.

The number and type of insects in that area also depends to a large extent on cattle-grazing practices. The number of dung beetles (family Scarabaeidae) in any locality may increase with heavy grazing, resulting in a temporary increase in the available food supply for

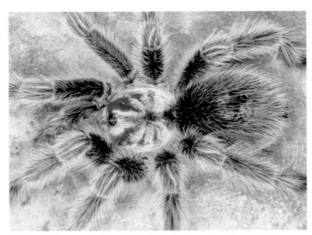

Phrixotrichus spatulata. *Male. This is the color phase most commonly imported.*

tarantulas. However, as soon as the cattle are moved to another range, the dung beetle population plunges (personal observations of these authors).

We presume that this type of food chain exists wherever tarantulas are found. In Tanzania, the predominant grazing animals may be elephants or wildebeest with some of the *Pterinochilus* species the benefactors. In Thailand, water buffalo and *Haplopelma* may occupy corresponding niches. The species and the ecosystems are different, but the working structure is the same.

During those times of relative abundance, the population of resident tarantulas increases. But, what happens to the tarantulas when the local food supply dwindles? In a laboratory, under controlled conditions, tarantulas have lived a year without food, providing they had access to water (Baerg 1958). There have also been anecdotal reports of *Phrixotrichus spatulata* in private homes voluntarily fasting for as long as two years with few signs of distress.

In the wild, however, they would not have unrestricted access to water, especially during a drought. Neither are environmental conditions such as temperature artificially controlled, although the tarantulas receive substantial protection from their burrows. Finally, tarantulas that are weakened from lack of food or water would be more vulnerable to predators or parasites. Under natural conditions, wild tarantulas probably would not survive nearly so long during an extended drought or famine. Even then, that is nothing short of amazing.

Entire colonies of tarantulas nearly disappeared in a drought that occurred in the 1980s in western Texas. However, by the spring of 1991, after several years of adequate rainfall, many of those colonies were regaining their original population levels. There seems to be much hope that when a colony suffers extreme but not total devastation from environmental forces or predation, it will be able to rebound once the devastating forces abate.

The Feeding Waltz. Tarantulas of all sizes and ages perform a peculiar little dance as they eat. These authors have witnessed *Avicularia avicularia* executing it on a vertical wall, and *Theraphosa blondi* performing it with a half-grown mouse which it had just killed. While there are rare cases when a tarantula won't waltz, nearly every tarantula in the authors' collection does when fed.

As soon as the tarantula grabs a cricket (or other food item) it immediately raises onto its leg tips, lowers the end of its opisthosoma, and begins to lay down a sheet of silk. All the while that it is holding and masticating its dinner it is turning in circles, weaving the feeding web. As time progresses, it will place the mass of food (as many as a dozen crickets for the larger individuals, or a half-

grown mouse for *T. blondi*) in the center of the mat and lightly cover it with another layer of silk. After allowing it to stand a few minutes, presumably for digestion to progress, the tarantula will pick up the whole assemblage, silk, digesting food, and even some of the substrate, and again begin to wheel and turn, creating another silken feeding web. These authors have grown to refer to this as the feeding waltz. Had he known of it, would Johann Strauss have written a waltz to commemorate it?

The hypothesis is that this behavior is a response to the uncertainty of food availability in the wild. Because most tarantulas do not leave their burrows to hunt for food, merely resting inside the entrance, waiting for some tender, juicy morsel to wander within striking range, their food supply is quite unpredictable. Then, with the arrival of a locust swarm or a pair of dung beetles rolling their ball of dung, food suddenly becomes temporarily abundant. Of the many options available to a spider, one is grabbing one prey item and allowing the remainder to escape. Another is developing some method for catching several and consuming them later at the spider's leisure.

Those spiders that live in circumstances where prey is more or less uniformly abundant have adopted the first strategy. The orbweavers (e.g., genus *Argiope*) are a good example. If several insects fly into the web at about the same time, the spider deals with each individually. Seldom is a second insect dealt with until the first is at least secured. After all are secured, each is eaten individually.

Tarantulas have adopted the second strategy. Their method is to grab as many of the prey items as they can, as fast as possible. Instead of being dispatched individually, they are lumped together in a common food bolus until the food supply runs out or the tarantula simply cannot deal with any more. Then all captured prey items are eaten at the same time.

Multiple prey capture is an opportunistic behavior developed to offset the insecurity of feast or famine food availability.

Diurnal Cycles

Some details of the daily existences (their diurnal cycles) of tarantulas are known. They are more active in the evening than during the day. Light intensity seems to be the most effective agent in influencing their activity. Minch (1977) also believes that surface temperature plays a large role, with disturbances by other animals also being important.

During the day, desert species may retreat deep into their burrows for protection from light, heat, and desiccation. They seem to become more active as dusk approaches, moving gradually up the burrow as light intensity diminishes. Finally, as darkness falls, if they had spun a silken veil over the mouth of the burrow, they will remove it by tearing it with their pedipalps and front legs, laying it against the burrow's mouth. Thereafter, they lie in ambush for passing prey. If they detect ground vibrations, as from a larger animal, they retire deeper into their burrows for a period of time. Eventually, they will return to the burrow's entrance. If they detect smaller prey, they attack, then drag their prospective meal into the burrow.

As night progresses, they may spend some time enlarging their burrows, or they may merely lie passively in wait at the entrance. As dawn approaches, they retire to the burrow's depths, usually

Aphonopelma moderatum *at the entrance to her burrow. She awaits prey or suitors. Tarantulas occasionally rest outside their burrows at dusk or on overcast days, especially if hungry.*

without first spinning the veil. After the sun is well up, in early morning, they may return to the burrow's entrance to spin the veil. Then they retreat into their *sanctum sanctorum* for the duration of daylight.

Occasionally, under an overcast sky, tarantulas may be seen out of their burrows during daylight, although they seldom move more than fifteen or twenty centimeters (six to nine inches) from their burrow. They often lay down draglines of silk to help them find their way home (Minch 1978). Breene (1996) reports that *Aphonopelma anax* from southern Texas can be seen just inside the mouths of their burrows most of the day, retreating into the depths only if they are startled by the sight of an approaching animal or a strong vibration, e.g., footfalls.

Minch (1978 and 1979a) reports an interesting behavior in wild tarantulas. During a downpour, *Aphonopelma chalcodes* use their bodies to plug the burrows' entrances, thus avoiding being flooded out. What other little behavioral tricks do they know that we don't?

Do tarantulas sleep during the day? We might be able to answer this if we knew what sleep really was. But even then, because their nervous systems are so radically different from ours, we probably couldn't tell if they experience anything like sleep.

Annual Cycles

In nature, tarantulas are subjected to a variety of seasonal stimuli that tends to entrain a basic, annual rhythm, their annual cycles. These stimuli are variations in day length, daylight intensity, temperature, moisture, and possibly the availability of food.

Breene (1996) reports that the tarantulas of southern Texas do not plug their burrows at any time during the year. And these authors have found *Aphonopelma moderatum* in open burrows in the upper Rio Grande valley in late December.

However, as fall approaches, tarantulas in more temperate climates (e.g., in Arkansas, or at an elevation of 1,350 meters [4,428 feet] in Pima county, Arizona) may plug their burrows with a mass of silk and soil (Gertsch 1949;

Baerg 1958; Minch 1978 and 1979a). Sometimes fragments of leaves may also be incorporated into this plug. The tarantula may do this several times as the season progresses, alternately removing the plug and replacing it as the weather changes. Finally, it leaves the plug in place and will remain dormant in its burrow until spring.

What do tarantulas do when they are sealed in their burrows? A good guess would be that they merely wait. We don't know. No one has ever reported watching one.

As spring approaches, the tarantula becomes more active, eventually removing the plug if one is present. If it is a mature female who had been bred by a male, it will produce an eggsac full of eggs, and tend it in the burrow. After the spiderlings escape the eggsac and eventually leave the burrow, the mother will molt, usually in midsummer.

Immature and unbred mature females of some species will molt in early spring. For the remainder of the warm months, they are active, excavating their burrows and waiting at the entrance for prey to pass. In mid-spring, mature males build sperm webs (see page 80) and seek females. Many are killed by predators. As winter approaches, the surviving males die of old age or exposure. This cycle is labelled the *fall mating strategy* by Breene (1996).

Breene (1996) reports that the seasonal cycle of *A. anax* in southern Texas follows a slightly different pattern, the so-called *spring mating strategy*. Here, the males mature in April, and leave their burrows to search for and breed with females in May and June. Females produce eggsacs in late June or July, then molt in August or early September.

Tarantulas in more tropical habitats seldom experience such severe changes

Aphonopelma moderatum. *A pretty tarantula from western Texas, but these bite readily.*

in seasonal temperature. In the dryer areas, rainfall and humidity are presumed to play more profound roles in their annual cycles, determining the season in which eggs are produced and molting occurs. The presumption is that spiderlings are produced at that time of the year when food and moisture are most plentiful, probably immediately following the rainy season. This hasn't been confirmed, however. These creatures have a knack for confounding us when we try to make analogies between them and more familiar animals. We must wait for some budding arachnology student to sit in the veldt or chaparral for a year or two, quietly observing these enigmatic creatures, and finally confirming our suspicions.

In tropical rain or moist forests where conditions are uniformly warm and humid all year long, seasonal cues may be quite subtle or imperceptible, and tarantulas' annual cycles obscure or nonexistent.

Arachnologists, either amateur or professional, have yet to compile a tabulation of annual habit patterns for most tarantulas, or determine what conditions are most important for entraining each species to its own annual cycle.

Life Cycle

Little is known of the details of the life cycles of most species of tarantulas. We can only assume that they parallel those of the few more thoroughly studied species and try to imagine adjustments for differences in seasons, temperature, moisture, and habitat. Be forewarned! These assumptions will surely lead us astray. The theraphosids have been around far too long to fit neatly into any prescribed formula. Surprises await us and our prejudices are to be used only as a starting point. Far more field

research is desperately needed. What follows is probably correct for most North American species, but is not necessarily true for any other species.

Maturation

There is one very significant molt that every tarantula experiences if it survives long enough—its maturing or ultimate molt.

The actual age of maturation can vary widely, depending on the species, the individual's sex, physical and nutritional condition, and other unknown factors. For instance, male tarantulas commonly mature a year or so before their sisters, and extensive fasting may delay maturation by as much as two years (Baerg 1928).

In one North American species this molt occurs during a tarantula's tenth, eleventh, or twelfth year (Baerg 1928). *Aphonopelma anax* males may mature at two or three years of age (Breene 1996), and some tropical tarantulas (e.g., *Avicularia* species) mature even more quickly, perhaps as soon as eighteen months (Charpentier 1992).

Among the individuals from any single eggsac, the males usually mature several months to several years in advance of their sisters. One hypothesis to explain this is that it precludes sibling crosses with the consequent loss of genetic diversity.

Another hypothesis holds that the males are of smaller body mass and require less time to reach a size necessary to reproduce effectively. The inference is that the females require more time to develop comparatively larger reproductive organs and cache greater reserves of body mass in preparation for ovulation. If this hypothesis is correct, avoiding inbreeding is only a secondary advantage.

A male Brachypelma smithi, *detailing the tibial hooks and the club-shaped pedipalps.*

Before the maturing molt, all tarantulas of the same species appear more or less alike, and after it, the mature female still appears much like a large immature.

The male, however, undergoes a radical transformation during his maturing or ultimate molt. He develops longer legs and a smaller opisthosoma than his sisters. In most species the first pair of legs now bear prominent hooks on each tibia, pointing forward. The male's personality has also changed (Petrunkevitch 1911). Instead of the sedate, reclusive

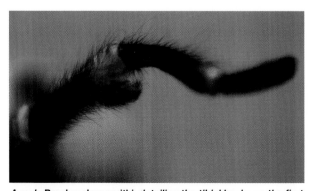

A male Brachypelma smithi, *detailing the tibial hooks on the first pair of legs.*

demeanor of a female, he has adopted a very excitable, hyperactive personality characterized by impetuous starts, quick flights, and a strong wanderlust.

For the male, this maturing molt is his final or ultimate molt. As we shall see shortly, this is the beginning of the end. His days are numbered.

One of the most important transformations occurs in his pedipalps. Whereas his sister's pedipalps still resemble walking legs, his appear like boxing gloves. But do not be mistaken, he's a lover, not a fighter! The bulbous ends of his pedipalps are intricately adapted for use as very specialized sex organs. The terminal segments on his pedipalps have changed from the relatively simple pretarsi and claws into complex secondary sex organs used to introduce sperm into the female

Sex Life

Little is known about the sex lives of wild tarantulas. Virtually all we do know arises from captive individuals, and life in captivity can radically alter habits and instincts. We report here what little we know about wild habit patterns, knowing that this will be incomplete. We can only await more field research.

Loading His Guns. Shortly after the maturing molt, the male tarantula spins a sperm web in preparation for his sexual career (Baerg 1928 and 1958; Petrunkevitch 1911; Minch 1979b).

The sperm web is a lean-to style silken tent, open at the ends. It comes in either one of two styles. Some species build it with only the two ends open. Other species construct it with a third opening at the top. If a top opening is present, the male will spin an extra little patch of special silk (presumably from his epiandrous glands) inside and adjacent

A pair of Brachypelma smithi, *male on the left and female on the right.*

to its edge. If no top opening is present he will spin this extra patch of silk inside and adjacent to the edge of one of the end openings.

Under the sperm web and upside down, he will then deposit a droplet of semen, containing his sperm, on the underside of the little patch of special silk.

After climbing back up on top of the web, he will reach with his pedipalps, first one and then the other, either through the top opening (if it is present), or over and around the end (if the top opening is not present) to load his bulbs with sperm. This process is known as sperm induction.

The sperm that he charges his bulbs with is not active. Shortly after the sperm are produced inside his testes their flagella wrap around their cell bodies. Thereafter they were encapsulated in a layer of protein and remain dormant through the remainder of their lives until they are called on to fertilize a female's eggs (Foelix 1982).

After loading his pedipalps, the male abandons the sperm web and goes a courtin'. During his wanderings, the male is fair game for any predator in the area, and he must be hyperactive merely to survive and mate. Thus, the hyperactivity

of the male is an important survival characteristic.

Where does the male produce his first sperm web? In the confines of his burrow before he abandons it or after he leaves the burrow, looking for females? The burrow would seem to be a very cramped place to perform the required movements, but it would be much safer than the great outdoors.

Males will build several sperm webs and charge the tips of their pedipalps several times. They are capable of mating several times during their sexual

A male Phrixotrichus spatulata *with the remains of a sperm web.*

Adult male Lasiodora parahybana *depositing a droplet of sperm on the lip of his newly constructed sperm web.*

careers. Very scant data has been published to indicate how many times a male is capable of recharging his pedipalps, or how many females he may inseminate.

Where does the male build additional sperm webs once he leaves his burrow? Do they prefer the seclusion of a space under a rock or other cover, or will they merely stop anywhere there is an object to use as a vertical support, oblivious to the rest of the world? The probability is

Adult male Lasiodora parahybana *picking up a droplet of sperm with the emboli and bulbs of his pedipalps.*

very high that the answers to these questions depend on the species. Obviously, (is this beginning to sound repetitive?) more field research is badly needed.

During the courting phase of his life, the male wanders freely, searching for females. Merely hiding during the brightest light of day, he no longer maintains a permanent home. The fair damsels he seeks normally stay home waiting for suitors. Of course, the more ground he covers, the better his chances are of finding a receptive female. Males have been found to wander almost two kilometers (Janowski-Bell 1995).

Baiting the Tiger. Females are probably first identified by the chemotactic qualities (we hesitate to call it taste or smell) of the webbing around their burrows (Minch 1979b). When located thus, the male will very cautiously tap at the burrow's entrance several times in an attempt to arouse interest in the female. If this has no effect, he will very warily crawl forward, head first (as it were) down the burrow.

At some point in his descent he will contact the female, and two scenarios are possible. He may be met with an almost explosive attack. In this instance, the female may charge him like a raging tiger with fangs bared and the clear intention of dinner instead of sex. The male must make a very hasty exit, backwards up the burrow, or become the entrée.

In another scenario, the female largely ignores him, playing coy and hard to get. In this instance, the male will lower his prosoma until it lies flat on the surface, with his opisthosoma held high in the air. He extends his first legs and pedipalps flat on the surface, and in this posture of extreme supplication, drags his body, forelegs, and pedipalps backwards. This sort of ingratiation almost always works to gain the female's attention. As the male drags himself backwards, she follows closely, demurely.

From time to time he will stop his retreat, still maintaining his posture, and push and pull his pedipalps and forelegs in an alternating fashion, first the left side, then the right, then left again, in an effort to maintain her interest. Slowly, they move in a peculiar procession up the burrow and out onto level ground.

Secret Password. The courting antics of the true spiders (Suborder Araneomorphae, families Araneidae, Pisauridae, Salticidae, and Lycosidae, for instance) are often very elaborate. In these spiders, a male performs a little dance or tweaks the threads of the female's web in some pattern that turns off the female's predatory drive and replaces it with a willingness to accept a mate. Some males in the family Pisauridae even go so far as to offer a freshly caught insect to the female before mating.

Courtship among tarantulas is relatively simple and straightforward. Males (and occasionally females) often twitch and thump their pedipalps and legs preliminary to mating. However, this is nowhere as elaborate a dance as that of the araneomorphs. To date, there have been no serious recorded attempts to determine differences in these antics between the species, nor even to verify that they are essential to mating. The possibility remains that they are, and that giving the wrong sign is a sure way for the male to be attacked and eaten.

Once on open ground, she is no longer in familiar territory, and he may approach her warily. By the time the male has seduced or baited the female from her sanctuary, she recognizes him as a suitor and remains quiescent. He may touch her with the tips of his first pair of legs, or tap the ground, or her, several times. There may be a brief pause, after which he may twitch his legs. He may alternate these displays repeatedly until he is convinced that the female means him no harm. The actual sequence of events, and the exact amount and type of foreplay, may differ with each species and may hold important clues to their phylogenetic relationships (Platnick 1971), as it does in other spiders. However, no one has yet made a serious study of this phenomenon in tarantulas.

Copulation. If the female is still passive, or if she approaches slowly, the male will move closer, sliding his front legs up between her pedipalps and over her chelicerae. At the same time she will rear up and extend her fangs. This is not an expression of hostility, but rather of willingness to mate.

The male then locks her fangs with his tibial hooks to steady both himself and his mate. The speculation is that this

Mating tarantulas.

immobilizes the female, disarming her. Quite the contrary. At this point, she is as eager to mate as he is. In fact, the authors have witnessed many instances in which it was the female who took the initiative, originating mating with the male!

After the male has securely locked the female's fangs, he pushes her prosoma up and backwards. At this point he reaches under her with his pedipalps, and gently strokes the bottom surface of her opisthosoma. If she remains compliant, he will unfold the embolus of one pedipalp, and carefully insert it into the gonopore in her epigastric furrow. This is the formal act of copulation. As he penetrates her, she bends sharply toward him at the pedicel, almost to a right angle. After emptying one pedipalp, he inserts and empties the other.

"I'm Outa Here!" After copulation, the male holds the female as far away as possible, until he can safely unhook his front legs, and makes a run for it! The female frequently chases him a short distance, but is seldom very intent. Although she is one of the predators that he must outrun, she is usually more interested in merely chasing him off. Contrary to legend, our lover usually lives to seduce another maiden, and there is good reason to suspect that he may return another evening to mate with a compliant female a second or third time.

Several weeks to several months after maturing, depending on the species, the male begins to slow down and eventually dies. Seldom do they live through winter, rarely beyond spring (Baerg 1958). At this time, no firm data are available on the life spans of the males of most species, although the authors have had several captive males that survived some fourteen to eighteen months after the maturing molt. Without question, older, failing males become easy prey in the wild and, therefore, would have a much shorter life expectancy.

The authors have collected numerous males in western Texas as early in the spring as the middle of April. Most such males were evidently survivors from the previous fall, judging from their badly worn appearance. A small but significant proportion (perhaps one in five or six) appeared neither emaciated nor showed signs of physical damage or bristle loss. This would suggest that they had molted that spring. This raised some suspicion that in warmer regions some species of tarantulas may molt and breed much earlier in the year than was once suspected. Subsequently, Breene (1996) described the mating cycle of *Aphonopelma anax* from southern Texas, in which the males matured and mated with the females early in the spring. See page 78 for a discussion. In many parts of the tropics, some tarantulas (e.g., *Avicularia* species) will molt and breed irrespective of the time of year because of the stability of temperature, moisture, and food supply (Charpentier 1992).

Baerg (1928, 1958) and later Minch (1978) both state that there does not appear to be enough time for a female to produce eggs between breeding in early spring and molting in midsummer. If this were true, such a mating would be inconsequential. However, Breene (1996) described a situation where precisely that occurs with *A. anax*. The authors' experience with captive *Brachypelma* species is that matings before December and after mid-winter (January in Canada) are usually fruitless. Thus, it would appear that the seasons of mating and egg laying vary with each species, often radically. These creatures have a way of pulling surprises on us, especially when we think we know all the answers.

Motherhood

Baerg (1928) reports that wild females of the Arkansas species he studied (Aphonopelma hentzi) that have been bred will plug the entrances of their burrows soon after mating and winter there. The sperm that the male transferred to her is carefully harbored in her spermathecae until the following spring. That next spring she will spin a walnut-sized eggsac holding as many as one thousand eggs or more. She will tend it carefully, airing it at the burrow's entrance and protecting it from predators. She can be quite aggressive while guarding it.

The time for egg laying seems to vary considerably. Some of the factors that determine the exact date are:

1. The species
2. The tarantula's original latitude in its native land (i.e., distance from the equator)
3. The prevailing climate patterns in its homeland
4. Its native hemisphere.

There may likely be other factors as well, so many in fact that generalizations are risky.

The tarantulas from Arkansas (Aphonopelma hentzi) usually lay eggs in June or July (Baerg 1958), those from western Texas a month earlier. In captivity, exotic species of tarantulas may lay eggs in early March. Presumably, this is the result of being kept in an artificial climate in a home.

Fertilization of the eggs occurs at the time they are laid, not internally during mating as one might surmise from the fact that the male must introduce his sperm into the female. Inseminating the female seems to serve at least two functions. It may stimulate the female to produce eggs, and it sequesters the encysted, dormant sperm in a convenient, protected location until needed.

The females of most vertebrate species ovulate whether or not there has been any contact with a male. Chickens lay eggs whether fertilized or not, and in the human species, women undergo ovulation and monthly periods in the total absence of sexual intercourse. It is unclear if this also occurs in tarantulas. The authors have had many females that did not produce eggs until after being bred by a male, being sleek and svelte before, and becoming swollen and heavy within weeks thereafter. This would suggest that the mating act or the presence of viable sperm in the female's spermathecae induced her to produce eggs.

On the other hand, Baxter (1993) believes that female tarantulas may produce eggs without mating. This may be due to the approach of the breeding season, the presence of an abundant food supply, or even the mere proximity of an appropriate male. These authors also have many female tarantulas that appear extremely gravid, but that have not been near a male of their species for years. If they are full of eggs, Baxter's hypothesis would be confirmed. If they are merely full of fatty tissue, the former hypothesis might be correct. These authors have not the heart to sacrifice one of their pets for this cause, and the question remains unanswered. These hypotheses are not mutually exclusive, and both could be correct, depending on any number of circumstances. These creatures have been around far too long to have not developed a vast repertoire of little tricks to confound us.

With a continuing population of 150 to 450 adult tarantulas, most being females, over a span of more than twenty-five years, the authors have had only one female lay eggs without being bred by a male. In the case in point, a female of the Aphonopelma species

Psalmopoeus cambridgei. *While this species is not brilliantly colored, it is still impressive in its subdued way.*

collected from the Del Rio, Texas, area had lived in captivity for more than three years and had undergone three molts. During the fourth spring, she produced an eggsac. The eggs did not develop. Baxter (1993) also reports the laying of sterile eggs by unimpregnated females of *Psalmopoeus cambridgei*. Breene (personal communication) reports that he has observed the phenomenon as many as thirty times.

We are not certain of the development time within the eggsac of most species in nature, but it undoubtedly varies with temperature and species. Somewhat more information is available about the developmental times of several species when the eggs are maintained in an incubator. Developmental times for various species, known to the authors, are presented in Table XII. It must be emphasized that these times are valid only in an artificial incubator.

Spiderlings of the Arkansas species *(Aphonopelma hentzi)* emerge from the eggsac in July or early August and usually

leave the mother's burrow a week or so later to fend for themselves (Baerg 1958). Shortly thereafter, the female will molt. If she didn't mate in time to lay fertile eggs, the female will molt somewhat earlier, perhaps in late spring or early summer.

Aphonopelma anax in southern Texas lays its eggs in June or July and molts in August or early September (Breene 1996). Thus, once mating has been accomplished, the schedule for the remainder of the female's summer is approximately the same as for the Arkansas species *(Aphonopelma hentzi)*.

Along with the rest of the exoskeleton, the linings of the spermathecae and any extra sperm they still hold will be cast off. Our lady will again be a virgin.

Wild Kids

Newly emerged spiderlings typically measure four to five millimeters (about one-sixth inch) in leg span and are light tan with a prominent black patch on their opisthosomas. These are the urticating bristles that they will need for self-defense. The authors have had newly emerged spiderlings of an unidentified *Paraphysa* species from Peru that were small enough to escape through three millimeter (one-eighth inch) holes in a jar lid. On the other end of the spectrum, *Theraphosa blondi* spiderlings emerge with a leg span of nineteen millimeters (three-quarters inch).

In nature, after leaving their mother's burrow, baby tarantulas are seldom found until they have quadrupled their size. We know little of this early period in their lives except that the rate of mortality must be staggering.

According to Baerg (1958), ants are perhaps the greatest menace to the eggs and newly emerged spiderlings. The adult, brooding female will abandon her eggsac almost immediately if confronted by marauding ants. These ants can then proceed to tear open the silken case and consume the eggs or baby tarantulas with complete impunity.

The interaction between ants and tarantulas depends almost entirely on the species of ant. In western Texas and the Mojave Desert of southern California these authors have found tarantula burrows within a meter of the nests of harvester ants. However, fire ants are reported to be voracious predators of tarantulas (R. G. Breene, personal communication).

While excavating the adults' burrows, neighboring burrows are occasionally found with baby tarantulas at the bottom. These burrows are typically ten to twenty centimeters (four to eight inches) in depth and less than six millimeters (one-quarter inch) in diameter. Spiderlings from these burrows often have a leg span of less than twelve millimeters (one-half inch). These smaller burrows are frequently more numerous than the adults' burrows. One must merely look for them carefully. Even small burrows are probably also present, but are extremely difficult to distinguish from minute insect burrows and irregularities in the soil.

But what do such tiny things eat? In the course of flooding adult tarantulas from their burrows, large populations of springtails, minute primitive insects of the order Collembola, are often found living with them as commensals. These could serve as the spiderlings' first food.

In addition, the soil contains a multitude of other minute creatures, and tarantulas have already proven themselves perfectly willing to attack anything small enough to overpower. For instance, the habitats where tarantulas are common also support large populations of termites. Although baby tarantulas have never been reported to eat them in the wild, we know of no reason

C ommensal: Any organism that lives with another (the host), gaining some advantage in doing so (most commonly food or habitat) without affecting the host.

why they couldn't, except for the termites' presumed inaccessibility. Perhaps termites also serve as an important source of baby food. If so, how would the spiderlings reach them?

McKee (1984a) reports that female *Avicularia avicularia* feed their babies for a few days with fluid that they appear to have regurgitated. This is not entirely unexpected. Scorpions and tailless whipscorpions are known to feed their young freshly caught prey. Furthermore, very young scorpions may be fed crushed crickets or even small morsels of canned dog food! Thus, there is some precedent for some mother tarantulas feeding their spiderlings, at least at the very first. In addition, there is some precedent for very young tarantulas eating nonliving food. The important question is whether tarantulas feed their newly emerged spiderlings in the wild, and if so, how prevalent it is. Only careful field research can supply an answer.

In spite of the fact that the mother tarantula tends the eggsac, tolerates the newly emerged spiderlings in her burrow, and may even feed them a little, her care is very brief. Within a few weeks of their emerging from the eggsac, certainly by the time the female molts, most species will ignore the spiderlings completely. There seems to be no long-term parental care as there is among some scorpions and humans.

Longevity

The male *Aphonopelma hentzi* from Arkansas that was studied by W. J.

Baerg has a total average life expectancy of little more than ten or twelve years in nature. Breene (1996) reports that *A. anax* reared in captivity under nearly ideal circumstances of plentiful food and warm temperatures can mature in less than two years. We can only guess at the life spans of the less well-studied species. Mounting experience indicates that those tarantulas that experience a cool, dormant period in winter live longer because their metabolism slows appreciably during the colder months. They don't "live" as fast during winter, don't age as rapidly as their tropical brethren, and therefore don't die as soon. (See page 22 for a discussion of ecdysis [molting], ultimate, and postultimate molts.)

In captivity, the males of most species of tarantulas will normally live only six months to a year and a half after attaining sexual maturity. No studies of the life expectancies of wild males have been done. However, Charpentier (1992) believes that the mortality rates of wild *Avicularia* males are extremely high; their life expectancies are surely much shorter than in captivity.

Phrixotrichus spatulata. *Male. This is the rarer, red color phase.*

Why do male tarantulas die so early in life, whereas the females live on for many more years? There is a clue. The authors and other enthusiasts have had male tarantulas that attempted a postultimate molt. In most cases of which the authors are aware, the males were unable to extricate their pedipalps from the old exoskeleton, and died as a result. Autopsies indicated that, had they molted successfully, they would have remained alive. The emboli and bulbs were present on the pedipalps of the new exoskeletons.

On three occasions the authors have had male tarantulas that were successful in their postultimate molt. One was a captive-bred individual of *Aphonopelma seemanni,* another was a wild-caught individual of one of the brown *Aphonopelma* species from the upper Rio Grande Valley of Texas, the third a male *Phrixotrichus spatulata*. In the first two cases they had lost their pedipalps during molt. Although they remained alive, they were effectively impotent, not having emboli or bulbs with which to impregnate females. That they were still fertile males is suggested by the fact that one of them built a succession of sperm webs even though he had no intromittent machinery to load with sperm.

In the third case *(P. spatulata),* the male retained his pedipalps, but they were trapped inside the cast skin. The male was cooled in a refrigerator to immobilize him, and the old skin was carefully removed. The male's cymbium, bulb, and embolus were distorted and probably could not have been used for mating.

In all cases, the males' legs were longer and more spindly after the postultimate molt than they were after the ultimate molt. While the tarantulas could walk around, they were visibly weaker.

None lived more than an additional six months before dying of apparent old age.

This poses several intriguing questions. Does the male die because he can't molt, or does he molt only if he doesn't die first? Might it be possible to alter the male's physiology through diet or pharmaceuticals to prompt him to molt again instead of die? If a male tarantula were recognized to be in premolt, could anything be done to help him shed successfully, retaining functional pedipalps? Once he shed, assuming that he retained functional pedipalps, would he be fertile and willing to continue mating for yet another season? Does this ever happen in nature?

For premolt care, dipping the ends of the pedipalps in a glycerine and water solution, and keeping the male tarantula in a more humid habitat might be suggested. Possibly, wild male tarantulas that survived the winter might instinctively seek a moist refuge in preparation for the coming molt. Just perhaps a few survive. (See also a discussion on page 153.)

The females of many species may live one or two decades or more (Baerg 1963) beyond their maturing or ultimate molt. The specimen of *Brachypelma emilia*, referred to as Duchess (see page 31), had a captive life span of almost nineteen years, but her total life span may have been well in excess of thirty-five years. Enthusiasts with experience with *B. emilia* suspect that the females may be the longest living spiders, perhaps approaching forty years.

Immatures of either sex and mature female tarantulas have few enemies. They are difficult to attack in their burrows, and as they grow they become larger and more powerful than most other predacious arthropods, the only significant exception being a few species of spider wasps. Animals such as foxes, coyotes, coatimundies, and mice may occasionally eat tarantulas, but normally hunt other prey. Once exposed to a face full of those irritating bristles, further contact is usually avoided unless driven by hunger.

Infamy

A brief word should be said about the famed tarantula hawk wasp, although a thorough discussion is beyond the scope of this book. The Entomological Society of America does not recognize *tarantula hawk wasp* as an official common name for these creatures. However, that is the name persistently used by the news media, as well as the one most familiar to the enthusiast. Therefore, we use it here, noting the exception.

These wasps are classified in several genera in the family Pompilidae. The adult wasps are not parasitic on tarantulas, as one would at first assume, eating plant nectar instead. The whole idea behind the wasp's attack on the tarantula is to secure incapacitated (though still living) tarantulas as a food supply for their developing larvae. The details of their technique and the apparent nonchalance of the tarantula when confronted by one of them is very interesting. However, although the phenomenon may be remarkable, it is by no means unique, as there are many smaller wasps the world over that routinely prey on spiders in a similar fashion. Indeed, this seems to be typical for several families of wasps. In the broad overview, the only really remarkable aspect of the hawk wasp versus tarantula relationship is their great size, a characteristic that has made them particularly vulnerable to exploitation by sensationalists.

For further reading on tarantula hawk wasps, read entries listed in the references by Petrunkevitch (1926 and 1952); William (1956); and Preston-Mafham and Preston-Mafham (1993).

Behavior

Sound

Many tarantulas from both the New and Old Worlds stridulate (see page 21 for a detailed description of the structures). Some of them can produce a rather loud hissing or buzzing sound. This sound is produced when the tarantula feels threatened, and it is usually accompanied by throwing the front appendages up and leaning back to expose the lower surface of the prosoma. The effect is intensified by the presence of bright or contrasting markings on the undersurfaces of the pedipalps and first pair of legs, or red or orange patches of bristles around the oral area, suggesting an open, snarling mouth. Long-term, tame captives often do not stridulate, whereas freshly caught or belligerent individuals might.

It is very difficult to describe the emotional reaction prompted by a tarantula that hisses. One of the authors (SAS) first encountered stridulation with a male *Theraphosa blondi* having a leg span exceeding twenty-two centimeters (nine inches). When first approached, it reared back with chelicerae, pedipalps, and forelegs spread, and made a hissing sound loud enough to be heard across the room. Several days passed before enough courage could be marshalled to attempt picking it up again!

Occasionally, tarantulas produce a swishing, brushing, or thumping sound when startled. This has not yet been reported in the scientific literature, but may be a ploy used to startle predators.

When a male tarantula encounters a female, he must convince her that he's a mate instead of an entrée. One of the things he may do is flex or twitch his legs repeatedly, in a series of two to four twitches at a time, with brief pauses between each series. During each flexion, these authors have noted a peculiar scratching or rasping sound produced in rhythm with the leg movements. That the sound is produced by the tarantula itself, rather than the tarantula scratching the substrate, is suggested by two lines of evidence. First, the same sound is present on different substrates, including soft fabric. Second, on one occasion a male *Brachypelma albopilosum* performed this maneuver while resting on a hand. A friend of the authors had been holding a female of the same species, then scooped up the male. The sound was barely audible, but the tactile vibration was startling.

This is not stridulation in the traditional sense, because those species that do not possess the traditional stridulating organs on chelicerae, pedipalps, or first legs are capable of producing the sound (e.g., *Brachypelma smithi, B. albopilosum,* and *B. emilia*). In those species that do stridulate (e.g., *Phrixotrichus cala, P. spatulata,* and *Theraphosa blondi*) the tarantulas do not visibly move their stridulating organs while producing this sound. These authors have not seen a reference to this sound production in the literature, and have not been able to determine its source. However, as a designation for purposes of future reference, we suggest the name of *sexual stridulation* for this peculiar activity.

How and where is it produced? Is this merely nervousness on the part of the male? Is he signalling his prospective mate? Is this part of the secret password required to prevent being eaten?

Many years ago, these authors were startled by individuals of *Aphonopelma seemanni* making vigorous thumping sounds from their cages in apparent response to the knocking of pieces of egg crate (packing used when shipping crickets) against the walls of an aquarium while unpacking crickets. This produces pulses of a low-pitched reverberating sound. The tarantulas were apparently responding to that sound.

Since that time, these authors have heard and seen female tarantulas of a wide spectrum of species signal with similar thumping sounds, presumably calling for mates, often with males in neighboring cages thumping in answer. As the state of the tarantula-keeping art progresses, other enthusiasts also report or refer to the exchange of thumping signals between individuals who are ready to breed.

These supposedly speechless, primitive animals even communicate with each other! Do they do this in nature? Probably, but no field worker has reported observing it.

How many different sounds can tarantulas make? Do these sounds differ with sex, species, or age? What other factors influnce them? Apparently, tarantulas can hear, but with what organs? Do they use these sounds in signalling each other of danger? Do they signal their rivals? Although this may seem a bit far-fetched, it is true that other spiders use sounds in courtship and in displays of rivalry. Why not tarantulas?

Here is a chance for the enthusiast to contribute to our knowledge. By careful observation and perhaps a strategically placed video recorder, we may be able to catalogue these sounds, determine how they are produced, and deduce if they have specific meanings.

Other Behaviors

These amazing creatures exhibit many other unexpected behavioral patterns if given the opportunity, and scientists and enthusiasts alike are just beginning to appreciate the size and complexity of their repertoire. It is unfortunate that we cannot present a full catalogue of these in this book. The enthusiast who has gained a little experience with keeping one or two species is encouraged to experiment with his charges to bring more of these to light. Of particular merit are the behavioral patterns exhibited in a natural setting. The inquisitive enthusiast might seriously consider allowing several tarantulas to build burrows in a very large community pen as an artificial colony.

If an adequately heated area were available for a project that would last for several years, for instance, one might set up a two meter by two meter by one meter thick (seven feet by seven feet by three feet thick) bin or *range* of soil approximating that in which a particular species of tarantula were naturally found. This range might be supplied with a few rocks and other obstructions and decorations in an effort to supply a natural ambience.

Several tarantulas of the same species might be encouraged to establish burrows in different parts of the range. Hopefully, unrelated females and immature males would be used. Thereafter, over the next several years, their behavior would be watched closely, notes and photos taken, even video recordings made to demonstrate their reactions and behaviors. Because tarantulas are most active in the darker hours of evening and night, equipment and accessories such as red lamps or infrared-sensitive cameras and films would have to be used for nighttime observations. We can only guess at what marvels would be revealed. (See also the discussion of cage arrangements that allow burrowing on page 116.)

The best news is that such an experiment need not be exorbitantly expensive. For instance, red bulbs are readily available from photographic supply stores, and most thirty-five millimeter, single-lens-reflex cameras are capable of using infrared-sensitive film if the appropriate filters are used. Neither the filters nor the film are unduly expensive. This experiment would have to run for several years to be truly fruitful, and it would require constant study and close attention to detail. Plan on spending lots of time watching the tarantulas in the wee hours of the morning.

Of course, the experimenter would be obliged to publish a detailed description of the structure's construction and its management, plus periodic progress reports, in an enthusiast newsletter or professional journal.

Remarks

Alien . . . Amazing . . . Bizarre . . . Exotic . . . Fantastic . . . Outlandish . . . Outrageous . . . Preposterous . . . Weird.

All of these terms have been used to describe the arachnids and their subgroup, the spiders. Had we not grown up among them, we might believe that we had been magically transported into some surrealistic science fiction story, or perhaps that we were hallucinating. The real world is often far stranger than any fictional one, and hallucinations are neither this intricate nor this well organized. From this time forward, you will never view spiders with the same arrogant ignorance of just a few pages ago. Whether you like spiders or not, you have lost your innocence of them.

Prepare yourself. Soon you will own a pet tarantula!

PART TWO
Tarantulas and Us

The human race evolved amidst the spiders, probably even amidst tarantulas. Surely, tarantulas were common in central Africa at the same time that our ancestors left the forests for the veldts and began the migration that succeeded in colonizing the planet. It should not be too surprising that, in more than two million years, tarantulas and humans have interacted countless times in a myriad of ways. The nature of those interactions is surprisingly diverse, and in some ways totally unexpected.

In the prologue, we promised you a long and winding journey. What lies ahead explores the core of our relationship with these phenomenal creatures.

Chapter Four

The Useful Tarantula

Some may have difficulty compre-
hending this concept. Of what use
could a large hairy spider possibly be?
We have some surprises in store for you!

Food

Prehistoric humans probably found
them to be a welcome source of protein. Even today, many of the world's
more primitive cultures find them nutri-
tious. For instance, the inhabitants of
the hill country of northern Thailand eat
them. They reportedly strip off the legs
and roast the bodies.

Smith (1990) reports that the bush-
men of central Africa tease them from
their burrows with a grass stem, then
roast them on a stick over glowing coals.

The native peoples of South America
also eat them. Documentary films by
Survival Anglia and Time-Warner (Brett
1993 and 1994), with Rick C. West as
scientific advisor, graphically illustrate
that *Theraphosa blondi* and *Pseudotheraphosa apophysis* are used for food by
the Piaroa Indians in Venezuela. The legs
are bent backwards over the body and
tied together for transportation. When
being prepared for eating, the spiders
are held with a leaf to protect the chef
from the intensely urticating bristles. The
animals are rolled in a leaf and roasted in
hot coals. The opisthosoma is discarded
and the prosoma and legs are eaten. If
the spider happened to be a gravid
female, the eggs may be squeezed from
the opisthosoma and cooked as an
omelette, as well.

"Pass the salt, please."

Cosmetics

In Indonesia, the more impoverished
members of the populace use tarantulas as an ingredient in homemade hair
dye. It seems that, although these people are proud to claim Western blood in
their family tree, they much prefer black
hair to blond or brown. Although the
exact recipe isn't known to these
authors, it involves boiling the tarantulas in oil, and may also include the use
of giant, black, Asian scorpions (*Het-
erometrus* species). As a result, the spider collector does a brisk business in
the bazaar.

"You look stunning today, my dear."

Mythology and Religion

Even apart from the old wives' tales
and misinformation that is rampant in
our cultures, tarantulas play an important
role in the religions and mythologies of
primitive peoples around the world.

Puzzled by scientific names? Read
Chapter 2: The Name of the Tarantula and Appendix A: Tarantula Species
as Pets for explanations and a cross-
reference between scientific names and
common names.

Mention has already been made to the film detailing the use of tarantulas in the Venezuelan forest (Brett 1993 and 1994). One of the principle players in that documentary is a native shaman whose patron spirit is the giant tarantula.

North American native peoples also have many legends and folk tales regarding spiders. Among some, the tarantula figures prominently.

> "The Zuni tell how 'old tarantula' entered into conversation with a handsomely dressed youth and asked him whether he would not like to see just how splendid he appeared. To this end the crafty old tarantula persuaded the youth, whose vanity had been aroused, to divest himself of his finery, even to the inclusion of his turquoise earrings and his anklets of sacred white shell, and then himself donned the raiment. 'Look at me now. How do I look?' asked the spider as he displayed the garments. The youth, finding the ugliness of the wearer somewhat detrimental to the appearance of the clothes, was not greatly impressed. The spider moved off a bit and, as distance lends enchantment or at least makes repulsiveness less obtrusive, the youth noted an improvement. Still a little farther off moved the spider, pretending that his only object was to gain the youth's approbation, but really intent on getting nearer and nearer to his burrow. At last he had arrived at the entrance. 'How do I look now?' asked the wily creature. 'Perfectly handsome,' replied the youth, but as he spoke, the spider dived into the earth with the stolen finery." (Schwartz 1921)

Arts and Entertainment

Tarantulas are also prominent in aboriginal art. The deserts near Nazca, Chile, are the home of the fantastic geoglyphs that were almost certainly produced by local native peoples many hundreds of years ago. One of these incredible works of art is a depiction of a huge spider, perhaps a tarantula. Although these were almost certainly done as part of a religious observance, they are now viewed as incredible aboriginal art.

Occasionally, the Zuni, Navajo, and other peoples of the southwestern United States will use the tarantula motif in their turquoise jewelry.

The tarantula has cropped up in Western art and literature, as well. They are mentioned in Nietzsche's *Also Sprach Zarathustra*. (See also page 3.) In addition, their role in contemporary film and television as subjects for science fiction stories is now becoming little short of outrageous. Still, beauty is in the eye of the beholder. The reader who appreciates low-budget sci-fi movies will, indeed, get along very well with tarantulas!

In our modern society, the spider and tarantula motif occurs time and again, as well. The authors have seen (and even possessed) belt buckles, boleros, earrings, pendants, and decorative pins done in the image of tarantulas, or even with preserved tarantulas (or their exuvia) mounted in clear plastic.

Commerce

Who would have thought that big hairy spiders would actually have a commercial value?

Several nightclubs use the name *tarantula* and the tarantula motif in their business name, logo, and advertising. Not too surprisingly, of the two these authors are aware of, one is in Mexico, the other in California.

Perhaps one of the most interesting roles for tarantulas is their use as pets. In this respect, they assume a significant financial importance to the native people who collect them and to a world-wide commerce through the pet industry. That trade has in turn prompted another use for tarantulas. They become the subjects of books such as the one you now read.

Research

Last, but not least, is their use in scientific research. Although their anatomy, physiology, and natural history seems exotic to us, they have many characteristics that are representative of arachnids in general. They also have interesting behavioral adaptions for meeting life's challenges and crises. They have adapted to a wide spectrum of ecologies using strategies different from most other animals, but still more or less representative of arachnids as a group. These characteristics hold important clues about the way that life evolved on Earth.

Witless Pranks

The human race is probably best characterized as being that species that has the proclivity to play stupid jokes on itself with no consideration of the results. We list here two such samples of our racial idiocy.

For a period in our history, some of the itching powder sold in novelty shops was, in reality, the urticating bristles from hapless tarantulas. This has now been replaced by a mixture of red pepper dust and fiberglass, thus saving the tarantulas, but introducing another potential health problem.

And, we all know too well the notorious pranks by those moronic dunces who put otherwise harmless tarantulas in teacher's desks and roommate's bunks.

Remarks

Once seriously considered, we find tarantulas hard to summarily disregard. They and other spiders hold a place in our culture and heritage that compels us to acknowledge them as important pieces in the vast jigsaw puzzle that is our civilization.

And you thought we had no use for tarantulas!

Chapter Five
The Pet Tarantula

Rationale

Before discussing the care of tarantulas, we must first ask ourselves why anyone would want to keep a tarantula as a pet. The following is a sample of some of the reasons that were actually given to the authors.

1. Status symbol. (Act now! Be the *first* on your block!)
2. Keeps mother/wife out of your room/workshop.
3. Conversation piece, not necessarily limited to *"Eek! A spider!"*
4. Satisfies a need to keep a pet when the lease says *"No Pets,"* because it can be hidden in a shoe box in a bureau drawer.
5. Satisfies curiosity. They *are* fascinating creatures, once one's initial apprehensions are overcome.
6. Scientific study. ("Well, actually I'm doing research on horror flicks . . .")
7. Your nephew bought one and his mother won't let him keep it in the house. So, you (poor gullible fool!) consented to keep it for him and let him see it every Saturday. Now you find out that they live twenty years!
8. You really hate your roommate, so you hope the spider's bite is lethal. *(Attack, Morte! Kill!)*
9. Your lifestyle and bank account require an inexpensive, undemanding pet.
10. You need a pet that *doesn't* come home with a litter of young every few months!
11. You need a pet that doesn't shed hair all over the living room.
12. Somebody told you that they make good pets, so you got one. And you know? *They were right!*

Ethical Considerations

The single most common mistake that pet keepers make is to buy a pet on impulse and with no consideration of how it must be cared for or even the simplest of ramifications of possessing it. As a result, countless thousands of animals from dogs and cats through the entire spectrum, down to and including tarantulas, endure miserable lives, or perish from miscare or no care at all. Read and heed the following pages *before* considering a pet tarantula. If these instructions cannot be observed, the authors strongly urge considering a different mascot, a plastic philodendron perhaps.

Do Your Homework!

Before buying your first tarantula, even before deciding to buy one at all, learn as much about these amazing creatures as possible. Because they are so outlandishly unconventional, a comprehension of the dissimilarities of their lifestyles, requirements, and weaknesses must be developed. Assumptions based on prior experience with the family dog are woefully inadequate. For your well-being as well as the tarantula's: *Do your homework first.*

Seek out local and international enthusiast organizations (see the listing beginning on page 248). Join one or more. Read every publication that they recommend. Ask them every question you can think of.

Read one or two books about them. The fact that you are reading this book is a good sign; it was written for precisely this purpose. As of this writing, these authors have a combined experience with tarantulas of well in excess of fifty years. Much of the information here is the direct product of hands-on, practical experience, and will not lead the tyro astray. But eventually even this book will be supplanted by more authoritative works. Keep reading.

If at all possible, try to locate another enthusiast with long-standing experience at keeping tarantulas. These may be found by casual encounters at local pet shops or by attending amateur herpetology club meetings. A surprising proportion of people who keep reptiles and amphibians as pets also keep tarantulas. If they don't, they surely know someone who does. Once contact is made with an experienced enthusiast, try to arrange for a few hours of consultation to gain a firsthand insight into the world of tarantulas and tarantula-keeping. Come prepared with some reasonable background knowledge, an appreciation for the subject, and a few questions that might stimulate the conversation. Don't waste this person's time. Again, do your homework first.

Lastly, if you have access to the Internet, the World Wide Web, or other Internet functions, seek out news groups and mailing lists that deal with arachnids in general and tarantulas in particular. Using this medium, you can communicate with some of the world's best-known arachnologists, amateur and professional, and you can do so almost instantly in an emergency. This subject is discussed more fully on page 249.

Pickin' and Choosin'

The Right Kind
The Broad View. How can the right kind be selected? Remember, these creatures don't live for only a few months like hamsters. They will live for years, perhaps for *decades*. Once purchased, it could be yours for a major portion of your life.

About eight hundred species of tarantulas are listed in the literature, fifteen alone from the state of Texas. However, for the reasons mentioned in the section on taxonomy, numbering the total species at eight hundred is dubious at best. An educated guess by the few scientists who seriously think about these animals places the real number anywhere between seven hundred and seven thousand.

During the entire course of the casual fancier's life, two dozen different species may not be seen. As avid collectors, and being closely involved with all levels of the pet industry for many years, the authors may have seen as many as one hundred different species. Not all of these are suitable as hand pets, however.

Ultimately, the enthusiast's first tarantula is usually the result of a trade-off between some characteristics that are highly desirable and some that are less desirable. For example, an exceedingly beautiful tarantula may not be handleable, one that is very docile and easily handled has particularly irritating bristles, or one that is otherwise an excellent pet is also exceedingly expensive. These authors counsel beginners to purchase relatively inexpensive, hardy, docile tarantulas as their first pet even though they may be comparatively somber in color. The more expensive, the less hardy, or the less docile tarantulas are best left until more experience is gained.

Here are some things to consider when making that fateful choice.

Not So Deadly Tarantulas. A few species of tarantulas (probably fewer than a dozen) may have a potentially harmful venom. Some of the *Pterinochilus* or *Heteroscodra* species from Africa probably fall into this category because there are references to people having been hospitalized after being bitten by "baboon spiders." The *Poecilotheria* species from India and Ceylon are also suspect.

It is important to note, however, that there are few or no references in the scientific literature that confirm this. Virtually every reference is anecdotal with no firm medical evidence or authoritative species identification. There are also allegations that some South American species are dangerously venomous (e.g., one or more *Phrixotrichus* species); but again, there is little factual evidence, merely unverified anecdotal reports, aboriginal myths, or unabashed attempts to impress the gullible tourist with giant spider stories.

Though brief, Breene (1996) gives a particularly good overview and extensive bibliography on this subject.

Too many people have cried wolf too many times. To say that these authors are skeptical is a vast understatement. With the exception of those listed above, none of the species commonly sold in pet shops are dangerous, and most make safe, reliable pets for the novice. The experienced aficionado may wish to acquire some of the rarer varieties, but is urged to take precautions when handling them until their identity is confirmed and verifiable evidence of the effects of their venom is obtainable. Other than that, neither the

Poecilotheria regalis *female. Dorsal view. This is their normal pose, head down on a vertical surface.*

enthusiast, roommates, the spouse, nor the mother need worry. Bites by tarantulas and their effects are covered more thoroughly on page 142.

Personality Types. Although the enthusiast need not be overly concerned about the danger of keeping a pet tarantula, some effort should be spent on considering the prospective pet's personality. As one might suspect, the spectrum of personality types among tarantulas is as varied as the tarantulas themselves. Some tarantulas are almost unbelievably docile. Others are simply too hostile to make handleable pets.

A few aficionados handle even the most malevolent tarantulas. The practice of handling hostile tarantulas is strongly discouraged by these authors, except by people who have years of experience with dozens of different species, and then only under the direst of circumstances. Handling tarantulas is discussed thoroughly, beginning on page 136.

There seems to be a broad correlation between personality and origin. Most species from the Old World are intractable and recommended only as cage pets, to be admired from a distance. The novice tarantula keeper is best steered away, leaving them for the experienced aficionado. On the other hand, many of the New World species become quite docile with minimal handling.

Superimposed in this broad tendency, each species also has its own typical personality. *Brachypelma smithi* and *B. emilia* from Mexico are so docile as to be arguably totally harmless (but beware the bristles!). In more than twenty-five years of handling literally thousands of them, keeping them as pets, breeding them, and selling them to enthusiasts, the authors know of only one instance when one attempted to bite.

Poecilotheria regalis female. Ventral view showing the brilliant yellow markings on the legs and the bright band across the opisthosoma.

Phormictopus cancerides from Haiti and *Haplopelma minax* from Thailand, on the other hand, are incorrigible scoundrels and bite at almost every opportunity. *Aphonopelma seemanni* from Costa Rica, though notorious for being highstrung and jumpy, seldom bears its fangs or attempts to bite.

The last level in the hierarchy of personality variations is the individual tarantula's personality. By way of example,

Brachypelma smithi. *One of the most sought-after species of tarantula in the world. Colorful and docile, but beware of the urticating bristles.*

the authors have had more than a dozen immature and adult *Brachypelma vagans* over the years. All except one have been docile, allowing themselves to be handled and caressed by adults and school children alike, with no spiteful reactions from the tarantulas. The single exception is a particularly large,

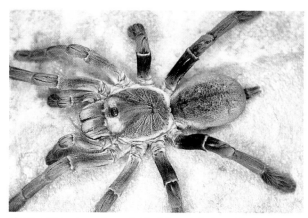

Haplopelma minax. *A nearly black tarantula from Thailand. These are eaten by the forest people. As with most Old World tarantulas, this one also has an attitude problem.*

colorful female called Mink, acquired from a close friend. Mink is completely unpredictable. On one occasion she will submit to being handled like a perfect lady. The next day she will bear her fangs and struggle fervently to escape the grasp or impale the nearest finger.

For the most part, the beginner's first tarantula should be one of the more mellow, New World species. The tarantulas from the United States, such as *Aphonopelma hentzi* and *A. chalcodes,* but not *A. moderatum,* are extremely docile and highly recommended in spite of their rather somber appearance. Many of the species from Central America, such as *Brachypelma vagans, B. albopilosum,* and others mentioned elsewhere, also make good hand pets. The Mexican species, *B. emilia* and *B. smithi,* now bred commonly in captivity, are also good pets and well worth the price. *Avicularia avicularia, Phrixotrichus spatulata,* and *Chromatopelma cyaneopubescens* are good examples of docile South American species.

There are some *caveats,* however. Many, if not most, New World tarantulas possess urticating bristles, and a number of people are allergic to them to varying degrees. It is best to handle a tarantula once or twice before its purchase to assess your sensitivity to the bristles. Dealers are often unwilling to refund the purchase price of animals once sold. This is entirely understandable as they are dealing in fragile, living organisms and have no way of knowing how well or poorly the animal was cared for, or what events it endured after its purchase.

Theraphosa blondi, Lasiodora parahybana, Pseudotheraphosa apophysis, and the other giants among the giant tarantulas should not be kept or handled by the novice. These are

Avicularia avicularia. *Adult female. While these seldom attempt to bite, they are a bit skittish, and will jump from the hand if annoyed too much.*

Phormictopus cancerides. *A plain brown tarantula with a bad attitude.*

enormous tarantulas that have special requirements for their care, and do not appreciate being handled. The effects of their venom are not well known, and the mechanical injury alone, resulting from a bite by one of these, is a matter of serious medical importance. The care and handling of these huge spiders is discussed throughout this text (see the Index) with particularly relevant passages on pages 127 and 139.

The Right Sex

The males of most species of tarantulas don't live as long as the corresponding females, and they are usually too hyperactive to make good hand pets. If the intention is not necessarily to handle the tarantula, or there is no great interest in having one that may live for

Brachypelma albopilosum. *The curlyhair tarantula. Still one of the best pets available. They appear to be having a perpetual "bad hair day."*

decades, a male may be acceptable, even desirable, especially if the price is acceptable. Freshly shed, mature males are in particular demand by enthusiasts who wish to breed them because new males must be acquired each year. Once they mature, they have only a limited time during which they are fertile. If the intention is to breed tarantulas, the males that others shun may be worth a premium. If the intention is to keep an interesting pet that might live a long time and may be readily handleable, a female is probably the better buy.

Before purchasing a tarantula, either immature or adult, if a shed skin is available from the individual, examine it carefully to ascertain the spider's sex. Science or biology teachers at local schools or colleges will be able to help with this sex determination if this book is brought to them with the shed skin. Recognizing a mature male tarantula is discussed on page 43. Sex determination in tarantulas is described in detail on page 194.

The Right Age

What age tarantula should be purchased? Following is a discussion of many of the pros and cons of purchasing spiderlings, immatures, and adults. Ultimately, you will have to decide which age is right for you.

Adults and Immatures. If the intention is to keep a pet tarantula for a long time, an adult or larger immature may not be a good choice. It is nearly impossible to accurately estimate an adult or large immature's age. A newly purchased mature female may live only briefly before dying of old age, and males seldom live more than twelve to eighteen months once mature.

Although adult and older immature tarantulas are very impressive on account of their size, the number of species of wild-caught individuals that are available is usually small and unpredictable, and as time passes will all but disappear due to ever-tightening export restrictions. The variety of smaller, captive-bred spiderlings is much broader and, as demand and breeding skills improve, will become more abundant.

There is no way of telling if adults or large immatures were captive bred or wild caught. Thus, these may represent a significant ecological loss somewhere on the planet. The purchase of a larger individual may be contributing to the destruction of their habitat and the extinction of another species.

The larger immatures are nearly as impressive as full grown adults, but the novice will have difficulty predicting their sex. For the novice with good luck, or by reading the section "Is It a Boy or a Girl?" on page 194, a female may be chosen, and her company enjoyed for many years. The enthusiast who wishes to try breeding tarantulas may prefer to look for males, however.

On the other hand, immatures have the advantage of being nearly as hardy as the adults, not as fragile as the baby spiderlings. The probability of survival to maturity is much greater.

Spiderlings. Spiderlings are more fragile than their corresponding adults. An indication of this is the terrible attrition rate that they must experience in the wild. An adult female may produce an eggsac every year or so for as many as fifteen years. In many species, each of these may hold as many as five hundred to one thousand spiderlings at a time. And, in spite of this impressive fecundity, the population in a given area changes little over decades. Why? Because they are ambushed by predators, annihilated by natural forces, or simply aren't strong enough to survive under the best of circumstances. They die by the thousands. Fortunately, captive-bred spiderlings have a much lower mortality rate. If twenty percent of the spiderlings die before they mature, the keeper considers the breeding attempt to be a disaster.

Although spiderlings are more fragile than adults, they have the potential of living for years, if not decades. Depending on the species, the males may live for three to fifteen years, the females from five to forty years. Spiderlings are probably captive-bred, and thus do not represent a pillage of some fragile natural habitat. And spiderlings of many of the rarer species are more likely to be found (rather than immatures and adults) because these originate in the more stable first world countries as the result of captive breeding.

One frequent objection to spiderlings and small immatures is that they aren't very impressive. To the uneducated eye, they resemble the spiders living in one's basement until they are nearly one-fourth grown. Although they will live decades, they will require many months before they even look like a tarantula, and there are those of the human species who simply cannot be that patient. For those who are so impatient, perhaps one-fourth grown immatures would be a better purchase, in spite of their greater cost.

If the intention is to breed tarantulas, half-grown immatures are the best size to start with. Although they are still young, they will mature soon, not requiring a decade of patience beforehand. But remember that as many as twelve to eighteen may have to be purchased and kept for several years to be assured of males at the appropriate times. Are you ready for such a commitment in time and effort, not to mention the cash investment?

There is one last advantage of buying captive-bred spiderlings or immatures. Wild-caught tarantulas may come with a load of parasites that are difficult or impossible to recognize, much less eliminate. In fact, we know almost nothing about tarantula parasitology. Captive-bred individuals have never been exposed to that threat, and therefore are in much better health than their wild-caught counterparts.

The Right Price

It is impossible to give actual prices here. Tarantula prices vary too widely at the whims and vagaries of politics, geography, availability, greed, and pure chance. It is hoped that this book will be useful for many years to come, adding yet another dimension of variability to prices. However, a few guidelines can be offered.

When the search for a pet tarantula is started, scout around to determine what species are available and at what prices. It's neither a bad idea nor bad manners to keep notes in a small note pad.

Enthusiasts and collectors tend to put too much emphasis on the tarantula's price, ignoring other, equally important considerations. Because of the time and effort required of the keeper, the captive-bred spiderlings and immatures may cost as much or more than wild-caught adults, but they may be the better bargain by far. It is much more important to acquire a reasonably vigorous individual with a long lease on life, and a healthy attitude, than it is to acquire a cheap one that might die next month, or one that can't be handled.

A last consideration involves increases in value over time. A baby *Brachypelma smithi* may cost US$30.00

in 1995. However, as an adult in 2005 it could be worth $300.00! Such a price increase may be due in part to inflation, but will almost certainly also result from its increase in size, maturity, and especially its scarcity. The tarantula purchased today must be regarded not only as a pet, but also as an heirloom and, believe it or not, an investment! Choose wisely.

The Right Source

Tarantulas can be purchased from dealers, pet shops, enthusiasts, and collectors. A few very fortunate enthusiasts even enjoy the opportunity of collecting their own tarantulas. Pet columns in bargain-finder-type publications and newspaper want ads often list tarantulas that other enthusiasts must dispose of. How does one go about choosing the most desirable tarantula from the most desirable source?

Mail Order Spiders. Yes, it is possible to purchase tarantulas by mail order! Dealers that specialize in exotic arachnids often advertise in the classi-

Haplopelma lividum. *The blue iridescence is extremely difficult to photograph. Many publications have resorted to "doctoring" the images of these to enhance the blue coloring, sometimes to ridiculous extremes.*

fied ad section of exotic pet magazines. The larger dealers sometimes buy display ads, too. In addition, most also advertise in the publications of international societies such as the American Tarantula Society (see page 248) and the British Tarantula Society (page 248), as well as those of many smaller hobbyist's clubs.

Most mail order dealers are honest folk, and will guarantee their stock. The occasional dishonest or careless one ordinarily develops a bad reputation very quickly, and soon perishes. The major risk is that the buyer may have too high expectations of what he should receive. In some cases this is induced or augmented by the description supplied by the dealer. The buyer has only two defenses. First, before placing the order, the buyer should speak with the dealer at length about the characteristics of the tarantula, its size, color, personality, venom strength, and the level of irritation to be expected from its bristles. Also, be sure to ask whether the description given is for the adult as it will look in five years, or the one-centimeter (half-inch) baby which will be shipped tomorrow.

The second defense is to adopt the point of view that there are risks involved, that this is clearly a gamble. You must adopt the attitude that even if the newly arrived tarantula isn't what you expected, it still won't be a major disaster. In fact, several of these authors' most prized pets at first impression were complete washouts. What you see is *not* necessarily what you get.

Lastly, be forewarned that bright blue or rainbow green and pink tarantulas seldom are. In reality they are most often black, brown, or dark gray with a blush, tinge, or iridescence that may not be obvious until the tarantula is held in bright light, and then only after it is almost fully grown or a mature male.

A good example of this is *Haplopelma lividum.* Except under perfect lighting conditions, this handsome tarantula is only charcoal gray with a few indistinct blue accents. See the photo on the previous page.

Neighborhood Pet Shop. Pet shops' priorities and enthusiasts' priorities are all too often completely different, and this has caused much consternation and discord between these two groups. We like to consider the neighborhood pet shop with a warm, fuzzy feeling inside. The pet shop, on the other hand, like any other small business, must answer to all the problems and pressures that any other small business falls prey to.

A pet shop must turn a profit. To do this, it must reduce its expenditures and increase its income. Realistically, tarantulas do not represent a large enough portion of the pet shop's sales to warrant a massive training program of its personnel. At the same time, to cut expenses, pet shops most frequently employ part-time help who are young people not interested in the pet shop as a career opportunity, and therefore with tarantula husbandry rather low on their list of priorities. The bottom line to all this is that nine out of ten pet shops know little more about tarantulas than the novices they sell them to.

This state of affairs is changing, but very slowly and not to the degree that tarantula-keeping veterans would prefer. The novices' only recourses are to read books such as this one in an effort to educate themselves before entering the store with money in hand and hopes held high. The following guidelines are offered to help avoid any misunderstandings or surprises.

When buying a tarantula from a pet shop, there are several important questions that must be considered. Are the tarantulas being cared for properly? Has the merchant been careful to remove from the public view any tarantulas that might be sick or weak? Are the cages clean, or have they not seen attention for months, with old shed skins and dead crickets lying about? Are the tarantulas kept away from very bright lights and sources of excessive heat? Do they have water dishes? Are the water dishes clean and reasonably full? Do the tarantulas appear plump and well fed?

Use caution in developing an opinion of the shop based on how well fed the tarantulas seem. Newly imported individuals are likely to appear emaciated for some time, in spite of the shop's best efforts. Emaciation is only important if all the tarantulas appear underfed or if they are all poorly cared for.

Next, talk to the personnel and the owner or manager, if possible. Do they seem knowledgeable about tarantulas? If they admit to ignorance, at least give them an extra point for honesty. If they are more interested in impressing the buyer with their eminence, be wary of an underlying ignorance. After reading this book, an informed judgment can be made of whether their advice can be trusted.

Will the staff handle the tarantulas? Do they pick them up *properly,* without anxiety or fear? Will they allow you, the prospective buyer, to handle a few of them? This must be allowed in order to determine your sensitivity to the bristles. Do they have all the items needed for the care of the tarantula? If not, perhaps the pet shop doesn't normally sell tarantulas. It is also possible that the staff is much more knowledgeable about other pets than tarantulas.

An assessment of the business's qualifications may indicate that it can't be relied upon for continuing support of your pet's needs. If a tarantula is purchased here, are competent advice and the necessities for its care conveniently available elsewhere?

Shows and Swap Meets. Here lies a great gray area, neither properly dealer or retailer, but not quite hobbyist either. Frequently, amateur reptile enthusiasts will hold shows and swap meets in an effort to sell excess livestock, their homemade cages and paraphernalia, or just to display their pets. These people appreciate exotic animals as much as any, and many also have tarantulas and other arachnids as pets as a result. Thus, it is not too unexpected to find tarantulas for sale at the larger events. Superficially, the displays in these shows appear to be businesses and many operate that way. Fundamentally, however, most are just hobbyists who enjoy doing things with their pets, including selling a few that they no longer need. Rarely, individuals will be found who actually order tarantulas from the wholesale pet trade for these shows. All this frequently allows for a relatively large number of varieties of tarantulas being offered for sale, much more so than in the local, retail pet trade; and these events offer excellent opportunities for the casual hobbyist to meet dedicated enthusiasts. Such contacts are often worth more than the business being conducted.

The tyro who is looking for a tarantula at one of these events must be as cautious about buying one here as they would be buying one from either a formal business (see above) or from another hobbyist (see below).

Enthusiasts and Collectors. Acquiring tarantulas from these people can mean reaping some incredible bargains.

However, the buyer must remember that once the sale is made, there is seldom any recourse, guarantee, refund, or return. The buyer will also have to seek out other, more reliable sources for caging, food, and supplies as well. After reading this book, an informed assessment can be made about the suitability of the tarantula as a pet, its condition, and what supplies and caging should be acquired on the way home.

Maintenance

Tarantulas are native to a truly wide range of living conditions, and each species has evolved to fit its native habitat, hand in glove. This implies that each species will have its own minimal, basic requirements, probably somewhat different from all other species.

Experience has shown that the living conditions that are most important include caging and substrate, presence or absence of a burrow, temperature and light intensity, water and humidity, and food. Each will be covered in its turn.

Caging

Necessity. There are no cages in nature. In captivity, cages are necessary to restrict the activity of the animal. Often, this is as much for the animal's protection as for the protection of the people around it. All sentimentalism aside, cages are an important requirement for life in captivity. The tarantula *must* be kept caged.

Cannibalism. Although tarantulas may live in groups that we call colonies, most are strictly antisocial. Keeping more than one per cage insures that only one fat tarantula will survive. They are *guaranteed* cannibals. A larger cage may be partitioned with solid dividers to allow holding several, but they must not be allowed to climb over, knock down, dig under, or squeeze around the barriers.

Possibly because of the very limited surface available to them, many of the arboreal tarantulas (e.g., *Avicularia* species, *Poecilotheria* species) have partially suppressed this cannibalistic tendency. This may allow a denser population to inhabit a much more restricted habitat. This suppressed cannibalism has prompted many enthusiasts to interpret these species as being semisocial, thus allowing them to save cage space by keeping several individuals together. As with most other stories that are too good to be true, so is this one.

Even under the best of circumstances, these authors are exceedingly distrustful of divided cages and communal living for tarantulas. Too many times we have heard the tales of woe because, to save twenty-five dollars on a new cage, the keeper lost a one-hundred-dollar pet! Much safer is a strict *one tarantula per cage* rule. Take heed!

Sizing It Up. The cage can be almost any container that will prevent the escape of the animal and its food. The width should be at least one and one-half times the tarantula's maximum leg span, and the length at least one and one-half times the width, or an equivalent floor area. Thus, a circular, hexagonal, or octagonal cage should be at least twice as wide as the tarantula's leg span. The height of the cage should be great enough to allow the animal to turn over and right itself easily during molting. For the average adult tarantula this would translate into a rectangular cage measuring about thirty centimeters long by fifteen centimeters wide by seven centimeters high (twelve by six by three inches). An equivalent circular cage might measure thirty centimeters (twelve inches) in diameter.

However, for a *Theraphosa blondi* with a twenty-centimeter (nine-inch) leg span, more reasonable dimensions would be thirty centimeters wide by sixty centimeters long (twelve by twenty-four inches) for a rectangular cage, or forty-five centimeters (eighteen inches) in diameter for a circular one. Huge, expensive tarantulas require huge, expensive cages.

The cage should not be too tall because tarantulas will occasionally climb the walls. But, because they are clumsy, they also fall, and any appreciable drop could kill them. As a rule of thumb, the cage should never be more than thirty centimeters (twelve inches) tall, and even less for some of the really huge species. They are exceedingly fragile because of their extreme bulk.

One exception must be noted to the preceding paragraph. The arboreal tarantulas (e.g., *Avicularia, Poecilotheria,* and *Psalmopoeus* species) have evolved for climbing and are remarkably adept at it. They should be given tall cages whenever possible, with a piece of rough bark, cork, a cardboard tube, or other device at the very top to act as an anchor for building a nest.

For spiderlings and immatures, ample room must be supplied to allow for future growth. As a coarse rule of thumb, the initial cage should be twice the size recommended above, and the growing tarantula should be moved to larger quarters whenever its leg span reaches half the smaller horizontal dimension of the cage.

An accompanying figure illustrates a progression of differently sized containers used for housing spiderlings. Some sizes are skipped for the larger or faster growing varieties of tarantulas.

All the Myriad Cages. Many different kinds of cages have been tried with

Examples of housing for spiderlings. As they grow, they are moved to larger quarters.

Cigar boxes are definitely not acceptable. If they have indeed held any tobacco products, it is almost certain that they are contaminated with nicotine. Nicotine is one of the most potent insecticides known. It is natural, organic, and deadly! Tarantulas are most definitely not immune to it.

Wooden cages are acceptable providing they are not constructed of cedar. The wood that comes from any of the cedars (various species of *Thuja, Juniperus,* and *Chamaecyparis*), contain aromatic oils that are toxic to most living organisms, especially arthropods. This is the reason for using cedar in the construction of closets and chests. It deters clothes moth and dermestid beetle infestations. Unfortunately, it is also dangerous to tarantulas and most other animals, as well. Never keep a tarantula in any container that has a cedar smell. Never keep a tarantula's cage on or near a cedar chest or closet. Never use cedar chips, sold for rodent bedding by pet shops, in a tarantula's cage.

Painting or varnishing a wooden cage is recommended. This seals the pores of the wood, making it easier to clean. The urethane-based products seem best because the finish is waterproof and very durable. Be certain that the paint is marked "nontoxic when dry." A semigloss or satin finish is recommended, as the flat finishes are almost as difficult to keep clean as the bare wood, and the high-gloss finishes appear too hard or harsh in a small cage. Lacquer and shellac are too fragile to be serviceable in these circumstances.

The major drawback to wooden cages is that their contents cannot be inspected without opening them. It would be possible to install a glass or plastic window, but the trouble might not be worth the effort.

varying degrees of success. Squat, eight-liter (two-gallon) goldfish bowls are inexpensive and have the required floor space for the smaller species (Perrero and Perrero 1979), but they are difficult to make escapeproof, the glass is seldom clear enough to allow a really good view of the tarantula, and the bowls hog much too much room if several are to be kept on the same surface.

Screen or wire mesh cages may be made at home from scrap materials, but they may allow the tarantula's food to escape. In addition, if the tarantula climbs up the sides, it could fall and injure itself. If the strands of wire are merely woven together rather than welded (as in hot-dipped, galvanized mesh), the animal could snag a claw between two strands. This could result in the loss of the claw or even a leg. Certainly the tarantula would be most uncomfortable, hanging there for hours until rescued.

Plastic boxes used for storing shoes and other household objects make inexpensive utility cages. These are popularly called plastic shoe boxes, and are usually available from variety and department stores. They measure approximately thirty-eight centimeters long by eighteen centimeters wide by ten centimeters high (fifteen by seven by four inches) and are an ideal size for all but the smallest and very largest tarantulas. They are particularly convenient because they are made to stack on top of each other when in use, and nest in each other when in storage. A series of small holes should be put in them to allow for ventilation. This is best accomplished with a red-hot carpenter's nail. Choose a nail that will produce a hole three or four millimeters (one-eighth inch) in diameter. A larger hole will allow the tarantula's food to escape. Melt eight to twelve holes high up, along each side of the shoe box, but just low enough so that the lid doesn't cover them.

One difficulty arises from the light weight of the lids. The larger tarantulas are capable of lifting them off and escaping. These authors have adopted the habit of placing small rocks or slabs of slate on top of them to prevent the tarantulas' escape. Another strategy involves lashing the lids down with the fabric straps used by hikers and campers.

The traditional plastic shoe boxes, made of transparent plastic that allowed easy inspection of the contents, are becoming hard to find. The newer boxes are made of a translucent plastic and are considered marginally useful because they must be opened to see the contents clearly.

Plastic bottle manufacturers make wide-mouthed (e.g., 110 millimeters in diameter, about four inches), two- and four-liter (one-half- and one-gallon) bottles out of crystal-clear plastic. These bottles come in a variety of shapes. The wide, squat shapes are excellent for the terrestrial species, whereas the tall, narrow shapes are acceptable for the arboreal ones. Because these are quite inexpensive, the enthusiast should acquire the largest sizes available. Holes may be melted or drilled in the lids, but these will be obstructed if the bottles are stacked upon each other. Melting holes around the top of the sides of the bottles will avoid this problem. For reasons of safety, drilling on a curved surface is not recommended. Although these bottles are serviceable for the smaller individuals in a collection, they are not acceptable for the giant tarantulas except when very young. Review the discussion of size requirements on page 109.

The ideal display cage is an aquarium. An eight- to twenty-liter (two- to five-gallon) capacity is adequate, a thirty-seven liter (ten-gallon) capacity is nearly the maximum size allowable because of its excessive height. The currently popular style, made of panes of glass held together with a silicone rubber, and with no metal frames, is relatively lightweight and easily handled. The convenient rectangular shape doesn't clash with most decors. They are also easily repaired if one pane is broken. However, they are so inexpensive in the smaller sizes that, if more than one pane is broken, it is often less trouble and expense to replace the whole aquarium than to repair it. Enthusiasts often make their own aquaria, but unless the glass is virtually free, it still may be less expensive, and certainly less bother, to buy the smaller sizes.

When making or repairing any aquarium, use only that silicone rubber that is specifically intended for aquaria. Most others contain a mildewcide that is extremely toxic and guaranteed to poison the inhabitant.

One of these authors' favorite styles of aquarium, complete with locking lid, is shown in an accompanying figure.

Keeping a Lid on It. A secure, utterly escapeproof top is an absolute necessity. Trying to save money by slighting this rule is guaranteed to lose an expensive pet. Various styles of screen or wire lids are manufactured to fit the standard-size aquaria, and some of these include locking mechanisms, an important safety feature.

Alternatively, these may be made in the home shop by the enthusiast. In North America the material to use is called hardware cloth. It is a coarse screening that has been hot-dip galvanized. The preferred mesh is three-millimeters (one-eighth-inch) square, although coarser meshes will work almost as well. In an emergency, a rectangle of mesh may be cut about four centimeters (one and one-half inches) larger than the cage top. Two-centimeter (three-quarters-inch) squares should be cut from each corner, and two-centimeter margins of the mesh should be bent down so that the corners meet. The result is a crude but effective lid that should fit snugly over the cage top.

Given a little more time and ingenuity, the enthusiast may build a more aesthetically appealing frame of wood and fasten a rectangle of mesh to it using staples or furring strips and brads.

It is important to stress that the mesh should be hot-dip galvanized, not merely woven. A nongalvanized, woven screen allows innumerable junctions where the tarantula may wedge a claw and become caught. It should be avoided at all costs. On any homemade cover, all sharp edges and points of wire should be removed or concealed to prevent injury to the enthusiast, guests, and the tarantula.

Other materials have been used as cage covers as well. Among them are sheets of aluminum (commercially stamped as decorative grills), heavy mesh nylon cloth, and thin boards or plywood with many drilled holes. All are acceptable as long as they produce an escapeproof lid that will not pose a hazard to either enthusiast or pet.

Some lids are of heavy enough construction that none but the largest tarantulas could move them. Even then it is better to be safe than sorry. If the lid does not come with a built-in method for fastening it down, a method must be improvised. Temporarily, a book placed crosswise on the lid will suffice, but it should be replaced with a more permanent security device as soon as possible. Weights left on the lid will eventually cause it to sag out of shape, or part the mesh from the lid's frame. Occasionally, clips are offered for sale in the pet trade that grasp the edge of the aquarium's plastic top frame and hold down the lid. These are usually made to work with only one or two brands of frames, however. For particularly recalcitrant tarantulas (who commonly end up being nicknamed Houdini), the authors use a cotton or nylon webbing strap of the sort used to tie down camping gear. If one isn't long enough, two are linked end to end. These are then looped and fastened securely around the long axis of the aquarium and lid.

Substrates

Enthusiasts have tried any number of substrates with their tarantulas. Some of them have been unqualified successes; most are of marginal performance;

some are unqualified failures. None are completely satisfactory. Below are listed the more commonly tested types with their relative merits and drawbacks. The novice is advised to use either well-tamped potting soil, vermiculite, or a mixture of these two at first. For the desert species, natural aquarium gravel is also acceptable. Only after much experience has been gained with the care of tarantulas should more exotic substrates be tried, and then only with much careful forethought and great trepidation.

Natural Substrates. Under this category we include nonorganic, natural products that have been tried by the tarantula-keeping community.

A commonly used substrate or bedding is aquarium gravel. Any of the natural (uncolored) aquarium gravels that are not sharp or coarse are acceptable. Colored gravels should be avoided unless they have absolutely no organic solvent odor whatsoever. Colored gravels that have already seen their stint in a fish tank are probably acceptable if rinsed thoroughly. Never use soap or any other cleaning compound when cleaning a tarantula's gravel.

Crushed gravel has too many sharp edges and points. It will abrade the tarantula's ventral surface, allowing a serious inroad for infection and disease.

Acquire enough gravel to make a layer two or three centimeters (three-quarters to one inch) thick. This is normally about 250 grams per liter of aquarium capacity (two and one-half pounds per gallon) if an aquarium of common proportions is used. Rinse it with room temperature tap water and allow it to drain thoroughly before using it in the cage. Don't worry about excess moisture as long as it evaporates in one or two days.

The major criticisms of aquarium gravel are that it is very heavy in quantity, relatively expensive, and difficult to clean. Additionally, it is more abrasive than many enthusiasts would prefer. Although it is one of the more commonly used substrates, especially by novices, it is hardly ideal.

Very coarse pebbles are not recommended. They are difficult for the tarantula to walk over, and they allow spaces for bits of food and waste to sift into and decay, promoting bad odors and vermin infestations.

Fine sand (e.g., blasting silica) is not recommended on the cage floor because it absorbs and holds moisture indefinitely, quickly turning sour in the process. Beach sand, even from freshwater shores, is not recommended because it is too fine and may contain harmful concentrations of salts, pesticides, or floating contaminants washed up on the shore. McKee (1986) warns that fine sand has a tendency to cake around the mouth, thus making feeding difficult, if not impossible. It is also accused of entering the book lung's spiracles with detrimental results. Do not use fine sand.

Do not use decorative crushed glass!

Use soil and peat with caution. They absorb and hold moisture and wastes, thus enhancing the probability of mold and mite infestations. If soil or peat are used, they should be the commercial, steam-sterilized product from a florist or garden shop. At the first sign of any mold or vermin, discard the soil and sanitize the cage.

McKee (1986) recommends using commercial cat litter. This is ground, baked clay that is used in cat pans as the cat's toilet. McKee quite rightfully warns against the use of those products that have been treated with odor retardants and other additives. Use only the unadulterated, natural product. These authors have several criticisms of this product. When dry, it tends to be very dusty, and is a powerful desiccant (drying agent). It should be used only with desert species of tarantulas, if at all. It will eventually break down to become sticky clay when kept moist.

In a personal communication, McKee has reported that a mixture of one part clay cat litter and two parts potting soil is also a serviceable substrate. It is reputed to hold moisture well for enhanced humidity, and the cat litter retards mite infestations. When kept dry, this mixture is also very dusty. When kept moist it behaves like unadulterated potting soil. Its mite-retardant properties could not be adequately tested.

Many veteran tarantula keepers recommend the use of vermiculite (expanded mica), available from flower and garden shops. Do not use the vermiculite that is intended as insulation. Most such vermiculite is treated with an antiwetting agent to prevent water absorption in walls or attics. At the very least, this treatment will make the vermiculite difficult to use, and it could poison an expensive pet.

Vermiculite is nonorganic and very clean. Thus, it doesn't promote disease or mite infestations of itself. It is also very light in weight, and a shelf of large jars or cages with vermiculite substrate will weigh only a fraction of the same containers with aquarium gravel. Because it is inexpensive, it may be thrown away when soiled, or used in the garden or in flower pots as originally intended, with little guilt.

In practice, the vermiculite is dampened slightly, but it should never be wet enough to allow any water to be squeezed out by hand. The present authors view such a moist habitat with some trepidation. Too much moisture for too long a time invites mite infestations and fungus infections. If moistened vermiculite is used, clean the cage often and inspect the tarantula frequently for signs of vermin or disease. If there are even faint suspicions of either, sanitize the cage and switch to a drier substrate.

Additional problems with vermiculite are that some tarantulas are not comfortable on the relatively loose, unstable substrate or the moisture. This is evidenced by burrowing species persistently hanging from the cage walls or pacing the container like a caged lion. Usually they recover from their unhappiness within a few weeks and settle into a normal routine on the vermiculite. If the problem persists, change to another substrate.

Another criticism that these authors have with vermiculite is its color, which is almost the same as newly emerged tarantulas. Thus, the tiny spiderlings are forever getting lost between the vermiculite grains, and the enthusiast has great difficulty finding them and assessing their health and growth. After some months, the spiderlings grow large enough and become colored enough to allow more or less easy recognition. The first few months can be trying, however.

One last criticism of vermiculite is that a mite infestation is all but invisible on it until the cage and the tarantula are almost completely overwhelmed by the mushrooming hordes. Refer to page 165 for a more thorough discussion.

Organic Substrates. There is something alluring about using products labelled "natural and organic" in a cage with a wild creature, perhaps because of some mystical, romantic presumption about their "natural and organic" needs. As demonstrated below, this is neither always true, nor necessarily the wisest strategy.

Newsprint is highly questionable in the tarantula cage. If the ink is old-fashioned lamp black and mineral oil, it might be safe. If it is derived from coal tar dyes, it is probably toxic.

Furthermore, a chemical in paper that is derived from fir trees resembles certain hormones that stop insect maturation (Slama and Williams 1966). It is suggested that virtually all paper manufactured in the United States possesses this substance. No one has shown a similar effect in tarantulas, but that might be because no one has looked. Do not take the chance with your valuable pets.

However, an experienced keeper might separate a few of the spiderlings from the rest and keep them on paper towels or newsprint, to compare their rates of development and maturation with those that are kept on various other substrates. Under any other circumstances, there are better alternatives for substrates.

Hancock and Hancock (1992) mention the use of forest bark, presumably the chipped or mulched bark used in landscape mulching and available from landscape and gardening suppliers. They hold the opinion that the tannin in such bark acts as a suppressant to mite growth and reproduction, but not to the tarantulas. In view of the information presented in the previous paragraph, these authors would recommend use of such bark only after further testing. For the novice there are other, less suspect alternatives.

Once again, never use cedar shavings. The oil of cedar is unquestionably toxic.

Hancock and Hancock (1992) also mention the use of coconut fibre. These authors have had no experience with this substrate and cannot offer an opinion. Enthusiasts who choose to experiment with it should do so sparingly at first.

Other organic substrates have been tried by the present authors and many other enthusiasts. These include crushed sugarcane pulp, chipped cocoa bean hulls, and even more exotic products. These all suffer from two overwhelming detrimental characteristics. They rot to produce a vile mess when they become moist, and they promote the rampant reproduction of mites and other vermin. If the enthusiast feels compelled to experiment with any of these, only one or two less highly prized individuals should be tried first. Only after many months of problem-free use should any more of the collection be switched to these exotic substrates.

Artificial Substrates. Some enthusiasts have tried the green, artificial turf carpeting used for patios and porches. This carpeting looks neat, is relatively inexpensive, and is easy to clean. Merely wash it with a mild detergent and rinse it well. The authors launder it in the washing machine using a delicate fabrics setting. It is entirely reasonable to keep several changes of such carpeting handy, just in case the cage must be quickly cleaned in preparation for polite company. An added bonus is that mite infestations are almost unheard of on such carpeting because humidity levels are normally quite low and there are relatively few places for the mites to hide.

If the enthusiast wishes to try this material, the variety with a rubber backing is much sturdier than the less expensive varieties that lack it.

Sooner or later, the tarantula will discover that it can dig in the nap of the carpet. Shortly thereafter it will have succeeded in tearing the corners and edges of the carpet to shreds, necessitating its replacement. *Do not* glue the carpet to the cage's floor! Not only is the glue potentially toxic, but it will make carpet replacement most difficult.

The authors are aware of two detrimental qualities of this carpeting. First, for moist forest species of tarantulas, it is difficult to raise the cage's relative humidity above the ambient room's value. This problem can be circumvented by restricting ventilation somewhat (but not blocking it entirely) and by using water dishes with larger surface areas. The other problem is that some tarantulas persistently snag their claws in the carpeting, with the ever-present potential of losing a leg. Most tarantulas seem to have little difficulty, however. Wherein lies the difference?

While artificial turf carpeting may make a good substrate for a temporary display cage at a show or in a pet shop, it has not been used long enough by enough enthusiasts to be recommended unreservedly. As an experiment, an enthusiast might use it with only a few individuals at a time, not changing the whole collection over to artificial turf immediately, or possibly ever.

The fibers in regular living room carpeting persistently snag the tarantula's claws, making movement extremely irksome for the creatures, and presenting the ever-present danger of losing a leg. Do not use this type of carpeting.

Burrowing

Every enthusiast wants the pet tarantula to live naturally in a burrow. Be forewarned. Unless done with great forethought, such an arrangement will make any interaction with the pet nearly impossible without tearing up the entire cage. It will neither be seen very clearly, nor very often. It will spend most of its time deep in its burrow, coming out only to catch food or when ejecting soil or detritus. In either circumstance, it will only be out for a small fraction of a second, and then only if there have been no disturbances for some time.

Experience has demonstrated that most pet tarantulas can get along quite nicely without a burrow. So, for the beginner, we recommend against a caging arrangement that allows for burrowing. After several tarantulas have been kept for some time, and the enthusiast has had some experience with their care, a special cage may be set up to allow burrowing for the sake of experiment.

The authors have seen a number of methods for allowing a tarantula (and other burrowing spiders) the luxury of a burrow in its cage. Undoubtedly, more will be devised by ingenious enthusiasts as time progresses, and at least one commercial design is already on the market. Virtually all of them suffer from one or two serious flaws. It is difficult, if not impossible, to clean the inside of any windows in the burrow's wall. Under the best of circumstances, the view will likely be obscured by layers of dirt or silk. Also, the average tarantula will spend all but a few moments at a time deep within the burrow. The owner will either have to be content with seeing the pet only very sporadically, or tearing up the cage from time to time just to check on its condition.

On the other hand, it is interesting to note that several species of tarantula have odd or interesting burrowing characteristics (Marshall 1997) which cannot be observed unless the tarantula is given ample opportunity to build such a burrow.

Lund (1977) gives instructions for using a smaller aquarium inside a larger one for allowing the construction of a burrow. The smaller aquarium is positioned in one corner of the larger, and the intervening space is filled with soil. Lund's method leaves the inner aquarium right-side-up, allowing the possibility of the tarantula falling into it and injuring itself. These authors would recommend that the inner aquarium be turned upside-down to prevent such injury. A little soil scattered on top of the inner aquarium will camouflage it from casual spectators. Standard potting soil may be too fluffy to work well, although this is what Lund used. Well-sifted garden soil might be recommended instead, or even a mixture of these two. If it contains too much clay, and packs or hardens too solidly, mix it with potting soil, coarse sand, fine aquarium gravel, or fine horticultural vermiculite. Choose soil that has not been exposed to pesticides, even if it means travelling some distance to acquire it.

A second caging method for allowing burrowing uses an arrangement similar to a formicarium.

"What in the world is a formicarium?" you demand. A formicarium is a thin cage used for the maintenance of an ant colony. An Ant Farm is a commercial product of this sort marketed by Uncle Milton Industries of Irvine, California. Although the walls are transparent, they are normally protected with opaque covers to prevent any light from reaching the inner workings. The cage is usually partially filled with soil or sand to allow the ants the ability to dig their tunnels and chambers. When being observed, the opaque covers are removed and the ants are viewed using either subdued or red light, which seems not to disturb them significantly.

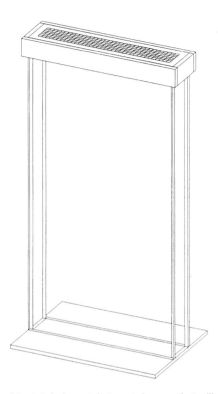

A tarantularium-style tarantula cage that will allow a burrow.

The tarantula-keeping enthusiast can use much the same arrangement for allowing and observing burrowing by tarantulas, a "tarantularium." Make a glass cage from four- or five-millimeter (three-sixteenths-inch) glass and silicone aquarium sealer. For a typical tarantula with a ten-centimeter (four-inch) leg span, the cage might measure four centimeters (one and one-half inches) thick (front to back), twenty centimeters (eight inches) wide, and thirty to forty-five centimeters (twelve to eighteen inches) tall. Scale the cage to match the size of the prospective

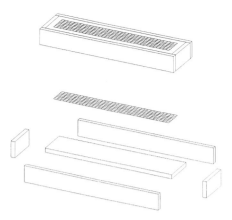

The tarantularium's lid, assembled (top), and exploded for clarity (bottom).

inhabitant. Leave one of the short, bottom end seams unsealed. In fact, a one-millimeter gap might be engineered into it. This will allow excess water to leak out in case of over-exuberant watering, without allowing the escape of the tarantula. Fill it three-quarters full of the same soil described above.

An accompanying figure is a drawing of a suggested lid. The finished lid is illustrated along with an exploded view to illustrate the parts and their assembly. The lid is heavy enough to foil most tarantulas, and possesses a screen window to allow for ventilation. A lid such as this, or a functional substitute, is absolutely necessary. In such confined quarters, air must be allowed to freely move in and out. To be strictly avoided is a tarantula that moves in and out!

A third caging method (de Vosjoli 1991) uses floral foam, available at florist's shops and greenhouses. De Vosjoli suggests drilling, carving, or sawing a mock burrow in such a way that it abuts a wall of the aquarium. The foam block is buried in soil with only the opening exposed. With careful arranging, the tarantula's habits can be observed through the aquarium wall.

Hancock and Hancock (1992) describe a cage made of a flat, soft mortar building block held in a frame. If the mortar is soft enough to work with hammer and chisel, a neat burrow may by gouged out of one face. Use safety goggles! A plate of glass can be fastened over that face of the block, to act as one wall of the burrow. The frame serves as a cage, to prevent the tarantula from wandering off.

Would a sheet of florist's foam work in place of the building block? Probably, but be sure to use a secure enclosing frame with a solid wood back. Otherwise, a burrowing tarantula might be able to escape if it burrows out of the foam block.

A more elaborate design was used by the Survival Anglia camera crew while filming *Theraphosa blondi* and *Pseudotheraphosa apophysis* in Venezuela (Brett 1993, R. West, personal communication). Actually it was a small movie set rather than a cage. It was built using the techniques of table top photography. The burrow was made of silicone rubber, camouflaged with soil, mosses, and lichens. One or more glass windows were constructed in the wall of the burrow to allow photography. The exposed end of the burrow *must* open into a secure cage, and provision must be made for safely cleaning the windows.

When the inhabitant is a possessive, adult *T. blondi* with an attitude problem, inserting one's arm into the burrow up to the armpit to clean the glass can cause stuttering, urinary incontinence, and several other equally disagreeable manifestations in the intruder! Careful advance planning is clearly prudent.

One scheme that shows great promise is to supply a sheet of florist's moss or sphagnum moss to the tarantula. If the clump were shaped to resemble a small cavern, the tarantula might be persuaded to accept it as a surrogate burrow. When the pet is to be inspected or shown to friends, gently lift the moss. When finished, merely replace it carefully. Spray the moss with a little water from time to time to raise the relative humidity in the cage, if needed. Such an arrangement has an additional benefit. Accidentally dropping the moss on the tarantula won't kill it.

For the individuals of *Theraphosa blondi* in the authors' collection, simple burrows were made from lengths of plastic pipe. Twenty-centimeter long sections were cut from ten-centimeter (four-inch) diameter, thick-walled, black PVC sewer pipe. Two longitudinal cuts were made to remove approximately one-fourth from the side of the cylinder to expose an open slot running its full length. All burs and sharp edges were filed off, and sawdust and manufacturing contaminants were washed off with hot soapy water and a thorough rinsing.

The pipe was then laid open side down on the substrate with one end butted against one end wall of the cage. This affords the tarantula a dark haven in which to hide. It also allows spectators a glimpse of the Goliath without a major upheaval in the tarantula's lives. Lastly, if the tarantula must be evicted from its burrow, the lengthwise slot allows it to be gently prodded out of the pipe without danger to either the enthusiast or the tarantula.

In Defense of a Burrow

Marshall (1997) lists at least two reasons why a tarantula might be allowed to burrow. The first is a matter of avoiding

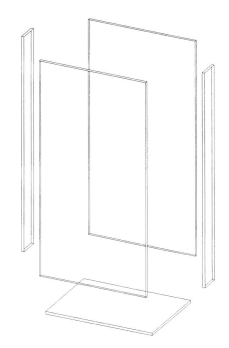

The body of the tarantularium exploded for clarity.

stress. We have few or no ways for determining when a caged tarantula is experiencing physiological stress. (It is unknown if they can experience psychological stress.) We do know, however, that some tarantulas pace their cages relentlessly or panic at the approach of their keeper. Marshall argues that these tarantulas are not at ease in their current home and should be allowed to make a burrow.

He also points out that many tarantulas make very interesting burrows, some multichambered (e.g., the species of *Harpactirella* and *Ischnocolus* of Africa), while others have elaborate turrets or flared collars at the entrance. Inquisitive enthusiasts might learn a great deal about their charges by allowing them to burrow.

Lastly, Marshall infers that tarantulas that are allowed to burrow may breed more readily, and that their breeding is more often successful.

These authors can offer no refuting arguments to Marshall's counsel. The rank novice might be warned away from allowing the first tarantula to burrow, and perhaps the second. Thereafter, that novice might even be encouraged to allow burrowing by problem individuals, by species that are reputed to make interesting burrows or have interesting behavioral patterns requiring a burrow, or by females of a species that is reputed to be difficult to breed in captivity. (See the section beginning on page 200 for a full discussion.)

Decorations

Decorations in the cage are largely for the enthusiast. The tarantulas don't seem to care, but then how would we know? Use attractive rocks; driftwood; curiously shaped tree roots; soft, artificial, plastic plants and cacti; or plastic and ceramic ornaments. Avoid sharp or pointed objects. When placing the ornaments in the cage, try to position them away from the cage's walls and flat on the substrate, even partially burying them. The various decorations must be moistureproof and easily sanitized or disposable.

If absolutely required, the cage may be planted with small tropical plants, but this is not recommended. For these, a light will be a necessity, but it can *only* be fluorescent, and it should be placed *outside* the cage. It should not be left on for more than three or four hours per day because tarantulas dislike bright light. Incandescent bulbs, even in very small wattages, will overheat the terrarium and kill the tarantula, and even a little sunlight will accom-

plish the same feat, only faster! Do not use incandescent bulbs near the cage. Never allow sunlight to fall on the cage.

Live plants will have to be trimmed back or replaced frequently, or they will either grow into such an impenetrable tangle that the tarantula will be all but invisible, or they will wither, die, and rot from poor care. To emphasize, it is strongly urged that artificial decorations be used instead.

Do not give a pet tarantula a place to hide or dig a burrow unless it doesn't matter that it is never seen again! The authors once tried to keep a tarantula in a cage with a ceramic skull, originally intended for a fish aquarium. The tarantula immediately took up residence inside the skull. It was quite happy, but could be neither seen nor handled thereafter. Think twice before using hollow ornaments.

Do not fall prey to the temptation of making little caves in which to hide unless the parts and pieces of the caves are securely glued (e.g., with silicone rubber) or otherwise fastened together. Tarantulas are great earth movers and will dislodge the ornaments, crushing themselves or becoming trapped in the process.

It is tempting to use cacti and other succulents in a tarantula's cage for atmosphere, but any with sharp spines are definitely to be avoided. Startled pets have been known to impale themselves on long cactus spines. Of particular menace are the cacti with small hooked spines, reminiscent of fishing hooks. Once impaled on the hook, the tarantula cannot easily free itself. In its struggles, it can do great damage to itself.

Other succulents that are devoid of spines might be acceptable except that they require bright light to survive. Tarantulas shun bright lights. If the two are kept together, either one or the other must suffer. Avoid the difficulty altogether by using nonliving ornaments instead.

Temperature and Light

The optimal temperature for pet tarantulas is approximately 23°C to 26°C (73°F to 79°F), but they can tolerate nearly any temperature that humans normally can without excessive protective cover, and most will live quite nicely at any room temperature at which people are comfortable.

During the hottest times of the year, care should be exercised not to shut them in a stiflingly hot room. If there is any question, they should be moved to a cooler location in the building. Be sure to allow them good ventilation and constant access to water. During the cooler months, move them to a slightly warmer room.

Those species that are native to truly hot, tropical areas (e.g., the deserts of Ethiopia or the rainforests of the Brazilian lowlands) should not be subjected to temperatures much lower than 21°C (70°F). Temperatures lower than this may be harmful to tropical species, but we have no data to support this. Those species that originate in more temperate climates (e.g., Texas, Syria, or the highlands of Mexico) can tolerate night temperatures as low as 16°C (60°F) or lower without fear, as long as temperatures are turned up to more reasonable values during the day. Because of the lower night temperature, these tarantulas won't eat as much as usual, but they will still have to be supplied with fresh water at all times. Freezing, of course, is fatal to any tarantula, regardless of its origin.

Be very careful about exposing a tarantula to bright lights or sunlight. At the very least, the animals abhor bright light. Far more important, however, is the accompanying heat. If they are exposed to direct sunlight or trapped in a container (even as big as a car) that is exposed to it, they overheat and die very quickly. Don't place their cage anywhere near a sunny window. Tarantulas don't benefit from the light and the heat can be deadly.

Be equally careful about placing the cage where it will unexpectedly receive sunlight during certain periods of the day or seasons of the year. For instance, placing the cage in a room opposite a window may serve to jeopardize the tarantula next winter when the sun rises lower in the sky and sunlight reaches the wall against which the tarantula's cage was placed in summer.

Several enthusiasts have reported that, during very hot weather, their tarantulas submerged themselves in a water dish for several hours. Accumulating evidence suggests that this may be a common practice. Like so much other tarantula behavior and natural history, the practice seemed so trivial or so far-fetched that no one had bothered to mention it until now. (See page 91 for additional comments on tarantula behavior.) The inquisitive enthusiast may experiment by supplying a large enough container of water to allow submersion, but definitely do not force a pet into it. The obligatory rock should also be included (see page 125).

There is mounting evidence that many, perhaps all species of tarantulas will grow faster and breed more often if kept slightly warmer than the usual room temperature. To this end, the people who have been most successful breeding them ordinarily keep the tarantula collection between 24°C and 30°C (75°F and 86°F). The devil must take his due, however. At this higher temperature, the males surely age faster and die sooner than their counterparts kept at slightly lower temperatures. Whether or not females suffer the same effect is still not clear.

If there are any doubts about the temperature in a tarantula's cage, purchase a thermometer from a tropical fish shop and keep it in the cage. Even better, though more expensive, is a combination thermometer and hygrometer (measuring both temperature and relative humidity) from a local hardware or electronics store. Check it several times during the day and night. It is particularly important that this be done when moving a tarantula into a new cage or the cage to a new location.

Bucking the Trend, Part I. Many enthusiast books on tarantulas admonish the keeper to supply supplementary heating to their tarantulas. To this end, a truly impressive array of contrivances and bizarre arrangements have been proposed for keeping them at some higher temperature. Based on the fact that these books are typically written and published in Europe, it is presumed that this is the result of Europeans keeping their homes cooler in the winter than North Americans. An additional common thread is that each of these books, tacitly, if not directly, assumes that every enthusiast who keeps a tarantula is automatically an aspiring tarantula breeder.

Let us be reasonable. It is unrealistic to expect everybody who wishes to keep a pet tarantula to pay the hard-earned cash required for a climate-controlled environment chamber. It simply isn't necessary.

Neither has everybody who has ever contemplated keeping a pet tarantula been interested in breeding it. In fact, the ratio of tarantula breeding enthusiasts to nonbreeding enthusiasts is probably on the order of one to several thousand. If the intention is to merely keep a pet tarantula for the fun of it, there is no need to build an elaborate cage with exotic heating appliances. Following the simple temperature guidelines outlined in the first few paragraphs of this section should allow the pet tarantula to live a long and happy life without all that extra expense and trouble, all other circumstances being equal. It's a lot more fun to spend the money on a second tarantula instead.

Besides the added expense and trouble, there is another very real reason to recommend against artificial heaters for the tarantula's cage: desiccation. More of this will be said shortly.

If You Just Have To, Anyway. If conditions in the home are felt to be so severe as to jeopardize a tarantula, if the intention is to try breeding a number of tarantulas, or if some very special conditions are felt necessary for some extraordinary species, heating the cage might be a defensible option, even with our admonition not to. In that case, be very certain to follow these guidelines:

Choosing thermometers: Fever thermometers will not work here, and liquid crystal thermometers are not accurate enough. Choose a red-alcohol aquarium thermometer instead. Compare the temperatures recorded by all that are in the store's stock. Choose any that register a temperature within a degree of the average for the group. When inspecting them in the store, be certain not to handle them by the temperature-sensitive end. The temperature reported by them would be perturbed by the heat of your fingers.

1. Always include a thermometer in each cage to monitor its temperature. Move the thermometers around frequently, perhaps daily, to monitor the temperature in various parts of the cage to ensure that they are not extreme anywhere in the cage at any time during the day or night. Few heat sources are absolutely uniform and predictable. Check the thermometer often, day and night.

2. Include a relative humidity gauge in the cage, and make some provision for maintaining a reasonable relative humidity in spite of the higher temperature. Increase humidity by using a wider water dish, more than one water dish, or closing off some (but not all) of the ventilation.

3. Make some provision for ventilation. This may mean allowing some warmth to escape, but that is unavoidable. Stagnant, warm, humid air allows a host of pests and infections to breed with reckless abandon. Without ventilation, your valuable pets are guaranteed to succumb to some pestilence within weeks.

4. All heat sources must be thermostatically controlled. If particularly valuable individuals are being kept, use two thermostats in series, one set a degree higher than the other. Using this arrangement, if one fails, the other will break the circuit before any damage is done.

5. If an intense heat source like a light bulb is used, place a dimmer switch in series with it to reduce the radiant heat's intensity. This will extend the heater's life and reduce its drying effects. Make certain that the dimmer switch's current carrying capacity equals or exceeds the current consumption of the heater.

The hobby out of control. One wall of the authors' spider room.

6. The tarantulas must be protected from the direct heat source. The intention is to heat the air in the cage and allow that air to gently warm everything else. The tarantula will not appreciate a constant glaring heat or light source in its cage all day. Besides tormenting the animal, a bare heat source will act as a powerful drying agent, desiccating everything, including the tarantula. Cover an incandescent light bulb with aluminum

A second wall of the authors' spider room.

A third wall in the authors' spider room.

foil and partially partition it off from the cage itself. A heating pad should be placed under only one end of the cage. A heating cable should be covered with a thin layer of vermiculite or soil. With either appliance, heat only one-fourth to one-third of the cage floor. Adequate retreats (e.g., plastic caves, plastic plumbing pipes) should be available on both the warm end and the cool end of the cage.

7. Heating many individual cages is inefficient. Instead, construct a cabinet that is large enough to hold several cages and heat this cabinet. An abandoned refrigerator might be pressed into service here. If a really large collection of tarantulas is amassed, seriously consider converting a spare room into a "Spiders' Lair," as these authors did.

8. Be ever cautious of fire hazards when using auxiliary heating devices. Install a smoke detector in the same room as the heated cage or cabinet or Spiders' Lair.

9. Clean and sanitize all cages and their contents often. Wipe down all

surfaces in the vicinity with a dilute chlorine bleach water solution. See the detailed discussion on page 148. Do not use this solution inside the cage unless extreme care is exercised to rinse the cage thoroughly with clear tap water, and dry it for a day in open air before putting the tarantula back into it.

The Importance of Wetness

Water. A water dish *must always* be included in the cage. Even desert tarantulas must be able to drink in captivity. Without the protection of a burrow, tarantulas lose water faster than they can acquire it from their food (Cloudsley-Thompson 1967). The water should be changed at least once a week, whether the tarantula is seen to drink or not. The dish should be wide enough to allow the tarantula easy access to the water. The tarantula should be able to immerse the entire lower surface of its prosoma in order to drink if it wishes.

The dish must be shallow enough that the tarantula will be able to easily reach over the edge and touch the water while walking. If the tarantula cannot touch the water with its legs, it may never find the water, and could die of thirst next to a full dish. However, the dish should be deep enough that it won't dry out too quickly. If the water disappears in only a day or two, the tarantula may not have time to find it when it really needs it. If an empty dish isn't noticed in time, a very sick or dead tarantula may be the result. A deeper dish may be pushed into the substrate to lower the edge to within easy reach.

The authors have used ceramic dishes from the local pet shop, measuring eight centimeters in diameter and four centimeters high (three by one and one-half inches) with good success.

Alternatively, small tuna fish tins also seem to work as well. Any rust that forms seems not to bother the tarantula. Ashtrays, plastic jar lids, and common petri dishes (from a biology lab, hospital, or scientific supply dealer) are ordinarily too shallow. However, with some searching, some of these that are deep enough to be serviceable may be found.

Put a small chip of slate in the dish, propping it against one edge as an escape ramp to help prevent the tarantula's food (usually crickets) from drowning. A small pebble will also work if it protrudes above the water surface, but a large enough water dish must be used to allow the tarantula plenty of room to drink around the pebble. This slate or pebble affords the crickets a means of climbing out of the water before they drown.

When tarantulas are shipped, they are usually transported in small plastic condiment cups. Included with them is a small moist sponge or a wad of moist cotton to maintain a high humidity in the cup. This prevents dehydration during a lengthy tour through the pet industry when it is impractical to give the tarantulas liquid water. Dealers and enthusiasts have assumed that this is the proper way to keep all pet tarantulas, and it is distressingly common to see tarantulas in pet shops as well as in private homes with water dishes holding small sponges or cotton balls. *This is wrong! Never use a sponge or a wad of cotton in any arachnid's water dish!*

The crickets defecate on the cotton and sponges, and lay eggs in them. These turn sour very quickly because of a growth of bacteria in their matrices. This sours the water in which they soak. Such a filthy cotton wad or sponge serves as a focus of disease in the cage. There is a real hazard of poisoning the pet with this foul water as tarantulas apparently have difficulty distinguishing tainted water from good (Baerg 1938). Indeed, the authors are frequently asked why a pet tarantula died unexpectedly. In a large proportion of cases, the keeper was using a sponge or cotton ball in the water dish. Although there is no proof to the hypothesis, there may be a correlation, and it is better to be safe than sorry. A pebble or chip of slate may be scrubbed clean. A sponge can never be thoroughly cleaned. (Crickets as food are discussed on page 127.)

Unlike some other arachnids (e.g., solifugids), tarantulas will not drown in their water dishes in an attempt to find a hiding place. They suffer a powerful aversion for getting wet. Therefore, if the cage is large enough and conditions warrant it, use a rather large container for water. Such conditions might occur during exceptionally warm or dry weather, if the tarantula's room is kept unusually warm, or in the case of an extended holiday. Just remember to include a slate ramp or rock to allow the tarantula and its food a means of rescuing themselves in case they fall in.

Humidity. Without the protection of burrows, tarantulas suffer some physiological stress from exposure to the desiccating conditions common in our homes. To minimize these conditions, reduce the open top of the cage to ten or fifteen percent of the floor area. Thin plastic food wrap is acceptable for this, but other materials may be used as well.

For the average enthusiast, the fifteen-percent rule will work quite well. However, as an experiment, a commercial relative humidity gauge might be placed in the cage. Deep desert species tolerate relative humidities between forty and sixty percent, or even lower, very se of high humidity to treat medical conditions is discussed fully beginning on page 149 under the topic "The ICU."

well. Rain or moist forest species do better in relative humidities of seventy-five to one hundred percent. Species living in intermediate conditions do best in intermediate relative humidities.

If the humidity remains too low, cover slightly more of the cage top, or increase the size of the water dish, or both. Under no circumstances should the open area be less than five percent of the floor area. If vermiculite is being used, moisten it slightly, and uncover a larger portion of the cage top.

If the humidity is too high, condensation will form on the cage walls as the room cools in the evening. Remove some of the covering material, use a smaller water dish, or exchange a portion of the moist substrate with drier material. Under no circumstances should the humidity ever get so high in the cage that it produces a condensation on the walls.

Bucking the Trend, Part II. Most enthusiast books recommend a humidity far higher than necessary. Too high a humidity promotes growths of mold on any organic substance left in the cage such as the tarantulas' feces, dead leaves on decorative plants, the discarded food boluses left by the tarantula, pieces of uneaten crickets, and even the tarantula itself. Too high a

The process of molting (ecdysis) is discussed thoroughly on page 22. The medical problems associated with molting are discussed on page 151.

humidity also encourages an infestation of mites and other vermin.

Relative humidity does gain importance under at least three circumstances: if the tarantula is weak because of poor care or a medical emergency, if it is a species native to a rainforest or other very humid habitat, and possibly if it is about to molt.

For some reason, rain or moist forest species have either never acquired the facility of withstanding aridity or they have lost that ability. In any case, a deliberate effort should be made to maintain a humidity of at least seventy percent for these tarantulas. If at all possible, purchase an accurate, commercial relative humidity gauge to monitor the humidity in the cage, and adjust circumstances accordingly. The price of such a gauge is seldom more than the cost of a moderately priced tarantula, and may save a valuable pet.

Food and Feeding

Up front. The first reflex after acquiring a new tarantula is to put it in its new cage and immediately throw in some crickets. After all it's been through, it should be hungry, right? Wrong!

After being more or less unceremoniously dumped into its new cage, it will be very confused and ill at ease. It will not be accustomed to the lack of its protective burrow, the change in lighting, the disconcerting shapes moving around it, or the confusing avalanche of vibrations sensed by every bristle on its body. The new cage will smell totally foreign, not like its old familiar home. The last thing it needs is to have a handful of crickets crawling over it, adding to its bewilderment and fright. If the tarantula seems to be in good health, give it the mandatory dish of clean water immediately, but wait at least a week before offering it food.

When first received in shipment, tarantulas often have very shrivelled opisthosomas. This is a sign of extreme dehydration and possibly starvation. Such individuals require immediate special care, but usually come through their ordeal with no apparent long-term effects. See page 149 for a description of the treatment of choice.

For the first several weeks or months after being brought into captivity, a tarantula will eat an astonishing amount. A dozen crickets a week is not unusual. As time progresses and they reach their full bulk of stored food reserves, their eating habits will also change. Within a few months, all but the very largest tarantulas will thrive on only six to eight crickets a month.

The very largest, giant tarantulas (e.g., *Lasiodora parahybana, L. klugi, Theraphosa blondi, Pseudotheraphosa apophysis*) require an unexpected amount of food compared to other more conventional tarantulas. One enthusiast feeds each of his collection of eleven adult *T. blondi* three live, subadult mice a week. (But see the discussion of live rodents as food on page 129.) These tarantulas are definitely neither for the rank amateur, the faint of heart, nor for the person with a limited income!

The Main Fare. The staple diets in captivity are the domestic or house cricket (*Acheta domestica,* Orthopotera: Gryllidae), and mealworms (*Tenebrio molitor,* Coleoptera: Tenebrionidae). Both may be purchased from fishing bait dealers and pet shops.

The crickets are accepted readily because of their movement. They may be allowed to run at liberty for extended periods of time in the tarantula's cage as long as a small dish of soft, dry cereal or dog food is supplied for them to eat. If this is not practical, the crickets should be removed within a day, or at most two days.

Tarantulas that are molting are unable to defend themselves, and crickets left in their cages will often nibble on the helpless spider, sometimes killing it. If a tarantula is suspected of approaching a molt, extreme caution must be used when feeding it, lest the eater become the eaten.

Mealworms will burrow out of sight if allowed their freedom in the tarantula's cage. Keep them in a shallow, flat, dry dish, similar to the water dish. A little dry oatmeal or bran flakes should be put in the dish for the mealworms to eat or they'll starve to death. Do not use enough meal to allow the mealworms to burrow out of sight. The meal is only intended as food for them. Mealworms will be taken if the tarantula is placed in the shallow dish containing them and left alone. The tarantula should be placed in the mealworm dish at least once a week to make sure that it can find the worms. An alternative is to place the tarantula and the mealworms in a flat-bottomed cage with absolutely no substrate whatsoever for one or two evenings a week.

The mealworms will eventually become black beetles if not eaten. These are also good food, even if a little hard.

Ordinarily, the tarantula may be given crickets whenever convenient for its owner, but at least once a month. If food is unavailable for several weeks, there is no need to panic. Tarantulas are capable of fasting for long periods of time without apparent harm (Baerg 1958, and see pages 75 and 131), as long as they have ready access to drinking water. This should not be used as an excuse for allowing one to starve through neglect, however. As food becomes more plentiful, feed the tarantula more heavily to allow it to regain its vigor.

In fact, one of the advantages of keeping tarantulas as pets is that they require so little care. Drop a few crickets in the cage, wash and refill the water dish. Now, a two-week holiday can be taken without worry. If you are detained for more than an additional day or two, try to find a friend who can refill the water dish. But, if no one is available for the task, there is still little need to worry. The tarantula probably can go an additional two or three days without water. Just be very certain to water and feed it immediately upon returning.

Spiderlings and smaller immatures should not be fed crickets that are larger than their opisthosomas. Feeding them crickets that are too large will expose them to possible injury in the resulting struggle.

Do not attempt to feed a pet tarantula if it is in premolt or molt. (The entire process of molting is discussed on page 22.) Several days after molting, during postmolt, you may try one cricket. If the tarantula eats immediately, give it the usual number of crickets to eat. If it fails to eat, remove the cricket and wait three or four more days before trying again. Very young spiderlings will often eat the day before they molt, and one or two days after. Older adults may not eat for several weeks before they molt and several weeks after. Enthusiasts who keep *Theraphosa blondi* report that the adults of these giant tarantulas may stop eating three or more months before molting, and may not eat for one or two months after.

Experience will be the best guide with any individual tarantula. In general, it is best to be conservative. Because of their ability to fast, it is seldom necessary to feed them on the last possible day before a molt or on the first possible day after a molt.

The practice of trying to raise most or all of the tarantula's food in a private home is not recommended unless the keeper has a truly large collection of tarantulas, or is routinely snowbound in a place like Umingmaktok, Northwest Territories, Canada, nine months a year. Too much time and effort is involved in the care of these insects. One enthusiast who tried it soon became so busy maintaining the cricket ranch that there was no time to care for the tarantula. The young entrepreneur was modestly successful in the fishing bait business however!

Up on the Roof. Arboreal tarantulas may pose a special feeding problem. Because these tarantulas seldom go to the floor of the cage, and crickets tend not to climb to the tarantula's lair, an arboreal tarantula may not get all the food it requires. The enthusiast has several courses of action to avoid this. Live crickets may be dropped into the lair or wild insects that normally live in the upper levels of grass or brush (e.g., moths, grasshoppers) can be caught and offered to the tarantulas as food. A special effort must be made to avoid insects that may be laced with pesticides, however. In a desperate situation, small lizards can be put in the cage with the tarantula, if such lizards are available and inexpensive.

One of the authors (SAS) has learned that, with a deft flick of the wrist, crickets can be catapulted in an upward arc in a vertical cage to land inside the tarantula's silken nest. This eliminates the concerns of both the tarantula not getting enough to eat and pesticide-laced wild food.

Alternate Foods. Wild tarantulas will eat almost anything that they can overpower. Captive tarantulas are no exception. Enthusiasts have tried feeding their pets cicadas, grasshoppers, katydids, flies and fly maggots, cockroaches, moths and caterpillars, waxworms, crayfish, small lizards, newborn mice, newborn rats, and many more things with varying degrees of success. Below, we discuss only a few of these foods. If something new is attempted, do so with great caution so as not to jeopardize a valuable pet.

The giant tarantulas (e.g., *Lasiodora parahybana, Citharischius crawshayi,* or *Theraphosa blondi*) are capable of taking newborn laboratory rats. The very largest are able to kill and eat adult mice. Beware: mice that are larger than one-third grown have learned to use their teeth as weapons. Feeding half-grown mice or larger, even to *T. blondi,* entails much risk for the tarantula. Some hobbyists have learned to stun the mice with a blow against a hard surface (brutal, but instantaneous and effective) before being offered to the tarantula. Other enthusiasts have taught their tarantulas to eat dead mice (see below).

Other, more normal-sized tarantulas may appreciate an occasional newborn laboratory mouse. These should be less than seventy-two hours old, however, to avoid the baby mouse or rat injuring the tarantula.

Be forewarned that not all tarantulas appreciate such fare. As an experiment, an attempt can be made to feed a baby mouse to the tarantula, but if it refuses to eat the mouse, be prepared to return it to its mother, or euthanize the rodent as painlessly as possible.

These authors have a personal aversion for feeding their tarantulas baby rodents, doing it very rarely. However, many enthusiasts feed baby mice to their tarantulas regularly. It's a personal choice. The inquisitive enthusiast might try it once. If it is too offensive, other less gruesome food can be used.

In recent years another beetle larva, a species called *Zophobus morio,* the so-called giant mealworm, have been offered commercially as arachnid and reptile food. While these are tenebrionid beetles related to the common mealworm, they have a much different natural history, living in moist soil and eating moist vegetation, not dry cereal grains or meal. They are partly carnivorous, eating other slow moving arthropods. While they require about the same temperatures for proper development, they require a slightly more moist habitat, and their life cycles are longer. They are several times larger than the traditional mealworm, seem to be more active, and presumably have about the same nutritional value. Use the same technique as with the traditional mealworm when feeding them to your tarantula, i.e., a shallow dish with a very thin layer of sawdust, placing the tarantula in the dish from time to time.

During the warmer months, tarantulas may be fed wild insects from a field or garden, but this is very risky because it is difficult to avoid pesticides in wild-caught insects. Do not feed a tarantula bees and wasps because of their weaponry. Other really huge insects such as lubber grasshoppers and stag beetles should also be avoided because they can harm the tarantula as they struggle. Do not risk a valuable pet in combat.

It may be very tempting to feed ants to a tarantula. After all, ants are among the most plentiful of insects. However, there is something about ants that nearly all tarantulas abhor, formic acid or some other chemical perhaps, or their proclivity to crawl over or attack the tarantula in vast hordes. Many ants are capable of delivering a potent sting. In nature, if ants invade a tarantula's burrow, it evacuates if it has time.

Ants come in many different types. Some are confirmed vegetarians, others are omnivorous; many are predatory carnivores. If omnivorous or carnivorous ants invade, and the tarantula cannot escape, it is dismembered alive, on the spot, and carried away piecemeal by the ants. **Don't try to feed ants to a tarantula!**

The authors know of one enthusiast who occasionally feeds spiderlings of species of tarantulas that are felt to be not worth marketing (e.g., *Phormictopus cancerides*) to other, larger tarantulas. "To each his own."

Another enthusiast is reported to have fed goldfish to a tarantula! When the tarantula was presumed to be hungry, a goldfish was netted from a holding tank and thrown onto the floor of the cage near the tarantula. The struggling goldfish was summarily dispatched. A major problem with this is that ornamental fish sold in the aquarium trade are routinely dosed with high concentrations of semi-lethal medications to prevent them from dying of transportation shock, disease, and overcrowding. These chemicals are absorbed and sequestered out of harm's way by the fish's liver and other internal organs. In eating several such poison-laced fish, a tarantula may receive a lethal dose from apparently healthy food.

Yet another instance involves feeding a tarantula common fishing worms or earthworms (e.g., *Lumbricus* species). In this case, the larger, so-called nightcrawlers were used. The major problem with this practice is one of pesticides. Such worms accumulate startlingly high concentrations of weed killers and insecticides in their tissues. On a steady diet of worms the tarantulas are at risk of acquiring lethal quantities of these pesticides.

Now and then, reports are received of tarantulas eating raw meat in one form or another. This is usually offered on the end of a string or a broom straw to mimic the movement of living prey. The interested enthusiast may try this as an experiment, or if food in any other form has been absolutely unavailable for months. The major problem with this is the lack of a balanced diet. No internal organs or skeleton (endo- or exo-) are included. Thus, many significant nutrients may be missing. Because we don't know anything about the dietary requirements of spiders, the best strategy is to supply a diet that is closest to the natural one and save the shortcuts for emergencies only.

Do not feed a tarantula cured meats such as smoked sausages or delicatessen meats. The chemicals used in their manufacture are toxic to humans and probably to tarantulas as well.

As time and experience have progressed, enthusiasts have discovered that, in direct contradiction to accepted dogma, many tarantulas will accept freshly killed or slightly warmed dead mice or rats, even without artificially induced movement. The enthusiast with easy access to such food from a local pet shop or research laboratory might consider trying this once or twice. Research animals must absolutely be free of chemicals, however.

Merely soak frozen mice or baby rats in very warm water long enough to thoroughly thaw and warm them through before offering them to the tarantula. **Do not use a microwave oven for warming a dead mouse!**

Even on very low intensity settings, the carcasses heat unevenly due to the uneven distribution of fat and protein. Within even a very few seconds they are likely to burst, a thoroughly disgusting situation.

The basic rule of thumb still holds. Don't give your pet tarantulas anything larger than their opisthosomas for food. Here, the admonishment holds, not because of danger of being hurt by struggling prey, but because many tarantulas cannot consume such large quantities of food at a single sitting. As a result, significant pieces of meat may be left in the cage to putrefy. Obviously, such an unwholesome condition will pose a serious threat to your pet tarantula's health.

Be very cautious, as soon as the tarantula seems to be finished eating, to thoroughly clean the cage of all uneaten remains, and remove and discard any soiled substrate.

Picky Eaters. Often, enthusiasts will report that their pet tarantula will refuse to eat mealworms or mice. This is not necessarily a sign that something is wrong. We presume that tarantulas can exercise food preferences the same as we do, especially if the food is unfamiliar. If your tarantula refuses to eat mealworms, for instance, return the mealworms to the pet shop and try another food. You should not necessarily expect a refund. Pet shops must of necessity be profit-making institutions, not lending libraries. They are often extremely reluctant to grant refunds.

Occasionally, tarantulas are reported to stop eating anything for extended periods of time. This is particularly true of *Phrixotrichus spatulata,* which are reputed to go as long as twenty-four months without feeding and without apparent harm. As long as the tarantula does not appear to be losing excessive weight, and appears to be in otherwise good health, the enthusiast should not become overly concerned. (See also pages 75 and 127.)

If a pathological condition is suspected, the enthusiast is referred to the discussion of dehydration and extreme starvation on page 150.

Fast Food Fetish. An important deficiency in the arachnid-keeping hobby is a variety of staple foods different from the house cricket. A more varied diet is badly needed to promote the health and vigor of our captive pets. Virtually every other live food tried so far has had one or more properties that make it unsatisfactory as a staple item in the tarantula's menu. The ideal food animal should have a short reproductive cycle, produce dozens or hundreds of offspring per female at each cycle, grow to a respectable size quickly, be easily cultured, be relatively odor free, not pose a significant threat to health and hygiene or agricultural and environmental interests, and be palatable to our pets.

Enthusiasts are forever experimenting with different foods, and from time to time new ones are offered in the pet industry. So far, none have been able to duplicate the success of the lowly cricket. Will you be the one who discovers another fast food for our tarantulas?

Cleaning

Timing. When to clean the cage is largely a matter of the keeper's judgment. In nature, the resident tarantula probably removes detritus that blows in, exuvia, and food remains as it grooms and enlarges its burrow. The authors have seen many burrows with cast skins outside the entrances in spring in the chaparral of western Texas, for instance.

In captivity, many but not all tarantulas are copious web spinners, laying down sheets of silk while feeding, molting, just moving around, and during various phases of breeding. They occasionally ball up portions of this webbing and deposit it in a corner as though they intended their keepers to remove it every Monday morning with the rest of the household rubbish! We presume that they do this in the wild also, depositing their trash outside the burrow's entrance or burying it somewhere in the back, but the authors are unaware of anyone studying this aspect of their lives.

When we acquire a tarantula as a pet, we automatically assume the responsibility for its well-being. It is our job to remove this waste. The only question is when. Dead crickets and discarded food boluses should be removed as soon as they are noticed in the cage. This cursory cleaning may help to retard the build up of mites and other vermin, but is probably much more effective at removing sources of bacterial and fungal infections.

A major cleaning, removal of all the substrate and thorough washing of the cage, must be done from time to time, as well. Probably one of the safest guides for knowing when to do this is your nose. When the cage develops an odor, assume that it is time for cleaning. Under any circumstances, a complete cleaning should be done whenever the tarantula sheds its skin. Of course, whenever a vermin infestation is suspected, the cage should be extremely thoroughly cleaned.

Many experienced tarantula enthusiasts (e.g., Marshall 1997) recommend against cleaning too often because this represents a source of great stress in the tarantula's life and may actually be counterproductive. These authors assume a middle-of-the-road stance. Clean the cage at least once a year when the tarantula sheds. In addition, when the cage smells, clean it.

Method. First, remove the tarantula to another container; then discard the soiled substrate (bedding). Wash the cage and its decorations with warm water and a few drops of mild dish soap; rinse it well with clear water. Dry it well enough to remove droplets of water and set it back up with new substrate.

Those enthusiasts who use aquarium gravel as a substrate frequently clean it thoroughly and reuse it, rather than purchasing new gravel. It is difficult to understand why mere rock should cost so much, until one has to carry it some distance. The fact remains that aquarium gravel is expensive. If the enthusiast is maintaining only one or two tarantulas in small cages and is using aquarium gravel, discarding the soiled gravel may be a defensible option. However, as the collection grows, this soon becomes inordinately expensive. At this point, the enthusiast must either change to a different substrate or clean the soiled gravel.

To clean the gravel, use a plastic bucket and lukewarm flowing water. Swirl the gravel around by hand until the overflowing water runs clear. A large sieve may be used to drain away the excess water. If one isn't available, melt several dozen very small holes in the bottom of a plastic container (another bucket, perhaps), and pour the cleaned gravel in this. When water ceases to seep from the holes, it may be assumed that it is ready for reuse. The cleaned gravel need not be dry to be used in the cage. It must merely not be wet to the point of dripping. A little moisture will do no harm as long as it is able to dissipate within a day or two.

Never try to merely rinse the gravel lightly by pouring water through it in a sieve or strainer. Intense mechanical action is required to abrade the tarantula's dried waste material from the grains of gravel. **Never use any household cleaner or chemical to clean the gravel.**

No amount of effort can rinse such cleaners completely away, and the residue will surely kill a prized pet. Do not bother to boil gravel in an effort to sanitize it. The heavy, hot gravel presents a serious safety hazard, it smells very bad, and it accomplishes little for all the trouble. If the gravel is that soiled, it is much better to merely purchase new gravel.

Other substrates such as vermiculite and potting soil should merely be replaced.

Rainforest Species

Rain- or moist forest species represent an extreme case in tarantula habitat and care. Mounting experience with these species suggests that they may have lost (or failed to acquire) much of the water-conserving properties of those species that come from more arid habitats. As a result, desiccation is suspected to be a major cause of death in captive rain- or moist forest tarantulas. This is particularly important because more and more of these species are becoming available as captive-bred spiderlings every day. It is urged that any tarantula that is suspected of being a rain- or moist forest species (because of avowed origin or reasonably reliable identification by a presumed expert) be kept in a cage with higher humidity.

A four-liter (one-gallon) clear plastic bottle with a wide mouth and laid on its side will work for the smaller individuals. For the larger individuals, and because

F ungus and mite infestations are covered under "Medical Problems" on page 147.

of the moisture involved, a larger leak-free aquarium would be a necessity.

Some portion of the cage's top or sides must be an open grill or bear numerous perforations for ventilation to prevent air stagnation. The humidity should never be high enough to produce a condensation on the cage's walls or top. If this happens, arrange for more ventilation as soon as possible. The cage must be inspected often because these conditions pose a serious threat of fungus outbreaks and mite infestations.

Arboreal Species

Those species that preferentially build their aerial webs in clefts in tree bark, tall grasses, or bunched leaves (e.g., *Avicularia, Poecilotheria, Stromatopelma,* and *Psalmopoeus* species) must be dealt with differently. These tarantulas should be supplied with taller cages with some provision for attaching their web. An appropriate-sized aquarium standing on end works well. The authors have also seen clever, custom-built cages.

A piece of florist's cork bark, curled or flat, is most often used as a foundation for their web. Various means have been used for fastening the bark securely in place, such as supporting it with heavy wire, wedging a large enough piece across the back of the cage, or semipermanently gluing it in place with silicone rubber. One lad used a clump of florist's moss wired to a slab of bark. The tarantula was quite happy with its silken burrow partially hidden in the moss.

Substrate in such a cage is of little importance to the tarantula. The tarantula seldom contacts it, and certainly

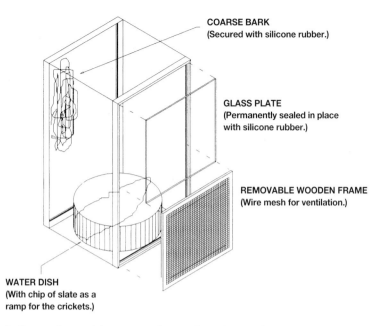

COARSE BARK
(Secured with silicone rubber.)

GLASS PLATE
(Permanently sealed in place
with silicone rubber.)

REMOVABLE WOODEN FRAME
(Wire mesh for ventilation.)

WATER DISH
(With chip of slate as a
ramp for the crickets.)

A schematic diagram for an elaborate cage for an arboreal tarantula.

will not use it to burrow. Damp vermiculite or soil will help to maintain humidity, but the cage must be inspected frequently for mite infestations. Much better is the practice of keeping the cage floor bare and using the largest water dish possible.

There is as much confusion about the proper habitat of arboreal tarantulas as there is about epiphytic orchids, and for much the same reasons. It is true that many of the arboreal tarantulas are also rain- or moist forest species, but it is not true that they must have an oppressively warm, stuffy, humid environment. These tarantulas typically live high in the forest canopy where they are treated to gentle breezes, dappled sunlight, and variable humidity. Their habitat could be best characterized as being breezy and of moderate temperature. Although the

humidity is often very high (e.g., during foggy weather or seasonal rains), it is just as frequently quite low (e.g., on a warm, sunny afternoon during the dry season).

An interesting variation on this theme is the species of genus *Poecilotheria*. These tarantulas originate in monsoon forests, which are dry and nearly rainless for a large portion of the year. When the forests are not on the verge of drought, they are being pelted with torrential rains. For these tarantulas, it is either flood or drought.

These tarantulas will not thrive in an oppressively stuffy container, and just as many of them die from such conditions as die from other forms of mishandling. Arboreal tarantulas must be kept in well-ventilated cages. If low humidity is a problem, a larger water dish or a second dish should be pressed into service. Do not compromise ventilation for the purposes of maintaining an exceptionally high humidity. Since tarantulas can adapt if conditions are close to those preferred, there is no purpose in risking disease or vermin in an attempt to duplicate fanciful jungle conditions. An accompanying illustration is a schematic diagram for a cage for arboreal species.

If there is great concern about the tarantula's ability to adjust to a drier cage life, its cage may be misted once every day or two with a small plant sprayer. Repeating our caution, make certain that the sprayer has never been used with pesticides or other poisonous substances. And, as always, an absolutely escapeproof lid must be used.

Cagemates

With one possible exception which we will discuss shortly, it is best not to try to keep other pets with the tarantula. American chameleons (actually *Anolis caroliniana*), European wall lizards (*Lacerta* species) and other small lizards will only make good, though expensive, food for the tarantula. Larger lizards will eat the tarantula instead. Other arachnids (e.g., scorpions and solifugids), being inveterate predators, can pose a serious hazard to the pet tarantula, or may be eaten by it instead. Some millipedes are notorious for exhaling traces of cyanide or other noxious gas, and will eat unsightly holes in the plants. Land snails will also eat holes in the plants and leave ugly trails of slime on everything. Centipedes have a toxic bite, are predacious carnivores, and are a threat to both the keeper and the tarantula. Land hermit crabs will tear up the terrarium arrangement faster than two wrecking crews *and* eat the tarantula!

By nature, tarantulas are confirmed recluses. Don't try to force them into communal living.

And now for the exception. Several enthusiasts have experimented with keeping woodlice with their tarantulas.

"Wood gets lice?" you cry. Well, not really, but that's what they're called, at least outside North America. Americans call them sowbugs and pillbugs. These are small crustaceans that are found under rocks and rotting logs, usually in association with rotting vegetation. The biologist calls them isopods (subphylum Crustacea, order Isopoda). Virtually all terrestrial isopods are scavengers, serving as recycling specialists. They have oval-shaped bodies and move like small army tanks. Some can roll into little balls and are called pillbugs. Others cannot roll up, and are called sowbugs. Most are marine, some inhabit freshwater. Many are terrestrial. The terrestrial ones are found on all continents and most islands, Antarctica possibly being the only exception. Most terrestrial isopods are less than a centimeter long (one-half inch).

These creatures require a moist habitat to survive, and they are photonegative, avoiding light whenever possible. Thus, they do well in tarantula cages which must be kept rather moist. Those enthusiasts who have experimented with them claim that they are harmless scavengers, cleaning up the discarded food boluses and other remains of the tarantulas, but never bothering the tarantulas themselves. In addition, the tarantulas apparently seldom or never eat the isopods. A further claim is that mite infestations seldom or never occur in cages populated by scavenging isopods, presumably because available food is kept to an absolute minimum by them.

Isopods as cagemates for tarantulas are still too new to allow making any hard and fast endorsements or recommendations. The enthusiasts who wish to experiment with them might consider setting up one or two cages with relatively inexpensive tarantulas and a few of the local pill- or sowbugs. If everything seems to be going well after a year, several more cages might be converted to isopod habitats.

Under all circumstances, careful records should be kept including detailed cage descriptions, a species determination of both the isopods and the tarantulas (done by recognized experts), population counts over time, behavioral descriptions, assessments of general cage conditions, descriptions of problems or concerns that arise, and their solutions. After several months, and at several intervals thereafter, reports should be written up and submitted to enthusiast publications (see Chapter 10: Publish! Publish! Publish!).

Handling

Personalities

There seems to be a clear dichotomy between the personalities of Old World and New World tarantula species. Old World species seem to have a perpetual attitude problem, resenting being touched or handled under any circumstances. The novice should not attempt to directly touch or handle any Old World species, for both the personal safety of the keeper as well as the kept. Experienced aficionados, and others with an inherent death wish, may attempt to handle the Old World species, but only when the benefits clearly outweigh the risks to both handler and handled. As has been pointed out many times by other authors, these tarantulas are best dealt with in the same fashion as tropical fish, perhaps even piranhas. They are to be kept in cages and admired only from a distance.

New World species, on the other hand, are typically more mellow. Few of them will struggle when picked up, and most will become quite accustomed to the practice. (See page 139 for a detailed discussion of picking up a tarantula.)

Yes, handling of the many, more mellow species of tarantulas is not only possible, it is to be encouraged. One of the most often stated reasons for keeping a tarantula is to be able to show it to guests and friends. If the keeper is accustomed to handling a pet, and the pet is accustomed to being handled, a performance will be carried off much more smoothly in front of the uninitiated.

This is not necessarily an exercise in vanity. The better we are at convincing our audiences that we know what we are doing, and that the tarantulas are nowhere near as dangerous as they appear, the better will be the chances of acceptance and appreciation of tarantulas and other "crawlies" by that audience in the future. Stripped of its euphemisms, it's propaganda pure and simple. Tarantulas need all the public relations help they can get.

Frequent handling will also keep a pet tarantula quite docile for those times when it must be handled, such as during cage cleaning, retrieval after an escape, and other emergencies. The keeper will survive those crises better, too.

Wrongly Accused

Several tarantula species have unfairly gained uncomplimentary reputations to the point where strong admonitions against handling them have appeared in enthusiast publications.

There may be several reasons for this. These reports may have been based on one intractable individual. Or the reputation may have originated with an enthusiast who was too faint-hearted to handle tarantulas at all and was concerned about concealing the deficiency.

Another possibility might be the result of an enthusiast handling them improperly. Something as elementary as the technique used to pick up an animal can have a major effect on its reaction and behavior. And, once badly spooked, the handled and the handler may never recover from the trauma.

Another possibility is that many of these reports started with enthusiasts who were first backed into a corner by a recalcitrant *Haplopelma minax*, a species of *Pterinochilus,* or *Citharischius crawshayi*. After being chased by a twenty-centimeter (eight-inch) spider that hisses like an enraged cat, almost anyone would be a little shy about touching tarantulas! This may be particularly true of those enthusiasts in Europe, where the most accessible tarantulas (from Africa and Asia) all seem to have an attitude problem, and some of whom have an arguably reliable reputation of being dangerous.

The last possibility involves an innocent initial report that is misconstrued and spirals indefinitely as an undeserved bad reputation. Thus, the record must be set straight for one species of tarantula, *Brachypelma emilia*. A reference appears in the literature describing an experiment in which one of these tarantulas was forced to bite a rat, whereupon the rodent quickly died (Baerg 1938b and 1958). On the basis of this simple experiment, many have concluded that *B. emilia* was dangerously venomous or even deadly. Worse yet, an allegation has appeared in sev-

Pterinochilus **species. The taxonomy of the genus** Pterinochilus *is still poorly understood. It seems as though every little colony in their range displays a different pattern or color.*

eral books that the species has an untrustworthy personality. This is accompanied by a firm warning against touching or handling them, or even placing oneself in a position where the animals could strike.

Once and for all, these authors wish to set the record straight. First, we are speaking with an experience based on more than twenty-five wild-caught individuals, plus scores of captive-bred individuals. Secondly, our experience spans a period of almost eighteen years with one female, and seven to twelve years for the remainder of the individuals. Thus, there is a sufficient base of experience on which to base a rational judgment, not merely rumor or conjecture.

B. emilia has demonstrated itself to be one of the most stable, most trustworthy species in the authors' collection. All the individuals in our care have been perfect ladies and gentlemen. Many are routinely taken to school programs and handled by six- and seven-year-old children. None have ever bared their fangs. None have even feigned an attack with the fangs sheathed. They are the stereotype *gentle giants*.

It seems that *B. emilia* has gained its bad reputation by conjecture and rumor alone, for the authors are unaware of any reports of humans suffering from their bite. This appears to be another case where the tarantula has been tried and convicted with neither a judge, jury, nor scientifically substantiated evidence. The enthusiast is admonished to *not* spread such stories without firsthand knowledge or reputable scientific evidence.

Caveats

Having said all that, the authors must also admit that there are instances when a tarantula should not be handled except under the direst of circumstances, if at all. We itemize them here.

Dubious Identification. If the tarantula is sold as an unidentified or questionably dangerous species, or you have good reason to doubt the reliability of the person providing you the name or the species' reputation, it should not be handled until it has been identified as safe by an independent, impartial authority. ***The novice should not keep this type of tarantula.***

Leave the suspect ones for the experienced aficionado. There are plenty of harmless varieties available to keep the novice satisfied. If there are any doubts, seek professional help, and in the meantime use a scoop (see "Getting Canned" below) to move the animal. There are probably fewer than a dozen species in the entire world that may be dangerous; the authors have seen verifiable reports of only three or four.

Until recently, the enthusiast could be reasonably certain that the tarantulas commonly offered in pet shops to the general public would be reasonably safe to handle. Not so anymore. With the tarantula-keeping hobby learning to breed more and more species, and with these species' availability increasing every day, the commercial pet trade is now offering some potentially dangerous species for sale to the public. Most notable of these are the *Pterinochilus* and *Heteroscodra* species of Africa and *Poecilotheria* species from India and Ceylon. If the novice finds any species sold as *baboon* or *monkey spiders* from Africa, or *ornamental, bird spider, birdeater,* or *tree* tarantulas from southern or Southeast Asia, an attempt should be made to identify the animal at least to genus before purchasing it. As a beginning, consult Baxter (1993) for approximate identifications. If still in doubt, contact experienced aficionados through one of the international organizations (see page 248) or one of the Internet mailing lists (see page 249) for help.

Be forewarned. Many tarantulas sold through wild animal dealers and the pet trade are wrongly identified, or are given nonsense names which effectively make them unidentified. This does not make them bad tarantulas, but it does raise serious questions about their suitability as hand pets. It also raises serious questions about the expertise or integrity of the vendor.

Sociopathic Little Fiends. The species that are intractable (e.g., *Phormictopus cancerides* and the species of *Pterinochilus*) can be most impressive in their displays of fear or rage. Such a tarantula may rear back, stridulate (if they possess stridulating organs, see page 21), and lunge when approached or touched. Because the tarantula has nearly 360° vision, it may turn to face a potential aggressor regardless of how it is circled to gain an advantage. Use a scoop (see "Getting Canned" below) to return it to its cage to regain its composure. If it exhibits this behavior repeatedly, write it off as an intractable cage pet. For its safety, as well as yours, disturb it as little as possible and seek a different species as a hand pet. Over many years of handling, these authors have noted that all or nearly all Old World species are not handleable. The novice should not make the mistake of keeping any tarantula from Asia, Africa, or any of the Pacific or Indian Ocean islands as a hand pet. Among New World species, *Phormictopus cancerides* and *Aphonopelma moderatum* are also poor choices for hand pets.

The *Tyrannosaurus rex* of Tarantulas. At this point a special note must be made of handling the truly huge tarantulas native to Central and South America, *Theraphosa blondi, Pseudotheraphosa apophysis,* and *Lasiodora parahybana*. These are the truly gargantuan of the giant spiders, and have several characteristics in common. These species are vying for the title of "World's Largest Spider." They tend to have extremely irritating bristles. They have exceptionally large fangs. They are reputed to have extremely bad attitudes.

These all have leg spans reported to be in excess of twenty-five centimeters (ten inches). As of this writing, the title of "biggest" is currently officially held by *T. blondi,* with unofficial reports of both *L. parahybana* and *P. apophysis* being marginally larger. When captive-bred individuals reach adulthood, the balance may swing another direction. We wait with bated breath.

From personal experience, these authors can vouch that thin latex surgeon's gloves are all but useless as a defence against their bristles. Much thicker household cleaning gloves must be used. These giant's fangs are large enough, and the tarantulas powerful enough, that a bite may cause mechanical damage of medical importance, irrespective of any effects of the venom. Lastly, no trustworthy medical data is available concerning the potency of their venom, and there most certainly is no antivenin available. All things considered, these monsters are best left to experienced aficionados.

Imminent Molt. Tarantulas that are suspected of being about to molt should not be disturbed, or should be moved most gently with a scoop (see "Getting Canned" on the next page). Molting is discussed on page 22.

Intense Allergic Reactions. It would be best if the prospective pet tarantula could be handled several times before being purchased. The buyer who is the one in a thousand who is intensely allergic to those urticating bristles might be advised to think twice about keeping a tarantula as a pet. See page 20 for a discussion of allergic reactions to tarantulas' urticating bristles.

The Wrong Ways and the Right Ways

Wrong Way #1: Squeezed. The popular notion, propounded by nearly every book on the subject, is that the thumb and index finger should be used to grasp the tarantula across the middle of its prosoma, between the second and third pairs of legs. This method is very insecure and we strongly recommend against it.

When picked up in this fashion, the fingers press against the basal joints (coxa and trochanter) of the second and third legs. This pressure is, in turn, transmitted to the sides of the prosoma. There is no sturdy purchase on which our fingers can rest securely, therefore we cannot obtain a stable grip on the animal without the danger of harming it.

If a claw has hooked the substrate, the tarantula may be pulled from the hand as it is lifted. Or, if the animal is unaccustomed to being handled, it may struggle from the grasp. If our grip is tightened in an effort to prevent its escape or fall, it may be injured or crushed because neither the leg joints nor the prosoma are constructed to resist lateral compression. If it does struggle free, it may fall to its death.

Wrong Way #2: Levitation. Another school of thought recommends picking up a tarantula by placing the hand over the top of the animal and sliding the thumb under its prosoma. Only a moment's consideration is necessary to establish that this is not very wise. It places the thumb in direct contact with the fangs!

One of the authors (MJS) was demonstrating this last method of "how-*not*-to-do-it" to a group of interested spectators when an otherwise docile, long-term captive *Aphonopelma* species from the Rio Grande Valley of Texas bit her firmly on the thumb.

Picking up a tarantula, I.

"This is how you're *not* supposed to do it."

"And this is what happens if you do!"

There are now seven or eight people in Calgary, Alberta, Canada, who are absolutely convinced that this is not the way to pick up a tarantula! Trust them.

Correct Way #1: Getting Canned. Perhaps the safest way of picking up a tarantula, both for the tarantula and the keeper, is with the use of an appropriately sized container. A drinking glass or a medium-sized tin can will usually work for normal-sized tarantulas, a large kitchen bowl may have to be used for *Theraphosa blondi* or *Citharischius crawshayi*. Use a piece of light cardboard to nudge the tarantula gently into the container, then use it as a lid to prevent the tarantula's escape.

This method is prudent if the species or temperament of the tarantula is uncertain, or the tarantula is too small to be manipulated with the bare hands. It is especially recommended for the recalcitrant species like *Phormictopus cancerides* and *Aphonopelma moderatum*. And it is a necessity for dealing with those species that are suspected of having potent venoms (e.g., the species of *Poecilotheria* from southern Asia and *Pterinochilus* and *Heteroscodra* of Africa).

The single most important consideration is that the person picking up the tarantula must neither be terrified of the creature nor on the verge of hysteria. (This may sound funny, but it is a definite possibility. Probability might be a better term!) Tarantulas are really not very large animals (compared to a Brahma bull, for instance), nor are they particularly aggressive or prone to attack (compared to a Bengal Tiger, for instance). Neither can they jump very far. At worst, they are merely rather small, nearly blind animals trying to fend off a perceived attacker. Even under the worst of circumstances you have at least two distinct advantages: larger size and better eyesight. Take a deep breath, calm down, and gently herd the spider into the can. If all else fails, merely lower the can gently over the tarantula and carefully slide the cardboard underneath. Voila! Canned spider!

Correct Way #2: Getting Scooped. If the tarantula is a long-term captive that is accustomed to being handled and not very flighty, it could be scooped up by merely sliding the hands under it from opposite directions. Don't try this with a newly caught individual or one that is not very tame (refer to Wrong Way #2, above).

Correct Way #3: Getting Palmed. This method works best for medium- to large-sized tarantulas that are accustomed to being handled, or those that are not but are known to not be dangerous.

Cup the hand slightly and come down quickly but gently over the tarantula's top as though an egg or a tennis ball, in danger of rolling away, were being picked up. For those tarantulas that are not accustomed to being handled, this must be done fast enough to not allow them time to react to the sight of your hand.

The thumb should be placed beside the animal's pedipalps and legs on one side. The index finger should come down over the top and front of the chelicerae. The fingers should enclose the legs on the side opposite the thumb. The animal's body should be cupped into the palm of the hand with its legs held firmly at its sides. The thumb and fingers should be at its sides, preventing its escape. Smoothly turn the hand palm up. The tarantula should nestle on

Picking up a tarantula, II.

its back, secure in the partly closed hand.

If it struggles, a fall can be prevented by merely clasping the legs to the body. If it tries to bite, the fingers are safely out of harm's way, but in a position to subdue the action of the chelicerae and fangs. And it doesn't appear as though the handler is terrified of the animal. The novice is strongly advised to practice on a docile, long-term captive before trying it on a wild one, freshly received at a pet shop.

Picking up a tarantula, III.

Two details are important when attempting to pick up a tarantula that is not cooperative or is not accustomed to being handled. First, one must be cautious not to injure the tarantula with too forceful or exuberant an attempt at grasping it.

Secondly, one cannot hesitate over the tarantula before grasping it. While the animal's eyesight is poor, they can still perceive your hand hovering menacingly over them. If they are inclined to defend themselves, a moment's hesitation is all that is required for them to turn and openly confront you.

After being picked up like this several times, many, if not most, New World tarantulas will become quite accustomed to being picked up and seldom struggle or object. For the naysayers in the readership, these authors often pick up *Theraphosa blondi* using this procedure, with heavy rubber gloves used as protection against the urticating bristles.

Don'ts

Don't Drop a Tarantula. A fall of more than a few centimeters will almost always kill a tarantula. If others are squeamish about tarantulas, do not allow them to handle the pet except on a table top or, better still, while sitting on a sofa or the floor. This might also be a good rule for the novice, as well, at least for the first several times that they handle the pet. This simple precaution is very effective in preventing a tragedy.

Don't Blow on a Tarantula. Its instincts immediately identify the blower as a predator and it will either broadcast those urticating bristles, jump to its death, or both. Having said that, it should be pointed out that it is equally unwise to hold your breath while handling the pet! Just breathe normally, but not directly on the tarantula.

Don't Scare Other People with a Tarantula. Shoving a huge, hairy spider at someone may seem like a cute prank and may be well nigh irresistible, but it jeopardizes the pet, opens the handler to serious liability suits, and is bad public relations for both tarantulas and keepers. Any way it is viewed, it's only a moronic stunt.

A surprising number of people are arachnophobes, that is, they have an overpowering, deep-seated, irrational fear of spiders. Attempts by the amateur to treat or cure such a condition may result in even more serious emotional problems for the victim, as well as a fractured friendship. Leave the problem to the professionals. When such a person is encountered, merely sympathize and keep the tarantula away.

Problems

Biting

One of the very first questions asked about a pet tarantula is "Is it poisonous?" *Poisonous* is perhaps not the correct term; venomous would be better. The fact is that, with very few exceptions, every spider on Earth possesses a venom, including tarantulas. So, yes, in that sense at least, they are venomous. The next question usually asked is "Have they been devenomized?" The answer to that one is "No." We will take each question in its turn.

Just How Dangerous? There are many characteristics which confound our ability to predict the seriousness of a tarantula's bite, the degree of reaction, or the time required for recovery.

Tarantulas are capable of exquisite control over the amount of venom they may inject with a bite. Most bites are *dry bites*, no venom is injected. Only when the tarantula is enraged and fighting for its life will it inject all that it has. The effect of a bite probably depends on how much venom was injected. With no venom, there will be no reaction beyond the purely mechanical stab wounds.

Tarantula venoms are almost certainly produced in varying concentrations depending on the species, the individual, and the length of time since the last use of venom, among other things. The reaction to a bite will depend in part on the concentration of the venom injected. A small dose of relatively dilute venom may produce almost no reaction at all. A small dose of a very concentrated venom may illicit a profound reaction.

Tarantula venoms are very complex mixtures of many substances that almost certainly vary greatly from one species to the next. This creates another level of variability in the reaction to a tarantula's bite. A large dose of a relatively concentrated venom may be without symptoms if the substances that it is composed of are relatively benign.

Our reaction to tarantula venoms also depends on where we are bitten and our physiological sensitivity to the venom. Being bitten in an area of relatively poor blood circulation, on the buttocks for instance, may tend to diminish the effects of the venom. Our sensitivity to the substances in a tarantula's venom may vary widely depending on a wide assortment of circumstances such as our degree of allergic sensitivity, degree of past exposure, and current emotional state.

All these things multiplied together produce a very muddled picture of tarantula venom toxicity and our reactions to their bites. It also serves to explain the extreme variability of reactions reported in the literature and anecdotally by enthusiasts who are bitten.

Many tarantulas, particularly the New World species, become quite tame when handled once in a while. Once accustomed to being handled, these captives rarely bite, and, with few exceptions, neither do the wild ones. If one does bite, venom is seldom injected (so-called dry bites), and the wounds are little more than needle pricks. They must usually be treated only with a mild antiseptic, and a little sympathy for the tarantula as well as the patient.

The comparison has been made between a tarantula bite and a bee sting, but there is little resemblance. A bee sting immediately swells, turns red, itches, and burns. If there is any reaction to a tarantula envenomation, it develops more slowly. The skin may turn slightly red, the wound seldom swells and usually only tingles or becomes numb as though the area had fallen asleep.

These authors have been bitten by a number of different species of tarantulas over the last thirty years. The species and the reaction to their bites are detailed in Table X. It is important to stress that these several bites occurred while handling several thousands of tarantulas. The true incidence of tarantula bites is so low as to be negligible.

A bite by **Aphonopelma moderatum**. *Right thumb of one of the authors with fang marks on the major knuckle.*

Table X
Tarantula bites.

Species	Reaction
Phormictopus cancerides	Bite #1: No reaction.
	Bite #2: Mild soreness for a day.
Brachypelma albopilosum	No reaction.
Aphonopelma moderatum	Bite #1: The little finger became numb, tingled for the afternoon.
	Bite #2: The knuckle ached slightly the next day.
Aphonopelma species (a brown species from the Rio Grande Valley of Texas)	The thumb became numb for the remainder of the day.
Pamphobeteus species from Peru	No reaction.
Poecilotheria regalis	The finger hurt for the remainder of the evening.

Conflicting reports do occur in the literature, however (Baerg 1922 and 1925; Bucherl 1968–1971; Maratic 1967). Of late, with enthusiasts keeping more exotic species, anecdotal reports are circulating of people who, upon being bitten, experience graver symptoms such as swelling and aching in the bitten limb, nausea and headaches, and even an onset of seemingly random allergies. These symptoms may last for hours, or days, or weeks, or more. In at least two instances during 1994 and 1995, bitten individuals were kept in the hospital for several days after being bitten. One individual, an otherwise healthy man in his late twenties, was bedridden for several weeks. The species that were implicated in these reports were the Asian ornamentals (*Poecilotheria* species) and some of the tarantulas of Africa (the species of *Pterinochilus* and *Heteroscodra*) .

The authors have heard two other anecdotal reports of people bitten by *Phrixotrichus spatulata* who developed symptoms of swelling and throbbing pain in the bitten hand or lower arm. Similar reports circulate by rumor through the pet trade and the tarantula-keeping community. Whether these reports are rare anomalies or whether these species really are that potent remains to be determined. If it were not for the fact that the overwhelming majority of individuals of these species exhibit such an extremely tame demeanor, we might be much more careful about handling them. Enthusiasts who keep *P. spatulata* should be suspicious if their trusted pet suddenly displays an unusual hyperactive reaction to being touched or handled. If it's having a bad day, perhaps it would be better not to provoke it until it has had time to settle its own problems.

So, You're Bitten. Now What? Upon being bitten by one of the suspected species, or an unidentified species, or if the victim is extremely allergic to insect bites and stings, or in the case of an unusual reaction to such a bite, a physician or local poison control center should be contacted immediately. If any suspicious symptoms arise, call an ambulance or have a friend drive the patient to an emergency clinic. **The patient should not attempt to operate a motor vehicle!**

Investigators have determined that the venom of common North American species closely resembles scorpion venom (both scorpions and spiders are members of the class Arachnida) and probably would be just as virulent if it were produced in similar concentrations (Stahnke and Johnson 1967). As of this writing, no antivenin for theraphosid tarantulas is being produced anywhere in the world. There is simply no need for it.

An Australian laboratory produces an antivenin for several Australian spiders that are related to tarantulas, but the delay in acquiring the Australian antivenin anywhere else in the world would make its usefulness dubious, at best. There is a high probability that it would have no effect at all. It is doubtful if the widow antivenin, currently available in the United States and elsewhere, would work against a tarantula's envenomation.

Under no circumstances should anyone allow the injection of any antivenin until a serum sensitivity test has been run. If the patient is allergic to horse or goat serum, from which most of these are made, the cure is surely more hazardous than the bite! Again, tarantulas as a group are normally not dangerous enough to warrant the use of any antivenin.

All of this sounds far and away more terrible than it really is. With the possible exceptions of those already noted, none of the tarantulas commonly sold in pet shops are considered dangerous. As was pointed out earlier, they rarely attempt to bite, rarely inject any venom, and the symptoms of an envenomation develop very slowly and seldom reach noteworthy proportions. To date, the authors are unaware of any fatal tarantula bites in the United States (Parrish 1959) and have heard only anecdotal reports of one death in Cuba and another in India. It is questionable if most doctors would even know what to do in the case of an envenomation. Tarantula bites are most remarkable for their rarity and extraordinary lack of symptoms. A bite from the family dog is more threatening!

Devenomized? From the foregoing discussion it is obvious that there is little or no cause for concern about the bite of the common pet tarantulas. So, it is even less reasonable to consider the removal of their venom apparatus. Worse yet, if it were attempted, it would almost surely result in the death of the animal because such an operation would require perforation of the chelicerae or removal of the fangs. Any breach in the tarantula's exoskeleton is very difficult to seal, and the animal would surely bleed to death.

If the species of tarantula or its venom potential is uncertain, merely avoid contact with it. If the keeper does not feel competent to care for it safely, it should be passed to someone who has had experience with uncommon species. There are too many safe ones available that make good pets. There is no reason for the novice to keep a tarantula that cannot be trusted.

The Peculiar Case of the Mouse. Rats or mice, however, have good reason for avoiding tarantulas. Rodents, it would seem, are abnormally sensitive to tarantula venom, and therefore are notoriously unreliable as predictors of toxicity in humans. Or, stated the other way, the venom of many tarantulas seems to be intended specifically for killing rodents (Baerg 1922, 1925, 1929, 1938b, and 1958).

This causes us to reflect on a peculiar aspect of tarantula biology. Over evolutionary time, what might have been one of the tarantula's most fearsome enemies? The answer is "Any predator that is quicker, fiercer, and smarter than a tarantula, and that could easily enter the tarantula's lair and do battle with it in the confines of its own burrow." Small rodents fit that bill almost exactly. Perhaps the tarantula's venom is not terribly useful for subduing insects or other small prey because the fangs alone are more than adequate. Perhaps their venom evolved as a means of defending them against their real archenemies, the rodents. This is all purely conjecture, of course, but very interesting conjecture indeed.

The Human Experiment. The only really good predictor of the toxicity of tarantula venom in humans seems to be humans. In the spirit of scientific investigation, Dr. William J. Baerg used himself as the guinea pig during the 1920s. In several articles, Baerg (1922, 1925, and 1938b) recounts his experiments with a number of tarantulas from Central and South America and the Caribbean. Among the species of tarantulas tested were *Avicularia avicularia,* *Psalmopoeus pulcher, Mygalarachne commune, Aphonopelma crinita, A. californicum* (see the notation on page 264), and *Crypsidromus breyeri* (now called *Metriopelma breyeri*). Not too surprisingly, Dr. Baerg did not die from any of them. In fact, the only symptom that persisted for more than a few hours was caused by *M. commune,* and that was a "lameness" in the joints of the bitten hand for two weeks.

Dr. Baerg also experimented on himself with scorpions, centipedes, and even widow spiders. One must admire his intestinal fortitude!

Pesticides

Tarantulas are reputed to be more sensitive to pesticides than the pests the pesticides are intended to kill. However, these authors are unaware of any definitive studies that reported the LD50s of the common pesticides for tarantulas. Regardless, the basic principle still is valid, and the following warnings are offered in an effort to help save a valuable pet's life.

1. Do not powder or spray the dog or cat for fleas in the same building as the tarantula.
2. Shower or bathe thoroughly after using any pesticides, especially dog and cat flea powders.
3. Keep the tarantula *at least* one room and two closed doors removed from any of the common, plastic insecticide strips. Better still, don't use the insecticide strips at all.
4. Remove the tarantula prior to spraying or fumigating for household pests, and keep it out of the building for at least forty-eight hours thereafter. Seventy-two hours would be better.

LD50: that quantity of a toxic substance which will kill 50% of a collection of laboratory mice. (Seldom are other animals used.) Usually reported as milligrams or micrograms per kilogram. Also, the method of exposure is usually given (e.g., subcutaneous, intramuscular, oral).

5. Identify all government agencies that are likely to spray the neighborhood for mosquitoes, flies, or other insect pests. Ask them for their spraying schedule and evacuate the tarantula at least one day in advance and keep it away for at least two days thereafter. In an emergency, seal it in its cage as described below.

6. Don't feed a tarantula any animals that may have been exposed to pesticides. See the discussion of alternate foods beginning on page 128.

There have been instances where tarantulas have been exposed to presumably lethal doses of insecticides in homes and survived. For instance, Breene (1996) reports that in Cameron County, Texas, the largest aggregations of *Aphonopelma anax* are found in golf courses and residential lawns where they are presumably exposed to frequent, high doses of the pesticides used for maintaining such lawns. At this point, no explanation can be offered for their apparent immunity.

We may hypothesize that either these animals did not get a fatal dose, or they had an inherent resistance to the pesticides used, but we have no way of knowing if we are correct. If they did receive a sublethal dose, we are unsure what the long-term effects would be. In any case, don't take chances with a valuable pet. It is far better to be safe than sorry.

In a crisis, a tarantula can be sealed, cage and all, in a double thickness of plastic trash bags to protect it from poisoning. Tarantulas easily can survive a day or two sealed like this because of their low oxygen demands. Do not blow into the bags to inflate them. Exhaled human breath contains four to five percent carbon dioxide, a powerful poison. The goal is not to kill the pet!

Medical Problems

We know little about tarantula medicine. These creatures are so different from more familiar animals it is difficult to draw analogies or work from parallel cases. Few people are willing to spend the money required to autopsy a dead tarantula, even fewer are qualified to perform such an autopsy. And, sadly, that is the only way that we can determine the cause of death and consider a remedy or cure for next time. We can only use guesswork and a little background knowledge to try to effect a cure. We know that they die, but few people (and mostly enthusiasts at that) have tried to determine why. Fewer still have actually tried to cure an ailing tarantula.

Below, we discuss what little is known or suspected of their maladies. The enthusiast should realize that this is folk medicine at best, and more probably little more than witch doctory. Any enthusiast who has any experience in diagnosing and treating any affliction, successful or not, is asked to contact the authors through the publisher, or to publish their own report.

Basic Considerations

Sterile Procedure. During the following discussion, frequent mention is made to sterile procedure. This may be a misnomer when used in this way, but it is the best means of describing a set of conditions that must be obtained.

The tarantula-keeping community needs to know what you have done and discovered. See Chapter 10: Publish! Publish! Publish! for a detailed discussion of getting your observations and ideas into print.

Whenever an organism has had its body wall opened or suffers a deep wound, it is subject to serious infections, and every precaution must be made to prevent them. Sterile procedure, when used here, means that the hands, all implements, bandages and dressings, and all drugs and medications be as clean and free as possible of infectious organisms.

Hands must be scrubbed with strong soap and, if possible, washed with seventy percent alcohol. All tools and implements must be washed in strong soap water. If possible, rinse them with boiling water, then alcohol. Ideally, use implements sterilized in an autoclave or pressure cooker, or purchased sterile from the manufacturer. Bandages and dressings and drugs and medications should be sterilized by the manufacturer. If at all possible, don clean clothes.

The animal's cage should be scrubbed with strong soap and hot water, and dried at a high temperature, if possible. The area around the place of treatment (e.g., the table top) should be treated likewise.

To prevent further infections and spread of disease, all implements should be thoroughly cleaned in hot soapy water and rinsed first in boiling water and then alcohol after the treatment. If possible, boil or steam sterilize the implements both before and after using them.

Sanitizing. Throughout this text, frequent mention is made to a chlorine laundry bleach solution as a means of sanitizing utensils, equipment, and surfaces. In reality this is merely a solution of two parts, by volume, of a plain, common, household, chlorine laundry bleach mixed thoroughly with ninety-eight parts, by volume, of clean, room-temperature tap water. Use a brand of unscented chlorine bleach that contains no soap or detergent.

This solution is also referred to by some authors as a two-percent v/v solution. Two percent means two parts per hundred and defines the final concentration, and v/v means volume per volume, as opposed to weight per weight or some other unit.

To make this solution, determine how much you will need. For one liter, measure approximately five hundred milliliters of water into a sturdy, one-liter glass or plastic container. Add twenty milliliters of chlorine bleach, cap the container and rinse any residue of bleach off the outside of the container. Shake the container vigorously. Remove the cap and fill the container to the one-liter mark. Recap the container and rinse off any residue. Then, shake the container vigorously again. Label the container for its contents.

We stipulate a glass or plastic container because chlorine bleach is highly reactive and might combine or react with other materials to produce toxic byproducts that could not be rinsed away effectively. We rinse off the outside of the container at each step to avoid splattering bleach or its solution indiscriminately around the area, a very dangerous situation. Because the bleach tends to adhere to any surfaces it contacts, thus interfering with its ability to mix well with the water, we add the bleach to the water, rather than the other way around, avoiding contact of the concentrated bleach solution with the container's walls. We mix it in two stages because the bleach is slightly syrupy, and requires vigorous agitation to become thoroughly dissolved. Such mixing would be difficult in a full container because there would be little extra room for the required agitation.

Great care must be exercised in the handling and use of both the original, concentrated bleach solution and the dilute solution just made. Chlorine solutions are extremely toxic and must be kept out of the reach of children. The concentrated solution is capable of producing severe chemical burns on unprotected skin, and will cause grave, irreversible damage if accidentally splashed into the eyes. Both solutions will quickly remove the dyes from any cloth on which they are splashed (hence the name *bleach*) and permanently damage the cloth. **Handle both the concentrated bleach and its dilute solution with great care. Safety goggles and rubber gloves are strongly advised. Do not allow contact with unprotected skin.**

In any case, with either the concentrated or the dilute solutions, first aid is the same. Flush with copious amounts of clear water. In the case of a chemical burn or having bleach splashed into the eyes, prompt, emergency medical treatment is absolutely imperative.

Both the concentrated and the dilute solutions will damage most varnished or stained surfaces and many painted ones. Before using this solution, test a small hidden area. If there is any sign of damage, replace the equipment, fixture, utensil, or surface with one that is either disposable or not so fragile.

Order of Treatment. In a collection of animals, in this case tarantulas, if one becomes ill, the first impulse is to care for the sick animal first, caring for the healthy ones second. **This is exactly wrong.**

A little forethought will establish that the healthy animals should be cared for first. Then, and only then, care for the sick ones. Impulsively going to the sick animals first contaminates you, your clothing, and any associated equipment with the pathogen. After that, every animal that is cared for is exposed to the disease.

Caring for the healthy animals first tends to isolate them from the contagion. One presumes that the keeper will have washed at least once, probably several times, and changed clothes after caring for the diseased animals, before tending to the healthy ones the next day.

The ICU

When a tarantula gets into serious medical trouble, it should be placed in a special container that we call the Intensive Care Unit. This is a scrupulously clean plastic container with a lid and a moist paper towel. A plastic cottage cheese carton is acceptable. Make two or three holes in it, each about four millimeters in diameter, for ventilation.

If the condition being treating is one where a contagious disease may be involved, or if there is a possibility that the ailing tarantula can acquire an infection (as in an open wound), sterilize a piece of clean, dry paper toweling in a microwave oven following the instructions of page 166, or in a conventional oven set at 120°C (250°F) for fifteen minutes. Moisten the sterilized toweling with cooled, boiled water and place it in the plastic container. Let the container set until everything reaches room temperature. If no contagion or infection is involved, merely wet the paper with clean water.

Place the ailing tarantula on the toweling and cover the container with the lid. Place the whole container in a warm, relatively dark location. This might be atop the refrigerator in the kitchen, but let common sense prevail. Check on the tarantula at least twice a day. Keep an extra container handy, and carefully switch the tarantula to a clean one every other day. Immediately clean the used one.

While the tarantula is in the ICU, its original cage should be thoroughly cleaned and set up with new substrate. When the animal begins to show signs of recovery, it may be moved back to its original cage. Be very cautious not to injure the tarantula during the move.

What sort of reasons would indicate using an ICU? Any set of circumstances when quiet, warmth, and a humid atmosphere would seem beneficial. The philosophy behind this ICU is merely to relieve as much environmental stress as possible from the tarantula.

Thus, the wet paper towel will raise the humidity, reducing the loss of water through its skin. And the slightly elevated temperature will allow its metabolic rate to function at a rate that will allow for a speedy recovery without undue stress from excessive warmth.

Does this really work? The authors use an ICU frequently when a tarantula appears in dire straights for various reasons. Many such tarantulas do get better. Some die. At this point, the philosophy is that it doesn't do any harm, and probably does some good. We feel compelled to do something to help an ailing pet, and this seems a viable route.

Dehydration

Occasionally, the authors will receive a tarantula that has suffered extreme dehydration and starvation, usually due to poor care or improper shipping. The very first strategy is to place it, prosoma downward, in a dish of water for at least forty-five minutes. It will be left there longer if it continues to drink. The animal must be watched closely during this time to keep the opisthosoma and book lungs above the water level to prevent drowning. After several hours, if the animal is

not faring any better, it will be moved to an ICU. The next day it will again be placed nose down, as it were, in the water dish. By the evening of the third day, it should be moved to its permanent, drier quarters and given the obligatory dish of water with a rock.

Extreme Starvation

Tarantulas may go without food for almost a year, sometimes even longer. However, this puts great stress on them, and they may be near death.

When extreme starvation is first recognized in a tarantula, it should be offered one cricket as food in the evening. If it fails to eat by the next morning, remove the cricket. Every second evening thereafter it should be offered one or two crickets until it begins to eat. If the tarantula seems active and able to fend for itself, the crickets may be left in the cage for several days if they are not eaten immediately, providing they are supplied a small dish (e.g., a bottle cap) of soft cereal to eat.

For a tarantula that is weakened from lack of food, an attempt at feeding should only be made in the evening. The room should be only very dimly lit or left in total darkness. Once the lights are turned off, no one, not even the owner, should go into the room or otherwise disturb the tarantula until the next morning. Most certainly, once the animal has been placed in its cage, neither it nor the cage should be moved or handled until the tarantula begins to eat regularly.

Occasionally, tarantulas are reported to stop eating anything for extended periods of time. This is particularly true of *Phrixotrichus spatulata,* which has been reported to go as long as twenty-four months without feeding and without apparent harm. As long as the tarantula does not appear to be losing excessive weight and appears to be in otherwise good health, the enthusiast should not become overly concerned.

The enthusiast who is faced with a tarantula that is on a long-term fast, several months perhaps, might try raising the tarantula's temperature by several degrees, keeping in mind that a temperature of 40°C (104°F) is probably the absolute safe maximum, as a means of breaking the fast. Another trick is to lightly spray the cage with room-temperature tap water from a plant sprayer. Be careful not to use a sprayer that has been used with insecticides, and do not spray the tarantula so forcefully as to hurt it.

The authors had one such tarantula (Brachypelma albopilosum) that had escaped and avoided capture for the better part of a year. One morning it was found all but dead. It was treated for dehydration (see above) and two days later was offered live crickets. It would not eat, presumably because it was too weak. It was then offered mealworms, and still refused food.

All live crickets were removed, and one was killed and partially squashed in order to expose its internal organs and body fluids. The dead cricket was placed in contact with one of the tarantula's front legs and left alone for the evening. The next morning the cricket had vanished. The same strategy was used the following evening. On the third evening several live crickets were offered and they were eaten sometime during the night. Thereafter, the tarantula made a complete recovery.

Molting Problems

Death Versus Molting. Before proceeding with this discussion, we must stress again that a tarantula that has turned upside down (i.e., is lying on its back) is definitely *not* dying! This is a normal prerequisite to molting. Dead tarantulas remain upright with their legs folded underneath them, somewhat in the manner of a clenched hand.

To Do or to Die. Molting is the most crucial act that a tarantula performs. Once it begins to molt, it must complete the process or die. In many respects the whole operation reminds one of a mammalian birth, with many of the same hazards. In mammals it only happens once in a lifetime. For tarantulas, it happens once a year. Experience suggests three reasons that may cause a tarantula to have trouble molting. (Molting is discussed on page 22.)

Dehydration Myth. A popular hypothesis holds that tarantulas that are kept too dry will have trouble molting. This has yet to be unequivocally demonstrated, and is still open to much controversy.

That these creatures are more than seventy percent water by weight (Stewart and Martin 1970) suggests that there should be ample water available for the molting process under all but the most severe circumstances. Because of this, these authors advance a different hypothesis. Unless a tarantula is nearly dead from dehydration, it can marshal all the water required from internal sources to maintain the old exoskeleton in a softened condition. For the purposes of molting, the humidity of the surrounding cage is all but irrelevant. This contention is supported by the observation that, as they emerge during a molt, the inside of the exuvium fairly glistens with moisture. There must be some other reason for molting problems (see below).

Having said this, these authors still admit to the advice of others. The practice of keeping pet tarantulas in circumstances drier than recommended by other authors is a means of vermin and disease control. However, in nature, terrestrial tarantulas spend most of their time in their burrows, especially just prior to molting. The burrows not only afford protection from enemies and the elements, but also maintain a significantly higher humidity around the animal than is normally encountered in captivity (Hadley 1970). This higher humidity might have a beneficial effect on the tarantula's molting by allowing the old exoskeleton to remain more pliable as it is cast off. Although this added pliability may not significantly effect the hardened rings, it could still serve to ease the job of the tarantula extricating itself from its old skin. Thus, the practice of lightly misting a pet tarantula and its cage once a day with room-temperature tap water from a plant sprayer certainly will do no harm during premolt, and may very well help the struggling tarantula, as long as the cage doesn't remain sopping wet for the remainder of the year. Be certain that the sprayer has never been used with pesticides or fertilizers.

Too Slow. The most common reason for a tarantula having trouble molting is physical weakness from extreme old age or disease. In this case, the trouble is due to a breakdown in the animal's physiological processes.

The greatest peril is that the tarantula will not be able to pull its legs through the hardened rings around the joints in the legs of the old exoskeleton. These constricting rings are as hard and inflexible on a fresh exuvium from a young tarantula as they are from a very old one. The same is true for tarantulas that have had no trouble shedding and those that have had to be surgically removed from the exuvium. The state of hydration of the old exoskeleton is irrelevant; the rings are hard regardless.

The physical condition of the tarantula is critical. If it hasn't the strength to pull itself out, from old age or disease, it will take too long to molt. If it takes too long, the rings in the new exoskeleton begin to harden. They will soon be unable to deform sufficiently to allow their passage through the hard rings on the old exoskeleton.

What does one do to help a tarantula molt successfully? Pure conjecture (these authors have not had the opportunity to try this) suggests that dabbing a little glycerine with an artist's brush onto the joints of the legs during premolt might be helpful. Glycerine might help to soften the constricting rings or lubricate them as they slip through. The key joints seem to be the femur-patellar and the patella-tibial joints. After the molt, it would be a good idea to gently wash off any remaining glycerine from the new exoskeleton.

Of course, great care must be taken not to damage the newly shed, and therefore extremely fragile, tarantula.

Beyond these simple actions, we can only hope for the best as the molting season approaches each year.

Getting Stuck. Another cause of an unsuccessful molt is injury. If a leg is damaged badly enough to cause a growth of scar tissue that penetrates the full thickness of the exoskeleton, it is possible that the scar tissue would interfere with the separation of the old and new exoskeletons during premolt. In effect, the scar tissue would serve as a weld between the two exoskeletons. During molt, the new exoskeleton and its associated appendage would not be free to slide out of the old exoskeleton, and the animal would remain trapped.

In this case, however, there is hope. The tarantula may be able to cast off the caught leg and complete the molt in spite of the problem. Indeed, the authors have had at least one tarantula cast off a trapped leg during molting. See the discussion of autotomy on page 31.

If the problem is recognized soon enough, the tarantula's owner may be able to amputate the leg. As gruesome as this sounds, spiders have a distinct advantage over humans in that they can lose a leg with relatively little harm. Once the offending leg has been identified by the enthusiast, a quick tug on the femur with a slight twist may be all that is necessary to remove it.

This is risky business however. It is entirely possible that such mistreatment will fatally injure the tarantula. The enthusiast must bear the full responsibility for this action.

Some Never Say Die. Among the rarest reasons for an unsuccessful molt involves mature males that attempt a postultimate molt. (Molting and postultimate molts are also discussed on pages 22 and 88.) The reason why mature males that attempt to molt are unsuccessful may be that their emboli and bulbs become entrapped in the old exoskeleton. If the enthusiast were alert to the possibility, the pedipalp tips of a molting male could be moistened with glycerine, and the whole tarantula kept in a humid container in preparation for the molt. With adequate care, it is just possible that the male would survive his molt intact. Would he be able to copulate with a female? Would such a male be fertile?

Orthopaedic Surgery as a Last Resort. If a pet tarantula is discovered to be having difficulty emerging from its old exoskeleton, it can be helped, if done very carefully. First, be absolutely certain that it is having difficulties, and not just resting. If it does not appear to be making progress after six or eight hours, the worst may safely be assumed and an attempt to help begun. ***Don't move the tarantula unless absolutely necessary!***

If it must be moved, do so very gently by shifting it onto a piece of stiff cardboard. After it is relocated, leave it on the cardboard.

Start by collecting the necessary equipment. This should include a pair of good-quality, sturdy, forceps or tweezers with small, but not sharply pointed tips, available from hobby shops, cosmetic counters in department stores, school science labs, and scientific supply houses. A large magnifying glass or a low-power jeweler's loupe is almost a necessity. A low-power binocular dissecting microscope (about five-power) from a biology lab would be ideal. The authors use a three-power headband magnifier, used by watchmakers and other people who do very fine work. A good light is an absolute necessity.

First, dissolve one or two drops of mild, liquid dish soap in 235 milliliters (one cup) of room-temperature tap water. Thoroughly wet the part of the tarantula that appears to be trapped with this solution. Gently drip the soap/water solution onto the tarantula with an eyedropper or pat it on with a cotton-tipped applicator. ***Do not allow any of this solution to get into the book lungs.*** Doing so might drown the tarantula. Within a half hour, this solution will begin to soften the exoskeleton. Wait for an additional half hour to determine if the tarantula can extricate itself. If it still isn't making progress, proceed.

Ordinarily, the tarantula will have already loosened the carapace and sternum, but either may still have to be removed. The individual plates are connected by relatively thin sheets of pleural membrane. If the tarantula has had difficulty loosening the plates, the pleural membranes on the cast-off skin must be torn or cut to allow for removal of each individual plate, and the thorough soaking of these membranes is crucial.

Once it has been confirmed that these plates are now off the tarantula, try to determine if the exoskeleton has come off the opisthosoma. If you are unsure, assume that it has been removed and proceed with the legs instead. If it is clearly still attached, an attempt should be made to remove it. Do not be overly aggressive about peeling off this skin. Be especially careful with the book lungs. No soap solution should enter them, and the inside membranes should be very carefully pulled out if they are readily obvious.

The legs pose a special problem. There is no way to determine where the real articulations with their delicate membranes are located in relation to the old joints because the tarantula has partially pulled its legs out of the old exoskeleton. Because these new membranes are still extremely fragile, there is

great danger that they will be injured in the course of removing the old exoskeleton from the legs. Extreme care must be exercised. The heavily reinforced rings of exoskeleton that border the articulations must be carefully chipped and broken away with the forceps. For this chore, at the very least, a jeweler's loupe or strong magnifying glass is obligatory; a binocular microscope is much better. Then, the thinner exoskeleton covering the remainder of the leg section can be carefully removed.

Work methodically, doing one joint and one leg at a time. Take frequent rests. The greatest danger is from a wrong move due to fatigue, stress, or impatience. Be extremely cautious not to puncture the exoskeleton. The new exoskeleton is still exceedingly fragile. Great care must be taken to *not* damage the underlying hinge membranes or exoskeleton. After removing the old exoskeleton, carefully rinse the soap water off the tarantula with a gentle stream of room-temperature tap water.

Congratulations. You are now an orthopaedic surgeon specializing in arachnid exuviectomy. (Try that one on your family physician!)

Postoperative Care. After a bad molt, a tarantula may not eat for several weeks to several months. Do not despair. The tarantula may be having trouble with the lining of its mouth, pharynx, and pumping stomach. These are normally shed with the old exoskeleton. If that is the case, the animal must work out its own problem. Tarantulas can fast an amazingly long time if they are given water and are in good physical condition in the first place.

After such a bad molt, and having to be surgically removed from the exuvium, the tarantula may be so crippled as to not be able to eat, drink, or even move

An unidentified Aphonopelma *species that became trapped in its exuvium during a molt. The new exoskeleton had already hardened before the spider could escape.*

itself. Such was the case with an extremely aged female *Aphonopelma* of unknown species belonging to the authors. The tarantula experienced a bad molt on May 17. One of the authors (SAS) spent several hours with a head-band magnifier and a variety of forceps extricating her from her old exoskeleton. Thereafter, the other author (MJS) adopted a regular program of virtually hand-watering her on a twice-weekly basis.

The tarantula was allowed to drink out of a shallow saucer. The saucer was propped up on one side to allow for the formation of a small pool of water along the other margin, the tarantula was placed in the saucer with its chelicerae and fangs immersed in that little puddle, and the remainder of its body uphill. It was watched very closely so that it would not slide into the water and drown. Great care was taken to prevent water from getting into the openings to the book lungs. After forty-five minutes to an hour, the tarantula was placed back in its cage. From time to time, averaging once a week, a cricket was killed and placed under her chelicerae in the evening, and the room lights were turned off. Occasionally the cricket was consumed by the next morning.

By September the tarantula had lost considerable weight but ate periodically. She had learned to drag herself around the cage by means of her fangs and was remarkably mobile. However, the following January she appeared to be having trouble moving around her cage, and she had stopped eating entirely. Sadly, she died on February 16.

This tarantula was a very old individual, having been acquired as a mature adult and having lived more than nine years in captivity. Without a doubt, her death was postponed some months by the heroic efforts made to save her. Sooner or later, the Grim Reaper must always be conceded his commission.

Injuries and Hemorrhage

Anesthesia. Little is known of the dosages or effects of anesthetics such as ether, chloroform, and halothane on tarantulas. We know that they will work because they have been used success-fully. We also know that they will kill if used improperly. Therefore, they should be used with great caution. In most countries they are controlled sub-stances, and the casual fancier is highly unlikely to have access to them. How-ever, small samples of these anesthet-ics or prescriptions that will allow their purchase may sometimes be acquired from medical doctors and veterinarians.

Ether is extremely, almost explo-sively, flammable; halothane is believed to cause liver disease and cancer in humans. Thus, both have their draw-backs and must be used in well-venti-lated rooms and with great caution. Under any circumstances, the novice is strongly advised to seek the help of a veterinarian when using any anesthetic.

To use either halothane, ether, or another inhaled anesthetic, place the ail-ing tarantula in a glass container with a lid. Because these are organic solvents, do not use plastic containers. A few drops of the anesthetic should be placed on a cotton ball, and this dropped into the container with the tarantula. If the tarantula is conscious and mobile it will immediately begin to pace or struggle. Monitor this activity very carefully. As soon as it begins to subside, the taran-tula must either be removed from the anesthetic entirely, or the vapor's con-centration greatly reduced with generous ventilation. During the remainder of the surgical procedure, a constant vigil must be maintained, increasing ventilation when the tarantula seems too deeply anesthetized, and decreasing it when the tarantula begins to struggle. In normal veterinary and human surgery, the sole job of the anesthesiologist is to maintain the patient in that gray world between feeling pain and dying from the anesthetic. A far safer plan is to take the ailing tarantula to a veterinarian for anesthesia and surgery.

Professional entomologists and arachnologists have known for decades that carbon dioxide is a safe anesthetic for insects and spiders. Amateur arachnologists are now also discovering that it will work on their pets. Carbon dioxide is readily available from a number of sources: carbonation in soft drinks, dry ice, and adding mild acids (e.g., vinegar) to baking soda (sodium bicarbonate). The major problem with using it is finding a way to apply it in sufficient concentrations to effect anesthesia but not endanger the tarantula with its precursory chemicals (e.g., vinegar fumes or direct contact with dry ice). Otherwise, the general technique and cautions outlined for ether are applicable here.

Professional entomologists and arachnologists also use nitrogen gas and report that it works much better than carbon dioxide. Nitrogen gas has the distinct advantages that it is nonflammable and is relatively nontoxic. The Earth's atmosphere is approximately seventy-eight percent nitrogen, however, it is relatively difficult for the enthusiast to acquire in concentrations that will work as an anesthetic. Cylinders of compressed nitrogen are available from companies that sell compressed gases for welding, but the associated hardware (e.g., cylinders, pressure regulators, hoses, valves) can be expensive. Liquid nitrogen (the gas that boils off the liquid is the anesthetic) is available from many of the same companies (or they can recommend sources) but requires special tools, equipment, and safety precautions for handling because of its extreme cold (–195.8°C, –320.4°F). Nitrogen gas can be produced in a laboratory from rather common chemicals (ammonium chloride and sodium nitrite), but this should not be attempted without the supervision of an experienced chemist because these chemicals can cause a fire or explode if not handled properly.

Some books recommend cold as a means of anesthesia. However, there is some question regarding the precise effect that cold has on animals. Many researchers who routinely use poikilothermic animals in their physiology experiments believe that cold does not effect pain sensation until near fatal extremes are reached. Cold anesthesia only blunts the motor neurons' ability to activate the muscles and the muscles' ability to contract. Thus, until the tarantula is almost dead from extreme cold, it may feel everything but not be able to react. If this is true, we should not use cold anesthesia.

A Breach in the Hull. If a tarantula's armor is ruptured, it will spring a leak, as it were. This is most common during molting, or if the tarantula is handled too roughly or dropped. If the injury is not too severe, the hemolymph that seeps out usually dries to become a clear scab.

If the injury is a minor one on the legs, merely put the tarantula back into its cage and do not handle it for four or five weeks to allow time for it to heal. It must still be offered food and water. The scab will be removed by the tarantula at the appropriate time or will be cast off with the next molt.

If the injury on a leg is severe enough, potentially resulting in much hemolymph loss, two options are available. The injury can be treated with the application of corn starch or tissue paper (see below), or the leg can merely be amputated. This last option may seem, at first consideration, to be very distressing and fraught with much danger. However, the reader is reminded that tarantulas' legs are constructed to allow removal as a last-resort survival strategy. (See page 31 for a discussion of autotomy.) While it is traumatic, it is not as traumatic as bleeding to death. Merely hold the tarantula securely in one hand and grasp the damaged leg by the femur and tug downward. Crushed or badly deformed legs should be removed as far in advance of the next molt as possible.

A rupture on the prosoma or opisthosoma is a crisis of the gravest proportions and usually results in death. Our philosophy is that it is better to try to save the animal and fail than not to try at all. Therefore, we offer these suggestions as experiments only. The enthusiast must realize that the damage has already been done and must accept the consequences whatever they are.

Of paramount importance is stopping the escape of hemolymph and preventing the rupture from growing. Adhesive bandages won't work on a tarantula because of the bristles. A bandage of unscented toilet tissue or very soft paper (kitchen) toweling might be improvised. The absorbent paper bandage is intended to hold the rupture together and to allow a firm matrix for scab formation. This same technique, using rice paper, is reportedly used by the Chinese peasantry on their own injuries, and any male humans living in our western civilization who have ever used a straight or safety razor have also used this principle with small bits of bathroom tissue. The dry paper may be sanitized by heating it in a microwave oven following the instructions on page 166, then laid on the open wound. The escaping hemolymph will moisten it. The paper will serve as the foundation for a clot, which, it is hoped, will seal the wound.

If the opisthosoma is ruptured, taking the animal to a veterinarian on an emergency basis may be a viable option, if one can be found who is broad-minded enough, capable, and willing to try! The veterinarian might be able to suture the rupture together because the exoskeleton on the opisthosoma is very leathery. However, great care must be taken not to disturb or puncture the internal organs, just the exoskeleton. The suturing material must be very fine and the stitches must be very small and precise. In addition, the suturing material must be of a type that will spontaneously dissolve and disappear because it will be impossible to remove the nondissolving variety once the exoskeleton begins to knit. Any remaining sutures will prevent subsequent molts, and the pet will die in spite of all efforts.

While this treatment may seem a bit unusual, at first thought, the human race has been suturing wounds on its domestic animals and itself for millennia. There is no obvious reason why the practice wouldn't work on a tarantula, too. To compensate for massive hemolymph loss in this instance, the enthusiast might also consider an intravenous injection of Ringer's solution, described on page 159.

Other methods of sealing wounds in tarantulas have been tried with success. Among them are triple nail hardener sold at cosmetics counters in department stores and pharmacies. Another product used with good success is New-Skin (Medtech, Inc., Jackson, Wyoming, USA) spread over the wound. These authors have heard of one anecdotal report of the use of a cyanoacrylate glue (Superglue or Crazy Glue) used as a sealer.

Any of these products that may use organic solvents must be used with great caution. Not only are they flammable, but the fumes could harm the tarantula. Use them in a well-ventilated space, and away from all open flames. Take special precautions to blow the fumes away from the tarantula until the product is completely cured and no longer smells of solvents.

Be forewarned that none of these products have been approved for use on animals or in veterinary medicine. Their use on a tarantula, or any other animal, must be viewed as experimental, with the owner bearing the full responsibility.

The medical supplies industry has developed several products that promote blood clotting when used during surgery in humans and other mammals. They are not routinely available to the laity, but can be obtained through the family doctor or veterinarian by prescription. The two that the authors are familiar with are Gelfoam (Upjohn) and Surgicel (Johnson & Johnson). Undoubtedly, similar products by other manufacturers are also available.

In the case of a minor breach in the tarantula's armor, or after a major breach has been surgically repaired, one of these products might be tried to reduce or arrest further bleeding. Merely cut off a small piece of the sheet with a razor blade or scalpel and apply it to the site of seepage. Thin slices work better than thick blocks. Use sterile procedure throughout. If at all possible, take the tarantula to a veterinarian for treatment rather than doing it at home.

Another strategy suggested to the authors has been the use of cornstarch, flour, or pure unscented talcum powder on the wound. The hypothesis is that it will absorb the escaping hemolymph and become a foundation for a developing clot, and later, a scab. We have no way of knowing what effect perfumes or other adulterations in cosmetic talcum powder may have on tarantulas. Thus, it is best to avoid them.

One enthusiast, a friend of the authors, had an *Aphonopelma seemanni* that had suffered a bad molt. One leg had become trapped in the old skin, and in the ensuing struggle the leg was cast off to allow the tarantula to escape. (See the discussion under the section "Loss of Limb" on page 31.) In the course of its struggles, the tarantula had managed to split its carapace, a life-threatening condition.

The owner called and asked for advice. He was told to sprinkle a little cornstarch or wheat flour on the crack and the hemolymph that was leaking out. On top of this, he was to place a small piece of paper toweling or unscented toilet tissue that had been cut very slightly larger than the length and width of the wound without covering the ocular tubercle or extending over the edge of the carapace.

The improvised bandage worked. The tarantula eventually recovered and molted without incident the following year.

An antibiotic ointment, such as Mycitracin Antibiotic Ointment (bacitracin, polymyxin, neomycin, and lidocaine, Upjohn Company) or any similar product, should be applied to any wounds to forestall infection. For serious wounds, such an ointment should be applied every second day. These are potent medications; not much is required on any application. These medications are often available at pharmacies without a prescription and are good additions for any medicine chest or first aid kit. Never use any of the strong disinfectants such as iodine, Merthiolate, Mercurochrome, alcohol, or peroxide. The risk of poisoning your pet is too great. **_Do not handle the tarantula until after the next molt!_**

For the first week or so, keep the tarantula in an ICU, discussed on page 149.

Ringer's Solution

Ringer's solutions are mixtures of chemical salts in a distilled water base, and for all practical purposes may be considered to be synthetic blood plasma. They are most often used in emergency medical situations to maintain electrolyte balance, blood volume, and blood pressure in the face of massive bleeding. They are normally used only when blood transfusions are impractical.

There are formulas for many different animals including humans, domestic cats, and frogs, for instance. Table XI lists a formula for tarantula Ringer's solution, devised by Schartau and Leidescher (1983). The present authors have not had the opportunity to try it on a tarantula, and it is described here for the desperate enthusiast on a purely experimental basis.

These authors can think of only two circumstances when the use of Ringer's solution could be justified. If the tarantula is badly injured and in grave danger from a massive loss of hemolymph, or if the animal has been allowed to go without water for such a long period of time that it is near death from dehydration and cannot drink on its own.

Those enthusiasts who wish to make this solution are strongly urged to enlist the aid of a chemist at a local college or university or a veterinarian. Making this solution requires experience with college-level chemistry, access to the required chemicals, and an accurate chemical balance (scale).

To make the solution, the chemicals must be weighed out with an accuracy of ±0.002 gram. College or university science labs, high school science labs in the larger schools, medical doctors, veterinarians, pharmacies in large hospitals, and large apothecary shops will likely have such balances. The chemicals will also be available through these same people and should be USP, reagent grade, or purer.

Be absolutely certain that the chemicals used are exactly as listed. Pay particular attention to the stipulated hydration (e.g., $7H_2O$) of the chemical. Make no substitutions unless you or a colleague have had extensive training in chemistry and know how to do so!

Sterile technique should be used at all times as it is unknown if this solution will be usable if sterilized in the usual manner under steam in an autoclave or pressure cooker.

Dissolve each chemical separately in a portion of sterilized, triple-distilled water (use 500 milliliters for the NaCl, one hundred milliliters for each of the others), then mix thoroughly and dilute to exactly one liter. Store the solution in a refrigerator with as little trapped air as possible in a tightly sealed, absolutely clean, sterilized glass bottle. Note carefully the date of manufacture, the contents, and the name of the person compounding the solution on a label on the outside of the bottle.

In theory, the dry chemicals could be weighed out, mixed, and then stored in

Table XI
Tarantula Ringer's Solution

Chemical Formula	Chemical Name	Formula Weight	Millimoles per Liter	Grams per Liter
NaCl	Sodium Chloride	58.443	190.0	11.104
KCl	Potassium Chloride	74.551	2.0	0.149
$CaCl_2$ + $2H_2O$	Calcium Chloride Dihydrate	147.016	4.0	0.588
$MgCl_2$ + $6H_2O$	Magnesium Chloride Hexahydrate	203.302	4.0	0.813
Na_2HPO_4 + $7H_2O$	Sodium Phosphate Heptahydrate	268.070	1.0	0.268
	Total		201.00	12.9220

small, tightly sealed glass bottles until needed. It is important that as little air as possible be included in the bottles. If facilities exist, storage under nitrogen might be advisable. Store the bottles in a refrigerator. Because the shelf life of this preparation is not known, the chemicals should probably be replaced with a fresh compounding every six months.

The authors know of no way to keep the water solution in concentrated or dilute form for very long. For safety's sake, plan on a shelf life of only two or three weeks. Over time, carbon dioxide absorbed from the air will precipitate the magnesium and calcium to a grey or white sludge that settles to the bottom. If this begins to happen, discard the solution and make a new batch.

To use Ringer's solution, one or more tuberculin syringes with fine needles, twenty-six gauge or finer, will be required. These are available from pharmacies, apothecaries, physicians, and veterinarians. If these are not available, use the smallest syringes and the finest needles that are available. Use each syringe and needle only once, using sterile technique, then destroy them.

Warm the solution to room temperature before use. Be certain to squirt out all of the trapped air in the syringe before making the injection. The exact amount to inject will probably depend on the size of the animal and the seriousness of its condition.

In tests on a tarantula which weighed between eleven and twelve grams, Stewart and Martin (1974) removed approximately one-half milliliter of hemolymph and replaced it with one-half milliliter of Ringer's solution. Upon removal of the hemolymph, the hemolymph pressures dropped to almost nothing and the heartbeat was barely discernable. Upon replacement with Ringer's solution, the hemolymph pressure and heart rate returned to near-normal values. Based on this data, a twenty-five gram tarantula might be able to accommodate as much as one milliliter of Ringer's solution.

Ringer's solutions are normally administered by intravenous injection. Because the few veins that tarantulas have are largely inaccessible, this is impractical. Because in arachnids there is little or no functional difference between a vein and the open body space, a slow injection into the opisthosoma is probably the most practical way to administer the solution. Care should be taken not to pierce the heart, which lies along the center of the top of the opisthosoma. The injection might better be made straight in, from the center of the side. *Do not* use a disinfectant such as alcohol on the injection site to forestall infection. The risks of getting it into the book lungs and killing the tarantula are too great. Instead, apply a small amount of antibiotic salve (see page 158) to the injection site after making the injection. Otherwise, use standard sterile procedure throughout.

The need for tarantula Ringer's is so infrequent and unpredictable that it is completely impractical to keep a stock solution on hand. Thus, this formula may be of no use whatsoever except to the physiological chemist who works in a large, well-equipped laboratory, or the research scientist or zoo keeper who maintains many very expensive, rare tarantulas. Furthermore, it is *most definitely not* a tested remedy for hemorrhage in tarantulas. It only offers a slight hope, not a promise. The enthusiast who wishes to experiment must clearly accept all responsibility and risk.

Paraphernalia

Lastly on this subject, many governments consider syringes and needles as *drug paraphernalia,* that is, items used by drug addicts. The mere possession of such items without a prescription may be punishable by law. If this is true in your case, seek a doctor's or veterinarian's prescription for syringes and needles, perhaps even for help in acquiring them. Keep several copies of the prescription safely filed away. Keep a copy of this book handy as well, as added evidence in your behalf. Better still, avoid all the complications by arranging with a local veterinarian for this as an emergency service.

The Hernia

One peculiar problem afflicts a very pretty species of tarantula from Central America, *Brachypelma albopilosum.* It seems that these large, docile tarantulas have a tendency to develop a scablike lesion on the lower surface of the opisthosoma. It may be in response to abrasion from gravel or other coarse substrate, or may merely be a congenital deformity. Once formed, this lesion grows and eventually ruptures and kills the animal. This rupturing usually occurs during molting, but the authors know of one instance when the tarantula apparently burst from eating too much.

The authors have had some limited experience with this problem, but minimal success in treating it. Other enthusiasts who have these animals as pets

Chapter 10: Publish! Publish! Publish!, beginning on page 252, is a discussion of the various means for publishing your experiences and observations with tarantulas.

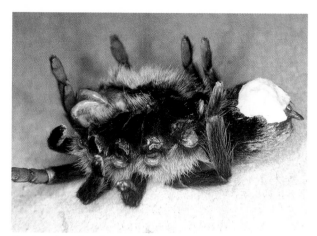
Brachypelma albopilosum *with a ventral opisthosomal scar that has ruptured during molt. The individual died shortly thereafter.*

are encouraged to experiment and report their successes or failures.

In an effort to prevent the development of this condition, it is recommended that the animals be kept on soft, nonabrasive substrates. Soft potting soil of the sort used for African violets, or vermiculite from a florist's shop is recommended. Those animals that are already suffering the condition should definitely be moved to such a substrate. In addition, the scab might be softened with applications of some moisturizing salve, especially during the weeks preceding a molt. The enthusiast might also try an application of pure glycerine with a cotton swab. Application should be done two or three times per week before a molt, and at least once a month other times. Be very cautious not to allow any glycerine into the book lungs.

Glycerine is sold in groceries in the baking supplies area, and in pharmacies and apothecaries. It is a clear, syrupy, colorless liquid with a biting, sweet taste, and is used as a skin softener (e.g., glyc-

erine and rosewater) and in the making of jelly candies.

Fungal Infections

When tarantulas are kept too moist, and especially with poor ventilation, they are (not too surprisingly) prone to die. On occasion, the dead tarantula may be seen to sprout the cottony strands of a fungus. It is only natural, though erroneous, for the enthusiast to assume that the tarantula died of a fungus infection. Little thought is given to the fact that a piece of bread placed in the same cage will also grow a fungal mycelium. Did the fungus also kill the bread?

The presumption that the fungus killed the tarantula has even crept into the literature, and it is now accepted as "scientific" fact. At the time of this writing, the authors have seen no published confirmation or identification of the infecting organism. In fact, the excessive humidity probably did contribute to the demise of the tarantula, but the pathogen could as easily have been a bacterium, parasitic worm, or protozoan. The fungus could have very easily been a secondary growth on a dying tarantula, or a dead carcass. Only histological examination in a competent laboratory and identification of the invading organisms by a competent microbiologist could offer an educated guess as to what caused the tarantula's death.

Making hasty, uninformed diagnoses such as these has two bad repercussions. First, it lulls both the diagnoser and followers into a false sense of confidence that is deceptive and disarming. Secondly, it confounds proper treatment. What is treated as a fungus may in fact be a bacterium that would easily respond to treatment by a different agent. The result is an expensive, dead tarantula.

The fact is, there are no reports of concerted, scientific attempts to diagnose or treat infectious agents in tarantulas. They almost surely suffer infections, but we haven't the foggiest idea of what they are and almost the same level of understanding of how to treat them. Proper care beforehand is the defense of choice.

Having said all that, it is possible that tarantulas kept too moist might contract fungus infections in the same manner as soldiers who must wage war in the tropics. These authors have heard of one anecdotal report of a living tarantula that had developed a growth of the telltale cottony mycelium of an authentic, pathogenic fungus. The growth was swabbed with a gentian violet solution, presumably of the same strength used to quash fungus infections in humans, and the tarantula recovered and shed normally thereafter. A solution of methylene blue might also work as well. Both dyes are well-known treatments for fungal infections, as well as staining clothing and skin. Both dyes are suspected or proven to be carcinogenic to some degree as well. Wear rubber gloves and old clothing when using them.

These authors have heard of anecdotal reports of common fungicidal medications used for athlete's foot being used successfully as well.

Parasites

In the broadest sense, a parasite is one organism that gains nutrition or sustenance from another without any compensatory return. And, sad but true, tarantulas are subject to some particularly gruesome parasites.

Tarantulas do not get fleas or lice. But, if cage conditions are appropriate, they are capable of developing a plague of mites. Mite infestations and their treatment are discussed fully on page 165.

An unidentified parasite that emerged from the body of a Texas tarantula (Aphonopelma species).

In addition to mites, tarantulas are subject to attack from a variety of insects. Perhaps the most famous are several giant wasps, often called tarantula hawk wasps by the news media. Occasionally, enthusiasts who live in areas where tarantulas occur will find a tarantula which has just been stung by one of these wasps. If the tarantula is rescued and kept in a protected environment with adequate humidity, it will often recover from the sting within two to six months (Breene 1996). See page 89 for more information.

Several other species of wasps in at least one other family can lay eggs on tarantulas. In these cases the larvae develop inside the still-active tarantula and emerge through the body wall just prior to pupation (Baerg 1958).

These authors have had two occasions when wild-caught tarantulas from the American southwest have died as parasitic insect larvae erupted from their opisthosomas. Both individuals had been in captivity for approximately a year before their death. The parasites

*Another unidentified parasite that emerged from a Texas tarantula (*Aphonopelma *species).*

could not be identified, and the specimens have now been lost.

At least one species of fly uses this strategy in parasitizing tarantulas. These are of the family Acroceridae (Baerg 1958) and are characterized by two hornlike protuberances on their thorax.

If the tarantula doesn't die from the stress of being parasitized, all of these insect parasites kill their weakened hosts as they emerge, much in the same fashion as the alien in the movies of the same name (Carroll, et al. 1979 and 1986, Swerdlow 1992). Gruesome is not a strong enough term for the phenomenon.

Doubtlessly, there are many other species of animals that parasitize tarantulas. Potential candidates may include protozoa, roundworms (Nemathelminthes), flatworms (Platyhelminthes), and a host of less well-known groups. The parasitology of tarantulas is very poorly known (is this beginning to sound repetitive?), and there is no exhaustive catalogue of the species of tarantula par-

asites, much less any knowledge of possible cures. For the most part, if a tarantula has a parasite, it has only two options. It must either outlive it or die with it.

Wild-caught tarantulas may have parasites acquired through predacious parasitism (e.g., the acrocerid flies), passive parasitism through their food (e.g., roundworm infections), and contact with each other during mating. (Yes, it is possible for tarantulas to suffer sexually transmitted diseases as well.) In fact, wild-caught tarantulas seldom display any obvious signs of parasitism. In the twenty-five years of collecting, importing, and selling pet tarantulas, these authors have had only two develop a recognizable parasite, although a small percentage died from unknown causes. The scarcity of such overt parasitism may be due to either of three phenomena. Either the parasitized individuals are weakened and do not survive the rigors of being caught, shipped, and sold, dying before they reach the consumer; or parasitism is rare in wild populations (from all reports, this is highly unlikely); or lastly, most parasites may be so covert that they simply haven't been noticed.

A distinct advantage of captive-bred tarantulas is that they are effectively free of parasites. Most are produced in countries where tarantulas, and therefore their parasites, do not exist in the wild. Thus, the tarantulas are not at risk from that quarter. In countries where tarantulas do exist in the wild and may act as a source of parasites, the breeders are kept in cages with screen covers, or even microscreen covers, thus preventing their exposure to parasitic wasps or flies.

Being fed on cage-raised crickets with only an occasional wild moth or beetle, cage-bred tarantulas are effectively isolated from food-born parasites. Because most cage-bred tarantulas will never have the opportunity to come into contact with other tarantulas, any infestations due to contact is effectively eliminated. We expect that this parasite-free status will improve the health of the tarantula, increasing their ultimate size and age over that of wild-caught individuals. However, because tarantulas have only been bred under parasite-free conditions for a decade or less (less than a complete lifetime for many species), there is no good data to confirm this supposition.

At this point, it should be noted that, as far as is known, no tarantula diseases or parasites are infectious to humans, or any other vertebrate species. The most paranoid among us has absolutely nothing to worry about in this regard.

Vermin

Mites. Occasionally, an enthusiast reports an infestation of tiny white or tan mites in a tarantula's cage (Browning 1981, Marshall 1996). There is some question about whether or not these are parasitic. Probably, some kinds are and others are not. Three things are certain, however. They are an unsightly nuisance; they irritate your pet; and they will eventually cause its death. Exactly how they kill tarantulas has not been established. However, possible modes of action include fouling and plugging the tarantula's book lungs and mouth with their cast skins and feces and irritating the soft membranes of the book lungs and the legs' joints. Most of these mites are normal commensals with the crickets that we feed to our pets (West 1995). When the tarantula's cage is kept too damp, the mites multiply uncontrollably. They can be suppressed, though seldom eliminated, with a thorough cage cleaning, stricter sanitation, and maintaining a drier cage. Like in-laws, once you get them, it's nearly impossible to get rid of them!

A common misconception by enthusiasts is that if the cage is kept clean, mites will have little or no food on which to live, and the tarantula keeper need never fear an infestation. This is blatantly wrong, and will only serve to lull the keeper into a sense of false security. The facts are that nearly microscopic bits of food are almost as large as the mites. Only a few such microscopic food particles are capable of supplying a bonanza of food for a host of mites because these creatures, like most other arachnids, have extremely low metabolic rates. As appendages fall off injured or dead crickets, as minute particles fall off the tarantula's food boluses, a nearly invisible pantry is stocked for the mites. All that is required is enough moisture to prevent them from dehydrating before they can breed.

This argument, of course, should not be used as an excuse for not cleaning a cage. A cage with dead crickets and discarded food boluses attracts mite and fly infestations and promotes bacterial and fungal infections.

How does one determine if a tarantula has a mite problem? Late in the evening, several hours after all household lights have been turned off, examine the walls and contents of the cage with a bright light and a hand lens. If tiny, light-colored specks that move slowly across the surfaces can be seen, the tarantula is keeping bad company, and they are almost surely mites. ***Never attempt to eradicate the mites with a pesticide!***

How does one exterminate the mites without harming the tarantula? Remove the tarantula to another container and throw away all of the old cage contents. Wash the cage with a chlorine bleach solution (discussed on page 148). Rinse the cage well until there is no smell of chlorine. Allow the cage to air dry for at least a day and check again for a chlorine odor. If one still persists, rinse the cage again and air dry an additional day. Set the cage up for the tarantula with new substrate and decorations, but this time keep it desert dry. Supply the obligatory dish of clean water with a pebble or slate chip.

Rain- or moist forest species cannot be kept indefinitely in such dry conditions without danger of dehydration. After one or two weeks in a desert-dry cage, they must be moved back to a more humid habitat. A new cage with all new decorations and appointments is highly recommended.

Nuking the Little Varmints. Nonmetallic ornaments and small amounts of gravel may be effectively sanitized in a microwave oven. Set the intensity on high for two to five minutes. If the items to be sanitized are dry, include a cup of water in the oven. The cup of water prevents damage to the magnetron tube that produces the microwave radiation. Never use metallic items in a microwave oven. They may spark and cause a fire, or may burn out the magnetron tube.

If the items to be treated can be moistened first, an additional cup of water is not necessary. Cover moist or wet things with a loose paper towel or light cloth to prevent splattering. Moistened gravel should be spread out in a thin layer on a glass or ceramic plate. Better still, replace it all with new, uncontaminated material.

Be certain to allow the sanitized objects plenty of time to cool before putting them back in the cage. Once sanitized, implements and supplies should be stored in a location that is frequently wiped with a bleach/water solution to reduce the probability of reinfestation by mites.

Obviously, it does no good to sanitize one or two items of the cage's appointments without thoroughly sanitizing the rest of the cage and its contents as well.

Saturday Night Bath. An excessive population of mites might be washed off the tarantula itself with a dilute solution of mild liquid dish soap. One drop to 235 milliliters (one cup) of room-temperature tap water is sufficient. Use a soft artist's paint brush dipped into this solution to gently wipe the mites away.

No tarantula will be impressed by this abuse! Do not be surprised at a display of aggression from an otherwise docile pet. Be careful not to get fingers or other body parts near the fangs, or you may discover what a tarantula bite is really like, firsthand! (This should not alarm you. The family dog will also bite if teased too much.) In addition, be very cautious to avoid getting water on or into the book lungs. Although tarantulas have very low oxygen demands, they can still suffocate or drown. After such a bath, try to rinse some of the soap water off the tarantula with clear water. Again, do not allow any water to get near the book lungs; merely rinse off the prosoma and legs.

Oil Slick. Occasionally enthusiasts will try to trap the infesting mites in droplets of oil. One such method involves placing a drop of mineral oil on the tarantula. The hypothesis is that, as the mites move around the tarantula's body, they will eventually contact the oil droplet and be drowned. There are at least two problems with this treatment.

First, we have no idea what effect the mineral oil will have on the tarantula as it cleans itself, smearing the oil around, or if it ingests the oil. Second, the oil droplet will only destroy those mites which get onto the tarantula and wander into the oil. That will leave a potential population of thousands of mites untouched in the cage to continue to harass the tarantula.

Fighting Fire with Fire. Within the last two decades another method of dealing with mite infestations in arachnid cages has emerged as an offshoot of the agricultural industry: predatory mites. The species that has the best reputation for controlling mites in a tarantula's cage is *Hypoaspis miles*. This mite preys on a wide range of mites as well as fungus gnats and other small arthropods living in the tarantula's cage (Elliott 1996, West 1995).

Under optimal conditions they will destroy all infesting mites within a few days. They will live for some time thereafter by preying on whatever other small creatures they can find, even eating algae and plant debris. While they have been observed crawling on tarantulas, they apparently do not irritate them (West 1995).

A major problem involves getting the mites across political boundaries. Some states or provinces within a country have strict regulations against the importation of any insect or mite. It is often very difficult to convince local agriculture and wildlife authorities that the mites you seek to ship from a neighboring state or province pose no threat to your state or province's agriculture or wildlife interests. If it is difficult to carry predatory mites across state or provincial lines, it is well nigh impossible to ship them across international borders.

Before ordering these mites from out of state, province, or country, contact local and national agriculture authorities about the necessity of permits. Such permits often require many weeks to be issued. If your tarantulas are at high risk of developing a mite infestation (e.g., you are keeping *Theraphosa blondi* or *Hysterocrates gigas* in a very moist cage), you should consider applying for a permit that is valid for a year or more, well in advance. In a crisis this will allow you to order a culture of the predatory mites without a lengthy delay.

For an enthusiast with one or two tarantulas and several hundred infesting mites, predatory mites may not be an economical solution. For the aficionado with several hundred tarantulas—or several tarantulas that are each worth several hundred dollars—and a rampant mite epidemic, predatory mites might be the treatment of choice.

Where does one get predatory mites? The pioneering company is Applied Bionomics in Sidney, British Columbia, Canada. As of this writing, they still market *H. miles* as well as other species intended for the agricultural industry. Predatory mites are now also sold by other companies, and enthusiasts who are interested in using them should contact local or international enthusiast organizations (listed on page 248) for local sources that do not require time-consuming, expensive permits.

In Living Color, Too. A similar problem concerns tiny, bright red or orange mites that frequently infest wild-caught scorpions from the American southwest. Occasionally, a tarantula will also be found with a few of these attached. Most of them will detach and wander off if the tarantula is placed in an ICU for a day or two. (The ICU is described on page 149.) Alternatively, these brightly colored mites may be carefully picked off the animal with a pair of high-quality forceps, or brushed off with a dry cotton swab. The authors have seen no reports of these forming an infestation in captivity. If one did occur, it should probably be treated the same as the mites described earlier.

Isopods. Several enthusiasts have reported that moist terrariums used for rain or moist forest tarantulas seldom, if ever, suffer mite infestations if isopods are allowed to cohabit with the tarantula. This is discussed more thoroughly on page 135.

The Fly. There are one or more species of small fly, belonging to the family Phoridae, that occasionally infest tarantulas. Because these are discussed in detail on page 229, no further mention of them will be made here.

Psocids. On several occasions, the authors' tarantulas experienced a plague of booklice.

"Books get lice?" you ask, incredulously. Yes, booklice. Technically these are called psocids (pronounced soak-ids) and belong to the insect order Psocoptera. They are minute, cream- or tan-colored insects that are most famous for living in very old books in libraries where the principle food is bookbinder's paste and the odd crumb left by the library's patrons. Psocids do not require liquid water. They will thrive quite nicely on minuscule amounts of water contained in their food and the water that their bodies produce as they metabolize the carbohydrates in the book's paste.

In the tarantulas' cages, these little varmints find a nearly infinite cornucopia of incredibly rich food. The psocids thrive by eating the remains of dead crickets, the discarded food boluses left over after the tarantula's meal, and perhaps even the tarantula's

feces. In even a spotlessly clean cage, there is a banquet, compared to some dry tome on a library shelf.

They became evident when many tarantulas stood up on the tips of their toes, so to speak, with their opisthosomas held high in the air. It was an odd stance for a tarantula at rest in its cage. Close inspection revealed the psocids hiding in the gravel and even crawling on the tarantulas.

Fortunately, they were easy to eradicate. Merely washing everything in the cage exterminated them.

Ants. The interaction between tarantulas and ants has always been a turbulent one at best. In nature, tarantulas almost never have anything to do with ants, generally avoiding contact with them. On only a very few instances have tarantulas been reported to eat ants, and tarantula burrows are seldom found near ant colonies.

Some ants are strictly vegetarians, seldom posing a significant threat to captive tarantulas. Those ants that are omnivorous or carnivorous pose a dangerous menace, however, forming marauding armies bent on dismantling anything edible, including a pet tarantula, and carrying it back to their colony piecemeal. While marauding ants are more often a problem in the tropics than in more temperate areas, it is possible for them to be serious pests as far north as southern Canada during warm weather.

The problem is that tarantulas have no defense against marauding ants except to abandon the burrow to escape them. In the confines of a cage, there is no escape, and once the tarantula is found by ants, neither is there any relief but death.

All is not lost, however, if the ant invasion is recognized soon enough.

Many ants cannot pass through common window screening. If this is true of your particular infestation, you must merely enclose the tarantula cages in antproof screen enclosures or fit the cages with antproof lids. Unfortunately, this is much easier said than done. *All* cracks and holes must be closed or sealed. There can be no gaps around doors, side walls, or vents.

If window screening is no barrier, a similar product called microscreen may be the answer. Microscreen is simply screen with mesh sizes much smaller than common window screen, and usually made of brass or stainless steel. Unfortunately, microscreen is not easily acquired. Small pieces of it are used in funnels intended for decanting gasoline, and it is used by industries as a relatively fine filtering or sifting medium in a variety of manufacturing processes. Some larger hardware stores and farm supply stores stock it.

Major problems with sealing tarantulas in antproof cages is that they are then much more difficult to clean, feed, and maintain, and the general appearance of the collection is degraded by the appearance of the antproofing.

There are other recourses, as well. Very few ants actually live in our homes. Most live out of doors in the vicinity. If the location of the home colony of the marauding ants can be located, it can be destroyed, thus cutting off the invasion at the source.

Ants seldom wander about haphazardly. Only the first scout wanders freely. All succeeding ants follow the scout's and each other's scent trails. Therefore, if every effort is made to wash away the trails, the invasion can be halted. Hot, soapy water with a touch of ammonia added and used liberally on the exterior surfaces of buildings, on interior walls and floors, and especially on the surfaces of the furniture supporting the tarantula cages, as well as the exteriors of the cages themselves, often works as a deterrent.

Additionally, in cases of really persistent or severe infestations, moving the tarantula cages to another building, or even setting their cages on small supports in pans of oil or soap water may protect the tarantulas. There are stories of eighteenth- and nineteenth-century explorers who were so fearful of driver ants (e.g., genus *Atta*) that they slept in beds whose legs were set in buckets of kerosene. The buckets of kerosene served as motes around the bed frame's legs to protect the sleeper. The veracity of this story has yet to be confirmed, but the principle is the important point. Setting the tarantula cage on several small blocks which in turn are set in a large pan of oil or soapy water might be a solution to a particularly persistent infestation. The major problem with this plan is the potential for accidentally creating a really distressing mess in the instance of a spill.

One hobbyist who was plagued by ants used a common brand of insect repellent on the vermin. The product contained a chemical called DEET (diethyl toluamide and related toluamides). Spraying it on the ants themselves produced instantaneous convulsions. Spraying it on their trails immediately halted their invasion. It should be sprayed generously wherever the ants are known to have active pathways, or areas that they are suspected of having used in the past. Pay particular attention to spraying the exterior of buildings from ground level to a height of forty-five centimeters (eighteen inches) or more.

Two important shortcomings are that these preparations evaporate quickly, having useful lifetimes measured in

Chapter 10: Publish! Publish! Publish!, beginning on page 252, is a discussion of the various means for publishing your experiences and observations with tarantulas.

hours, and they are quickly rinsed away by rain. They must therefore be applied frequently in order to be effective.

It is also important to stress that DEET is probably as repellent to tarantulas as it is to insects. Do not use any insect repellents near your pet tarantulas. Be very careful to thoroughly wash or bathe after using insect repellents and before working near your pet tarantulas.

As a last ditch stand, calling a professional exterminator might also be necessary. However, in this case the tarantulas must be entirely removed from the building for at least a week after the ant infestation has been terminated to avoid the poisoning of the tarantulas too. There have been anecdotal reports of tarantulas dying from the exterminator's insecticides as long as two months after his visit, but apparently no tests were performed to determine toxin levels in the tarantula's tissues. To be forewarned is to be forearmed.

Entourage of Your Favorite Nightmares. In a humid cage used for a rain- or moist forest tarantula all manner of organisms are likely to materialize. When these are noticed, they should be taken to a biology teacher at a local school or college for identification, or the enthusiast could invest in several good, college-level, invertebrate zoology text books (e.g., Barnes 1980 or Meglitsch 1972). A ten-power hand lens or a binocular microscope would also be a good investment. Most of these organisms are harmless to pet tarantulas. A few are harmful. All are exceedingly bizarre.

When in doubt, clean the cage. Under any circumstances, report your findings in an enthusiast publication.

Welcome to the wild, weird, wonderful world of creepy crawlies!

Making a Break for It

What can be done if a pet tarantula escapes? The very first thing is to usher both the cat and the dog out of doors. Both are likely to try to eat the tarantula if they find it, and that crisis is best avoided.

Next, tarantula psychology must be examined carefully. The terrestrial species of tarantulas seldom climb, and if they perceive themselves to be *up,* they almost invariably try to get *down.* The key word here is *perceive.* Tarantulas have such limited powers of long range perception that they instinctively assume that any horizontal surface under them is down, even if it is the top shelf of a bookcase in the attic. An exception is the tree-dwelling, rainforest species. These will almost invariably attempt to climb to the highest level attainable, and must be dealt with accordingly.

Next, tarantulas are the archetypal recluses. Even wandering males will hide during the light of day, and females and immatures will hide in a dark place almost indefinitely, moving to a new location only when they become thirsty or hungry, and then only after dark.

Because of their limited long-range senses, they are not attracted by what they may see, smell, or taste. Therefore, they cannot be baited. Neither will they return to their cage, for they simply have no way of finding it except by blind chance.

To find a lost tarantula, a good flashlight (torch) and a mechanic's mirror will be required. A mechanic's mirror is a small mirror attached to a long handle with a swivel, and is used by mechanics for seeing into difficult places. Other tools may be necessary, depending on circumstances.

The chances are excellent that the tarantula is within thirty centimeters (twelve inches) of the floor, hiding in some dark recess, in the same room where it escaped. Choose some convenient landmark, a doorway for instance, and systematically search the room, always going in the same direction (e.g., to the right). The key to finding a lost pet is the thoroughness of the search.

Be extremely cautious about shifting furniture and other appointments until spaces behind or next to them have been investigated to ensure that the tarantula won't be innocently crushed. Don't slide books into a shelf without searching behind them first. Don't open reclining chairs and hide-a-bed sofas until their mechanisms have been thoroughly inspected.

Be very careful to look into every nook and cranny into which a tarantula may squeeze. Keep in mind that tarantulas are amazingly adept at concealing themselves. Check inside the cheesecloth bottoms of sofas and easy chairs. Don't forget the spaces inside the arms of these as well. Check behind all drawers in bureaus, dressers, and cabinets. Look into any hot or cold air ventilating registers or any other spaces into which something the size of a finger might be squeezed. Carefully look into all boots and shoes. Inspect the full length of floor-length drapes, as the tarantula might have assumed it was in an extra-long burrow when it found a fold. Don't miss the false bottoms that many items of furniture conceal.

Look into stereo cabinets and speaker housings and into the insides of radios and televisions if they are near the floor or on the same surface as the cage. Be very certain to unplug these from the electric mains before opening their cases. Be very cautious about touching any of the circuitry. Electronic appliances possess capacitors that are capable of storing a dangerous electric charge for long periods of time. They may still be dangerous for hours after the unit was unplugged.

If the tarantula can't be found the first time, take a break, then search the same room again, even more thoroughly, extending the search limits to waist level or higher. If the second search doesn't reveal the errant pet, move to the next room and do it all again, twice. Tarantulas will go down stairs, but seldom up. If it can't be found on the floor where it was lost, search on the next lower level. Search once a day until it is found. After retrieving your pet, **don't put it back into its old cage!**

It has already amply demonstrated its ability to escape from it. Either reconstruct the old cage to prevent further escapes or get a new, escapeproof one. Having to crawl all through the house on your belly to find a pet tarantula is uproariously funny, but forgivable, once. Having to do it twice is inexcusable stupidity.

These authors have an individual of *Brachypelma albopilosum* that made persistent attempts to escape. On each of those occasions when it was successful, it was found hanging from the wall only a few centimeters from the ceiling, well above head level. Clearly this creature had not read this book! If you are not successful at finding your pet near the floor or downstairs, extend your search toward the ceiling and to upper levels of your home.

The lid to this tarantula's cage is now strapped down with a nylon web strap of the sort used by campers and hikers for securing their belongings, and Houdini's career seems to have come to an abrupt end.

Remarks

So now you know that caring for a tarantula is not a very complicated task. Their requirements are simple and they are undemanding. After the initial briefing and set up, their care merely becomes a matter of not doing anything that might harm them. The danger is that, because they are so different, it is sometimes hard to perceive their Achilles' heels, and we may do something imprudent and lose a valuable pet out of benign ignorance.

If, after reading this, you decide to keep a pet tarantula, you will be most welcome to the club!

Chapter Six
Catching Your Own

Occasionally, through accident or design, the enthusiast will be presented with an opportunity to collect tarantulas. The following comments are offered to help the amateur collector. Because the authors have had most of their experience with species from the dry areas of the American southwest, these suggestions are biased heavily in that direction. The tyro in a rain- or moist forest or other exotic habitat must be innovative.

Gear and Trappings

The recommended equipment list is not too long.

1. A pair of light leather work gloves for protection from sharp rocks, thorns, and the smaller animals that sting or bite. Be cautious about using exceptionally heavy gloves such as those intended for use when welding. Their extra thickness offers no additional security. They are too coarse and clumsy, and will only result in injured and killed specimens. Relatively thin, supple leather gloves of the sort used in light garden work are much preferred.

2. A garden trowel and a stout tablespoon, used in the event of having to dig out a recalcitrant tarantula. Both should be of solid construction and with a comfortable feel or grip.

3. A collection of plastic containers with lids to carry the catch. The authors use small yogurt and delicatessen cups). Perforate them with four to six small holes for ventilation.

4. Jugs of water for flushing the tarantulas to the top of their burrows. The authors prefer four-liter automobile radiator antifreeze bottles with horizontal handles at the top. Alcohol and glycol antifreezes are poisonous, so they should be flushed out with copious amounts of water before being used.

5. Suntan or sunblock lotion. This is the only hedge against skin cancer. The higher the sunblock rating, the better. Use it copiously and often. A wide-brimmed hat is a definite asset as well.

6. A piece of light clothes hanger wire sixty to ninety centimeters (twenty-four to thirty-six inches) long. It is used to tease the tarantula out of its burrow once it has been brought to the top by an inrush of water. The wire should have some sort of handle on the end. A simple loop in the wire will work just fine. Anything more elaborate may actually be an encumbrance. Wrapping a little brightly colored yarn or tape around the handle will help avoid jabbing yourself in the face when distracted by a rebellious tarantula. The other

end should be filed smooth and blunt. The idea is not to shish kebab the tarantula, just tickle it! The authors have found that a slight curve on the terminal one-third will help it accommodate a curve in the burrow. During impromptu collecting expeditions, stout grass stems or very light, flexible twigs will work instead.

7. A potato rake or a stout snakestick is optional but very handy. These are used for turning over logs and rocks from a safe distance. If they are the correct length, they will also make convenient walking sticks in rough country.

Where to Collect

One cannot simply walk out into any field or pasture and pluck a tarantula from under a rock. Within any range, their distribution is spotty and unpredictable. Much real estate must be trudged to find a few and collecting them can be a labor of love.

With sufficient advance warning, the trouble of a little research about the area to be visited will be repaid many times over. What is the geography like? The altitude? What are the seasons like? Is the planned visit during a hot, warm, cool, or cold season? Wet or dry? The tarantulas are likely to be sequestered in their burrows during bad or cool weather.

If time permits, locate descriptions of the tarantulas that are found in the area, or talk to an expert. Local children can also be helpful. What species occur there? Are any of them dangerous? What are their habits? Do they prefer desert, dry uplands, scrub brush lands, or wet rainforests? Some other habitat? Are they arboreal aerialists, terrestrial vagabonds, or burrowing recluses? If the search is spontaneous, be creative and imaginative. Do not presume a habitat as unsuitable until a search establishes it to be.

When searching for the burrows of tarantulas, a major source of confusion involves discriminating between a burrow occupied by a tarantula and those of other animals. Among the animals that dig burrows that resemble those of tarantulas are Wolf spiders (family Lycosidae), small rodents, large beetles, and small lizards. Snakes do not dig burrows, although they frequently appropriate them from other animals.

Any burrow that exhibits a neat, circular entrance deserves a closer inspection. If the mouth of the burrow is touched lightly with the fingertip and an almost invisible web is seen holding soil particles together around the lip, or if there is a silken ring or collar around the entrance, the burrow almost surely holds some species of spider, though not necessarily a tarantula. In the middle of the day, or during inclement weather, the burrows may be covered with a thin veil of silk. Few other spiders use this method to ensure their privacy. But don't ignore unveiled burrows. During warm weather, tarantula burrows may have an indistinct, radiating web (draglines) at their entrance, but these are also produced by some other kinds of spiders. Once one tarantula's burrow has been located, look for similar ones in the same area.

Dry soil is not the only place to seek tarantulas and their close relatives.

Chapter 3: Natural History contains a lengthy discussion on tarantulas' habitat preferences and lifestyles.

Vagabond species may lurk in or under fallen logs, cactus stumps, or mats of dead vegetation. Others prefer the interstices in piles of rocks. A few theraphosid tarantulas and many other mygalomorph spiders favor thick mats of moss on forest floors and rotting logs, clay banks in canyons, or cracks and crevices in cliff walls. Arboreal species often live in bromeliads, hollow tree trunks, clefts in bark, holes in tree stumps and fence posts, hollows at the base of palm leaves, or silken tubes built in bunches of leaves or tall grass. Some tarantulas are commonly found around the footings or in the thatched roofs of homes and outbuildings.

When to Collect

Usually tarantulas can be hunted and collected at any time of the year. However, two periods in the year pose special collecting problems. If possible, avoid these periods when collecting tarantulas.

In the colder months, the tarantulas are semidormant and unable to escape their burrows (see page 48 for a discussion of cold torpor). During these times, attempts to flood them from their burrows are futile and may only drown them. Digging is the method of choice, providing the disturbed soil is replaced and firmly tamped after removing the animal, to prevent erosion.

In spring to midsummer, tarantulas are normally molting. If they are in molt, they may not be able to leave their burrows or move out of danger. They may also be extremely fragile until they complete their molting cycle. Do not be too persistent about trying to flood them out, and be especially careful while digging for them and handling them.

How Many to Collect

Do not wipe out a population of tarantulas. This is probably the single-most important rule to heed when collecting tarantulas. When you locate a colony, do not remove more than one-twentieth of the total population; fewer would be much wiser. Base your estimate on a defensible, realistic estimate of the colony's size, not an emotionally inflated guesstimate. If there are any doubts, err on the conservative side, collect fewer rather than more.

There is one situation when collecting every available tarantula is justifiable. If an area is found with signs or public notices that it is scheduled for development (e.g., a new shopping center) or is offered for sale for development (e.g., for sale, zoned multiple residence), there is a very strong argument in favor of collecting every tarantula on the premises.

In the overwhelming majority of cases, such property is indeed sold or developed, in which case any resident tarantulas (and all other wildlife as well) are summarily destroyed. For all those that are collected, that fate is postponed for a time, at least. Most will find their way into the tarantula-keeping community or the pet industry through you. With any luck, a few will be kept and bred by serious enthusiasts, thus conserving their genetic legacy, and your pets, for a little longer.

Techniques

There are basically three techniques used to catch burrowing tarantulas.

Collecting Rule #1: Do not over-collect!

Flooding a tarantula's burrow.

Flush them out, dig them out, or catch them as they wander after dark. The vagabond and arboreal species require special techniques that are covered later.

Flooding

The basic technique is very simple. Merely pour large amounts of water into their burrows to flush them out. This works because most tarantulas abhor

Tickling the reluctant spider out of its sanctuary.

getting wet, and has the advantage of not tearing up the landscape. The disadvantage is that lugging the water all through the countryside is very tiring.

To implement this technique, kneel or sit so as to shade the burrow's entrance with your body. Then use the clothes hanger wire to *gently* probe into the burrow to determine if it is more or less straight and vertical or which way it bends or slopes. Leave it in place. Then pour a large amount of water down the burrow. The sudden inrush of water will startle the tarantula, and as the water level rises, the tarantula will move up the burrow to escape it.

However, upon beholding the light of day it will halt a short distance below the entrance, even if it must endure submersion. Watch for the tips of the tarantula's forelegs several centimeters down the burrow. At this point, jiggle the wire a little. This disturbance will encourage the tarantula to exit its burrow. While prodding, it is usually helpful to cover the entrance carefully with a cupped hand, as the tarantulas intensely dislike bright light. Some practice is necessary to become proficient, but it is well worth the effort.

If no tarantula appears or if it dives back down into the burrow instead of exiting, flood the burrow again, cover the burrow's entrance with something to diminish the glare of daylight, and move on to another burrow. Several minutes later, upon a return inspection, the quarry may be waiting near the entrance. If there is no success after the third flooding, find another hole. If the burrow never fills with water, it probably is either a meandering rodent burrow appropriated by the tarantula, or it connects to a large crack in the subsoil, a common condition. In either case, further flooding or digging is futile.

Once a tarantula is removed from a burrow, place a few grass stems in the burrow or place a small stick lightly in the entrance. This will mark it, forestalling another attempt to flood the same empty burrow the next day. Any vagrant tarantula may set up housekeeping in the burrow by merely digging out the marker.

Digging

Tarantulas may also be dug out of their burrows. This has four serious drawbacks. It's hard work. It's terribly time consuming in the hot sun. There is a very good chance of killing the tarantula if *extreme* care isn't used. And such excavations can lead to serious erosion and habitat destruction.

The method that works best for the authors involves some strategy. First, probe the burrow with the wire as before, and leave it in place during the excavation. It will mark the location of the burrow in case of a cave-in.

Next, dig a small pit twenty-five or thirty centimeters (ten to twelve inches) away from the burrow's entrance and to the side *away* from the burrow's slope or bend. When this shaft is some thirty centimeters or more (twelve inches) deep, carefully excavate a crosscut, tunneling sideways from the bottom third to intersect the tarantula's burrow. Extreme caution must be used at this time to insure that the burrow doesn't collapse and that the tarantula isn't wounded with the trowel. As the burrow is approached from the side, switch to using the spoon.

Careful removal of all loose soil is of paramount importance to avoid burying the animal alive. When the lower portion of the tarantula's burrow is exposed, the tarantula can be carefully teased out with the wire or spoon handle. Be

Devon Seitz and his newly captured pet.

very cautious not to injure it with these implements, or allow the burrow to collapse on the newfound pet.

The instructions given here are for burrows that are approximately thirty to forty-five centimeters (twelve to eighteen inches) deep. If the burrow is deeper, make corresponding adjustments in the position of the starting point. As a rule of thumb, estimate the depth of the burrow

Collecting Rule #2: Always leave the habitat the way you found it or improve it. If you dig, replace and firmly tamp the soil. If you move rocks and logs, replace them. If you can rearrange other rocks or logs to make more habitat sites, do so. If you can clean up someone else's mess, do so proudly.

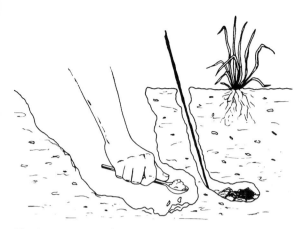

Digging out a tarantula.

and move away from the entrance an equivalent distance. In the Mojave desert where tarantula burrows are often more than a meter and one-half deep (more than five feet), the starting excavation would have to be at least one and one-half meters (five feet) from the burrow's entrance. Such an undertaking soon becomes a major construction project, and digging is a great waste of time. Flushing them out in early morning or late evening, when they are already lurking near the entrance, is a much better strategy.

Those species that construct elaborate, many shafted burrows (e.g., the genera *Harpactirella* and *Ischnocolus* of Africa) can only be extricated by digging.

Driving up and down lonely country roads late at night is guaranteed to attract the attention of local residents and the police. In some political districts it may be illegal to hunt any animals using this method. Be sure to check with local authorities before embarking on a road cruising expedition.

After removing the tarantula, it is absolutely imperative that all the disturbed soil be carefully replaced and solidly tamped in place. Pits from such digging, left exposed, will act as foci for erosion, causing irreversible damage. When an excavation is begun, the excavator must automatically accept the obligation to protect the habitat of the animals that are prized so highly. ***If you cannot accept this responsibility, don't dig!***

What is to be done if the burrow collapses or the tarantula can't be found? Feeling a moral obligation to the creature entombed below, these authors make a concerted effort to exhume the tarantula, often at the expense of much sweat and malediction. The pit is carefully extended to at least the maximum known depth of burrows in the area, and approximately the same distance in diameter. All removed soil is carefully searched for the tarantula. This represents a huge expenditure of time and work and is perhaps the greatest incentive not to dig.

Road Cruisin'

The third method is to drive very slowly down rural roads after the onset of dusk with the car's headlamps turned on. During summer and fall, many tarantulas may be found by using this method, but they will probably all be males. If acquiring males for stud service is the goal, this is the method of choice as these have already built their sperm webs and are seeking females. See page 80 for a discussion of sperm webs.

An amazing assortment of other creatures can also be found, some of which are dangerous (e.g., some types of snakes and scorpions).

The Noble Vagabond

Some species of tarantulas do not inhabit permanent lairs. Instead, they bivouac in a convenient cavity or scrape (Hancock and Hancock 1992) for the time being, and move on to another refuge whenever they feel a wanderlust or are disturbed or evicted. Finding these tarantulas may be as simple as waiting in a convenient area after dark with a flashlight (torch), or as difficult as turning over every stone and rotten log in the surrounding one hundred hectares (two hundred fifty acres). Be very certain to return turned logs and stones to their original condition after searching under them. If possible, move others to produce more refuges for these creatures.

Other much less hospitable creatures are likely to be encountered while hunting in this manner. Use great caution.

Up on the Roof

Arboreal tarantulas pose a special problem. The authors know of only two ways to reach them. You may either chop the tree down or climb up there after them.

Chopping down a fifty-meter tree is definitely to be discouraged. Killing a tree that has stood in a rainforest for decades, even centuries, to satisfy one's greed for tarantulas is the epitome of lunacy. Climbing up such a tree is probably equally insane, unless the climber has experience in rock climbing and the requisite equipment. For the inexperienced or unwary, one slip of the hand or foot could be the last.

However, if an area is found where the trees are being felled and freshly fallen ones can be safely examined, there is the possibility of acquiring some remarkable specimens. This has

*A*s a naturalist who appreciates and values all life, you are committed to *not* killing any creatures you find, snakes included. Enjoy them from a safe distance and leave them alone.

the added advantage of saving animals that would be killed as soon as they were seen by the workers in the area or that would eventually die because their habitat was utterly decimated.

The authors have heard of a chap who, while touring the tropics, would contract with the local boys for tarantulas from the area. They were equally adept at retrieving them from treetops and subterranean burrows.

Transitory Lodging

Containers

The containers that work best for carrying adult and immature tarantulas are the small cartons used by delicatessens for chip dips, dressings, and condiments. The ideal ones hold about 235 milliliters (one cup). They measure about twelve centimeters (four and three-quarters inches) in diameter and about four and one-half centimeters (one and

*C*aution. If you aren't accustomed to handling harmless snakes and haven't been trained in handling venomous ones, it's best to admire all snakes from a respectful distance and leave them alone.

*C*aution. In areas where spitting cobras exist, a respectful distance may be in excess of three meters!

Caution. Never attempt to handle a snake while wearing gloves. Gloves offer no protection whatsoever against a snake's bite and allow a snake the fraction of a millimeter of freedom required to break from one's grasp.

three-quarters inches) deep. Also, be certain to acquire the lids. If possible, use the transparent variety of both so that the captives can be inspected without opening the container. An advantage of using the deli cups is that forty-five of them will fit snugly in the standard styrofoam boxes used by the pet industry for shipping tropical fish and reptiles throughout the world.

The next best containers are common plastic yogurt cups or cottage cheese cartons. The individual serving sizes (175 to 225 milliliters, three-quarters to one cup) are best, unless really huge tarantulas like *Theraphosa blondi* or *Hysterocrates hercules* are being collected. These cups may be had most readily at delicatessens and dairies. If not, these businesses may be able to recommend a source.

Packaging

Put one tarantula into each cup and supply it with three or four air holes for ventilation. The authors carry common, single-hole paper punchers for the purpose. The models that punch the smaller, three-millimeter (one-eighth-

Puzzled by scientific names? Read Chapter 2: The Name of the Tarantula and Appendix A: Tarantula Species as Pets for explanations and a cross-reference between scientific names and common names.

inch) holes work best because they do not allow the food crickets to escape during shipping. In each cup, insert a piece of moist sponge measuring about two centimeters (three-quarters inch) on a side. Each sponge should be wet enough that it just barely drips once. These are to prevent the dehydration of the captives and should be remoistened at least twice a week, until the tarantulas can be moved into more hospitable caging. Read the admonition against using sponges or wads of cotton in the tarantula's water dish in its permanent quarters on page 125.

Hazards

Temperature Extremes

While in the field, extreme care must be taken to keep the tarantulas out of direct sunlight. This is the third most important rule of tarantula collection, after maintaining the habitat. Not only are they very uncomfortable in bright light, but they will be quickly cooked by the heat. When they are brought back to the car, be *extraordinarily* careful of extreme temperatures as well. While the outdoor temperature may be quite comfortable, the car's internal temperature (both trunk and cabin) can skyrocket into the cake-baking range! The same is true in a rainforest clearing, a desert, and a city parking lot. It's the same sun everywhere. Try very hard to park the auto in the shade. At the very least, keep the tarantulas in the shade. Keep trunk lids and cabin windows open to allow for as much ventilation as possible.

Alternatively, move all of your captured specimens out of the car and into deep shade under dense shrubbery or next to a building. Beware of marauding ants, however, in these locations.

The Law

The authors have known of many people who ship their tarantulas through domestic mail. Before this is done, however, check postal regulations with the local postmaster. Until recently, the U.S. Postal Service, for instance, prohibited mailing spiders! If the tarantulas cannot be mailed, they will have to be sent by an independent freight agency or courier. Look in the local telephone directory for their names and locations.

Many national and state governments have restrictions or prohibitions against the collection, exportation, or importation of wildlife. But many such regulations only refer to *animals* and this is often interpreted to mean only vertebrates. Before collecting tarantulas, consult with local authorities. If you break the law, knowingly or unknowingly, the penalties can be severe. Some countries are now treating such cases as poaching with the same sentences as drug smuggling! Beware!

In addition, shipping livestock across international borders involves meeting rigid permit requirements, including an inspection by wildlife and agriculture officers. Often, this requires setting up appointments in advance, filling out numerous forms in quintuplicate, paying inspection fees, and (sad but true) sometimes even offering a gratuity to the inspecting officer. All this can become complicated enough to require a broker to handle the details, adding another dimension of expense, inconvenience, and foreplanning to the project.

At the time of this writing, all species of the genus *Brachypelma* are prohibited in international commerce without a CITES permit. (See page 240 for a thorough discussion of the CITES treaty.) As natural habitats around the world are

Collecting Rule #3: Always ensure the health and safety of your collected tarantulas. You have removed them from a home in which they have survived for many years. It is your obligation to care for them so they survive comfortably in captivity for many years to come.

decimated by development and pollution, more species are bound to be added to the list. Eventually, the collection and exportation of all wild-caught tarantulas may be prohibited. Those who wish to collect tarantulas and transport them across international borders should speak with national authorities both in the country of origin and the country of destination to determine the legality and requirements of such transport.

If living or dead tarantulas are to be transported across international borders, acquire one copy of the current CITES appendices for your records and another to be mailed to the recipient beforehand. It never hurts to be too careful.

Violating the "Olde Homestead"

Never go on private property without the owner's permission. Cattlemen, for instance, are perpetually suspicious of rustlers. And landowners are very defensive of their property. Trespassers are occasionally used for target practice! Under any circumstances, tarantulas and their collectors both have serious

Warning. There are severe penalties for bribing government officials in most developed, and many third world, countries. Do not attempt to offer a gratuity to any official unless you are absolutely certain that the practice is acceptable and requisite.

public relations problems. Do not intensify it by trespassing.

Personal Safety

On a collecting trip such as this, the novice can expect some nasty surprises. Temperatures in tarantula country may exceed 45°C (113°F) in the summer and fall below freezing in the winter. In deserts and rain- or moist forests, the relative humidity is often extreme (high or low) and combined with a high temperature can make a deadly combination.

In most wild spaces virtually every plant is bedecked with spines or thorns, or laced with offensive chemicals. Wild creatures are many and varied, and most of them have some effective method of defense. If the animal you've just stumbled onto isn't immediately recognized as harmless, give it a wide berth. Venomous snakes are common in tarantula country, as are other spiders, scorpions, stinging ants, bees, wasps, blister beetles, and a host of other unwholesome creatures. The same clump of grass that shelters the taran-

*A centipede (*Scolopendra heros, *class Chilopoda: Scolopendromorpha) from western Texas. Though not deadly poisonous, the bite is severe and the gloves are clearly warranted.*

tula's burrow will often conceal a hornets' nest. The rock that acts as the tarantula's roof may also protect a scorpion. What appears to be a classic tarantula burrow may, in fact, hold a fifteen-centimeter (six-inch) centipede with an attitude problem. It's a jungle out there, even in the desert!

In western Texas, with one's head down looking for tarantula burrows, it is possible to stumble upon a Brahma bull. In the Serengeti plain of Africa it might be a rhinoceros, in northern Thailand a wild water buffalo.

Trust us on this. Similar habitats and similar situations exist on all continents. Only the details are different. Be ever careful of your own safety and the safety of those who accompany you. The following basic rules are strongly recommended as a starting point.

1. Do not take undue risks.
2. Avoid hazardous situations. In an awkward predicament, take the coward's way out.
3. Be careful not to overexert or overextend yourself.
4. Go prepared for the terrain and climate.
5. Always use a sunblock lotion copiously and frequently.
6. Always wear long-sleeved shirts as protection against the sun, weather, insects, and spiny or irritating plants.
7. A wide-brimmed hat is suggested in the heat of day to prevent sunstroke.
8. A container of drinking water is recommended even if the excursion is not far from civilization.
9. A first aid kit and the minimal training necessary to use it are also highly recommended.
10. Carry a referee's whistle. Their sound is unique in the wild and

carries very well. This is used to signal a cohort that you're in trouble, to give other important information (e.g., "I've found one!"), and to indicate your position. Agree on a set of standard signals (similar to Morse Code) in advance.

11. Be ever cautious of dangerous wildlife.

12. In venomous snake country, wear reasonably snakebite-resistant boots. *Do not* use a snakebite kit on a snakebite without previous training. Instead, consult with local medical personnel on the approved field treatment for such a bite *before* leaving on the excursion. Carry a snakestick.

13. Always stand *behind* a log, rock, or other object that is to be overturned for inspection, never in front. Lift them toward you with a potato rake or snakestick so as to protect yourself from the lunge of an irate snake.

14. Never place fingers or hands anywhere that has not been thoroughly inspected for contentious occupants.

15. Make a concerted effort to avoid large or dangerous animals (e.g., venomous snakes, bull elephants, crocodiles, Brahma bulls, stinging ants, ranchers with rifles).

16. Always take a buddy. As one seasoned field tripper once sarcastically pointed out, "Somebody's gotta write the epitaph!"

17. Always tell someone of the expected route and an estimated time of return. Never walk out of sight, or at least earshot, of the road in terrain that is not intimately known. When in doubt, take a guide. Sometimes the local children are best for this purpose. They know where all the best hunting

Red Diamond Rattlesnake, Crotalus ruber. *Venomous snakes are arguable the most dangerous creatures the tarantula collector may meet.*

spots are, and are often your best guides.

18. Make certain that your vehicle is in good repair. Before venturing into primitive areas, inspect the condition of fan belts, radiator hoses, bumper jack, tire iron, and tires including the spare tire. Fill the fuel tank to capacity. In extreme cases carry extra fuel, water, and engine oil. Carrying a small shovel is highly recommended, as well.

The **Good News.** Most venomous snakebites are not fatal, especially with prompt, adequate medical care. For instance, deaths due to rattlesnake bites are actually quite rare.

The **Bad News.** A venomous snakebite may leave the victim incapacitated and in agony for weeks or months, and often scarred or impaired for life. You may not die, but you may wish you would!

19. Before venturing into primitive areas, acquire detailed maps and inquire locally about routes, road conditions, and weather.
20. In extreme cases, enlist the services of a professional guide.

Ecological Etiquette

A very important, absolutely indisputable point is that, as a naturalist, you are merely *harvesting* an important, renewable natural resource. Although this may be viewed as exploitation, it is harmless, even beneficial, if done wisely. This implies the responsibility to not plunder the landscape for the sought-after animals. These animals' habitats are already under attack and far too fragile to survive much abuse. Instead, purposely try to improve their habitat and even produce more, where possible.

Ripping up a 150-year-old shrub to get a tarantula is sheer folly. Pouring noxious chemicals down burrows to roust out the inhabitants, thus poisoning the spot for decades, is nothing short of criminal. And littering the landscape with a host of craters from digging is unforgivable.

Instead, always replace overturned stones and logs, and reposition any others to allow more habitat sites. If digging is absolutely necessary, do so conservatively, and replace and firmly tamp all turned soil when finished.

Be very cautious about telling others the location of tarantula colonies. All your finest efforts can be ruined by one thoughtless, irresponsible fool.

Only the most boorish dolts witlessly scatter their waste throughout the landscape. Unfortunately, the world seems replete with them. Do not become a part of that group. Instead, carry along a bag for trash. In it, not only put your own trash, but clean up the mess left by our slovenly brethren.

One of the authors (SAS) wages a holy war concerning discarded mattresses and carpets. These should not be burned or buried in a landfill. They should be scattered at random throughout all wild spaces.

"How ugly!" you cry. They are only ugly to human tourists. To the legions of small creatures living in all the hostile places on our planet, they are badly needed refuges. Mattresses are thick pads of material that soak up and hold large quantities of moisture with every rain and dew, releasing it parsimoniously over remarkably long spans of time. During that time a mattress affords hundreds to thousands of small organisms a moist place to hide, to live, to breed.

A mattress also affords relief from extremes of temperature. The thick pad of insulating material shelters the creatures hiding in its shade from the scorching sun, and at the same time absorbs the warmth for a slow release through the cool night. In the dark, moist warmth, the little folk of our planet live and breed in relative comfort and safety.

While a rolled carpet is not so dense and will not hold warmth or moisture as well as a mattress, it affords a myriad of little cavities and interstices in which these small creatures can hide. Rolled carpets are also havens for wildlife.

To the tourist, a discarded mattress or carpet is a loathsome thing, prompting visions of myriads of hostile crawly things. To wildlife (and now you and us), they are sanctuaries, oases in a vast hostile world. Only a true naturalist can appreciate how important this can be, and how really useful and beautiful an old mattress or carpet really is.

Museum Specimens

Sending specimens to museums is a great idea. Live specimens, preserved dead specimens, or the exuvia of living specimens may all make museum material. Such specimens serve as the starting point for nearly all tarantula research. Thus, they are the most important part in the process of learning about these intriguing spiders.

Seeking the Savant

Before shipping any specimens, call ahead to a large museum or university entomology department to inquire if anyone there is currently doing research on tarantulas. If the answer is no, inquire for the name and location of someone who is. Most museum personnel will be glad to give a reference to an appropriate expert.

International hobbyist organizations are also very good sources of information about the location of competent arachnologists. See page 248 for a listing of the organizations that are known to these authors.

When an expert arachnologist is located, ask to speak directly to them. Inquire if they would have an opportunity to look at your specimens. Ask where the specimens should be shipped and what methods for packing and shipping should be used. Be prepared to pay for the shipping yourself. Such individuals' operating funds are usually extremely meager and probably already stretched to the limit. It would be inappropriate to expect these people to pay the shipping fees from their personal funds.

If living specimens are available, ask if living or preserved specimens would be preferred. If living specimens are preferred, make arrangements to ship or carry them to the arachnologist fol-

Methods for humanely killing live specimens, preserving, and shipping them are covered on page 187.

lowing the instructions on pages 180 and 190. If living specimens are not available or preserved ones are requested, confirm that the methods used for preserving, labeling, packaging, and shipping are acceptable.

Ship or personally carry the specimens directly to the arachnologist. If they are hand delivered, be sure to make an appointment first. With luck, an invitation may be negotiated to see the inner workings of the museum or research lab. If they are shipped, include a cover letter reminding the arachnologist of your call and supplying all necessary information.

As a service to its members and an aid to science, the American Tarantula Society (see page 248), among others, will accept properly preserved and packaged specimens of any arachnid for forwarding to a competent arachnologist for identification. All specimens submitted should be accompanied by as much of the following information as possible. Be certain to include your exact return mailing address, phone number, facsimile number, and e-mail address if available.

The Facts, Ma'am, Just the Facts

As they collect, professional scientists usually attach a collection number to each specimen and keep a logbook in their pockets in which they make notes on the specimen's collection data. Often photos are taken of the surrounding habitat and the location where the animal was found. Later, back in the laboratory, the scientist transfers the number and information into a formal register that becomes part of an official record system, and the corresponding log number is then attached to the photos when they come back from the developer.

When specimens are donated to museums or sent to other scientists for study or identification, they are accompanied by the collection number and any information recorded in the register, including duplicates of the photos. The serious amateur collector is urged to adopt a similar system. It is only through such a formal record system, executed with nitpicking diligence and accuracy, that we can gain information about these animals in nature and in captivity.

If the tarantula was purchased from a pet shop, no collection data will be available. Sending it to a museum as a specimen is often worse than useless; it wastes the museum staff's time and resources. Doing so is acceptable if a positive identification is required for a legitimate reason, however.

Collection data must be included with each specimen. These include the collector's name and address, the date of collection, the place of collection, the characteristics of the burrow, habitat, climatological and environmental information, and any other notes available about the animal's living conditions. Our lack of knowledge about most species' intimate lives and habitats is distressing.

Do not use any abbreviations. Spell out all names, locations, and addresses in full. Three hundred years from now, *Blvd.* may not mean anything, or something entirely different than what it means today. Spell out the date to avoid all ambiguity. Three hundred years from now, scientists may not be able to tell if 4/11/93 was April 11 or November 4, seven months and two seasons later.

Neither will they intuitively know that the year was 1993 instead of 1893 or 2093. Use 1993-April-11, instead. The place of collection should include country, state or province, county or parish, and nearest city or town if available. Additionally, an approximate distance and well-defined direction from that town or city is very desirable.

Describe the diameter, depth, and shape of the burrow or lair, and whether it possessed a distinct atrium at the top or chamber at the bottom. Did it branch? How so? Was it hidden under a clump of grass, bushes, rocks, or logs or in the open? Was it positioned on level ground, a slope (How steep, "rise over run?"), in a vertical bank, in a tree, brush, or bunched grass? Was anything to be found around the burrow's mouth, a silken turret, a shaped grass funnel, radiating strands of silk, or a silken veil perhaps?

Describe the habitat, the identity of the dominant vegetation and what plants were growing nearby. Could the area be best characterized as deep desert, desert scrub, chaparral, savanna or prairie, scrub forest, open forest, deep forest, rain- or moist forest, or some other habitat? What kind of soil (e.g., clay, loam, gravel, sand, cracks in large rocks or cliff faces) was the burrow made in?

Describe the burrow's physical relation to the nearest body of water or dry wash, its distance and height above or below the highest apparent water level. Was the burrow on the top of a hill where it would be high and dry during a storm, on a slope where it would receive water runoff, or at the bottom of the slope where it could be inundated? What was the tilt or slope of the terrain?

If at all possible, find a topographical map of the collection area and make a best guess at the altitude of the collection site. Because climate depends so dramatically on altitude, this can be very important data. Such maps are often available in local libraries, police stations, military installations, large book stores, and the geology departments of local colleges and universities.

Describe the climate and the weather at the time of collection. Talk to the locals or consult official records if there is time. If possible, include notes on the average rainfall in the area by season and by the year, the average high and low temperatures by season, and whether there are distinct dry and wet periods (e.g., drought and monsoon).

What was found inside the burrow besides the tarantula? Exuvia, food remains, blown-in detritus? The dry, nonliving contents of the burrow should be saved in a sealed glass or plastic vial and labeled in some way that unambiguously associates it with the tarantula that was living in the burrow. Labeling will be discussed shortly.

Small living arthropods sharing the burrow with the tarantula may be placed in small vials of alcohol. Living commensal organisms of substantial size might be euthanized as humanely as possible and given their own bottles of alcohol, labeled to unambiguously associate them with the host tarantula. Alternatively, an attempt might be made to keep them alive until they may be handed to an arachnologist who will, in turn, find an authority who can identify them.

If the tarantula is from a colony, how many burrows could be counted? How far apart were they? What were their diameters? What other animals, vertebrates as well as invertebrates, were common in the area? Can a food chain be deduced, beginning with the local plants and continuing through to the tarantula? Is there any indication of what the predators would be for the local tarantulas? Are there any other remarkable or unexpected facts to report?

Preparation and Submission

Shipping dead, preserved tarantulas presents several problems, including how to kill them humanely, preserve them, and ship them properly.

Euthanasia. Among the most humane methods of killing a tarantula or any other small invertebrate, and certainly the easiest to arrange, is to cool it in a refrigerator overnight. The next step is to transfer it to a freezer. Presumably, it becomes numb and feels no pain as it cools because tarantulas are cold-blooded and experience the same phenomenon in nature during cold weather. When it is placed in the freezer, it is unconscious and doesn't experience any discomfort during death. There is some doubt about this process, however, and the reader is referred to the discussion of cold anesthesia on page 156. If available, asphyxiation with nitrogen gas would probably be better, with carbon dioxide being a close second best. These are discussed on page 155.

Pickled Tarantulas. Museum curators argue hotly and heavily about which preservatives are the best for spiders. Generally, ethyl and methyl alcohols, obtainable from high school and college biology labs, pharmacies, hardware stores, and chemical supply houses, are conceded to be among the better ones. Their availability makes them the choice of the amateur. Other chemicals have been tried with limited success, such as isopropyl (rubbing or athletic) alcohol, glycol, and even strong whiskey, but the amateur is discouraged from using these except as the last resort. These do not preserve the specimens satisfactorily, making identification very difficult or impossible.

Tarantulas are massive creatures and hold much water. If the alcohol's concentration is too low, the alcohol diffuses poorly through the exoskeleton, allowing the internal organs too much time to decompose. At the same time, the alcohol remaining in the bottle outside the tarantula becomes too dilute too quickly as the excess water diffuses out of the tarantula. The result is a specimen that is partially preserved and partly decomposed. The internal organs, the genitalia in particular, can be largely useless in identifying the specimen, and the characteristics of the genitalia are the most important features in identification.

The best method for preserving a tarantula is to pickle (i.e., preserve) it in alcohol of at least seventy percent, with eighty to ninety percent being superior. If only seventy percent alcohol is available, it must be drained away and replaced with fresh alcohol every second day for three changes for smaller specimens, more for larger specimens, to ensure adequate preservation.

If ninety percent alcohol is available, the specimen should be soaked in it for at least three weeks, then moved to seventy percent for permanent storage.

The pickled tarantula should only occupy one-fourth or one-fifth of the bottle's volume. The remainder should be filled with alcohol and with as little air as possible. One or two drops of glycerine per specimen bottle will help to maintain pliability over time.

Place only *one* specimen in each bottle. Placing more than one specimen from a single location in a single bottle is done occasionally, even by professional arachnologists, as a cost-saving measure, but is to be strongly discouraged. The individual specimens rub important bristles from each other or damage each other in other ways as they float around in the bottles. In addition, placing more than one specimen in a bottle makes the reporting of data for each individual most difficult. If the specimens are of different species, any data collected may result in unresolvable ambiguities. Theraphosid biology is far too confused as it is, and doesn't need any more uncertainty.

Packing and Shipping. It is unwise, and sometimes illegal, to ship preserved specimens in liquid. After they have soaked the appropriate time in the preservative, carefully drain off all the excess liquid and ship them in a moist condition. Wrapping them loosely in soft paper (kitchen) towels, moistened with preservative, inside tightly sealed, sturdy glass bottles will protect them from damage and prevent them from drying out. Several bottles can be included in one package, but each should be generously wrapped

DATE: 1995-April-07
LOCATION: Val Verde County, Texas (United States of America). Twenty kilometers south of Del Rio on Highway 277.
COLLECTOR: Marguerite Jane Schultz; Calgary, Alberta, Canada
PRESERVATIVE: 90% Ethyl Alcohol w/glycerine
LOG NUMBER: 950407.010A

separately in thick newspaper or other soft wrapping material. Be certain to incorporate generous amounts of padding between the bottles as well as next to the carton walls.

Some arachnologists have shipped specimens preserved and prepared as described above, but wrapped in double Zip-Loc plastic bags instead of glass bottles, with good success. If possible, use the heavy-duty variety intended for freezer storage. The bags are then generously padded and shipped in a sturdy cardboard box. This arrangement saves courier costs without jeopardizing the specimens.

Most postal services prohibit shipping dangerous substances, formaldehyde and alcohol being very near the top of the list. There are serious penalties for violating these regulations. Shipping the specimens by courier may be somewhat more expensive, but usually more reliable and certainly more legal.

Labeling. Labeling requirements are rather rigid and should be followed carefully.

1. Each specimen *must* be accompanied by its own accurate label. It is all too easy to confuse labels and bottles if they are kept separate, even if boldly cross-referenced.
2. Each label *must* be with its specimen *inside* the bottle. Labels that are attached to the outside of their bottles invariably fall off in time, allowing for great confusion and loss of important data.
3. Each label *must* be printed heavily in "lead" pencil or India ink on sturdy white, high-rag content paper. Over time, even waterproof inks will smear, fade, or dissolve in the preservatives and light, cheap paper will turn to formless pulp in a few months. The whole idea is that these specimens and the associated information will last for eternity!
4. Each label must contain the date and place of collection, the collector's name and address, a collection number if available, and the type of preservative used.
5. If collection numbers are used to cross-reference additional collection data, be certain to enclose a complete copy of all such data, including duplicates of all photos. Need it be mentioned that such additional data be closely referenced to its corresponding specimens, but packed alongside the appropriate specimen bottle, not in it?

Exuvia. The exuvia of pets may be useful to a museum if collection data is also available. At the very least, they are a good way to have a professional scientifically identify a pet's species without the necessity of killing it. As the tarantulas molt, the fresh exuvia may be carefully posed to make pleasing displays. However, doing so may obliterate some key characteristics of the animal's anatomy. Special bristles may be broken off or other structures distorted. On the other hand, leaving the skins to dry in the crumpled state makes the museum staff's work much harder because they must soften and rearrange them before examination. Call the arachnologist well in advance to ask if time is available for examining them and what requirements must be met when submitting the shed skins.

Shed skins are best sent by mail. Merely place the dried skin, posed or natural, in a box that is just large enough to hold it without breaking it. Carefully cushion the skin with a few pads of cotton. Be certain to include a data label and all associated collection data. Tape the box securely, wrap it in heavy wrapping paper, and mail it as a first-class parcel.

Shipping Long Distances

Live tarantulas should always be shipped in a styrofoam box of the sort used in the tropical fish industry. These are available free or for a small fee from tropical fish stores and wholesalers. If the boxes are stored in a cool or cold storeroom, several hours should be allowed for the boxes to come to room temperature before being packed. In extreme temperatures (e.g., –30°C, –22°F) a one-liter (one-quart) plastic bottle of warm water may be placed in the foam box as thermal ballast. Every effort should be made to keep the box in a place of moderate temperature. If possible, wait until milder temperatures to ship.

Check the weather reports on both ends of the shipping route. While it may be sunny and 30°C (86°F) in Houston, Texas, it might be –30°C (–22°F) and a raging blizzard in Fargo, North Dakota. The tarantulas must survive inclement weather both at the point of departure and the point of arrival and must therefore be packed for both conditions.

When shipping living tarantulas long distances, crumple a piece of soft paper (e.g., a piece of kitchen paper toweling) in each cup to act as a shock absorber. See page 180 for a description of these cups. These cups should be placed in a styrofoam box of the type used for shipping tropical fish. Try to get the corrugated pasteboard box that the foam boxes fit into, for added protection. If the correct cups were acquired, forty-five of them will fit comfortably in each styrofoam box. For fewer cups, the surplus space may be filled with crumpled newspaper or plastic peanuts to stabilize the contents.

Plastic peanuts are small bits of plastic foam used specifically for packing delicate cargo.

Baby tarantulas are best shipped in plastic pill vials. The vials' diameters should be about the size of the spiderling's leg span. Acceptable vials may be available at a local drugstore or apothecary. The depth should be relatively short to conserve space in the shipping box. The inside of the vials should be loosely stuffed with paper toweling and a few drops of water added to maintain adequate humidity. Holes should be punched in each lid for ventilation. Be sure that the holes are small enough to prevent the spiderlings' escape. Pack one spiderling per vial. Wrap the whole mass of vials containing one species in a paper bag and label the bag with the number contained and the correct scientific name. Pack the bags into a styrofoam box and fill any empty spaces with crumpled newspaper or insulating packing.

Be absolutely certain to securely tape the boxes shut, using an appropriate packing tape. The last thing needed is to find out that your tarantulas, so carefully collected or reared, are wandering at liberty throughout some major international airport in some foreign city! This is the sort of thing that "B" horror movies (or comedies) are made of!

Every shipping box must be labeled with at least two sets of labels. Such labels must appear on all six sides (four lateral sides plus the top and bottom). Commercial carriers (e.g., bus, truck, plane) do not supply such labels for your use. If you will be shipping only one or two consignments of animals, you can merely write clearly on the sides of the shipping boxes with black or red felt-tip markers. If you plan to ship several consignments of animals or plan to ship animals on a regular basis, you should have formal adhesive labels printed for the purpose.

The first set clearly specifies the shipper's (your) name, address, and phone number and the consignee's (the recipient's) name, address, and phone number. Including facsimile, night, and alternate numbers when available is also strongly recommended.

The second set of labels must list the statements as shown in the accompanying example.

If the boxes must pass through a foreign country, a third set of labels and marks should be included with the same warnings and information, but in that other country's official language or in an alternate international language, such as French or Spanish.

The waybills that accompany the shipment should be marked with the same information as the labels. Whenever possible, get blank copies of the waybills in advance and type them up before leaving for the airport or carrier's warehouse.

Commercial carriers must follow specific, rigid guidelines when transporting any livestock, especially when crossing international borders. As a result, many simply decline the business. Others charge exorbitant prices for the service. It is the *shipper's responsibility* (yours), not the carrier's, to determine and meet those requirements well in advance. If a commercial carrier is relied upon to transport the tarantulas, discuss both shipping regulations and fees with the carrier well in advance of showing up at the loading dock with the box.

It is also the *shipper's responsibility* to make certain that the animals are packaged appropriately, and that the

> **Harmless Live Animals**
> **Protect from Cold**
> **Protect from Heat**
> **Protect from Sunlight**
> **Notify on Arrival**
> **Hold for Pick Up**

recipient is called as soon as the boxes are accepted by the carrier. The recipient is to be given the carrier's name, the flight or route number, the waybill number, and the estimated date and time of arrival. The recipient must also be reminded that it is their responsibility to pick up the shipment at the freight hanger or warehouse. It will not be delivered. Make certain that the recipient knows how to contact you (the shipper) in case of an emergency.

Whenever possible, live animal shipments should be shipped by air freight. Bus lines and couriers should only be relied upon for shipments that are too small for economic transport by air freight or for short-distance transport.

The mail should only be used in those countries that have a well-organized and efficient postal system and only for shipments within the national boundaries. Before considering your postal service as a carrier, you should discuss the legality of shipping living organisms by mail, especially live tarantulas, about the various types or levels of service available, and their costs.

Remarks

Probably fewer than a dozen people reading this book will ever have an opportunity to hunt for tarantulas. The remainder must content themselves with merely reading and dreaming. Even then, reading this chapter was not a futile exercise, for the reader now has a far better grasp of the problems and rewards of catching your own pet tarantula.

If done wisely and safely, catching one or two wild tarantulas can be a very rewarding experience. The collector will find it much easier to develop a personal bond with them as pets, something that is much harder to accomplish if the tarantulas were collected by some stranger ten thousand kilometers or miles away. The collector will also know more about the way the tarantula lived in nature because of firsthand experience. Lastly, the collector can contribute to our understanding of these creatures by donating the shed skin or even the body of the dead animal to a museum.

Who knows? Perhaps you too will soon catch your own pet tarantula.

Chapter Seven
The Well-Bred Tarantula

A Difficult Project

Until the 1980s, successful attempts to breed tarantulas were almost unknown. The great-grandfather of tarantula keepers, William Baerg, apparently was unsuccessful in getting them to mate, lay eggs, and have the eggs develop in captivity. All the eggs that he procured were from newly caught females that had been impregnated in the wild (Baerg 1938a). Only now, more than one-half century later, are we learning enough about these creatures to be able to breed them with any hope of success. We are still learning, and as our knowledge and experience advance, what is written here will soon be out-of-date. One of this book's readers may even be responsible for making it obsolete!

We did not know why tarantulas would not breed readily in captivity. Baerg (1958) thought they required beetles in their diet. But there is some question as to whether they merely require a variation in diet or if beetles have some magic property for tarantulas. If they do, what could it be?

Conditions other than nutrition may also effect breeding, such as light intensity, temperature, moisture, substrate, handling, and time cycles (diurnal, lunar, and annual). If we knew each species' exact origin and the details of each one's habitat, we might be able to guess at reasonable parameters for

these variables. We might also be able to guess at other conditions that could have an effect.

Over the decades, as more was learned about tarantula biology, more and more earnest attempts were made to breed them in captivity. Nearly all such attempts ended in failure. Certainly the few successes were not reproducible. If tarantulas did breed in captivity, it was purely accidental rather than a carefully planned project with some realistic probability of success.

The first edition of this book reported a successful breeding by Mr. John Blue. Although Mr. Blue's success was not the first such instance, it was particularly noteworthy because he was able to pass living spiderlings on to other collectors. This had been done very rarely before that time. Even then, Mr. Blue's success was not reproducible. Family planning had not yet arrived at the realm of the tarantulas!

Success at Last

The year 1984 saw a major event in the breeding of tarantulas. Mr. A. W. McKee of Seattle, Washington, published a book (McKee 1984a) detailing a technique that he had developed and used for some time. Shortly thereafter, he published a second book (McKee 1984b), and then a third (McKee 1986). However, because they were privately published, the press run was very modest and their distribution low. Copies are now very difficult to acquire. Still, the few serious collectors who did acquire copies of those books were able to make great advances in breeding tarantulas.

What is presented here is a distillation of the experiences of the authors and several other successful enthusiasts, including Mr. McKee.

Not Another Get-Rich-Quick Scheme!

Acquiring and maintaining a breeding population of tarantulas can be a very expensive proposition. Because of the number of tarantulas that must be individually housed and cared for, and because of the long period of time required by these creatures to mature, it is virtually impossible to turn a profit. The enthusiast must be resigned to doing it only for the love of it.

With this in mind, the enthusiast who resolves to breed tarantulas could make an inestimable contribution to their preservation. Even if unsuccessful, at the very least a greater insight into the lives of these remarkable creatures will be gained. Whatever losses incurred are well worth the risk.

Breeding Stock

The casual fancier may not have the time or resources to set aside a special stock to be used exclusively for breeders. However, those who become truly obsessed, as the authors have, will find themselves one day with literally hundreds of tarantulas, and should seriously consider the practice. This special stock may appropriately be called the breeding stock. The enthusiast is advised to choose these very carefully. It should be of species that have admirable properties as pets or some other truly exceptional characteristic. Additional emphasis should also be placed on the species' rarity and endangered status. The individuals chosen should be free of defects. Because we have little idea of which defects are inheritable, and which are merely accidental, we recommend weeding out *all* defects.

Obviously both sexes are needed. New, mature males must be had every year because they tend to lose their breeding vigor within a few months after maturing and die within a year or eighteen months. Several males are recommended in case one is sterile or impotent.

In order to ensure a steady supply of mature males, the enthusiast will have to maintain a number of tarantulas of different ages. The larger the number of individuals, the more matings can be made, and the greater will be the probability of success. But large collections of tarantulas can be expensive to amass and time-consuming to maintain, and the enthusiast's limitations must be recognized. One possible solution to the problem might be a cooperative effort by a group of enthusiasts, a club perhaps. But do not allow the lack of resources to stop an attempt if the opportunity presents itself.

Is It a Boy or a Girl?

It is very important to be able to distinguish between male and female tarantulas. It is also very difficult to accurately determine the sex of immature or small, adult female tarantulas by casual inspection. Their secondary sexual characteristics are obscure at best. Although, over the years, several subtle differences have been noticed between the appearance of immature male and female tarantulas, there are only two or three relatively infallible ways of determining their sex. We examine the various methods here. The reader is referred to Chapter 1: The Physical Tarantula for an explanation of the various body parts mentioned here.

1. Adult male tarantulas possess clubbed pedipalps, although these may not be readily obvious, being small or hidden under an extension of the cymbium. The males of most species also possess tibial hooks. A discussion of the secondary sex organs of male tarantulas appears on page 43.

2. Adult males are usually smaller and lighter bodied than the corresponding adult females. Their legs are usually markedly longer and more slender, as well.

3. There may be a slight difference between the sexes in the size of the chelicerae compared to the sternum, with the prospective male's chelicerae and fangs being smaller in proportion than the female's.

4. The well-fed female's opisthosoma tends to be wider at the pedicel and more globose than an immature male's. The male's opisthosoma tends to be more ovoid and narrower at the pedicel.

5. Immature males that are approaching their maturing molt may exhibit a more hyperactive personality, but this is far more obvious in retrospect than in foresight.

6. Immature males in the last year or two before their maturing molt may exhibit an indication of their adult coloring, if this is markedly different from the female or immature. Examples of this are several species of *Pamphobeteus* from Columbia and Peru in which the males glow with a beautiful blue, purple, magenta, or pink iridescence under almost any light. Males begin to exhibit this iridescence several molts before they mature.

7. Immature males may develop a telltale clue to their sex by the appearance of a small patch of bristles on the epigynal plate of the opisthosoma several molts before actual maturity. The epigastric furrow is the rear border of a triangular or trapezoidal plate bounded by the forward book lungs on the sides and the pedicel toward the front. This plate is called the epigynum or epigynal plate. Arachnologists have noticed that in immature male tarantulas, this area has a central patch of bristles with a color, luster, or sheen different from those that immediately border it. A good light and a small magnifying lens are helpful in searching for it, not to mention a proper grip on the tarantula. The enthusiast must be careful not to confuse the surrounding bristles with the actual coverings of the book lungs. A distinct patch is good evidence of an immature male. Lack of such a patch is inconclusive.

8. In many species the sex of immature females may be verified by examining the area immediately forward of the epigastric furrow. In females, this plate, the epigynum (see page 51), protrudes above the surrounding surface, and the distance between the two anterior book lungs is greater than in males. When viewing the tarantula's profile from the side, the female has a distinct little pot belly that the male lacks. If the tarantula can be held, the enthusiast can often detect this bulge by gently stroking the area

with a fingertip (Hancock and Hancock 1992). The presence of such a bulge, especially on older individuals, is strong evidence in favor of a female. A lack of a distinct bulge, however, is inconclusive.

9. When a female tarantula molts, it sheds the linings of its spermathecae along with the rest of its exoskeleton, and these can be seen in the shed skin. Because males possess no spermathecae, none are present in the male's exuvium. If the enthusiast has access to the cast skin of a tarantula and if that tarantula is old enough to have undergone about six molts or more, its sex may be determined with a very high probability of success.

Moisten the shed skin. Usually, a solution of one or two drops of mild, liquid dish-washing detergent to a cup of water works better than pure water. Use small-tipped forceps and common straight pins. Carefully open the skin from the lower surface of the opisthosoma and pin it flat, with the inside facing upward, on a piece of cork or styrofoam.

With a suitable magnifier, a binocular microscope for young or small individuals, a hand lens for larger individuals, find the inside aspect of the epigastric furrow. It will run transversely between the rear margins of the forward book lungs. Females will have an inward pointing leaf or fold of exoskeleton that resembles a little fence running between the book lungs. Actually, upon close inspection, two such leaves or fences may be evident. The forward one will bear either two hooklike spermathecae or one or two small swellings along its forward margin. The leaves may have to be separated with the tip of a pin to distinguish these structures.

Males will have a slight fold or wrinkle between the book lungs, but not a definite leaf or signs of the spermathecae. They may also have two little glandlike structures (called accessory organs or epiandrous glands) normally lying outside the central area, not on a leaf. Do not confuse these with spermathecae. A school biology lab is a good place to do this work.

10. The authors have seen one offhanded reference, in one scientific paper to a second paper, regarding a difference between the tips of the pedipalps of immature males and females, but has neither seen any additional descriptions, nor been able to find the second paper. It is likely that, if the presence of a telltale difference were valid, the trick of determining the sex of immatures by this method would be widely known by now. Or perhaps this is another piece of information that languishes in the dim reaches of some vast library, awaiting rediscovery.

11. The last and very surest way to recognize a female is when she is carrying an eggsac, or has an older one still in her cage or burrow. If it lays eggs, by definition, it's female!

Care and Maintenance

Maintaining tarantulas for breeding purposes is somewhat different from keeping a pet or two around to impress the gang. Among other things, the requirements for care and feeding are augmented. For the most part, the instructions given for keeping pet tarantulas elsewhere in this book must be viewed as the absolute minimum requirements. All aspects of that care must be upgraded.

Temperature

Most tarantulas will not breed successfully unless their temperatures are elevated above room temperature. Some provision should be supplied for maintaining a uniform, moderately high temperature, e.g., from 25° to 30°C (77° to 86°F). There are many ways to do this. The one way that should not be used is to place an incandescent light bulb above the cage. Tarantulas abhor strong light and radiant heat.

For a single cage, or a very few cages, a good system is a standard medicinal heating pad placed under one end of the cage. Do not place it under the entire cage bottom. The tarantula must be allowed some place of refuge in case the cage bottom becomes too hot. Be sure to place an insulating board under the heating pad. Such heating pads can get warm enough to damage the finish on a spouse's (or parent's) favorite antique table.

Several red alcohol thermometers, purchased from an aquarium shop, should be placed in strategic cages in the collection of breeders and checked frequently during the day.

Place one thermometer on top of the cage floor that lies above the heating pad. Place another on the cool end. The thermometer above the heating pad should never read higher than about 38°C (100°F). If it does, either reduce the setting on the heating pad temperature control or wire a standard rotary-type dimmer switch in series in the power cord. The dimmer switch is the type used for mood lighting in a dining room. Just be very certain that its current rating is equal to or greater than

> **P**icking reasonably accurate thermometers can be very challenging. A serviceable method is described on page 122.

the current consumption of the heating pad. Such wiring is best left to a professional electrician.

The thermometer on the other end of the cage should read the desired temperature. If it is too low, move more of the heating pad under the floor of the cage (but no more than fifty percent of the cage floor) or sheathe the cage in sheets of styrofoam insulation.

A major drawback of this system is that the temperature is uncontrolled. With the arrival of an unexpectedly warm day, the tarantula could easily be cooked! The obvious solution to the problem is the incorporation of a thermostat in the power cord. Such a thermostat must lie on the cage floor. It must also be protected from moisture, the cage's substrate, living and dying crickets, and from the tarantula itself. For this modification, the enthusiast is strongly urged to seek a professional electrician's help.

Humidity

A commercial relative humidity gauge is a very good investment for the aspiring tarantula breeder. Choose the gauge carefully. Most of the less expensive models are so inaccurate as to be all but useless. If at all possible, consult with a local heating and air conditioning firm about which are the better models or have a newly purchased unit calibrated against a standard. To save money, one or two such gauges can be moved from cage to cage, rotating through the breeding stock every few days or weeks.

Because the breeding stock will be kept at a higher temperature, it will automatically be exposed to a lower relative humidity unless a special effort is made to compensate. Although pet tarantulas can usually tolerate the ambient relative humidity found in the average home, the goal here is to bring the breeders into prime condition. The correct level of humidity can often be deduced by reading books on tarantulas written by enthusiasts who have bred them. Some idea of the relative humidity in the tarantula's homeland can be gained by consulting books written on their habitat or books written about tarantulas which contain references to habitat (Smith 1985, 1990, and 1994). Look for wildlife or natural history books written about the appropriate country or district in a local library. Some geography books and tourist brochures can also offer important clues.

Once the temperature in a cage is stable, the humidity can be adjusted by opening or closing the ventilation gaps (e.g., covering more or less of the cover with plastic food wrap) and by using larger or smaller water dishes, even using two dishes if necessary. In extreme cases a water dish may be moved into the warm end of the cage where the elevated temperature will cause greater evaporation. Always allow the humidity gauge eight hours to equilibrate before making a reading.

Because of the higher temperature and humidity, the chances of experiencing a mite infestation are greatly increased. The cages and all adjacent surfaces must be cleaned and sanitized with a dilute chlorine bleach solution often, perhaps as often as once a week. (The manufacture of a chlorine bleach solution and its use are detailed on page 148.) In addition, the aspiring tarantula breeder must be ever watchful for tiny white dust motes that crawl over cage fronts and dark surfaces, particularly after the lights have been off for several hours in the evening. At the slightest hint of a mite infestation the offending cage must be thoroughly cleaned and the entire room must be sanitized with the chlorine bleach water solution. Refer to page 165 for detailed directions for dealing with a mite infestation.

Diet

Herein is another big difference in the breeder's care. Its diet should be varied as much as possible. Offer the breeder mealworms and perhaps pinkie mice, as well as crickets. Caterpillars and other wild insects are acceptable, but only if they are certified pesticide-free and are not toxic or armed with dangerous mandibles, spines, or stingers. Another approach is to fortify the breeder's diet with vitamin-mineral supplements.

Lacing Their Food. Fortifying the tarantula's food with vitamin and mineral supplements has been suggested for some time. McKee (1986) recommended feeding crickets on a fortified mash before giving them to the tarantulas. The popular wisdom in tarantula breeding follows his dictum and these authors can see no reason why it could not be true. There is only one caveat we would offer, which we will come to shortly.

For several days before being offered to the tarantula, the food animal should be fed on food that has been slightly doped with a vitamin-mineral supplement. Ordinarily, such food animals are the domestic house cricket. For this purpose, they should be fed on chick mash that has had vitamin-mineral supplement thoroughly mixed into it. One or two teaspoonfuls of supplement per kilogram (two pounds) of mash should be sufficient.

The aspiring enthusiast will have to improvise with other species of food animal.

Powder Room. The authors have also heard of enthusiasts who dusted the crickets with a powdered vitamin-mineral supplement. Place the crickets in a small glass jar with a small spoonful of powdered supplement and shake them gently once or twice before offering them to the spiderlings. Small paper bags will also work. Save the powdering container. It need not be thrown away after each use, but can be reused repeatedly, thus not wasting the extra, unused supplement.

Snake Oils and Universal Panaceas. In the pet industry as a whole, and especially among dog breeders, the fortifying supplements that have been exhorted have ranged from the sublime to the ridiculous, and any number of commercial names have been heatedly recommended. In all honesty, it is doubtful that there really is a big difference except in the packaging and the price. The animal for which a supplement is advertised is not the only one for which it can be used. The authors know of at least one brand of vitamin–mineral supplement that made separate packages for cats, dogs, and guinea pigs. However, when their ingredients, analyses, and appearances are compared, it is obvious that the only difference was the photograph on the label!

Natural-source vitamin–mineral supplements are preferable to synthetic ones. Human metabolism, and to some extent that of dogs, is capable of using some synthetic vitamins, and supplements intended for human consumption are usually based, at least in part, on them. We know absolutely nothing about a tarantula's dietary requirements or whether they are capable of metabolizing the same synthetic supplements that we can. Indeed, there is every reason to believe, based on our experience with other aspects of tarantula biology, that their requirements and tolerances would be quite different from ours.

Natural food stores may be a good place to look for these supplements, but many common grocery stores, drug stores, and apothecaries also carry such products. If natural-source vitamins cannot be found, look in a pet shop for those made for other animals. The animal listed on the label is almost irrelevant. Compare the ingredients, not the artwork. Very little will be used over time, so buy only a small portion.

Purchase a powdered form rather than a liquid. Those supplements that are dissolved in the drinking water are all but useless. Because drinking water must always be present in the animal's cage, and because water solutions of these supplements have a very short useful life span, they must be changed every day. The result will only be fouling a lot of water and wasting a lot of supplement.

Too Much of a Good Thing. Now for the caveat mentioned earlier. It is important to understand that reinforcing the diet of an animal does not work miracles in ten minutes or even ten days. To overcome the effects of poor nutrition, months of careful work are required. Good nutrition is a lifelong pursuit. If the plan is to breed the tarantulas next year, the fortification of their diet should have started last year, or earlier still.

Care should be taken not to overdose the tarantulas. Remember, the natural food of tarantulas contains all the vitamins and minerals on which the tarantula will thrive for decades. Massive

Metabolism, thermoregulation, and food consumption are discussed at length in Chapter 1: The Physical Tarantula.

malnutrition is not being fought here, only a little boost is being given. In fact, because tarantulas have a metabolic rate dramatically lower than humans (see page 49), it is reasonable to assume that they require proportionately lower doses of vitamin supplements.

It is better to be too conservative than too liberal. An acceptable compromise might be to supplement the tarantula's diet no more than once every three months. No nutritional information is available for tarantulas, and we aren't even certain that we could recognize either malnutrition or hypervitaminosis in tarantulas if we saw it!

A much better approach would be to vary the tarantula's diet as much as possible. Using crickets as the mainstay, pinky mice, mealworms, waxworms, and pesticide-free wild insects as food supplements makes much better sense. It is difficult to conceive of any circumstance where such varied fare would pose a nutritional overdose problem.

Caging

At this point in this discussion, the care of breeder tarantulas suffers a clear dichotomy based on the way in which the females are maintained. This, in turn, has significant ramifications on the way in which the eggsacs and eggs are treated. These authors adopt a middle-of-the-road stance, acknowledging that each method has its uses and problems.

Burrow Brooding. One group of enthusiasts maintain their breeder females in cages that allow burrows or limited retreats that they apparently interpret as burrows. Because of the limitations imposed by living in a burrow, the eggsac is generally left with the female and the entire cage is considered to be a large incubator. This places the eggsac and its eggs in jeopardy of being eaten by a nervous female and greatly increases the possibility of a rampant mite infestation at the worst possible time. On the other hand, this is often the only way that a particularly highstrung or difficult-to-breed species may be bred successfully. Enthusiasts who wish to study the brooding behavior of tarantulas, or who are simply infatuated with motherhood, are attracted by this method, as well.

Maternity Ward. The other group of enthusiasts maintain their tarantulas in relatively spartan cages, not allowing burrows. In this case, the eggsac is usually removed from the female and cared for artificially in one of several different ways described a little later in this chapter. While this method largely removes the possibility of both the female eating the eggsac and its eggs, or the eggsac being overrun with mites, this sort of caging is not favorable for the breeding of highstrung species. Obviously, maternal brooding cannot be studied and compared by this method either.

Strategy Session. There are several different strategies for dealing with the day-to-day care of the breeders leading up to breeding, leading up to making the eggsac and caring for the eggsac after it is made.

On a day-to-day basis, the style of the cage in which a mature male should be kept is almost irrelevant because mature males ordinarily are wanderers anyway, and will seldom permanently retreat to a burrow.

On a day-to-day basis, leading up to and during mating, the females may either be kept in display cages with little substrate or they may be kept in cages that allow them to create a burrow. Not allowing them to burrow facilitates moving them to the male's cage for mating. Allowing the female to burrow complicates this task immensely and may require moving the male to her cage instead. Males are prone to temporarily losing their libido when handled in this fashion, thus foiling any mating attempts. This will be discussed more fully below.

The enthusiast will have to decide how the female will be caged after the breeding season is finished until it is time for egg laying, based on consideration of the enthusiast's goals and requirements and a careful assessment of the pros and cons outlined in the discussion above.

For females that are not allowed to burrow after the mating season, the eggsac is almost always removed and cared for artificially.

For females that are allowed to burrow after the mating season, the enthusiast may either leave the eggsac with the female to incubate, or the female's burrow can be sacrificed for the sake of removing the eggsac to artificial care. Leaving the eggsac with the female puts it at risk of being eaten by her. Digging up the burrow puts the eggsac at risk from damage by the enthusiast in the course of excavating the burrow.

Basic Principles. Breeders should be placed in better cages. These might have more floor space, half again or more than that recommended for the average pet. The male must have room to maneuver and out-maneuver the female during breeding. The substrate should be of a type that allows better hygiene (e.g., easily replaceable horticultural vermiculite, sterilized potting soil, or a mixture of these) instead of garden soil or aquarium gravel. In a breeder's cage, cute decorations are not advisable. The tarantula doesn't appreciate them and they allow a place for mites to hide. An additional consideration is the maintenance of a higher-than-normal humidity. The cover should have some provision for allowing easy adjustments of humidity and ventilation.

The Brood Case. If several tarantulas are to be kept as breeders, consider making a brood case. This is merely a heated case in which several individual tarantula cages are kept. A discarded refrigerator makes a particularly good brood case, but any cabinet or case that can be closed and insulated is acceptable.

Inside, near the floor of the case, a dual incandescent lamp fixture is mounted. Two incandescent bulbs (start with twenty-five watt bulbs) should be tried at first. It may be helpful to cover them partly with aluminum foil to block much, but not all of the light. A standard, household-style dimmer switch is almost essential to adjust the current going to the bulbs, and therefore, the intensity of the heat that the bulbs produce. Using a dimmer switch will also lengthen the bulbs' lives. A standard, household furnace thermostat that draws from the main power source is also essential. This should be mounted inside the case, about midway between top and bottom. It is important to mount the thermostat in a position that will not allow heated air from the light bulbs to rise directly to it. The dimmer switch, the thermostat, and the lamp fixture should be wired in series. The enthusiast is strongly urged to seek the assistance of a professional electrician for wiring these circuits.

A false floor or shelf should be suspended above the light bulbs in such a way that it will block all direct heat from radiating up into the body of the case, but ample space (e.g., two and one-half centimeters, one inch) should be left around the margins, or a dozen or more two-centimeter (three-quarters-inch) holes bored across the floor to allow easy airflow. All heat should be carried by convection only. A second shelf, preferably made of a grating and positioned slightly above the bottom one will hold the lower tarantula cages and a flat baking dish of water for humidity. A commercial relative humidity gauge should be kept one or more shelves higher.

Several holes should be cut toward the bottom and top of the case to allow for slight ventilation. The exact size and shape of these will be a matter of experimentation and experience. Plan on at least four near the bottom and four toward the top. Use a diameter of about one centimeter (one-half inch). Excess holes can be easily plugged if not needed, and holes that are too large may be partially plugged more easily than dismantling the whole case and boring additional ones or enlarging the ones already present. Make more than would seem necessary at first.

Screened ventilation plugs can often be found in hardware and larger department stores. If these are available, make the holes a size to accommodate these plugs. Or improvise a method of covering the holes securely with a layer of fine screen. This will prevent the escape of any errant tarantulas and invasions by mice or ants.

The enterprising enthusiast may even be able to carefully fit a glass or Perspex (Plexiglass) plate in the front so that the on-off cycle of the bulbs can be monitored and the cages inspected without the necessity of opening the

door. If a refrigerator is used, great care should be made not to pierce the coolant conducting tubes that are often built into the side walls. A refrigeration technician should be contracted to safely drain off the refrigerant and locate the tubing for you. Usually the doors are safe.

Thermometers should be placed at varying levels in the case. The thermostat should be set at the target temperature and the dimmer switch turned to produce the strongest light from the bulbs. Several hours later, the thermostat should be checked and readjusted if necessary. Then the dimmer switch should be adjusted so that the bulbs will be on about one-third of the time. This may require experimenting with larger or smaller bulbs. These adjustments and use of a dimmer switch reduces sudden, dramatic temperature fluctuations in the case and prolongs the life of the bulbs.

Once the temperature has been adjusted, the size of the water dish and the number of ventilation holes should be adjusted to maintain a proper humidity. The wider the water dish, the higher the humidity will tend to be. The more ventilation holes or the larger the holes, the lower the humidity will tend to be. The deeper the water dish, the less often you will have to refill it. Use of distilled or demineralized water will avoid a mineral build-up in the water dish. Do not block all ventilation; leave open at least one ventilation hole toward the bottom and one toward the top at all times.

The Guest Room. If a spare bedroom is available (the guest room perhaps) and the project becomes all-consuming, consider turning that room into a tarantula room, as the authors did. (See photographs beginning on page

123.) In this case, the honored guests have eight legs each, instead of two!

Temperature is controlled in this room with a standard thermostatically controlled electric space heater. Humidity is controlled cage by cage with the use of water dishes and plastic food wrap applied to the cage lids to retard (but not completely block) ventilation and loss of moisture. For rain- or moist forest species, moist soil, vermiculite, or extra large water dishes are used. Lighting may be controlled by an automatic timer. In effect, the entire room becomes a brood case.

Maintenance

To control infestations of mites, flies, and other organisms, hygiene must be improved in the breeders' cages. Dead crickets and consumed food boluses must be removed promptly. In anticipation of the laying of eggs, the entire cage should be cleaned and set up anew, giving the female plenty of time to set up housekeeping before she begins to build her brood web.

A special effort should be made to clean and refill the water dish at the slightest sign of stagnation.

In maternity-ward-style cages, the only cage ornament should be a coconut shell or a small bowl. Its purposes are outlined below.

Seclusion

The breeders' cages should be placed in a part of the house away from major disturbances. The breeders should only be disturbed by the keeper and only when necessary. Frequently disturbed males may be too nervous to breed the females, and females that feel insecure may destroy their eggsacs before the eggs can be removed to an incubator or have an opportunity to develop and emerge. Most successful enthusiasts keep their breeding tarantulas in quarters that are off limits to casual spectators and never attempt to handle them except in emergencies.

The Male

Once a mature male is obtained, he must be given better-than-average care in order to maintain his vigor. The longer he is kept in good condition, the more females he will be able to breed.

A higher humidity may help prevent the drying of the sperm in his pedipalps and may retard his aging. A lid should be used on the cage that allows for a smaller exchange of air to maintain the desired humidity. A plastic shoe box (see page 111) is nearly ideal. Give the male a wider water dish. Be careful that the substrate does not become wet, however. Excessive dampness invites bacterial, fungal, and mite infestations.

Care should also be taken to feed him more often than normal, but perhaps not so much at a time. Remember to vary the diet as well. An occasional vitamin-mineral supplement may also be desirable.

The Female

All the foregoing comments regarding the care of the male also apply to the female. She is the one who must harbor the sperm for months, produce a mass of eggs, and spin a large silken case to hold them. She needs to build up large reserves of stored fat and protein in advance to allow her to complete the program.

If caging resources are limited, give the females the larger cages. Because of their size, females that are heavily laden with eggs can be easily injured when handled. When a bred female begins to put on weight, it is best not to handle her. Females that are producing eggs often develop ravenous appetites. Once a female has been bred, it is a good idea to check the cage daily and keep one or two crickets with her at all times.

Pedigrees and Inbreeding

We simply do not know what effects inbreeding will have on a population of tarantulas. We do know that other, more familiar animals like dogs and tropical fish cannot be inbred to any large degree before serious defects become obvious, and the population loses its vigor and ability to breed at all. The population geneticist explains this by saying that this reduces the genetic variability below a critical level.

Other scientists have pointed out, however, that many insects and other creatures reproduce parthenogeneti-cally generation after generation with no apparent adverse effects. In this case, the genetic variability is reduced to zero in the population and the species seems to survive, even thrive, anyway.

There are many differences between the two examples given (e.g., vertebrate versus invertebrate, sexual reproduction versus asexual reproduction, the intensity and type of selective culling or natural selection on the populations) that cloud the issue, and their relative importance cannot be properly assessed. For lack of definitive data, these authors assume a very conservative stance and recom-mend strongly against inbreeding, know-ing full well that this opinion will be open to severe debate and possible criticism.

Parthenogenesis: reproduction wherein an unfertilized female gamete develops into an individual.

It is beyond the scope of this book to deal fully with the topic of inbreeding, its consequences and remedies. The enthusiast is referred to books on the subject in the genetics, agriculture, and animal husbandry sections of a univer-sity library. We give here only a few basic guidelines.

A pedigree should be maintained for each individual to be used for breeding. This is merely an itemization of the tarantula's ancestry, if known, and a list of the individuals with which it has mated and produced offspring.

Under ideal circumstances, no given individual breeder should be allowed to mate with any relative closer than second cousin (defined as the children of the children of their aunts or uncles). Similarly, they should not be allowed to mate with parents, grandparents, great-grandparents, or between parents and children, grandchildren, and great-grandchildren. Periodic attempts should be made to breed the members of your stock with totally unrelated members from the stock of another enthusiast. Hopefully, the other enthusiast will also be maintaining pedigrees and be able to verify that the individuals in question are not related to yours. This is particularly important as the tarantula-breeding hobby develops and the web of cross-breeding becomes more complex.

These rules may be violated under extreme circumstances. One such case might be where an enthusiast pos-sesses the only surviving captive indi-viduals of an extremely rare species, perhaps all being siblings from one eggsac. The population that would arise from such a situation would be so intensely inbred that their survivability would be in serious jeopardy, but at least there would be some possibility of survival. Especially in this case, every effort must be made to secure additional, unrelated breeding stock.

Another case where limited inbreeding might be allowable, if not advantageous, is the circumstance where a hobbyist is attempting to develop a hereditary line of tarantulas that display certain desirable features such as a remarkable color pattern, the absence of urticating bristles, or excessive size. The human race has done this innumerable times with other domestic animals, and as the hobby progresses there is no reason to doubt that we will do it with tarantulas as well.

Nuptials

Timing

The male tarantula should have built his first sperm web shortly after his maturing molt. (See page 80 for a discussion of sperm webs.) Males are often very secretive about this, so the only evidence might be an otherwise clean web trampled to the floor of the cage or a few tatters still adhering to the cage wall. Try to use the male for breeding anytime after he is suspected of building a sperm web or anytime after about two weeks following his maturation, whichever comes first. Thereafter, he will probably be able to breed every four to seven days for several months. After six months, males seldom breed successfully. Although they go through all the motions, they are usually sterile. In some tropical species, the males pass their prime even sooner. This should not be used as an excuse to not attempt a breeding, however, especially with particularly rare species. It does little harm to try to breed an older male. The worst that can happen is that he will be eaten by the female. This sounds gruesome, but it is a quick death. On the other hand, an exceptional male with a long, productive life span may be a real bonus, and prejudging him may preclude a successful breeding.

The females will accept a mate most of the time, as they apparently do not suffer a heat period. It does no harm to breed the female, even if it is likely that she will molt before laying eggs. With rare species it is well worth the effort, just in case.

Wild North American tarantulas employ at least two strategies for determining the proper mating period. The species from Arkansas that Baerg studied (putatively *Aphonopelma hentzi*) mated in late summer or fall (August through October). The females produced eggsacs in March through May. Breene (1996) calls this strategy the *Fall Mating Strategy*.

In that same publication, Breene reports that *Aphonopelma anax* from southern Texas employs a *Spring Mating Strategy*, whereby they mate in late May. The females produce eggsacs in June and July.

The authors have successfully bred *Avicularia avicularia, A. versicolor, Brachypelma smithi, B. emilia,* and *B. albopilosum* as late as the first week in January (mid-winter in the northern hemisphere), with female *Avicularia* species producing eggsacs in February and *Brachypelma* species producing eggsacs in March or April. This could be interpreted as yet a third mating strategy, or an intergrade between the two. Little has been reported about the breeding seasons of most other exotics.

The authors note that most individuals of *Phrixotrichus spatulata* brought to North America from Chile (in the southern hemisphere) molt in October or

November the first year, then again in midsummer, and again the following spring. That is, they shorten their inter-molt, molting more frequently until they lock step with the northern hemisphere's seasons. Enthusiasts who wish to breed species from the opposite hemisphere should carefully consider this reversal of seasons. In April, it will do little good to breed a newly imported and matured southern hemisphere male to a female who is already acclimated to the northern hemisphere. This may be his prime time for breeding, but she's preparing to molt (a variation on "Sorry dear, I have a headache").

Those imported males that shed the previous fall are probably too old and weak to mate by the following summer, but those that mature in the spring are vigorous and willing through the entire coming breeding season.

While this resetting of the biological clock occurs in many individuals, there seem to be a significant number of instances when the resetting has not occurred. What proportion reset their clocks? Wherein lies the difference? There is still much to learn about these enigmatic creatures.

Baxter (1993) infers that some species of tarantulas will breed and subsequently produce fertile eggs at almost any season of the year. While these authors have had greatest success breeding tarantulas during the traditional breeding season (late summer through early winter), they have heard of several successful attempts at breeding during the presumptive off-season. These out-of-season breedings occurred with long-term captive or captive-bred tarantulas. It is suspected that these had lost their strongly entrained link to an annual cycle because of their relatively protected cage lives. These reports lend further justification to attempting breeding regardless of whether or not timing and other conditions seem to fit the rules.

Baxter also mentions that *Psalmopoeus cambridgei* and many of the Indian and Sri Lankan ornamental tarantulas (genus *Poecilotheria*) will produce a second eggsac with fertile eggs before they molt. Furthermore, Smith (1990) reports an instance where *Pterinochilus murinus* produced a second eggsac before molting. The one eggsac per molt cycle rule is not as hard and fast as was once thought.

So, when is the best time to mate a pair of tarantulas? There are two answers. Discuss mating strategies with other enthusiasts who have bred the same species and check authoritative texts to determine when they have mated successfully for other people. The international enthusiasts' organizations and local hobbyists' clubs (see page 248) are good places to start. The second answer is to mate them as soon as it is suspected that the male has built a sperm web, regardless of the state of the female.

The Main Event

A rectangular piece of light cardboard should be acquired to act as a shield between the prospective breeders if the female attacks. Several prods should also be handy. These authors prefer chopsticks, but any other light stick may work as well. R. G. Breene prefers small artist's brushes (personal communication).

The authors have found that males are much more enthusiastic about breeding in the evening rather than during daylight hours. This is completely understandable because in the wild they would be easy game for any predator within sight during daylight. In addition, tarantulas are much more willing to breed if their temperature is relatively high than if it is lower. The authors have had much more success breeding them at 30°C (86°F) than at 21°C (70°F).

At this point, the dichotomy in maintenance and breeding methodologies, described earlier, begins to play an important role. Whichever system is employed, the boudoir must be large enough to allow the male to outmaneuver the female lest he be killed by her.

In either caging arrangement, the female must be well-fed several days prior to mating lest she prefer dinner to sex.

Out in the Open. The authors prefer keeping the females in relatively spartan cages without burrows (but see the discussion of burrows on pages 116 and 200 and the discussion that follows). The male's cage is used as the boudoir by moving the female into it. The reasons for this are outlined below.

The five-hundred-milliliter (one-pint) plastic containers used for cottage cheese and yogurt are good for this purpose. First, carefully trap the female under the container. A piece of light cardboard can be slid under it to act as a lid. Be careful not to injure the animal (e.g., trapping and ripping off a leg). This method reduces the possibility that a human odor would upset him.

Place the female toward the opposite end of the cage from the male, but as near as possible without touching him. If the male does not take the initiative after several minutes, gently stroke her pedipalps and first legs with a chopstick, then gently stroke the male's, then the female's again. The scent that is picked up by the chopstick from this gentle stroking serves to let them both know that there is a member of the opposite

sex very near. This may precipitate a mating. If all else fails, gently nudge her closer until she touches him.

Be prepared to separate the two tarantulas, especially at the end of copulation when the male is trying to make good his escape. Use the piece of cardboard, not the hand, to avoid being bitten by the female. (The male seldom tries to bite at this point.) Be gentle but firm! The female is seldom intent on harming the male and either might be injured if too much force is used.

With a Burrow. If the female is allowed to live in a burrow, the sole recourse is merely to put the male in her cage. Place the male toward the opposite end and watch both his and the female's actions carefully.

Sudden Turn-offs. As a defensive warning system, the fine bristles on tarantulas are exceedingly sensitive to the slightest air movement, much more so than the hair on our arms or the back of our necks. When trying to mate tarantulas, do not make sudden movements that might create little eddies or breezes that would disturb them. Move slowly and deliberately. Most certainly, do not breathe heavily on them. The authors have found little that will turn off a male tarantula's libido faster than a careless breath of air!

Often the male will panic at any contact from either the chopstick or the female and attempt to bolt up the wall of the cage. Try again the same evening, but be forewarned, once spooked (so to speak) the probability of a successful mating on the same evening is slight. If all goes well, however, he will perform his nuptial duties without hesitation, even in public.

It is not uncommon for a male to absolutely refuse to have anything to do with a female. The authors have found this to be particularly true of newly caught males or those that were acquired only one or two seasons before maturing. They apparently had not the time to fully adjust to captive life.

If the male and female are of different species, the male will probably refuse to have anything to do with the female, often standing absolutely stark still as though frozen in stone or cowering in the corner or making every effort to escape the cage. Continuing such a mating is futile and dangerous to the male.

Another possible reason for the male's lack of interest in sex is that the excitement of being caught and transported ruins the male's ability to concentrate on sex, hence our preference for moving the female into the male's cage. If the male appears to be distressed by any disturbance, place him in a larger cage (perhaps thirty by seventy-six centimeters, twelve by thirty inches) and do not disturb him for several days. Later, when the breeding is to occur, the male's cage is opened quietly some time in advance (assuming that he isn't trying to escape) and a period of time is allowed to elapse for him to "chill out." The female is then carefully lowered into the male's cage and placed some distance from the male, so as not to alarm him. After another passage of time to allow the male to relax, the female may be gently prodded toward him if they haven't already found each other. If a male is hyperactive enough to require this treatment, keep spectators and all other disturbances away from the room during the entire breeding season.

When mating tarantulas, the authors firmly position a chopstick, point down against the cage floor, between the two breeders, very close to the female, as they are introduced. The chopstick serves as an obstacle that the female must get around in case she attacks the male. On many occasions, it has foiled her assault long enough for the male to escape. The chopstick is removed as soon as the female indicates by her submissive actions that she is willing to accept the male as a mate rather than a handy meal.

Because we have no idea how sensitive a male tarantula's sense of smell is or what his reaction will be to the scent of another tarantula, it is best to clean all equipment and tools that come into contact with other tarantulas before using them around a prospective breeding pair. Use a different set of clean containers and prods with each pair. The authors suspect that several of their earlier attempts to breed rare species may have failed because the males were just too apprehensive about the odor of other tarantulas on the implements.

Use each male with as many females as possible, including those belonging to other enthusiasts. Little or nothing is known of the fertility rates in tarantulas and this practice will weigh the odds in favor of a successful breeding. Swap wives, so to speak. Use the males to their fullest, at least once a week, whether a sperm web is seen or not. A short life, but a merry one!

Never try to mate a female tarantula after she has laid eggs, until she has again molted. After she has laid her eggs, her maternal instincts assume command and her drive to reproduce is suspended. At that point the male is merely food. Her willingness to accept a mate is apparently reinstated after molting.

Hybridization

Breeding tarantulas of the same species is difficult enough that no attempt to mate tarantulas of different species should be attempted by the novice. Ordinarily, the female will not recognize the male as a mate, either because he bears the wrong scent or because he doesn't know the secret password. The result will be a single, very plump, unimpregnated female.

Attempts at hybridizing tarantulas should be left to the seasoned veteran, and then only with grave trepidation. The experienced enthusiast might try hybridization as an experiment, but only with the firm resignation that the male will most likely be sacrificed in the process, with virtually no probability of any offspring.

The authors are aware that intergrades of closely related species of tarantulas exist in nature. It is entirely possible that, if a mate of the correct species is unavailable, a lonely tarantula will accept a close substitute. It happens with other animals. Can the veteran enthusiast convince two tarantulas of different but closely allied species and opposite sex to mate?

McKee (1986) reports that he tried hybridizing *Brachypelma auratum* with *B. smithi* on several occasions. They did copulate and eggs were produced but were infertile. Turbang (1993) displays photos of hybrids between *Ceratogyrus brachycephalus* and *C. darlingi*, and between *Brachypelma smithi* and *B. emilia*, and mentions hybridization of *B. vagans* and *B. albopilosum*. These authors have also heard rumors of hybrids between several species of *Avicularia*. The authors have had neither the opportunity to examine any of these hybrids, nor have seen them offered for sale to the general public.

Why would we want to hybridize tarantulas? Is there any virtue or advantage to doing this? There are a number of reasons why hybridization might be attempted. Hybridization might give us

Brachypelma auratum. *Compare the yellow markings on the legs with those of* B. smithi.

a better idea of spider genetics, for instance. At this point, the science of arachnid genetics simply doesn't exist. Any ideas that we have concerning the way that spiders inherit color, color patterns, web designs, and habits and behavioral patterns, to name a few characteristics, is based almost completely on data from other animals, and pure surmise.

Assuming that the offspring were not infertile mules, there is the possibility that hybridization and selective breeding could produce unique color patterns, less irritating bristles, or significantly larger sizes. The imagination runs amuck with the thought of hybrid tarantulas the size of *Theraphosa blondi* and with the colors of *Chromatopelma cyaneopubescens* and *Brachypelma smithi* combined, or hybrids of *T. blondi* and *Lasiodora parahybana* with forty-five-centimeter (eighteen-inch) leg spans! Such thoughts make those of us who are obsessed with these fabulous creatures fairly drool with anticipation.

These authors are not qualified to discuss the philosophical, moral, or ethical ramifications of hybridization, selective breeding, or domestication, but must go on record as making several observations.

Throughout history, the story of humankind's involvement with domestic animals has been one of altering their inheritable characteristics for humankind's own purposes. In the process, these animals have, as a continuing genetic line, survived, whereas many of their wild brethren are imperiled or have disappeared entirely. Whether or not the hybrid individuals are the same or a different species, are better or worse than their wild ancestors, or are somehow impure because of hybridization and selective breeding depends entirely on one's point of view and the standard against which they are measured. The fact remains that those domestic breeds with which humans have tampered have survived and often increased in numbers, whereas their natural kin have not.

Hybridization occurs frequently in nature among a wide assortment of plants and animals, and survival of the fittest is actually nothing more than a form of selective breeding by nature, if not by humankind. It doubtlessly has occurred in tarantulas without our intervention in the eons before this and, providing tarantulas manage to escape the current great extinction, will occur in the future. The question is not so much one of whether we should, but what benefits to the animals as well as humankind will be the result of the practice.

Ultimately, the whole discussion concerning hybridization and selective breeding in tarantulas by enthusiasts may be a moot point, and possibly of little merit. Both will almost surely occur, with or without any individual's or group's approval.

Maternity and Prenatal Care

At the end of the breeding season, before the eggs are laid, the female's cage should be thoroughly cleaned to reduce the resident mite population. If the intention is to allow the female to brood her own eggsac, this is the best time to set up a cage that will allow a burrow.

For tarantulas acclimated to the northern hemisphere, depending on local climate, weather patterns, and the species, egg laying usually occurs from February through July. (See the discussion on page 205 for more information.) In the southern hemisphere, these months are probably reversed. Between the time of mating and eggsac production, the female does not appear to undergo any significant changes in personality, but she may grow in bulk. Although nothing obvious shows, she is actually very busy. Her ovaries become distended with the job of changing stored body mass into eggs.

If the female is supplied with a burrow, no further alterations need be made or cage appointments added as the egg-laying season approaches.

However, if the eggsac is to be cared for in an incubator, the female should be given a place in which to lay her eggs, in effect, a temporary burrow. A coconut shell is very handy and works well for all but the largest tarantulas. Choose one that is more oblong than spherical. With a hacksaw (metal saw), cut about one-third off one end. After the liquid and pulp are removed, the hull should be washed with a very mild dish soap solution, then rinsed thoroughly several times to remove all traces of soap. It should then be dried completely to avoid a fungus growth.

Place the dried coconut shell on its side in a back corner, with the opening aimed straight out toward the center of the cage. It should be oriented horizontally or aimed slightly upward providing a bowl-shaped hollow in which the female may construct her eggsac. It should be absolutely stable and oriented so that the female can easily find her way into it. The aspiring tarantula breeder must be able to see into it easily as well. Putting a small amount of the cage's substrate (e.g., gravel, vermiculite, or soil) into the shell has been recommended to give the female the opportunity to dig a nest (McKee 1984b). The hypothesis is that she will benefit in some way from this domesticity. The practice surely will do no harm and we wish to do everything we can to expedite egg laying.

Some enthusiasts use small cereal bowls instead of a coconut shell. The bowls are not tipped on their sides, but rather merely set into the substrate.

If the female suddenly begins a major earthmoving project in March or April (perhaps September or October in the southern hemisphere), especially if it is accompanied by a burst of web spinning, egg laying may be imminent. By the time she is going to lay eggs, the female may have spun webbing everywhere in the cage, and either thoroughly barricaded herself in her coconut shell with a densely opaque wall of silk or tried to construct a nest in the corner of her cage.

The Blessed Event

She will spin a bowl-shaped web, lay the fluid-laden eggs in its center, and roll

A **Brachypelma smithi** *female has barricaded herself into a coconut shell to lay eggs.*

the egg-filled bowl into a ball. The curved hollow of the coconut shell or cereal bowl is intended to mimic the curved inner surface of the female's burrow in nature. The upturned walls collect the egg mass in the center, allowing the

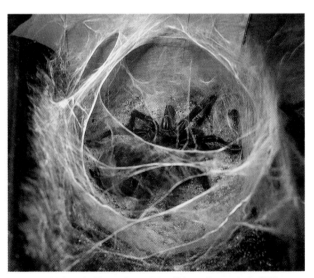

This gravid female **Theraphosa blondi** *has chosen to build her egg-laying web in the corner of her cage, out in the open. When completed, the silk will be so dense that it will be almost opaque.*

A female **Aphonopelma chalcodes** *laying eggs.*

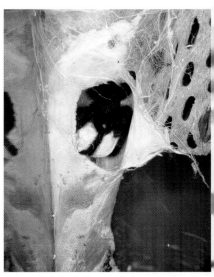

A female **Avicularia avicularia** *protecting her eggsac. A hole has been cut in her silken retreat to reveal her at her station.*

mother to securely wrap the eggs in silk to make the eggsac. Without such a bowl-shaped vessel, the eggs are likely to merely drain away, and the mother's efforts to produce an eggsac are futile (O'Brien 1997).

A female **Aphonopelma chalcodes** *protecting her eggsac.*

If the mother can still be seen, look for an eggsac held by her fangs and pedipalps. If she cannot be seen, wait twelve hours and then carefully cut a small slit through all the webbing. Look for the eggsac. If one is not present, beat a hasty retreat. Don't try to repair any damage that may have been done to the silken wall. The added disturbance may cause her to destroy the eggsac once it is made.

If an eggsac is present and if it is to be incubated apart from the mother, it must be removed very quickly. Unless great pains have been taken to ensure a very high humidity in the cage with the mother, the eggs will desiccate within a few hours. This, of course, is fatal to them.

Removal of the eggsac is best done with the aid of a large spoon to ward off the female's protective efforts and a long pair of forceps or tweezers to reach into her boudoir. (Do you know how to use chopsticks?) Carefully, so as not to hurt the female, reach into the cage with the forceps and attempt to grasp the eggsac by a fold or edge. Be careful not to grasp it across the middle or some of the eggs will be ruptured. This would precipitate a rampant bacterial growth, killing the remaining eggs.

At the same time, try to slide the spoon between her and the eggsac. The spoon will also serve as a shield in case the female becomes too aggressive. She will guard the eggsac adamantly. If she grabs the spoon with her fangs, quickly remove the eggsac with a pair of forceps. Be very cautious not to injure either the female or the eggsac. Keep your fingers clear! Most tarantula bites are harmless, but they can still hurt. It is best not to take the chance.

Life's Little Necessities

Three characteristics are necessary for the development of tarantula eggs, and these must be permitted, if not actively supported.

Humidity

If the eggs are allowed to become too dry, they will shrivel and die. This can happen in a matter of hours. If they are allowed to remain too damp or allowed to get wet, they are attacked by fungi or bacteria and rot. This may happen in less than a day. Thus, more or less precise control of humidity is crucial.

Temperature

In nature, temperature is the one variable that is hardest to control. The developing embryos must be tolerant of varying temperatures or surely perish. But the limits of tolerance differ with different species. The tropical rain- or

The female **Theraphosa blondi** *is brooding her eggsac.*

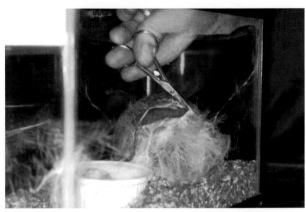

To retrieve the eggsac, the silken barricade is carefully cut away with a pair of scissors.

The mother guarding her eggsac. **Brachypelma smithi.**

moist forest species are perhaps the least at risk in nature because the ambient temperature seldom changes by more than a few degrees. Therefore, they are probably also the least tolerant.

The tarantulas inhabiting more temperate climates must be able to tolerate fairly wide ranges of temperature. Even then, although the developing eggs may be able to tolerate brief episodes of too cool or too warm temperatures, the temperature must moderate toward the ideal within a day or two or the embryos may die. In captivity, tarantulas are kept in homes whose temperatures are thermostatically controlled, often in both summer and winter. This amounts to nearly tropical conditions. However, it turns out that for most species this temperature is too cool for the developing eggs. Therefore, an additional controlled source of heat is required.

Agitation

This last item is unexpected by the novice. When female tarantulas first lay their eggs, the eggs are suspended in a slurry of fluid that resembles fresh, warm tapioca pudding. If they are not rolled around somewhat as they dry, they will remain glued in a solid mass. Those in the center begin to die almost immediately, possibly from asphyxia. Because the clump cannot dry properly, bacterial growth is very rapid, soon killing any of the survivors on the periphery.

If the initial drying is successful, but a bit later in their development the eggs are allowed to lie in a pile too long without being turned over or stirred up, the eggs in the center or at the bottom of the mass will also die. The exact reason for this is still open to conjecture. The fact is that it is a real phenomenon, not just a figment of someone's imagination.

In nature, the female frequently rolls the eggsac around with her fangs and pedipalps, massages it tenderly, and carries it up and down the burrow. This serves to keep the eggs stirred up and moderates temperatures and humidity toward acceptable values.

The Paths to Nirvana

These authors are aware of at least four techniques for caring for tarantula eggs, differing principally in the amount of artificial care they are given. Each has its advantages and disadvantages and will be discussed in turn.

Au Naturel

Many people, particularly novices breeding tarantulas for the first time, merely leave the eggsac with the mother. This method is also used by experienced enthusiasts who wish to allow their mothers to live in a burrow, as well as by those who are studying the mother's brooding behavior.

A high relative humidity (sixty to seventy percent at ambient temperature) is maintained in the cage throughout the entire incubation period. The cages usually are covered so as not to admit much light, or they are kept in rooms that are dimly lit, often cellars or closets. Ambient temperatures are usually maintained quite high; 27°C (80°F) or higher is typical. Preparatory to egg laying, the cages are scrupulously cleaned to reduce fungus and mite infestations to the absolute minimum. And finally, only the keepers enter the room, and then they are cautious to keep disturbances to an absolute minimum. The public is forbidden, lest they provoke the female to destroy the eggsac.

While this method works on occasion, it has a high failure rate because many times the mother eats the eggs, despite all efforts on the keeper's part, or because of a scourge of mites or mold. In the hands of an experienced keeper, this method offers a relatively trouble-free method of allowing the eggs to develop; however, it is almost always unsuccessful in the hands of the novice.

Pedestal Method

The next change from *au naturel* is to remove the eggsac from the female and maintain it separately.

A cage (primitive incubator case) is set up under much the same conditions described above and with a thick layer (two and a half centimeters, one inch) of moist vermiculite or sterilized potting soil on its floor. A plastic shoe box (see page 111) works well. A short, squat jar (e.g., a baby food jar) or a plastic jar lid of suitable size is turned upside down in the center to act as a small pedestal. The eggsac is placed on top of this pedestal, thus preventing contact with the moist substrate. Allowing the eggsac to contact the moist substrate or otherwise get wet surely spells the eggs' death. The incubator case is kept at about 27°C (80°F). Several times a day, the eggsac is turned over in order to loosen and rearrange the eggs inside.

This method removes the eggsac from the female, thus precluding her destroying it. However, since a firm control of temperature and humidity is not maintained, the eggs are still at great jeopardy from being allowed to cool too much, overheat, or develop mite or mold overgrowths. In addition, the necessity of having the keeper constantly turn the eggsac makes this method a bit onerous. If this task is skipped even just once or twice, or if the eggsac is handled roughly enough

to burst some of the eggs, the whole brood is placed in great jeopardy.

While the success rate of this method is higher than *au naturel,* it is still far from ideal.

Over Easy

An additional step towards complete artificial control of incubation of the eggs involves removing the eggs from the eggsac altogether. Pierre Turbang (1993) describes this process in some detail. The eggs are removed from the eggsac and suspended over moist potting soil in a sling of soft cloth stretched over the mouth of a common canning jar.

In another method the eggs are removed to small, plastic condiment cups that are kept in the same sort of brood case as detailed above. Each cup holds three to twelve eggs, depending on their size. On a daily basis, each cup is picked up and the eggs are gently swirled around to mimic the gentle kneading of the mother.

No information is available regarding the success rate of this method. There is no apparent advantage to removing the eggs from the eggsac, and the added manipulation increases the probability of damaging the eggs. The lack of a protective eggsac would also allow more rapid desiccation of the eggs, thus decreasing the probability of success even further. Unless unequivocal evidence of some overwhelming advantage or of a high success rate is forthcoming in the future, these authors would definitely counsel against this practice.

There is one instance when this method must be relied upon. If a female were caught in the act of destroying an eggsac, and apparently viable eggs were evident, this system would constitute the last hope of saving them.

Mechanical Mom

This is the method with which the authors are most familiar, and the one that is most strongly recommended. Using such a full-fledged incubator has resulted in an approximate two-thirds success rate for successfully caring for tarantula eggsacs, higher than that which can be expected from any of the other methods described. It also does not require daily attendance. Only highly experienced or extremely lucky aficionados can boast similar or better success rates with the other methods. From this point forward, it will be assumed that an artificial incubator similar either to the original McKee or the Fostaty/Schultz models will be used. Should one of the other methods be used for caring for the eggs, suitable and appropriate adjustments will have to be made by the enthusiast.

This style of incubator was first devised by Al McKee. Detailed plans for its construction were published in McKee, 1986. Subsequently, Michael Fostaty and the present authors devised alterations and improvements on that original design. Detailed plans

for construction of the Fostaty/Schultz incubator can be found in Schultz and Schultz (in preparation). The reader is referred to both these publications for specific construction details and operating instructions. A photo of an incubator built by the authors is given.

After the female has been bred, an incubator should be constructed in anticipation. The incubator allows precise control of the conditions that are essential for the survival and growth of the developing eggs, and precludes destruction of the eggsac by a high-strung or strung-out mother.

As soon as the incubator is constructed, it should be plugged in and the appropriate adjustments made. These include adjusting the temperature and establishing the necessary humidity. When these are made and verified, the incubator should be allowed to run indefinitely, with weekly checks, until needed. If it were to be turned off, it might require too much time to reset and a valuable eggsac could be lost.

McKee (1986) reports that the ideal humidity for most nondesert species is about sixty percent. The ideal temperature is about 26.7°C (80°F). Rain- or moist forest species may require a slightly higher humidity (e.g., seventy percent) and desert species a slightly higher temperature (28°C, 82°F), but the use of such an incubator has not been widespread enough to allow confirmation of this. These authors have had good success with various species of *Brachypelma* with temperatures between 25.5 and 28°C (78 and 82°F).

The incubation time for tarantulas varies with species and temperature, with higher temperatures reducing the incubation time. This effect is not linear, however. In an incubator, the eggs may

The working mechanism of the McKee/Fostaty/Schultz incubator. Note the eggsacs in the brood cups.

ail to develop entirely if kept below about 25°C (77°F) or above about 32°C (95°F), but even these limits depend on the species. Table XII lists those incubation times that the authors are aware of and the source of the information.

Perinatal Care

Place the eggsac in the incubator. Double-check the water level in the water cup and the temperatures. Close the incubator and throw a party. You are about to become a stepparent to dozens, maybe jillions, of baby spiders!

As soon as an eggsac is in the incubator, start collecting small jars to hold the babies. Any small jar will work, and many tarantula breeders buy plastic pill bottles from pharmacy supply houses for the task.

Baby food jars were first recommended by McKee (1984a) and later by Schultz and Schultz (1997a). They are preferred for terrestrial, burrowing species because they have a more substantial weight and shape, not tending to tip over or roll off a table as easily as light plastic vials. If there are no babies (human babies, that is) in the house, start canvasing the neighborhood for families with infants. At least in the developed nations, the jars are plentiful and free.

For arboreal species, tall narrow jars, either pill vials or the taller-style baby food jars, are recommended because they give the spiderlings a place to hang away from the substrate.

Each spiderling will require its own jar. Each jar should have five or six small (two-millimeter or one-sixteenth-inch) holes punched in its lid. If the lids are plastic, use a fine hot wire or very small nail to melt holes of the appropriate size. It is even possible to make a small tool

with several such wires secured to a heatproof handle. Heat all the wires at once in a broad flame and melt all the holes in a cap at the same time. If the lids are metal, either drill the holes, one by one, or punch them with a very small nail. The inventive enthusiast may be able to improvise a tool with several little nails that will punch several holes at once.

Each bottle should be one-fourth to one-half filled with well-tamped, moist, commercial, sterilized soil of the type used for houseplants. Try to choose a type of soil that purports to be steam-sterilized rather than chemically sterilized. In fact, if there are any suspicions that any pesticides or chemicals have been used in or near the bag of soil, it is best to abandon it and go to another dealer.

The soil should be slightly moist, so that when it is squeezed in the hand it retains its shape. No moisture should be able to be squeezed from it, no matter how hard the hand is pressed.

Many tarantula breeders use horticultural vermiculite. This should be thoroughly moistened, but very well drained. As with potting soil, no water should be able to be squeezed from a handful, no matter how hard the hand is pressed.

Vermiculite remains very loose and unstable. As the baby tarantulas attempt to burrow into it, the burrow walls collapse, burying the spiderlings. This does not seem to hurt them, but makes inspection of the jar and the spiderlings very difficult. Because the spiderlings are the same general color as the vermiculite, they are difficult to inspect among the granules. In the case of a mite infestation, the light-colored mites will not be at all obvious against the light-colored vermiculite, as well.

Table XII
Incubation times for various species of tarantulas.

Species	Incubation Period (Days)	Authority Cited
Aphonopelma caniceps	64	McKee, 1986
Aphonopelma chalcodes	94	Schultz & Schultz
Aphonopelma hentzi	76	McKee, 1986
	56	Baerg, 1958
Aphonopelma seemanni	86	McKee, 1986
Avicularia avicularia	52	McKee, 1986
Brachypelma albopilosum	72	McKee, 1986
	75, 77	Schultz & Schultz
Brachypelma auratum	76	McKee, 1986
Brachypelma emilia	92	Schultz & Schultz
Brachypelma smithi	91	McKee, 1986
	92	Schultz & Schultz
Brachypelma vagans	69	McKee, 1986
Cyclosternum fasciatum	52	McKee, 1986
Eucratoscelus longiceps	25	Rick C. West (verbal)
Phrixotrichus cala	54	McKee, 1986
Phrixotrichus iheringi	67	McKee, 1986

Nominal temperature is 26.7°C (80°F) and sixty percent relative humidity except for *A. hentzi,* as reported by Baerg (1958), which is unknown.

Phrixotrichus cala may in fact be *P. spatulata.* See page 274.

On the other hand, soil looks dirty and weighs more. If hundreds of jars must be dealt with at a time, this weight can be important. Spiderlings will burrow in the soil almost as soon as they are placed on it. When they are very small, spiderlings may not be able to be seen in their burrows, even with the aid of a flashlight (torch), by peering through the jar's wall. A saving grace is that the white or tan mites that occasionally cause infestations in these jars are readily apparent against the dark soil.

How many baby food jars are required? There is no way to tell in advance. The species of *Avicularia* ordinarily produce an eggsac about the size of a walnut that may contain fifty to one hundred and twenty-five eggs. The newly emerged babies ordinarily have one-centimeter (three-eighths-inch) leg spans. A fully grown female of one of the *Brachypelma* species can lay more than one thousand eggs in an eggsac the size of a golf ball. The babies will have three-millimeter (one-eighth-inch) leg spans. *Theraphosa blondi* will produce an eggsac almost the size of a tennis ball but containing only seventy-five to one hundred fifty eggs. The babies have nineteen-millimeter (three-quarters-inch) legs spans as they emerge from the eggsac!

For the first effort, having one-quarter of the eggs develop into spiderlings would be expected. With greater experience and some fine tweaking of the temperature and humidity, a seventy-five percent development rate would not be unreasonable. One jar will be required for each spiderling. But it is better to have too many jars than too many spiderlings. The authors keep about five hundred, cleaned and ready for use, stored for these special occasions. If a particularly large eggsac is produced by a species that is notorious for laying many eggs, this stock is doubled in anticipation.

The Grand Debut

Some advance preparations must be made for the time when the eggsac will be opened. One of the most important items to be procured is something that will act as a corral for the hundreds of baby spiderlings that are anticipated. For the authors, an aquarium laid on its side works best.

In preparation for that magic day, commandeer an empty aquarium of at least a thirty-seven-liter (ten-gallon) capacity, larger if possible. Also very useful are the following: a teaspoon, a large dinner plate or a shallow pie plate, one or more pairs of good-quality forceps, a pair of small, good-quality scissors (nail scissors may work well), several file cards, fine black sewing thread, and a sewing needle. Do not neglect to have several hundred baby food jars or vials with moist potting soil or vermiculite prepared as well.

On the appointed day, first double-check the baby food jars. The addition

The theater in which the eggsac is opened: an aquarium turned on its side.

of a little clean tap water may be required to regain the proper level of moisture. A twenty milliliter hypodermic syringe with a fifteen-gauge needle is helpful for this task.

The OK Corral

The well-cleaned aquarium is laid on its side on a table, with the opening facing the enthusiast. If the babies are ready to emerge and the eggsac is opened, there is usually a stampede of dozens, even hundreds, of baby spiderlings in all directions. The aquarium impedes their escape. It is better than a cardboard box because it allows plenty of light to enter, thus making it easier to see supplies, equipment, and spiderlings. The spiderlings will have greater difficulty climbing the glass walls, and will have no crevices in which to hide. These authors use a desk lamp, outside the aquarium, to illuminate the work area inside. Excellent lighting is essential.

> ***W**arning.* In some political jurisdictions possession of hypodermic syringes is illegal. Read the discussion of "Paraphernalia" on page 161.

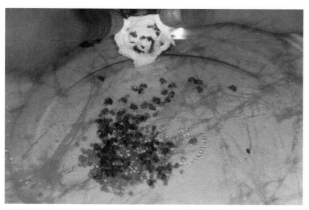

An eggsac a moment after being opened. Brachypelma emilia.

Shallow cardboard boxes, used as trays, with the prepared baby food jars or vials are placed within easy reach. The jars' lids should be removed and stacked nearby. A number of baby food jars, depending on available space, may be put inside the aquarium. The other tools and utensils mentioned earlier are also placed near at hand. Everything should be laid out as in a surgical theater, arranged neatly and in easy reach. Speed and efficiency are paramount to deal with the potential stampede.

Carefully think through the whole process in advance. If the system doesn't work well, there will be little opportunity to regroup and switch to another method.

Hello, World!

Finally, all is set and the eggsac is ready to be opened. Internally, the eggsac is composed of crumpled sheets of silk folded, wrinkled, and rolled

See Chapter 10: Publish! Publish! Publish! for a more complete discussion of getting your discoveries into print.

around each other. The baby tarantulas are scattered throughout this labyrinth.

Place the eggsac on the plate and carefully snip a small slit in its outer wall. Carefully spread the layers of silk, cutting only where necessary. If the spiderlings are colored and actively moving around, it's time for them to meet the world. Cut the eggsac open by carefully snipping part way around its circumference. Be very careful not to cut any of the spiderlings. It is time to stop cutting when the spiderlings begin running in all directions. At that point, the primary objective is to prevent those that are headed toward the open side of the aquarium (toward you) from escaping. Use a file card as a barrier and a scoop to coerce the spiderlings, by hook or by crook, one at a time, back into the corral or into a baby food jar. In the rush, do not neglect to install the lids on the jars. An assistant is most helpful at this juncture.

Hancock and Hancock (1992) recommend doing the transfer in a bathtub. A good light is essential, and be very certain that the drain is plugged.

If the incubation time for the species isn't known, check the eggs at fifty days. If the spiderlings are still white or immobile, carefully stitch the opening closed with the needle and thread, and try again at weekly intervals. When the incubation date has been determined (when the baby spiders are pigmented and actively moving around) it is time to move them to their own baby food jars. Then, be very certain to write a letter to the editor of an appropriate publication (e.g., the American Tarantula Society's *Forum Magazine,* see page 248) describing the details of incubation (i.e., a brief description of the incubator's construction, temperature, and humidity) and the incubation time. You've done a good job and deserve the notoriety.

A Developmental Thing

Lack of space precludes a detailed discussion of spider embryology here. Suffice it to say that the embryology of spiders is as unconventional as the rest of their biology.

During the course of their development, they undergo a type of first molt in which the egg membrane (the chorion) is cast off. Thereafter, they remain in the eggsac for several additional weeks to experience at least one true molt before finally emerging. (Spider development is discussed more fully on page 28.) The emerging of the spiderlings from an eggsac is roughly equivalent to a fledgling bird leaving its nest in the sense that the exact day on which they are released from the eggsac is not critical. The tarantula breeder may be able to open an eggsac a day or two later than recommended with little harm to the spiderlings. It is far more important that the tarantula breeder be prepared for the release of the spiderlings than for the spiderlings to be prepared for their own release.

Feeding

Feeding such small spiders poses some special problems. One of the first questions is "What do you feed them?" For the most part, any small insect might qualify, providing they can be acquired in large enough numbers and can be easily handled. These authors have used two species, house crickets and fruit flies (*Drosophila melanogaster,* Diptera: Drosophilidae).

Jillions of Little Flies! As a first food, common fruit flies are worth considering, but as the spiderlings grow in size they will require something considerably larger. It is possible to use the wild, winged varieties of fruit flies, but only if cohabiting with the hordes that

Newly emerged spiderlings of Avicularia avicularia.

escape isn't a serious problem for either you or your roommate or spouse. The flightless varieties, used in genetics laboratories, are much easier to manipulate. Such laboratories euthanize literally thousands a day, and may give away a starter culture for simply asking. Seek out such laboratories in biology, zoology, genetics, or biochemistry departments in local colleges and universities. Failing that, ask a biology teacher at a local school for permission to thumb through any biological supply catalogues that may be available and order a culture by mail. These same people may be able to demonstrate the techniques required to continue the culture through several generations.

Several strains of these flightless fruit flies are available and are superior to the traditional vestigial-winged

Ordering insects of any species by mail often requires special permits from local, regional, and national agriculture, health, or wildlife authorities. Contact these government agencies well in advance of placing any orders.

strains. The major problem with the vestigial-winged characteristic is that it is lethal to the flies after a few generations. To maintain the fecundity of a culture of vestigial-winged fruit flies they must be out-crossed with wild fruit flies every few generations. This requires experience using an anesthesia jar and ether. Ether is difficult to acquire and store. It is also explosively flammable at room temperature, much more so even than gasoline (petrol). Either procure a different type of flightless fruit fly or plan on frequently returning to the genetics laboratory for replacement cultures.

Besides the toil involved in breeding fruit flies, there is another, nutritional problem. Studies with species of true spiders have shown that fruit flies by themselves are not a complete diet. Baby spiderlings fed nothing but fruit flies will develop deformed legs and suffer great difficulty molting. The aspiring enthusiast is therefore urged not to rely on a steady diet of fruit flies alone for their pet baby tarantula, but rather should use a mix of both fruit flies and very small crickets or other insect food.

Congratulations. You are now in the fruit fly business!

Jillions of Little Crickets! For the remainder of this discussion, it will be assumed that crickets of appropriate sizes are being fed to the spiderlings. Although the same basic rules apply, some improvisation will have to be made if fruit flies or other insects are used instead.

The more the spiderlings are fed, the faster they will grow and the larger they will get. The better fed they are, the sooner they will mature as well. This may be particularly important with the giant varieties (e.g., *Theraphosa blondi*, *Pseudotheraphosa apophysis*, *Lasiodora*

parahybana, *L. klugi*, *Citharischius crawshayi*, *Hysterocrates gigas*, and *H. hercules*) whose exceptional size is highly desirable.

It is clear that the spiderlings should be fed very often. Some enthusiasts do this as often as twice a week, but few of us can afford to spend that much time on them, especially when they number in the hundreds. Perhaps a reasonable compromise would be to feed them every week or ten days. If they are fed once a week, give them three or four crickets. If they are fed less frequently, give them four to six crickets per feeding.

No cricket should be larger than the spiderling's opisthosoma. Acquiring very small crickets for the new spiderlings may not be a simple matter. If crickets are already being purchased from a pet shop or bait dealer, several hundred (several thousand in the authors' case) baby crickets might be special ordered every few weeks. If the enthusiast orders crickets directly from the cricket farm, a wide spectrum of sizes or ages are usually available.

The next problem involves distributing food to all those baby spiderlings. Obviously this will be a very labor-intensive operation. The easiest method that these authors know of employs a large jar, a deep funnel, and a small jar with a tapering neck.

The baby crickets are placed in a holding cage upon arrival, assumed here to be an aquarium. Pieces of the *papiermâché* egg cartons used in their packaging for transport or the cardboard tubes from toilet paper and paper towel rolls are kept with them as a place to hide. Many crickets will climb onto the lower surface of the egg crate or into the cardboard tubes in an attempt to hide. Hold a squat, wide-mouthed jar carefully n one end of the cricket cage, being careful not to crush any of the crickets. Carefully pick up a piece of egg crate and tap it across the mouth of the jar to knock the hiding crickets into it. After enough crickets have been collected in the jar, use a deep funnel to pour the crickets into a smaller bottle for final distribution to the spiderlings.

These authors use a standard one-liter plastic soda pop bottle with the bottom removed, as the funnel. The jar used for final distribution of the baby crickets is a 125- or 250-milliliter Erlenmeyer flask. This particular style of flask has a conical shape that tends to line the baby crickets up single file, making it easier to apportion them to the spiderlings.

To speed the process, one may be tempted to open several baby food jars at a time. Be very cautious. The more open bottles, the greater the probability of the spiderlings' escape.

Watering

As time progresses the bottles will become dry. The speed at which this happens is unpredictable because it depends on ambient relative humidity, temperature, air circulation, the number and size of ventilation holes, and whether the bottles are stacked atop each other so as to block the vent holes, among other things. At first, compare the soil's dampness to a sample of similar soil that has just been prepared for new bottles. If the spiderlings' bottles are significantly drier, add one or two milliliters of water and allow them to set a day. Then compare them again. If the soil in the older bottles is still significantly drier, add a little more water. Repeat if necessary. After the second or third trial, enough experience will have been gained to allow an estimate of the amount of water required without the necessity of experimenting. Check the bottles for water at least every two weeks. In an exceptionally dry climate, check them every week.

Be ever careful that the bottles do not dry out completely. The baby tarantulas have only a very thin cuticle and cannot tolerate desiccation. At the same time, do not allow them to live in an excessively wet environment. In the bottles there is not much air circulation, and mite, fungus, and bacterial outbreaks are a constant menace. Under no circumstances should the soil in these bottles be wet enough to allow any liquid water to be squeezed out of a sample. If a bottle is accidentally over watered, immediately move the spiderling to a new, dryer container.

A handy way of watering large numbers of baby food jars involves the use of a pump. The one that these authors use was purchased at an auto supply store and was originally intended for pumping small quantities of engine oil out of a standard one-liter (one-quart) plastic oil bottle. Presumably, a hand pump intended for liquid hand soap would also work. A one-liter glass bottle was rescued from the recycle bin, cleaned and pressed into service with the pump. Once primed, each stroke of the pump delivers about a teaspoonful of water. When you are looking for such a pump, only purchase one in an unopened package. It must not have been used for anything else beforehand. Once used on any suspect or dangerous substance (even soap), the pump is poisoned forever.

Temperature

Some tarantula breeders place much importance on keeping the spiderlings at higher than room temperatures. Various temperatures have been suggested from 24° to 35°C (75° to 95°F) or higher. There are some disadvantages to this practice. Raising the temperature of an entire room above normal house temperature will also raise the fuel bill. The use of auxiliary electric, gas, or oil heaters increases the risk of fire. Higher ambient temperatures will also cause the spiderlings' jars to dry out faster. This translates directly into more time spent tending to the spiderlings.

For small numbers of spiderlings, construct a brood case (see page 201). For really huge numbers of baby tarantulas, devise a means for safely heating a closet or even an entire room.

Keeping the spiderlings at elevated temperatures would have the advantage that they would grow faster and be marketable or breedable sooner. For the casual fancier, however, maintaining the spiderlings at a higher temperature is probably more trouble and expense than it is worth. Experience has shown that the spiderlings will do quite nicely at room temperature, nominally 22°C (72°F). Some North American homes and many European homes are kept cooler than this during the winter months. If the home temperature drops below 20°C (68°F) some provision should be made to maintain the spiderlings at a somewhat higher temperature.

Alternatively

Dormitory Living. To reduce the amount of labor involved, the authors have adopted a different practice for the initial care of the spiderlings on the advice of several other tarantula breeders. Instead of placing each spiderling in its own baby food jar immediately upon emerging, they are placed, *en masse,* in one or more four-liter (one-gallon) glass pickle jars. These are available for free, or for a very small sum, from restaurants, delicatessens and cafeterias. Glass is almost a necessity, as opposed to translucent plastic to allow easy examination of the spiderlings without opening the jar.

Put moist potting soil in the bottom of the jar and tamp it firmly. Vermiculite will also work, but can not be tamped well. The final depth should be between two and three centimeters (about one inch). Some tarantula breeders also put a handful of moistened, coarse moss into the jar to provide additional hiding places. This may be particularly important if the brood numbers more than two hundred spiderlings.

Each jar may either be kept covered with several layers of nylon mesh held with rubber bands (elastics), or the original metal or plastic lid may have a large hole cut in it and covered securely with fine screening, or the lid may have several dozen very small holes melted or drilled through it.

The spiderlings of some species can be very fast runners, and one problem that may be encountered is that a few will always try to make a break for freedom every time the lid is removed. This can be thwarted by smearing a ribbon of petrolatum (petroleum jelly) around the inside of the bottle's mouth. This ribbon should be at least as wide as the spiderling's leg span. The spiderlings cannot cross it, but are strong enough to free themselves if they make contact with it. This method is not without its risks, however. If the petrolatum covers or enters the book lungs, the spiderlings could suffocate. Not enough experience has been gained with this method to assess the danger.

The baby tarantulas are all put in this jar together for the first three to five weeks, making their care much easier. The secret to success is copious feeding with baby crickets or fruit flies to prevent cannibalism.

Virtually all spiderlings from a given eggsac will molt within forty-eight hours of each other for the first several molts. If left together too long in a communal jar, those who molt too soon may be eaten by those who have yet to begin, and those who lag too far behind are eaten by the first ones to molt as they recover.

At other times, those spiderlings that are cannibalized by their siblings are presumed to be the weaker ones and therefore would have likely died eventually anyway. Practice has shown that losses due to cannibalism are minimal during these first few weeks.

Magic Dancers. Ordinarily, the spiderlings arrange themselves around the jar, on the walls, the floor, and in the moss, equidistant from their neighbors, in an effort to maximize the distance between them. They have an instinctive behavior pattern that prevents them from being eaten by their litter mates. When they make contact with each other, they perform a peculiar little dancelike maneuver with their pedipalps and forelegs, fending off the other individual without harm to either. This instinct is well known in their true spider brethren (Araneomorphae) (Foelix 1982), but the authors are unaware of it being reported for theraphosids before this.

Mass Mess Hall. The primary reason for keeping baby tarantulas in a communal setting is to reduce, for a time, the labor involved in feeding them. If they are kept together in large jars, baby crickets do not have to be given to each spiderling separately.

To feed the horde, a piece of egg carton or cardboard tube is carefully removed from the crickets' holding cage (see page 222), held over the pickle jar, and tapped gently. Several hundred baby crickets will fall into the jar with several hundred baby tarantulas.

The result is chaos. As the spiderlings and the crickets dash around in hot pursuit or dead flight, the spiderlings bump into each other and immediately take defensive action. The resulting pandemonium could be an arachnophobe's nightmare! Within a few minutes, however, the spiderlings will have their chelicerae full of crickets and the jar settles into a peaceful banquet.

If the spiderlings are kept copiously fed, they seldom attempt to prey on their litter mates, and their social etiquette is maintained for several weeks. The authors have witnessed spiderlings of *Phormictopus cancerides* with a leg span of nearly two centimeters (three-quarters inch) living more or less in harmony. This obviously eases the burden of being a stepparent to hundreds of tarantulas. Be forewarned. If they fail to be fed even one day, one-half of the brood may eat the other!

If it is suspected that the spiderlings are beginning to attack and eat each other, or by five weeks of age at the absolute latest, the spiderlings should be removed from the community jar to their individual containers to prevent rampant cannibalism. By this time, several to many of them will have started to burrow. Be very careful not to inadvertently throw them away. Meticulously sift through the substrate for these little troglodytes.

Communal Living. Again, the arboreal species prove to be an exception to the general rule. Many breeders report that these species' spiderlings will cohabit in containers like pickle jars and other confined quarters for excessive lengths of time without cannibalism. *Poecilotheria* and *Avicularia* babies are reported to live and grow together for months, sometimes reaching leg spans in excess of five centimeters (two inches) before there are any fatal conflicts, providing they are kept very well fed. While these authors do not approve of communal living for any species of tarantula, the enthusiast with limited resources might use this tactic to buy more time for acquiring proper, individual housing.

Growth Rates

How long do the spiderlings have to be kept before they begin to look like tarantulas? How long must one wait for them to mature? How big will they ultimately get? At least two variables are known to affect the growth and maturation rates of tarantulas: feeding and temperature.

Feeding. Maturation times, at least for males, can be delayed several months to a year or two by not feeding them to the maximum (Baerg 1958; McKee 1986; Baxter 1993). Thus, if the aspiring tarantula breeder has spiderlings of a rare species with little or no prospect of finding additional males for breeding, the males can be fed significantly less than their sisters, delaying their maturation until the females are mature. The devil must take its due, however. Underfed males do not grow as large as well-fed ones and may not be as vigorous. Slightly malnourished males may mature when needed but either be too small to handle their mates or sterile.

The techniques for determining the sex of a tarantula well in advance of its maturation are discussed on page 194.

On the other hand, tarantulas can be induced to mature more quickly by power feeding. Power feeding is defined as the practice of feeding the tarantulas as much as they can consume. If a few crickets are kept in the cage with them at all times so that they may eat whenever hungry, the tarantulas may mature several months to several years earlier than expected. At the same time, they will be much larger and more vigorous.

Temperature. Maturation times can be delayed several months to several years by keeping the spiderlings at slightly lower temperatures than normal. Two or three degrees can have a profound effect over a period of three to ten years. The devil's due is that they will have to be maintained months to years longer than ordinary before they can be bred, increasing the amount of time, money, and effort spent on them.

Optimal Strategy. Depending on the rarity of the species and the resources of the enthusiast, some number of spiderlings should be kept until at least their sixth molt. For common species, a dozen might be suggested. For rarer species, several dozen is recommended. At that age their exuvia should be examined to determine each one's sex.

If there is no question that unlimited numbers of unrelated males and females of any given species will be available for the indefinite future, it will not be necessary to maintain an excessively large breeding stock.

If, on the other hand, the supply of breeders is unpredictable in the long run, the aspiring tarantula breeder will have to be more conservative.

First, cull out any with defects. Thereafter, as soon as possible, determine the remaining spiderlings' sex. To retard development and maturation, one-half to two-thirds of the males should be kept two or three degrees centigrade cooler than normal. The remainder might be kept in normal temperatures so that they mature more or less on schedule. At the same time, two-thirds of the females might be kept two or three degrees centigrade warmer, perhaps in a separate brood case, to accelerate their maturation. The remaining females would be allowed to develop normally. This strategy will almost ensure that the majority of females will mature before their brood mates.

If the probability of acquiring breeders in the future is nonexistent, an extreme strategy is required. Examples of this situation might be where the tarantula breeder possesses the last few surviving members of a species in captivity, or if the enthusiast were unbelievably fortunate enough to acquire, as a wild-caught specimen, one female of a very rare species that produced an eggsac. The tarantula breeder might eventually possess two hundred of the only individuals of this species in captivity. (The authors know of at least one instance when this happened!) Now, what does one do? If they are cared for normally, the males will all mature one or two years before the females. Although they may mate with their sisters, no offspring will be produced because the females are still immature.

The recommended strategy is to identify and separate nearly all of the males and keep them cool. Only a few should be kept at normal temperatures. (One should avoid putting all of one's eggs in one basket!)

Similarly, nearly all of the females should be kept warmer than normal. If only a few individuals are available instead of dozens, all of the males should be kept cool, and the females warm.

In all cases where the future availability of breeder tarantulas is questionable, the strategy is to retard the development and maturation of some proportion of the males, and accelerate the development and maturation of some proportion of the females. As the number of available breeding tarantulas becomes smaller, the larger must be the proportion of individuals that will have their developmental times retarded or accelerated. Decreasing numbers of potential breeders decrease the probability of success and extra efforts must be made to diminish that decrease as much as possible. In extreme situations, the aspiring tarantula breeder may have to modify the developmental rates of all individuals, like it or not.

If members of the same species become available while this is being done, the brood mates should not be interbred. Crossbreed the unrelated stock instead. If no unrelated stock becomes available, and none will be available in the foreseeable future, inbreeding must be accepted over guaranteed extinction as the lesser of two evils.

As They Grow

Eventually the spiderlings must be moved to larger quarters. A good rule of thumb is to compare their leg spans to the smallest horizontal dimension of their container. When they can reach halfway across, it is time to move them to a larger dwelling. A representative progression might be pill bottles or baby food jars, then one-half-liter jars, two-liter jars, and finally adult housing. A thorough discussion of caging begins on page 108.

As the spiderlings grow, they will require larger crickets for food. If commercially bred crickets are being used, this will merely involve ordering larger sizes as time progresses. If home-grown crickets are being used, this will entail setting up a full-scale cricket-ranching operation. If at all possible, it will be much more convenient, if not more economical, to have crickets shipped in from commercial sources. Speak with local pet shops or fish bait dealers about the possibility of special ordering the crickets that you require for your pets.

If you find yourself consuming 500 or more crickets every two weeks, you would be well advised to either negotiate more reasonable fees for the crickets from the dealers, or ordering them direct from the cricket farm. You can find the names and addresses of the major cricket farms accessible to you by speaking to members of amateur arachnological and herpetological societies (see page 248) or by looking for advertisements in amateur arachnologist and herpetologist publications.

Spreading the Seed

Any spiderlings with defects, however small or seemingly inconsequential, should be culled from the breeding stock and either sold strictly as pets or summarily destroyed. Any babies to be kept as breeders should be kept in a controlled environment case or room and fed as much as they will consume. The successful tarantula breeder is advised to keep only a few dozen of the spiderlings, distributing the remainder to other enthusiasts, local pet shops, or dealers. This has the affect of scattering the spiderlings to many places, increasing the probability that at least a few will be acquired by other enthusiast breeders, thus continuing the genetic line.

Other enthusiasts can be found by frequent haunting of local pet shops that stock tarantulas, through local amateur herpetological societies (herp club members often keep tarantulas, too), by advertising in local newspapers and bargain-finder-type publications, or through the Internet and World Wide Web (see page 249). Dealers can be located by perusing magazines intended for amateur herpetologists as well as the newsletters of amateur herpetology and arachnology clubs and societies.

Just for the Record

Hot Dates. Keep an accurate, detailed log of each mating, successful or not. These records should include the identity of the pair, the date, exactly how they were set up, what you did, how they reacted, what they did, how you reacted, and all the time spans involved, any unusual circumstances or occurrences and a complete description of the event if possible. The more information recorded, the better. These notes will be invaluable in years to come, as other attempts are made at breeding tarantulas. We don't know enough details of the mating habits of the various species except to suspect that they do differ. Such records are our only evidence that they do.

If possible, photograph and time the entire spectacle. The enthusiast who is lucky enough to own or borrow a video camera might tape the entire sequence, complete with recorded comments. Such a tape library will become an invaluable resource as time progresses, as well as an indispensable help to other enthusiasts. With good-quality equipment, professional-level photography, and proper editing, there is always a potential for a commercial application as well.

Prenatal Records. When an eggsac is produced, keep accurate, detailed records of its history. The minimum should include the identity of parents, the dates on which they mated, the date the eggs were laid, how you cared for them (e.g, *au naturel* or in an incubator, at what temperature and humidity), the date on which the eggsac was opened, and an estimate of the total number of eggs produced and the number of eggs that developed. Also keep a record of the number of spiderlings that died. Include any clues to the cause of death.

Vital Statistics. For several individuals, also record molting dates; what, how much, and how often they eat; and their cage or room temperatures. Photograph them against a ruler and weigh them with a sensitive balance after each molt, before they begin to eat again. Such balances may be found in nearly all high school and college chemistry and biology labs. Many of the teachers, professors, or their assistants would be glad to help or demonstrate their use. Keep a complete set of labeled and dated cast skins, correlated with the written data. These data will comprise a continuous record of the growth and development of a set of individuals and can be of great value to anyone who seeks clues to the growth or developmental rates of each species.

Keep in Touch. A record should be kept of as many enthusiasts as possible who receive the extra spiderlings. Attempts to breed your stock or theirs should be made at every opportunity (but beware of inbreeding).

The Scourge

On one occasion, these authors had three broods of tarantulas, totaling almost a thousand, in plastic vials. In keeping with the practice of the day, the vials were loosely filled with sphagnum moss and were kept very moist.

Coincidentally, a shipment of adult tarantulas was received from a dealer. When they arrived, a number of small brown flies, resembling fruit flies *(Drosophila melanogaster),* arrived in the shipping containers with them. The adult tarantulas were unpacked and placed in their respective cages. No particular attention was given the flies.

A week later, in the coarse of feeding the spiderlings, an abundance of fly larvae were noticed in the vials, and an inordinate number of spiderlings had disappeared. Within another two days, before clean empty vials could be set up and the spiderlings moved, all but about one hundred spiderlings had been killed by the fly larvae. Those spiderlings that were kept in drier vials survived. The more moist vials allowed the fly larvae to thrive and kill the spiderlings.

The flies and their larvae were also seen to infest dead and dying crickets, both in the crickets' holding cage and in the tarantulas' cages.

Now we are much wiser. Spiderlings are kept on moist potting soil, not wet moss. Although not absolutely dry, their bottles are kept only slightly moist and checked often, both for moisture and fly larvae. For the last several years no such flies have been seen in the authors' collection.

Subsequently, these flies were identified as belonging to the family Phoridae, and have been reported by other enthusiasts as well (Marshall 1996).

It may be argued that this was a peculiar, even unique event, hardly worth mentioning. However, these authors have received several additional shipments of tarantulas from different dealers over the years that were infested with the same flies. In fact, in some dealers' warehouses, adult tarantulas were found that were being eaten alive by the flies' maggots. Furthermore, a friend of the authors who collects and breeds *Theraphosa blondi* reports that virtually every individual that he receives through the pet industry is infested with phorid flies and must be picked over very carefully to remove the maggots. He also reports that as many as one in five or six die within a few days of receipt because their infestation has progressed beyond hope with the maggots infesting the tarantulas' internal organs. Clearly, this is a problem of great gravity, especially when the tarantulas in question are as expensive as *T. blondi*.

Because dealers often trade stock and sometimes order cooperatively to gain a price advantage, the probability is high that they will also, sooner or later, also inadvertently trade starter cultures of these carnivorous flies. Thus, phorid flies represent a distinct, continuing threat to the tarantula-breeding hobby and business.

Unpack all newly acquired tarantulas in a building that is separate from your main collection of tarantulas. If the containers are transparent, inspect the tarantulas before opening them for signs of eggs or maggots among the bristles near the pedicel, median fovea, or leg bases. Inspect the containers for signs of small flies or maggots. Only after the tarantulas are certified free of them should they be brought into the same building as the main collection.

If at any time small brown flies resembling fruit flies are noticed around the collection, and especially if small fly maggots are seen in the vials or bottles with the spiderlings or on dead or dying crickets, immediate action is required. Clean each cage, bottle, and vial to remove all traces of dead crickets and other detritus. Immediately move all tarantulas, especially the spiderlings, into cleaner, drier quarters.

Now might also be a good time to order a starter culture of predatory mites. See page 230.

Thereafter, inspect daily all tarantulas in the collection for eggs or maggots among the tarantulas' bristles, near the pedicel, the median fovea, and the bases of the legs. Remove them carefully with a fine-tipped artist's brush dipped in mild soap water, or gently scrape them off with the blade of a small knife. (Need we say "Be careful not to cut the tarantula?") Be careful. The tarantula will not appreciate such abuse and may lose patience with your ministrations. Do not be alarmed by this. The family dog will bite if teased too much as well.

Remarks

For the casual fancier this chapter is offered merely as a means of quenching one's curiosity. For the serious enthusiast, it represents the greatest and most important challenge: to establish a successful, long-term captive-breeding program for these remarkable creatures. Such a program would have many benefits. It will ease the collecting pressures on the natural populations. It will likely save very rare species from extinction. It will increase the availability of these most interesting pets to other enthusiasts around the world. The complete breeding habits of another species of tarantula will be known, and another part of the mystery of these incredible creatures will be solved.

The individual tarantulas in any enthusiast's collection are not merely pets. They must be viewed as priceless, irreplaceable treasures. There are currently so few people in the world who are actually breeding tarantulas that the total captive-breeding population of a rare species may be wiped out by one disaster, a fire or flood, for instance. Although many of the tarantulas in an enthusiast's collection may be common and relatively inexpensive today, in ten or twelve years, as the older individuals die, as political winds change, or as natural or human-made catastrophes hit their homeland, only three or four people in the world could have the only surviving breeding members of the species. This is not so far-fetched as it sounds; it has happened time and again with other species. Sadly, it may happen with tarantulas as well.

PART THREE
The Cause

These creatures and our hobby are under siege and in grave peril. The threat assaults tarantulas and us from at least four directions.

The giant spiders that we prize so highly are in danger of being driven to extinction by the sheer press of humanity.

Our ignorance of these creatures is staggering. All through this book we have pointed out shortcomings in our understanding of their natural history. We aren't even certain how many kinds there really are.

We are so poorly organized as a community that we are totally unable to voice an argument on our behalf or on the behalf of the spiders that we prize so highly.

Lastly, those of us who do learn some little detail of a tarantula's natural history, one that no one else has ever recorded, are frequently unwilling to tell the world for fear of appearing foolish or just for fear alone.

Chapter Eight
Ravaging the Planet

Their Peril

It is a pity that after almost 400 million years of evolving and surviving holocausts and natural disasters whose nature we can only guess, many kinds of tarantulas are now in imminent danger of being wiped off this planet by only one other species. This other species is not a predator, a pathogen, or even a direct competitor. This other species is merely indifferent.

This other species is *Homo sapiens,* the human race.

Humankind's attack against nature continues unabated in spite of all efforts by government agencies and conservation groups. The result is that species of plants and animals are being exterminated from our planet at the rate of thousands per year. Indeed, the current rate at which species are vanishing has prompted biologists to call this extermination the greatest mass extinction of all time! Tarantulas are not escaping this massacre.

The irony is that the very species that is threatening their survival may also hold the key to their survival. In all the history of this planet, this state of affairs has never before existed. It is hoped that the information presented in this book will help the casual fancier to care for these animals well enough to prompt attempts to breed them, for only in such captive-breeding attempts can many species of tarantulas survive the onslaught of extinction.

Serious Attitude Problem

Everything that we do is tainted with our humanity. Western civilization has, as a built-in feature direct from the factory, a spoiled brat ethnocentricity that is nothing short of astounding. We view everything on planet Earth as belonging to us. As pointed out by J. A. Livingston (1981), the very practice of considering all of nature a *resource* carries the connotation that it is a possession of the human race to manage, to use, to exploit, to abuse, to squander, to destroy. Nothing could be further from the truth. The human race is a product of the vast biological system that we call Mother Nature, a subpart of it, not its overseer. We are very much in the position of the impudent child attempting to domineer its parents. The tail is wagging the dog.

With its newfound intelligence and technology, the human race has found itself with the power of minor gods. Unfortunately, these *nouveau dieu,* like the *nouveau riche,* have no genetic proclivity, no training, no experience, and not a shred of the common sense required to wisely use all this power. Like a spoiled kid with a box of dynamite, it is an even bet which we shall do first, blow ourselves to smithereens or die a ghastly death as we level the house around us. The absolute worst part of this whole scenario is that all but a few of us fail abysmally to appreciate this basic fault in our cultural character.

Beware, Civilization Ahead

Civilization as we practice it is the primary instrument of destruction. The demands of civilization, like a starving dragon, gulp as much of these natural resources as possible and corrupt whatever is left to foil any return, recovery, or reuse by the original or future occupants.

No plant or animal on earth is capable of surviving the onslaught of these new gods. Not the least of these are tarantulas. All too commonly, the habitat that tarantulas require is thoughtlessly squandered or obliterated by humans, and any tarantulas that survive are sprayed with pesticides or merely squashed under a boot when found.

Agricultural Nemesis

Agriculture is responsible for most of the damage and it attacks on two fronts. The first front involves one of agriculture's most basic attributes: the plowed field. The Achilles' heels for tarantulas are the great length of their life cycles and their need for a long-term, stable home. It is impossible for a colony of tarantulas to establish itself in a field that is often tilled. Once a colony is seriously molested, it will require years, perhaps decades, to recover, if ever. Being plowed under spells certain death for both the individual tarantula and the colony.

Rampant poisoning comprises the other front in agriculture's war on wildlife. The reckless abandon that humankind displays in spraying its environment with pesticides is nothing short of criminal. Agriculturists overuse pesticides to increase crop yields with little or no thought about long-term or global repercussions. Even if a plot of land is allowed to lie fallow, it may be hopelessly poisoned for decades to any animals, tarantulas included, who must live intimately with the soil.

Urban Chaos

Urbanization is the other major offensive thrust. Realistically, no suburbanite or apartment dweller is going to willingly cohabit with a colony of giant hairy spiders (in spite of this book), and tarantulas would find the task of setting up housekeeping in a shopping center parking lot impossible.

As an example, consider the fate of a colony of tarantulas on the south side of Dallas, Texas. In the spring of 1983, the authors collected a few individuals from a colony on the upper margin of the flood plain on the south side of the Trinity River. Within the next two years a developer had deposited a ten-meter (thirty-three-foot) thick layer of dirt on the site and erected a condominium complex. Civilization struck that colony very hard indeed. At the time of this writing, the three individuals in the authors' collection are probably the sole surviving members of that colony!

Getting the Wrong Impression

In many locales, tarantulas appear quite numerous and in little danger. However, this impression may be based on the laity's casual observation of wandering males. These observations are imprecise and extremely misleading. Attempts are seldom made to keep an accurate count of the number of individuals sighted, and the unenlightened are sure to exaggerate the numbers for the sake of drama. We lack reliable quantitative data.

Because of the appalling state of tarantula taxonomy, no serious attempt can be made to identify the species sighted, except by experienced professionals. Such experts are rare indeed and their time and resources stretched to the limit. Thus we have little or no qualitative data.

The males are notorious for wandering many kilometers, and the exact position of the colony is almost surely not where the males were found. Thus, any data about the presence of a population of tarantulas in any region may not be representative. What data we do have is probably misleading. Mother Nature often throws us a red herring!

Lastly, little correlative data exists that would indicate which species are common and which are endangered in any given area, and any data that does exist may be decades out of date.

For the nominal species of North America (variously estimated from twelve to forty), there are no reliable maps or range records to give trustworthy distribution data, and we certainly have no real idea of how common or rare any individual species really is. Without rigorous scientific data, the abundance of one species may mask the peril of another, and a major disturbance of one or two colonies might have little overall effect on the common species but could decimate a rare one.

Exploitation

Exploitation is not a dirty word!

The pet industry is responsible for the capture of literally tens of thousands of tarantulas per year (Browning 1981). If this collecting were done with discretion, the wild populations could easily survive. We have learned to harvest and manage deer, waterfowl, and fish populations, for example, to actually increase their numbers. It is easily conceivable that the same could be done with selected populations of tarantulas.

The Bad News

The tragedy of the situation is that the collectors are usually unsophisticated folk who, because they are living in extreme poverty, must use any and every means at their disposal to maintain life, however meager. Such is the case of *Brachypelma smithi,* for example. As late as 1985 this handsome species was *the* pet tarantula to own. Now it is on a *Convention on International Trade in Endangered Species of Flora and Fauna* (CITES) list (see page 240). Adults are only rarely available and prohibitively expensive, and even though captive-bred spiderlings are readily available, they are costly.

The problem was not so much a matter of the numbers that were exported, though they were significant. The problem was that the peasants catching them took no care to maintain the habitat. Now, large tracts of land are not only devoid of these noble tarantulas, but that land is pitted with the excavations of their burrows and their habitat is literally washing away with every storm. In many areas where it was once

Puzzled by scientific names? Read Chapter 2: The Name of the Tarantula and Appendix A: Tarantula Species as Pets for explanations and a cross-reference between scientific names and common names.

common, there is little hope that the wild population will ever recover.

The Good News

A few farsighted enthusiasts have managed to accumulate a number of adult *B. smithi* and have succeeded in breeding them in captivity. Babies are now available in the pet industry. With any luck, the wild population may be saved by the current restrictions and the fancier will still be able to acquire this queen of the tarantulas as spiderlings.

Droughts and the Road Crew

The authors have been taking part in an unofficial and clearly unscientific observation of the effects of collection of tarantulas from several parts of western Texas. For a period of twelve years they have been collecting tarantulas persistently from several well-defined areas. The number collected varies but amounts to a total of approximately seventy-five to one hundred tarantulas per year of at least two species. In addition, the authors are aware of at least one other collector who takes an additional two to four dozen at intervals of two or three years from the same areas.

During that ten-year period, the greatest single cause of reduction of individuals in these colonies seems to have been a severe drought, exactly as one would expect. However, as the drought ended and moisture once again became available, all but one of the surviving colonies have gradually recovered in size and population, in spite of the pressures of arguably heavy collecting. The one colony that totally disappeared was destroyed when road crews overhauled a roadside rest area. Collecting had nothing to do with the colony's extermination. Civilization struck again!

There are a number of messages to be gained from all this. First, habitat destruction is absolutely the most important threat to the survival of tarantulas. Without a secure place to live, all else is hopeless. Second, the colonies can withstand continued losses (e.g., by predation, natural disaster, collection) over long periods. If the losses are not too great, they pose no threat to the colonies. Even if these pressures become extreme for a brief time, the colonies will recover once the pressures are eased or removed, provided the colonies are not totally obliterated. Lastly, continued collection, done at appropriately controlled levels, and using environmentally sound techniques, does not significantly endanger a colony or a species.

The "E" Word, Again

Thus, we work our way around to the word *exploitation*. The authors were exploiting the animals, pure and simple. Was this necessarily bad? Probably not. In this case, the species collected were not threatened or endangered, and only limited numbers of individuals were taken. Those that were taken were flooded from their burrows, not dug. Thus, their habitat was not jeopardized. Taking them from the wild did not threaten the natural populations. In fact, the three individuals from the site in Dallas would not be alive today if it were not for such collection.

"What good did it do to collect them?" you demand. It helped to foster an interest in these fascinating animals. It helped a large number of people in this world understand and appreciate an animal that is radically different from a goldfish or the family dog, and one that is much more poorly understood. Only through such exposure will the true value of these fascinating animals be realized by the public. Only after they are understood and appreciated can we gain public support for saving the individuals left in the wild.

"What defense have you for the exploitation of those species that live in the forests of South America, Borneo, Sri Lanka, or the Caribbean islands where habitat is being ripped up at a rate of forty hectares (one hundred acres) per minute?" Our defense is quite simple. The enthusiast-fancier is the only hope that these creatures have. To depend on political pressure or economic aid to stem the tide of habitat destruction is to delude ourselves (Livingston 1981). To date, these strategies have proven to be absolutely worthless. Those efforts are forty hectares and two species per minute too little and too late. Leaving these animals in their habitat condemns each of them to death and guarantees their species' extinction.

Mind you, this is not an excuse for wanton, wholesale collecting. But a controlled exploitation may very likely be their only real hope for survival. We have proven that we can breed many tarantulas in captivity. After nearly four hundred million years, it would be immoral, even criminal, to forbid them this last chance for survival.

Historical Perspective

Historically, exploitation of many species of wild animals has led to both the species' survival and enrichment of the human condition. One must only recite the list of domesticated animals to prove the point. There are many other less-obvious animals whose numbers we have increased markedly in captivity, if not saved outright from extinction, merely as a result of exploitation. The list

is too long to recite here in its entirety but includes the Argentine Pearlfish, the Syrian Golden Hamster, the common Canary, the Guinea Pig, the Mongolian Gerbil, the Andean Chinchilla, and the Burmese/Indian Python. There is a fascinating story behind each of these, stories that, for lack of space, cannot be recounted here.

Exploitation coupled with the enthusiast's passion is very likely the only real hope for survival that many small animals have in the face of civilization's onslaught. To ignore or suppress this means for species conservation or salvation is ludicrous.

The Plan

Probably the best solution would be a four-pronged management effort. First, fund the necessary research to develop the data needed for intelligent decision-making.

Second, identify colonies of remarkable character and establish preserves to protect them. Realistically, this would only be possible if done ancillary to other, higher-profile wildlife interests.

Third, rigorously control, but not prohibit, the collection of tarantulas from those areas where unique or rare species are found. In extreme cases, limit collecting to people who have proven themselves proficient in breeding tarantulas. From those areas where tarantulas are plentiful, more liberal collection quotas should be established to allow limited exploitation without seriously endangering the wild population.

Fourth, actively promote the captive breeding of these animals, especially the rarer varieties, by enthusiasts. Thus, private industry could maintain its market, enthusiasts could acquire and keep their pets, and collecting pressures on the wild populations would be eased.

An added bonus is the possibility of reintroducing captive-bred individuals to habitats from which the species was originally exterminated. This, of course, assumes that their habitat still exists at all. This has been done with elk in Michigan, for instance.

The enthusiast can have a significant part in this. By actively seeking the appropriate legislation, a continued supply of pets for our hobby can be ensured while still protecting a valuable wildlife resource.

In addition, a concerted effort should be made by enthusiasts to discover the tricks required to breed these animals in captivity. Without doubt, a captive-breeding population of the rarer species would remove the pressures of collection from the wild populations. As pointed out above, more than one species of animal has been saved from extinction by this principle.

Lastly, all information that enthusiasts and professionals alike discover or develop should be freely disseminated.

An Admission of Abject Ignorance

A persistent theme throughout this book has been that we know far too little about tarantulas. Only a handful of people have ever really studied them and very little of the information gathered so far has been corroborated by other researchers. What we do know only leads us to ask more questions. If we continue to exterminate our wildlife

> Chapter 10: Publish! Publish! Publish! contains a detailed discussion of ways to get your ideas and experiences into print for the rest of us to read.

heritage at its current rate, we may never know what questions we might have asked, much less discover their answers.

Although hundreds of theraphosids have been scientifically described, only a dozen or so species have been intensely studied. All that we have for the others are poor to nonexistent physical descriptions and equally poor to nonexistent collection data. Their phylogenetic relationships and taxonomy are so poorly known and so confused that no one is even certain how many species there are.

Until quite recently, no one had made a concerted effort to publish a comprehensive listing and key to the genera and species of tarantulas, using rigorous, modern standards. Smith (1985, 1990, 1992, and 1995) is attempting that feat, but as this book goes to press the correctness of his effort remains to be substantiated or its completeness confirmed.

Regardless of the final outcome, Andrew Smith must be commended for his effort. He is treading where no one else has dared.

Convention on International Trade in Endangered Species

Of all the things that have been done to halt the current great extinction, this international treaty has probably had the greatest effect. Praised by some, damned by others, no one denies that it has worked a profound change in the way that the human race conducts international trade in wildlife. Because of its importance, and because few understand it, we take the time to briefly discuss it here.

The environmentalist fad of the 1960s bore fruit in 1973 with the creation of a treaty entitled *The Convention on International Trade in Endangered Species of Wild Flora and Fauna,* otherwise known by its acronym *CITES* (pronounced *SIGHT-ease*). It took force in 1975. Today, there are approximately ninety-five countries, or *States* as they are termed in the treaty, who have signed this treaty, thereby agreeing to support and enforce its provisions. In this treaty, these member States are termed *Parties* to the convention. The fundamental concept of CITES is to control or protect from international trade any organisms that were threatened or endangered in any of the signing countries. Both the living organisms and any readily identifiable parts are covered by the treaty.

CITES established three appendices or lists of organisms. Each list affords a different level of protection to the organisms listed on it, with Appendix I being the most strongly protected. Appendix I lists those organisms that are currently threatened with imminent extinction and are affected by international trade or are likely to be so affected.

Appendix II, on the other hand, lists plants and animals that are not currently threatened with imminent extinction, but for which there is some evidence that they might be in danger if international trade is not curtailed. Furthermore, these organisms must currently be a part of international commerce or there must be a likelihood that they will become part of that commerce. Lastly, there should be some evidence that such trade, real or anticipated, will be great enough to pose a significant threat to the organism's survival.

Appendix III lists those organisms that are restricted or protected from exploitation in individual countries and for which international cooperation is required in order to make such protection effective, but do not qualify for either Appendix I or Appendix II.

A committee composed of representatives of the member States, termed a *Conference of the Parties,* meets every odd-numbered year to review the implementation of the treaty and consider amendments to it, as well as status changes of the organisms listed in the appendices. These status changes may include listings (additions), delistings (removal from all lists), uplistings (changes to a list of higher protection, e.g., from Appendix III to Appendix II), or downlistings (the reverse of uplistings).

An organism may only be proposed for listing or a status change by a member Party, and only if it is native to that member Party's country. The proposed amendments to Appendices I and II must go before a Conference of the Parties during a regular biennial meeting. If sufficient evidence is presented to justify the change, the proposal is adopted. Thereafter, the world has ninety days to be informed and prepare to take the appropriate action to enforce the provisions of the treaty.

Appendix III is an exception to this process. Amendments to this list must still be performed by member Parties but are not reviewed and approved by the Conference of the Parties. While there are controlling guidelines, listings and delistings are entirely the prerogative of the proposing country.

The Good News

Of all the treaties ever signed, of all the laws ever enacted to protect threatened and endangered species, CITES is probably the most effective. Numerous statistics are quoted to verify the impact of CITES (World Wildlife Fund 1986, Hemley 1988, and Favre 1989). Any of those people who deal in the international trade in animals or animal products will agree that, for good or for bad, CITES has dramatically reduced the number of the protected species that are shipped around the world.

CITES, because of the scope of interests that its founders represented, is a very flexible instrument for protecting wildlife in international trade. Provisions were incorporated to allow amendments to its structure, exceptions to its provisions, and frequent modifications and updates of its lists. As a result, it is capable of reacting to changes in the condition of any covered organism or any organism that should be covered, the international wildlife trade, and political and socioeconomic conditions of its member Parties.

A large portion of it deals with the captive breeding of threatened and endangered organisms and under what circumstances these may be transported through international commerce for the purposes of exploitation or reproduction.

To date, the implementation of CITES has tended to be even-handed and justifiable on the international level. The Conference of the Parties has been careful not to abuse the powers of CITES for the sake of political reasons or due to excessive pressure by rabid special interest groups.

The Bad News

CITES has come under attack for a number of reasons. A few of the more important ones will be itemized here.

CITES leaves many terms and concepts poorly defined. As an example, the term *threatened with extinction* is used as a criterion for an organism placed in Appendix I, but no definition is given for what constitutes such a threat or when such a threat becomes significant.

The treaty does not specifically stipulate what actions must be taken once an organism is listed, although there are guidelines and political pressures from the member Parties. CITES leaves the details of enforcement to the member States. In each case, whatever action is to be taken is dictated by the individual government of the member State in which a violator is caught, and this enforcement is far from uniform. This variation in enforcement is the result of several phenomena. In poorer countries, there simply aren't the resources to enact appropriate laws and hire or train competent enforcement personnel to implement them. In other states, graft and corruption in the legal systems make enforcement problematic at best, a joke at worst.

In the United States, violators of the laws that enforce CITES can be jailed and heavily fined. In another country, all that is required to gain one's freedom upon being caught is the presentation of an appropriate gratuity to the arresting officer. In yet another country, the same infraction may simply be overlooked.

The method for originating any actions to be presented to the Conference of the Parties within any given country are not dictated by CITES but is left entirely to the discretion of the Party State's government.

CITES does not protect habitat, control wildlife management, or govern human interaction with the controlled organisms, except when those organisms cross an international boundary. While CITES controls or prohibits international trade in endangered species, it does absolutely nothing to protect individuals or species that don't cross an international border or organisms that are not listed on one of the three appendices.

Thus, while *Brachypelma smithi,* the Mexican redknee tarantula, is now protected from export from Mexico (as indeed all Mexican *Brachypelma* species are), CITES can do nothing to protect the individuals living within that country. Reports are rampant of the efforts of the Mexican peasantry to eradicate these noble creatures, stories of gasoline being poured down their burrows to route them out, stories of peasants risking their lives and limbs, not to mention those of their families, at the opportunity to veer across a highway with their car to run down a wandering male. CITES is powerless to influence this.

Similarly, the rape of the Brazilian rainforest is out of CITES jurisdiction in spite of the fact that more species are becoming extinct there every day than anywhere else on the planet. As long as none of those species are exported, the problem is an internal Brazilian one that CITES cannot affect. Even if those organisms were exported, CITES's terms can only affect the individual specimens that are in international trade and the people who are transporting them. Neither the last individuals of that species that are being exterminated in the rainforest nor their exterminators can be touched by CITES.

While the Conference of the Parties makes every effort to base its actions on valid scientific input, that input is often inadequate. This may arise in the instance where the affected organism is so rare that next to nothing is known of its natural history or population or in the case where the proposing Party lacks the funds to adequately determine an organism's true status in the wild and must rely on secondhand or anecdotal data.

While great efforts are made to fill these gaps, there is always the potential for error. The results of such mistakes can have grave consequences. If an inappropriate decision is made, the extinction of an organism could be sealed; the survival of a native people who rely on the organism as a source of sustenance or a basis for their economy could be jeopardized; or collectors, exporters, and importers could be jailed or fined inappropriately.

The provisions of CITES are based on the plights of high-profile vertebrates and flowering plants. The lesser-known vertebrates, invertebrates, and plants are dealt with in the same manner as the high-profile organisms on the tacit assumption that the same rules will fit all organisms. Thus, tarantulas and a rare moss are dealt with as though they were white rhinoceroses and orchids. While the basic philosophy may be the same, the details of maintaining a two-metric ton rhino, requiring forty hectares of scrub forest or veldt for grazing, are vastly different from the details of maintaining even a *Theraphosa blondi*. White rhinos do not lend themselves readily to the establishment of large captive-breeding populations, while all indications are that *T. blondi* very likely could.

CITES makes provisions for the maintenance of captive-breeding populations of endangered and threatened organisms, including tarantulas, and even purports to encourage it. However, those in the international wildlife trade, zoos, and dedicated enthusiasts will vouch that CITES and the associated national laws actually are counterproductive in this respect. The paperwork, the time required to acquire CITES permits, and the monetary costs of obtaining those permits makes the establishment of enthusiast-based efforts very difficult and improbable. The bureaucracy and the red tape become as burdensome as a white rhino.

Remarks

Because we view all of nature as our property, disposable at our leisure; because our business institutions measure their profits in dollars per year rather than in genetic diversity or species diversity over eternity; because our governments are much more sensitive and responsive to the immediate, imprudent demands of its populace and its economic institutions rather than the long-term requirements of the planet as a whole, we are faced with a future world as bleak and unvarying as any foretold in the grimmest of science fiction stories.

The very most that we can hope for is to save a few small parts of nature to bequeath to our offspring and to hope and pray that those offspring will somehow acquire the wisdom to treasure those few small bits of nature before they too are gone.

Historically, political pressure from environmentalist groups and wildlife conservationists has had very little affect in either conserving wildlife habitats or saving species. By way of example, rain- or moist forests around the world are still being raped, pillaged, and burnt to the ground, and the rate is increasing, not decreasing, in spite of all their efforts. As many as two species of plant or animal per minute may be exterminated in the name of progress or development, in spite of all their efforts. For all their media attention and public posturing, they are largely impotent.

The prognosis looks grim indeed.

Unless a solution is found to the greed and deplorable economic conditions that drive this destruction, it will not stop. It is entirely probable that the champion of the world's wildlife and wild spaces will not be a politician, government bureaucrat, or conservationist, but rather a social scientist or pet-loving enthusiast.

Wildlife's one hope is that one day our government and economist magi may gain the wisdom necessary to see through this idiocy and correct it. This will require someone or some group of people to instruct them, or even coerce them, into a more rational approach to the problem. You are as good a candidate for the position as anyone. Will you accept the challenge?

Chapter Nine
The Enthusiast Conspiracy

The Necessity

At this point, a word must be said about enthusiast organizations that have dealt with arachnids in general, spiders in particular, and tarantulas specifically. The tarantula-keeping community, although not new, is remarkably unorganized. These large, hairy spiders have been known by the peasantry for millennia, and by science for at least two hundred and fifty years. Baerg wrote the first book devoted exclusively to tarantula biology in 1958, and Dale Lund wrote the first book specifically for the enthusiast in 1977. It is astounding that over this span of time enthusiast organizations haven't sprung up all over the world. Even now, at the end of the twentieth century, very few exist. Those that the authors are aware of are listed on page 248.

Such organizations are of paramount importance for several reasons. First, they represent a pool of knowledge and experience about tarantula care and breeding that is available to any who seek it, which is very inexpensive if not free. They offer resources that are not available from any other source, including professional arachnologists.

Secondly, local organizations hold regular meetings, and often publish newsletters. Thus, they are an important focus for the community. International organizations can often publish high-quality journals reporting signifi-

cant advances in research and husbandry (e.g., *Forum Magazine* and *Mygalomorph* of the American Tarantula Society [see page 248]).

Lastly, but certainly not the least important, these organizations are also a source of input to the various governmental institutions that pass and enforce legislation and regulations affecting the collection, breeding, and keeping of these animals. These organizations afford the enthusiast the strongest tool for influencing those laws and regulations.

The Local Gang

Unfortunately, such enthusiast organizations do not have a very high expectation of survival. From time to time they are started, flourish for a while, then perish. Historically, they all seem to have the same attributes and fate. They are founded by one or a very few enthusiastic individuals. Most of the work and responsibility for running them is born by the founders. After the initial excitement wears off, little responsibility is shared by the membership. The founders simply are unable to bear the work and responsibility in addition to the other demands of living, such as holding a job and maintaining a family life. The organization is continually at risk of running out of operating capital. The founders become disenchanted with the organization itself, the membership, and sometimes even the hobby as a whole. The organization stagnates and eventually dies, usually leaving hard feelings and debts that must be personally borne by the few remaining members or the founders themselves.

In spite of this dismal general tendency, many enthusiast organizations (of a wide variety of interests) last for remarkable lengths of time, making significant contributions to their areas of interest. These authors have watched several such groups function for thirty years or more. These survivors seem to exhibit many of the following qualities.

1. The organizations are kept small. The more people in an organization, the more likely the organization is to suffer from personality conflicts, petty politics, and a lack of camaraderie. An organization with up to about twenty members seems to be ideal. At about forty members, the organization begins to require leaders with the wisdom of Solomon, the patience of Job, the leadership of Caesar, and the organization of the British Empire to persist. Such people become national leaders, not club presidents.

2. The organization is kept very local. If the members must travel more than thirty minutes to attend a meeting, their interest soon lapses. Instead, the establishment of sister organizations in neighboring localities is encouraged. Although this may seem redundant, even self-defeating, it has the distinct advantage of not "putting one's eggs all in one basket." If one club begins to falter, a neighboring club is still there to pick up the effort or offer support.

3. The political organization is kept as simple as possible. The more opportunities there are for petty politics,

the sooner the organization will fail. The potential for such conflicts rises exponentially with the number of officers. Three officers (e.g., president, secretary, treasurer) seems to be the maximum. Combining secretary and treasurer seems to work well, eliminating one more individual to grandstand and one more potential source of discord.

Establishing a board of trustees may be suicidal. If a board of trustees is deemed imperative, it should be kept small to reduce the probability of conflicts and should be composed of an odd number of voting members (e.g., three) to reduce the probability of tie votes.

4. Spouses should never hold collateral offices (e.g., president and secretary).

5. Newsletter mailings are generally kept to an absolute minimum. The labor and costs of production, printing, and distribution of a newsletter can be staggering. Newsletters are issued as seldom as possible, three or four times per year maximum. They are confined to a one- or two-page meeting announcement with a synopsis of the business of the last meeting, any important announcements such as elections and special events, the meeting schedule for the next several months, and an agenda for the next meeting. At the very most, only one significant article is included. If the meeting is used as the principle forum, attendance is almost obligatory to all who are interested in the organization.

6. Interesting programs are offered as the substance and core of each meeting, avoiding as much politics and business as possible. The reading and discussion of interesting

chapters, books, and articles (scientific as well as popular), the invitation of local and visiting speakers, and the viewing and critiquing of educational films (possibly acquired through the interlibrary loan program from a local library), are all ways of maintaining member interest and attendance. An annual or semiannual tarantula show, perhaps held in conjunction with a sister herpetological club, is always a big event.

7. Often two types of meetings are held. One is an executive committee meeting where business is conducted. While it is open to any of the general membership who are interested, their attendance is not necessary or expected. Typically, these are held two or three times a year as the need arises. The meetings of the general membership include a brief summary of the executive meeting, then promptly move on to the program.

8. Meetings are held no more frequently than once a month. Often, no meetings are held during the summer months. If nine meetings are held per year, and one of those is a spring or summer picnic, another is a yard sale, swap meet, or show, and a third is a holiday party (e.g., Christmas in predominantly Christian countries), the executive committee must only fill six meeting spots creatively, a much less onerous chore. A conservative meeting schedule accomplishes the task of maintaining interest but doesn't squander the membership's free time or overtax its attention.

9. In one or two places, an arachnid division is incorporated into a local herpetological club. Because most amateur herpetologists also have an interest in other exotic pets, there is immediate support and interest. The organizational framework is already in place, thus saving a lot of work. The larger organization also adds merit and clout to any actions taken on behalf of either the amateur herpetologists or amateur arachnologists.

Big Brother

National organizations must operate differently than small, local groups because of the membership and geographic base that they represent. Memberships are often quite large, making them very difficult to coordinate effectively. Because the membership is usually scattered over a very wide geographic area, the meetings must be much less frequent. The meetings must also be much better structured to accomplish any meaningful business. All this translates into higher operating costs, and fund raising becomes a major priority.

The greater size and complexity of these super clubs requires a more sophisticated, formal executive structure. More talented and experienced executive officers are also required. At the very least, the expenses incurred in the course of their duties must be covered by the organization, and these people must often be compensated for their talents, time, and effort, adding to the organization's financial burden. National and international organizations are big business, with big budgets, big responsibilities, and big headaches.

The enthusiast is warned not to attempt to found or hold office in a national organization without considerable experience in managing large organizations, the more experience the better. For ordinary folk, the local enthusiast group is challenge enough.

Having said all this, it is important to stress that national organizations are critical to the hobby and the enthusiast is strongly encouraged to support them. Among other attributes, these organizations form a backbone for the hobby, serving to disseminate news and knowledge over a much wider base than the small local group ever could. Some may even publish high-quality journals in place of the more mundane newsletter. The larger organizations may be able to support some original research. These national organizations are the only entities that will have the funds and the political clout to influence legislation and regulations on a national or international level.

Below is a listing of the few organizations, enthusiast, semi-professional, and professional, that concern themselves with arachnids, spiders, or tarantulas of which these authors are aware. Doubtlessly there are more regional and local organizations that are not listed here. Enthusiasts are encouraged to contact them for information about memberships, current projects, programs, and publications. This information is current as of July 1997 but, because of the factors outlined early in this chapter, may change unexpectedly. Once one active organization or society is found, inquire about any others with similar interests.

As a matter of courtesy, and sometimes necessity, membership dues for foreign organizations should always be submitted in the form of an international money order in that country's currency.

American Arachnological Society
American Museum of Natural History
Central Park West at 79th Street
New York, NY 10024
USA

A professional organization. Publishes *Journal of Arachnology* and a newsletter.

American Tarantula Society
P.O. Box 1617
Artesia, New Mexico 88211-1617
USA
E-mail: miep@compuserve.com
Website: www.concentric.net/Dmartin/ats/
A combined professional and enthusiast organization. Publishes *Forum Magazine* and *Mygalomorph*.

Arachnologischer Anzeiger
Sandstrasse 31
8000 Munchen 2
Germany
An enthusiast organization.

British Arachnological Society
71 Havant Road
Walthamstow, London E17 3JE
England
A professional organization. Publishes *Bulletin of the British Arachnological Society* and a newsletter.

British Tarantula Society
81 Phillimore Place
Radlett, Hertfordshire WD7 8NJ
England
An enthusiast organization. Publishes the *British Tarantula Society Journal*.

Central California Arachnid Society
2732 E. Griffith Street
Fresno, California 93726-4559
USA
E-mail: dld18@csufresno.edu
An enthusiast organization. Publishes a quarterly newsletter.

French Tarantula Society
F-94191 Villeneuve St. George
Cedex
France
   An enthusiast organization.

H. O. T. S. Reptile Research
P.O. Box 12252
Hamtramck, Michigan 48212
USA
   Publishes a monthly newsletter.

Northern Tarantula Society
17 Commercial Street
Hyde, Cheshire SK14 2JD
England
   An enthusiast organization.

Rockhampton Arachnological Society
50 Naughton Street
Wandal, Rockhampton
Queensland 4700
Australia
   An enthusiast organization. Publishes
a quarterly journal.

Sonoran Arthropod Studies Institute
P.O. Box 5624
Tucson, Arizona 85703
USA
   A combined professional and enthusi-
ast organization. Publishes *Instar, Back-
yard Bugwatching,* and a newsletter.

We wish to emphasize again that this
list is extremely ephemeral. The
addresses and the very existence of
these organizations may change at any
time without notice.

Wired, Netted, and Webbed

It's an odd twist of fate that a book
about tarantulas should contain a section on the Internet and the World Wide

Web, but this one shall. Enthusiasts
who wish to take advantage of the Net
and WWW are advised to seek information on them at the local library, with
particular reference to Internet etiquette
(netiquette).
   The advent of the Internet and the
World Wide Web promises to be both
an unequaled boon to humankind as
well as one of the world's greatest time
wasters. The incredible complexity and
the amount of information and misinformation offered by this medium is so
great and disorganized that merely
attempting to find one small datum can
take significantly longer than the entire
trip to the local library.
   Another major problem with the
Internet is that none of the information
to be found on it is copy edited, peer
reviewed, or censored. There is no guarantee that what is found is true or
believable, and the unsuspecting novice
can easily be led astray. Any information
found on the Internet or World Wide
Web should be checked with experienced enthusiasts or professionals
before being taken as truth or used in
making decisions about your pets.
   There is no crystal ball for the
Internet and its future is totally unpredictable. There is every reason to
believe that before this book goes to
press, many websites, news groups,
and mailing lists will have been created,
a respectable number will have disappeared, and perhaps a totally new
mode for exchanging information and
ideas will have evolved. Enthusiasts
who wish to tap this wealth of information are warned that any information
presented here must be viewed as
ephemeral at best.
   As of July 1997 at least two mailing
lists for arachnids in general, and one
devoted more or less exclusively to

scorpions, exist on the Internet. In addition, there seem to be an ever-burgeoning multitude of websites that contain anecdotal or professional information. There is every indication that the numbers of these will grow exponentially as time progresses.

Mailing lists are maintained on a computer (the listserver), which accepts all electronic mail postings (e-mail) sent to the mailing list's address and automatically forwards them to every e-mail address in its address listing. Subscription to these mailing lists is usually without charge. They are managed by some interested enthusiast or professional as a public service, using hardware and facilities supported by university budgets.

The three mailing lists follow. In all cases, "name" is your name, using capital letters in the usual places, as you want it to appear on all forwarded postings. Your personal e-mail address is enclosed in angle brackets and looks like this: <e-mail@address>. All characters except those in your name are lower case.

arachnid@bga.com

A mailing list intended principally for enthusiasts. Professional arachnologists frequently monitor its postings and, time permitting, contribute technical information.

To subscribe, send an e-mail posting from your personal e-mail account to: majordomo@bga.com with the only text being the single message: subscribe arachnid "name" <e-mail@address>.

arachnology@zi.biologie.uni-muenchen.de

A mailing list intended primarily for professional arachnologists. Enthusiasts are allowed to subscribe, but it is strongly recommended that they refrain from posting messages here unless the messages have some technical merit or require a technical response.

To subscribe, send an e-mail posting from your personal e-mail account to: majordomo@zi.biologie. uni-muenchen. de with the only text being the single message: subscribe arachnology "name" <e-mail@address>.

Scorpion-Enthusiasts@wrbu.si.edu

A mailing list for enthusiasts primarily interested in scorpions. Professional arachnologists frequently monitor its contents and, time permitting, contribute technical information. This list is mentioned here because of the close association between spiders (including tarantulas) and scorpions, and because many topics discussed here concern tarantulas as well as scorpions.

To subscribe, send an e-mail posting from your personal e-mail account to: macjordomo@wrbu.si.edu with the only text being the single message: subscribe Scorpion-Enthusiasts "name" <e-mail@address>.

Note that *Scorpion-Enthusiasts* contains both a capital *S* and a capital *E,* an exception to normal e-mail addresses. Also, the letter *c* in *macjordomo* is not a typographical error.

We wish to emphasize again that this list is extremely ephemeral. The addresses and the very existence of these organizations may change at any time without notice. Once contact has been established with one, the interested enthusiast may inquire about the existence of other similar mailing lists and news groups.

A Plea for Help

The hobby needs your help. Find a local club. If there are none, consider starting one. If a local club exists, you are strongly urged to offer help to the people who are running it. Something as simple as managing coffee and doughnuts for each meeting can be an inestimable benefit to the organization. If nothing else is possible, contribute to its financial support.

Under all circumstances, join one or more of the large national organizations. Their membership dues are seldom oppressive, and they offer many benefits that are beyond the capability of a smaller organization. Enthusiasts who have the experience or talent to help in the running of such organizations are well advised to donate their services. These organizations need all the help they can get as well.

We cannot afford to lose front-line, top-notch enthusiast organizations because of overwork, indifference, or neglect. We can't afford to allow our hobby to slip away because of inattention. If we persist in our apathy or indifference, we will soon find ourselves unable to pursue our hobby altogether.

Remarks

Here are some things which you can do to help. Some of these require more work than others, but will be well worth the effort for those with the talent and time.

1. Support enthusiast organizations.
2. Try very hard to breed your pets.
3. Experiment *gently* with your pets.
4. Keep accurate records of all of your observations.
5. Write articles about your experiments and observations for enthusiast newsletters and magazines.
6. Present programs to schools, scout, and youth groups
7. Advise pet shops on the proper naming, care, and husbandry of tarantulas.
8. Hold "Tarantula Days" at local pet shops. These are publicity and sales events held in cooperation with local businesses. They enhance public awareness of tarantulas and help the business as well.
9. Raise funds for scholarships for budding arachnologists (a good project for any club).
10. Raise funds to sponsor research by professional arachnologists (another good project for any club).
11. Become a professional arachnologist. (These jobs are very few and far between!)
12. Aggressively work for more enlightened laws and regulations. Lobby government agencies for those projects that will help to preserve areas that contain tarantula colonies, and for laws and regulations that will promote rather than inhibit the keeping of pet tarantulas and the establishment of captive-breeding populations.

Chapter Ten
Publish! Publish! Publish!

The Photographic Tarantula

The Art and Science of It

It is assumed that the enthusiast who seriously reads this section already knows something about the basic mechanics of photography and artistic composition. If this is not the case, beat a hasty retreat to the nearest public library or camera store and acquire one or two books on the basic principles of photography, and on close-up, table-top, and macrophotography in particular. A good comprehensive book for both beginning and experienced wildlife or scientific photographers is Blaker (1976). For in-depth treatments of the subject, refer to the books by the Eastman Kodak Company (1969a, 1969b, 1970a, and 1970b) in the bibliography. These last four references are very good, but are also very heavy technical reading.

Reference and text books on the art of wildlife photography should be consulted, once the aspiring photographer is familiar with the physics and mechanics of close-up photography. Reading several of them before any film is loaded into a camera will save a lot of time and money, not to mention frustration. Do not ignore the magazine counter in the corner news shop either.

In the larger cities, some camera stores sponsor periodic seminars by well-known professional wildlife photographers. The cost of admission is seldom very high and they have much to offer in practical experience.

Who in your area has been an amateur wildlife photographer for many years? Perhaps a school biology instructor? Perhaps they would be willing to sit down one evening to offer a few pointers or a demonstration of their equipment and techniques.

Lastly, do not forget about adult education, photography courses offered by the larger public school systems, some junior colleges, and many universities. Again, the fees are usually modest, and an hour spent in a structured course can save many hours of vexation, and many rolls of worthless photos.

Tarantulas Specifically

Tarantulas pose some special problems to photographers. Among them are their aversion for bright lights. It is unlikely that a tarantula will pose long enough to get a good photo in sunlight. In fact, the heat might hurt the animal if it is forced to stay in direct sunlight for more than a few seconds. Strobe flashes or the very brief use of floodlights indoors are the viable alternative.

Second, because tarantulas are covered with a dense layer of bristles, they photograph like black velvet. Unless the film is overexposed, often severely, they only appear as dark silhouettes.

The exact amount of that overexposure must be determined by experimentation and it differs with different tarantulas and light arrangements. Perhaps the easiest way to solve the dilemma is to take several shots at different levels of overexposure.

The problem with this is that any other subjects in the frame are likely to be seriously overexposed. Careful arrangement of subjects and background is necessary. With an automatic flash, one trick is to photograph the tarantula on a surface that is as dark as it is, but a different color for contrast (e.g., dark velvet or felt).

Avoid glossy surfaces. The reflection can fool the electric eye in the automatic flash, if one is used. Another problem is the presence of a bright flare in the photo or a mirror image of the tarantula in the glossy surface. Such shots may be attractive with a scenic mountain lake but are only confusing with tarantulas. The authors once witnessed a photo of a pair of tarantulas mating on a glossy table top. There appeared to be four indistinct masses which represented the bodies and their reflections, plus thirty-two entangled legs. Tarantulas and surrealism do not go well together.

Avoid busy settings. The authors have a photo of a *Brachypelma smithi* on an onyx chess set. The exposure is perfect, but the chess pieces around the tarantula are an incredible distraction. Cute, but not art.

What if the tarantula insists on walking off the stage? One technique is to put an opaque container over it for several minutes, to give it an opportunity to settle down.

If a settling down period won't work, postpone the photography session for a day or two. If that still doesn't work, try putting the tarantula in a small container and placing it in a refrigerator for thirty minutes. This won't harm it, but it will slow it down a little. *Don't forget about it in the refrigerator!*

The End Result

Now that we have all these great tarantula photos, what will we do with them? Try getting them published, of course! But first, we must digress a bit.

The Written Word

For most people, the thought of writing anything for publication instills a terror second only to going to the dentist. Yet this is the only means that the rest of the world has of knowing what we have seen or done. If we have something to say, we say it, don't we? Well, why not write it?

The Enthusiast Newsletter

Stories, reports, and any other relevant material may be submitted to any newsletter published by enthusiasts' clubs. They may be found by talking with other tarantula fanciers, amateur herpetologists, and amateur photographers who are encountered in pet shops, camera stores, or at hobby shows. Often, watching the "Pets for Sale" columns in the want ads of local newspapers will supply contacts as well.

Such articles normally are very short, one or two pages at most. Therefore, the subject must be well focused. This is not necessarily bad. Short articles are easier for the amateur to write. Most enthusiast newsletters are unable to handle halftone prints. If illustrations are to be included, they should be pen-and-ink line drawings, not photos. Semiprofessional and good amateur artists are available through local colleges and are not expensive. Current copyright laws dictate that, once drawn, the commissioned illustrations belong to the person who paid to have them made.

If photographs are to be submitted to enthusiast publications, they should be black and white. Such photos can be made into PMTs (photomechanical transfers) and printed relatively inexpensively. Color photos require a lengthy, and therefore expensive, process to be turned into a number of plates (usually four, one for each primary color plus black), then must be run through a printing press capable of printing the four colors simultaneously. The technology, time, and effort, and therefore the expense, required for this is usually well beyond the resources of the neighborhood club.

Color photos may be copied onto black-and-white paper, but with great loss of definition and crispness. Most color photos rely on color differences to distinguish the parts of the image, not contrast. Black-and-white copies tend to become neutral grey with little contrast between the individual parts of the image. The conversion process also requires several intermediate copies. Each copying step degrades the image quality, resulting in an out-of-focus appearance. To solve the problem, these authors make a practice of photographing their subjects with two cameras. One is loaded with color film, the other with black and white.

Popular Magazines

Many popular nature and sporting magazines would be interested in publishing good-quality thirty-five millimeter transparencies, and possibly any associated stories. Their names and addresses may be found in their publications by perusing newsstands, pet and hobby shops, or in special listings at the local library. Write to the prospective publishers for their requirements.

Magazines commonly maintain want-lists of photos of subjects for upcoming articles written by their reporters. They also maintain lists of photographers to whom they regularly mail these want lists. The enthusiast who is interested in becoming an amateur nature photographer should inquire about being placed on these mailing lists.

The Mechanics of Writing

But how does one write such an article? As a start, get several pieces of paper, take a pencil firmly in hand, and write down the first word. Follow it with the second. Good! The most difficult part has been mastered, the beginning. Don't give up now. *Keep going!* Don't worry about punctuation, spelling, or grammar. The most important step is to get it all down in black and white before getting cold feet, getting tired, or forgeting.

The article will probably have to be rewritten two or three times before it is right, but don't be too fussy at first. Eventually, the result will be a neatly typed copy. You can't type? Don't despair. In most colleges and universities, the bulletin boards are bursting with signs advertising word processing and the rates are remarkably reasonable. Although every effort should be made to use correct English, don't let that be a barrier either. Merely do the best job that you can. The publisher will have an editor or proofreader copyedit the article to correct the errors.

Here's a little tip that may help. Begin the article as though the conversation had already started, as though someone else's question were being answered or a comment was being made on what they said. After having reached the very end of the article, write a closing paragraph of only two or three sentences that sums it all up in a general way. Then, and only then, go back and write an introductory paragraph of two or three sentences that leads the reader into the dissertation.

Although your *magnum opus* can be in letter style, most publishers prefer essay style. Number the pages and make sure that the author's name (presumably yours) and the article title appears in a top corner of each page. The author's full name and address should go on the first page. Don't forget to include a cover letter telling the publisher that this material is being sent in the hope that it will be interesting enough to print.

Write as simply and as compactly as possible. Don't try to be too flowery. Very long sentences will try the reader's patience. Don't despair about any questions or trouble writing. Free help is plentiful. The local library will have many books and pamphlets giving detailed instructions on everything from correct spelling to the fine points of writing prose. Just ask the librarian where to find them. Many English and literature teachers in public schools will gladly spend an hour to help a budding young author. Use this time wisely and don't abuse their generosity. But if you need help, don't be afraid to ask.

Have faith, the first endeavor is always the hardest. Once an article has been published, beginning authors catch the fever. They have even been known to sign up for creative writing courses at local schools. They are then forever hooked.

Copyrights and Royalties

Before an article or photo is submitted, ask the publisher about the copyrights. Publishers of enthusiast newsletters often request that submitted articles be accompanied by a letter stating that all claims to copyright are being released to the public domain with the single exception that the author must be given credit. This means that the article may be republished endlessly without the author's permission. This also means that, although no royalties or other payment will be received for it, and no other claim of ownership can be made to it, the article may eventually be distributed among enthusiast newsletters around the world. The author still gains the notoriety, and enthusiast newsletters gain another article to print. But far more significantly, the author's ideas, experiences, discoveries, innovations, and creations are disseminated for others to benefit from worldwide. Without this, we would remain in the Dark Ages forever.

Other arrangements are used by commercial publishers (e.g., magazines and books). One common practice is "work for hire," whereby the publisher merely buys the article or photo for a fixed, one-time-only fee. This practice is usually used for smaller works (e.g., magazine articles and photos). For larger works (e.g., this book), elaborate contracts are usually signed and royalties paid, commonly based on the cover price.

The copyright laws are complex and confusing and cannot be reported in detail here. Suffice it to say that once an individual creates a graphic or written art (e.g., photograph, magazine article, book) the work is protected for the duration of that person's life plus fifty years. For more precise information or counsel, consult a copyright or intellectual properties attorney.

Translating the Word

The enthusiasts who are fluent in more than one language can translate scientific papers and popular articles from one language to another so that their cohorts may also benefit from them. Arrange to publish these translations. Enthusiast journals are excellent places to publish. Be certain to check the copyright date, and obtain written permission for publication if necessary. Often, the publisher of your translation can help with this.

Remarks

Never think that what you have to say is too dumb or of little interest. Let the publisher worry about such trivialities. If you fail to report a fact because you prejudged it as insignificant, it will never be printed, and the rest of the world may never learn about it. There are few details about tarantulas' lives that are too trivial to be told.

Similarly, reporting negative results (i.e., what didn't work) can be as important as reporting what did work. Publishing the negative results will help the rest of us avoid duplicating the same unsuccessful trials. Never be afraid to report your failures.

Tell it all. Tell it like it is!

Epilogue

We started out with some very clear prejudices about spiders in general, and tarantulas in particular. We discussed some of the myths and old wives' tales about them, and gradually began to suspect that what we thought we knew may not be entirely correct.

Then we examined their anatomies and physiologies rather closely. That's when we began to realize just how strange these creatures really were, and how absurd our original preconceptions were.

When we reviewed the way they were named, we found that not even the experts were really certain about what tarantulas really were.

As we explored their private lives, we discovered that a lot of rather knowledgeable people had many of the same problems that we did trying to understand these remarkable animals. Tarantulas seemed hell-bent on confusing everybody any way that they could.

As we explored their interrelationships with humans, how we use them for food, how they figure into our religions, art, and philosophy, it became clear that spiders in general, and tarantulas in particular, were intimately associated with humans in many parts of our world. Our western civilization alone seems to have missed that relationship because our civilization evolved and matured principally in Europe, where tarantulas are all but nonexistent.

We learned how to keep them as pets, that many species were really comparatively docile and good subjects for the pet keeper who hadn't the time or resources to keep more demanding pets like dogs or birds. We even found out how to hunt and catch wild tarantulas, just in case the Fates find us in east Africa, western Texas, or Amazonia.

We learned that many tarantulas, like most other wildlife, are threatened with extinction because of humankind's assault on their habitat. We discussed how solving the underlying problems of poverty, greed, and ignorance might help all wildlife in general, tarantulas in particular.

As you read this book, your attitude about these giant spiders has undergone a great metamorphosis. These things often are not obvious at first, but your life is changed, whether you believe so or not. Along the way, you have lost your innocence of these creatures. You no longer hold the prejudices and preconceptions that you once did. Where once you looked upon tarantulas as something to be feared and destroyed, you now see them as fascinating creatures, worthy of a great deal of respect. You now realize that tarantulas aren't demonic fugitives from Hell, or visitors from an alien world. They're just different, so different that you have trouble imagining their lifestyles and their concepts of the world we share with them.

From now on, when you see a tarantula on television or in the movies, you will criticize the filmmakers for their inaccuracies, and you will feel disturbed by their misrepresentations and deceptions.

When you pass a pet shop, you will think that you might stop in to see what kinds of tarantulas they have. Perhaps you will meet someone who actually has one for a pet.

You cannot go back. You will never look at a tarantula the same way again. Whether you admit to it or not, not only do you understand them better than before, you now *enjoy* them.

"Come into my parlor," said the spider to the fly . . .

Welcome, indeed!

PART FOUR
Appendices

Here we collect important things for your reference that didn't fit well into the body of the book.

Appendix A
Tarantula Species as Pets

The following is a cross-reference between scientific and common names for many of the species of theraphosid tarantulas sold in the pet industry over the last twenty years. In this book, the authors use the scientific names, occasionally giving common names only parenthetically. However, in many other works (e.g., other enthusiast publications, how-to books, dealer's price lists), as well as in pet shops, common names are often used almost exclusively. This list is intended to give the enthusiast a cross-reference, however tentative, for these names.

The scientific to common name correlations given here are not to be trusted. Because of the wholly arbitrary, undisciplined, often whimsical manner in which common names are applied, the correlations are only best guesses. To emphasize the point, the reader will note that several species often bear the same common name and the majority of species bear several common names.

The entries are listed cardinally by the scientific name. The subfamily is given under the scientific name as a point of interest for the aficionado. Common names of which the authors are aware are listed in alphabetical order after the scientific name and subfamily, so as not to infer any priority or preference. However, those names that are the approved, official common names as listed by the American Arachnological Society's *Common Names of*

Arachnids (Breene 1995, and pages 67 and 248) and updated frequently in their *Forum Magazine* are emboldened in the following list. It is expected that new, revised editions of the master list will be published regularly, and the enthusiast is encouraged to contact the American Tarantula Society (see page 248) to request a current edition.

This list is intended to itemize all common names that have been used for tarantulas that the authors are aware of, whether officially accepted by the American Arachnological Society's Committee on Common Names of Arachnids and listed in *Common Names of Arachnids* or not. Their appearance on this list should not be construed as acceptance of these names as official common names, and the authors are not proposing that they should be officially sanctioned. The sole purpose of this list is to serve as a cross-reference between the various common and scientific names, official or otherwise, that pervade the community and the industry.

The Vernacular Tarantula

A number of nicknames are misapplied ruthlessly. In the tarantula-keeping community, *tarantula* and *spider* are

Puzzled by scientific names? Read Chapter 2: The Name of the Tarantula for a detailed discussion.

often substituted for each other whenever convenient or to conserve the poetic meter of a name, e.g., baboon tarantula and monkey spider. *Common Names of Arachnids* accepts neither baboon nor monkey spider as a correct name for any spider. *Bird spider* and *birdeater* should be restricted to refer to any spider (here, any theraphosid spider) that is known to eat birds, but often is inappropriately used for nearly any species of theraphosid spider. *Common Names of Arachnids* does not accept *bird spider* for any spider and accepts *birdeater* to mean only one species of spider in the world, *Theraphosa blondi*.

Tree spider usually refers to any spider (here, any theraphosid spider) that ordinarily dwells in trees or even in tall brush, weeds, or grass. *Common Names of Arachnids* does not accept it for any tarantula.

Aficionados often abbreviate names mercilessly in the heat of discussion. A species may be referred to merely by a condensed form of its common name (e.g., redknee for the Mexican redknee tarantula, *Brachypelma smithi*) or by a specific epithet alone, with the listener left to assume the genus (e.g., versicolor for the Antilles pinktoe tarantula *Avicularia versicolor* and smithi for *Brachypelma smithi*). Because the same word or name is not often used as the specific epithet for more than one species, and because the listener is free to request a clarification in a verbal discussion, this last system works well in casual conversation.

Enthusiasts who write articles and books, however, must be ever careful not to fall into that trap. Whenever a species of tarantula is discussed, its scientific name should be specified at the beginning of the discussion, possibly with the corresponding common name, to avoid confusion.

In the written word, and the spoken word as well, only the common names as listed in *Common Names of Arachnids* (or its successor) should be used to avoid confusion in the future.

Thereafter, unambiguous abbreviations of the scientific names, or the common names if defined at the beginning, are acceptable. Having said that, these authors have blithely broken their own rule in this text, leaving the reader to refer to this appendix for clarification. This book represents a special case where so many species are mentioned in so many scattered references that, for reasons of economy of time, effort, and print, this system seemed a preferable alternative.

Systematics

In the following list, Raven's (1985) and Platnick's (1989) systematics are followed as closely as possible. A few former names are given in parentheses where appropriate to help the interested enthusiast track them through the literature. The complete nomenclatural history of any genus or species can be determined by first consulting Platnick (1989), then backtracking through Raven (1985), Brignoli (1983), Roewer (1942), and finally Bonnet (1945–61).

These reference books are often very difficult to find. Seek them in the libraries of major universities, in their entomology and arachnology departments, or in major museums that hold extensive arachnid collections. A few fortunate professional entomologists and arachnologists at these institutions may also have copies. The novice should not be offended for not being allowed to remove them from the sight of the owner. Be prepared to offer a spouse or first-born child as a security deposit for the privilege of examining these books!

Two Cases of Whiplash

Recently, two of the most popular genera in the tarantula-keeping community experienced name reversals after their names had been revised by Raven (1985). Simon created the genus *Brachypelma* in 1891, but in 1985 Raven, after examining specimens sent to him by various museums, determined that it was synonymous with the genus *Euathlus,* created by Ausserer in 1875. Thus, upon publication of his findings, the official name was changed. Since that time, new information has indicated that the type specimens that were supplied to Raven were incorrectly labeled. It has been determined that these two generic names are *not* synonymous, and *Brachypelma* is the correct name for the affected species after all.

The second reversal of a revision involves the genus *Rhechostica.* Raven, upon examining a number of type specimens, determined that there were no significant differences between the members of the genera *Rhechostica, Dugesiella, Eurypelma,* and *Aphonopelma.* Therefore, he grouped (*lumped* is the informal, but most often used, term) the members of these genera into one large genus and used the oldest (most senior) name for it, *Rhechostica.* However, this move rankled many arachnologists who had grown up thinking of these creatures as *Aphonopelma* or at least some name that was easier to pronounce. Petitions were submitted to the Zoological Nomenclature Committee recommending that the better-known name, *Aphonopelma,* be reinstated. The

argument held that *Aphonopelma* was so firmly ingrained in the literature that changing it would cause much more confusion than it was worth. (Many of us will agree heartily!) The arguments were compelling enough, and the signatures important enough, that the Committee did indeed adopt *Aphonopelma* as the correct name in place of the senior name, *Rhechostica.*

The scientific community and the hobby have been experiencing a type of intellectual whiplash in trying to keep abreast of the changes. Unfortunately, *Euathlus* and *Rhechostica* had already been used in the literature following Raven's revisions. Any who read those papers must now remember yet another revision of revisions in order not to be confused by the nomenclature. Here, *Brachypelma* is used with *Euathlus* in parentheses, and *Aphonopelma* is used with *Rhechostica* in parentheses.

To save space in the bibliography, the references for the species names are not supplied. The enthusiast who wishes to examine the initial scientific paper describing any species should consult the references listed above, in the order presented, for the exact citations.

If the correct scientific name for any tarantula must be unequivocally determined, seek assistance from a professional arachnologist at a major university or natural history museum.

The Hit List

Acanthogonatus pissii (Simon 1886)
Family Nemesiidae
Chilean red rump tarantula
(This species does not belong to the family Theraphosidae. It is included here because it occasionally appears on price lists.)

Acanthoscurria antillensis (Pocock 1903)
Subfamily Theraphosinae
Pinkpatch tarantula

Acanthoscurria musculosa (Simon 1892)
Subfamily Theraphosinae
Brazilian black velvet tarantula
Mato Grasso birdeater
Mato Grasso black velvet birdeater

Aphonopelma (Rhechostica/Dugesiella) anax (Chamberlin 1940)
Subfamily Theraphosinae
Kingsville bronze-brown tarantula
Rose carapace red rump tarantula
Texas tan tarantula

Aphonopelma (Rhechostica) burica (Valerio 1980)
Subfamily Theraphosinae
Central American cinnamon tarantula
Costa Rican blue front tarantula
Costa Rican chestnut brown tarantula
Costa Rican chestnutzebra tarantula

Aphonopelma (Rhechostica/Eurypelma) californicum (Ausserer 1871)
Subfamily Theraphosinae
California blond tarantula
California brown tarantula
California tarantula
Common brown tarantula
Mojave brown tarantula
(This species is probably not valid, and probably doesn't exist. This raises the question of what is the true identity of all the tarantulas that have been called *A. californicum?*)

Aphonopelma (Rhechostica/Dugesiella/Eurypelma) caniceps (Simon 1890)
Subfamily Theraphosinae
Big Bend gold tarantula
Gold carapace red rump tarantula
Golden orange rump tarantula
Texas Big Bend gold carapace tarantula

Aphonopelma (Rhechostica) chalcodes (Chamberlin 1940)
Subfamily Theraphosinae
Arizona blond tarantula
Cinnamon tarantula
Mexican blond tarantula
Palomino blond tarantula
Palomino tarantula
Southwestern/Mexican blond tarantula
Tucson blond tarantula

Aphonopelma (Rhechostica/Dugesiella/Eurypelma) crinita (Pocock 1901)
Subfamily Theraphosinae
Gold carapace red rump tarantula
Mexican green tarantula

Aphonopelma (Rhechostica/Dugesiella) hentzi (Girard 1854)
Subfamily Theraphosinae
Arkansas brown tarantula
North American palomino tarantula
Oklahoma brown tarantula
Texas brown tarantula
(The status of this species is the subject of much controversy. Some arachnologists hold that it is only found in Oklahoma and Louisiana. Others believe that it is also found in Texas and that many of the new species of tarantulas named by Smith [1994] are actually this species, or a subspecies of it. Because all the variants have very nearly the same appearance and the same personalities,

the argument is of importance only to the scientist and the enthusiast who is trying to breed them, in which case the confusion is maddening!)

Aphonopelma (Rhechostica/Delopelma) moderatum (Chamberlin and Ivie 1939)
Subfamily Theraphosinae
Rio Grande gold tarantula
(This species was first given this common name by one of the authors [MJS] on Saturday, April 16, 1982 [Easter weekend] when she first encountered them in the Falcon/Zapata/Roma, Texas, area. It was called Rio Grande because of its origin [literally in sight of the Rio Grande River] and gold because of the remarkable golden-beige color of its dorsal surfaces [the venter is jet black]. Subsequently, that name was first published in the 1984 edition of this book and has since been accepted by the Committee on Common Names of Arachnids of the American Arachnological Society as the official common name for this species [Breene 1995].)

Aphonopelma (Brachypelma/Euathlus/ Dugesiella/Eurypelma) pallidum (F.O.P.—Cambridge 1897)
Subfamily Theraphosinae
Mexican gray tarantula
Mexican rose tarantula
Rose gray tarantula

Aphonopelma (Rhechostica) seemanni (F.O.P.—Cambridge 1905)
Subfamily Theraphosinae
Bamboo tarantula
Costa Rican zebra tarantula
Skeleton tarantula

Avicularia avicularia (L. 1758)
Subfamily Aviculariinae
Orange tipped bird spider

Pinktoe tarantula
South American pink toed tarantula

Avicularia avicularia variegata (F.O.P.—Cambridge 1896)
Subfamily Aviculariinae
Grizzled pinktoe
South American yellow banded bird spider
Yellow banded bird spider

Avicularia bicegoi (Mello-Leitão 1923)
Subfamily Aviculariinae
Manaus brick-red rump tree spider

Avicularia juruensis (Mello-Leitão)
Subfamily Aviculariinae
Brazilian yellowbanded tarantula

Avicularia magdelenae (Karsch 1879)
Subfamily Aviculariinae
Cinnamon pinktoe tarantula
South American yellow banded bird spider
Yellow banded bird spider
(Tarantulas sold in the pet trade with this name may actually be *A. juruensis* [Mello-Leitão].)

Avicularia metallica (Ausserer 1897)
Subfamily Aviculariinae
Metallic tree spider
Surinam birdeater
Whitetoe tarantula

Avicularia nigrotineata (Mello-Leitão 1940)
Subfamily Aviculariinae
Pink toed tree spider
Yellowtoe tarantula

Avicularia pulchra (Mello-Leitão 1933)
Subfamily Aviculariinae
Tigerrump tarantula
Tricolored tree spider

Avicularia purpurea (Kirk 1990)
Subfamily Aviculariinae
Ecuadorian purple tarantula
Purple pink toed tarantula
Purple tree spider

Avicularia "peruana"
Subfamily Aviculariinae
Fuzzy tree spider
Peruvian fuzzy tree spider
Peruvian tree spider
(These authors and several professional arachnologists have not been able to locate a formal description bearing this species name. The best guess is that this is a pseudoscientific name contrived for use in the hobby.)

Avicularia urticans (Schmidt 1994)
Subfamily Aviculariinae
Peruvian pinktoe tarantula

Avicularia versicolor (Walckenaer 1837)
Subfamily Aviculariinae
Antilles pinktoe tarantula
Martinique bird spider
Red bird spider

Brachypelma (Euathlus) albopilosum (Valerio 1980)
Subfamily Theraphosinae
Costa Rican curly hair tarantula
Costa Rican woolly tarantula
Curlyhair tarantula
Honduras curly hair tarantula
Honduras woolly tarantula
Orange hair woolly tarantula
Woolly tarantula

Brachypelma (Euathlus) angustum (Valerio 1980)
Subfamily Theraphosinae
Costa Rican red rump tarantula
Costa Rican red tarantula
Guatemalan red rump tarantula

Brachypelma (Euathlus) auratum (Schmidt 1992)
Subfamily Theraphosinae
Flame knee tarantula
Mexican flameknee tarantula

Brachypelma (Euathlus) boehmei (Schmidt and Klaas 1994)
Subfamily Theraphosinae
Boehm's red leg tarantula
Mexican beauty tarantula
Mexican fireleg tarantula
Mexican rust leg tarantula
Red leg tarantula

Brachypelma (Euathlus) emilia (White 1856)
Subfamily Theraphosinae
Bottle brush red leg
Emilia's red leg tarantula
Emilia's tarantula
Mexican redleg tarantula
Mexican true red leg tarantula
Painted red leg tarantula
Panamanian red leg tarantula
Red banded tarantula
True red leg tarantula
(In decades past, *B. smithi* was called "Mexican red leg." However, when the present species was imported *en masse* in 1985 or 1986, it became apparent that *B. smithi* really wasn't a "redleg," but an "orange knee" or "redknee," instead. Thus, even though the hobby had been calling *B. smithi* "redleg" for decades, *B. emilia* was given the moniker officially.)

Brachypelma (Aphonopelma/ Rhechostica/Dugesiella) epicureanum (Chamberlin 1925)
Subfamily Theraphosinae
Yucatan rustrump tarantula

Brachypelma (Euathlus) sabulosum
(F.O.P.—Cambridge 1897)
Subfamily Theraphosinae
Central American cinnamon tarantula
Guatemalan redrump tarantula

Brachypelma (Euathlus) smithi
(F.O.P.—Cambridge 1897)
Subfamily Theraphosinae
Mexican redknee tarantula
Mexican red leg tarantula
Orange knee tarantula
Red leg tarantula
True red leg tarantula
(Traditionally in the hobby, this species was known as the "Mexican red leg tarantula." However, with the importation of *B. emilia,* the present species has lost that title. While *B. emilia* has vivid crimson or scarlet legs, *B. smithi* only has orange and yellow knees (patellae). As a compromise, *B. smithi* has been given the official name "Mexican redknee tarantula," and will be forever known by that nickname. "All glory is fleeting.")

Brachypelma (Euathlus) vagans
(Ausserer 1875)
Subfamily Theraphosinae
Black velvet tarantula
Guatemalan black velvet tarantula
Guatemalan red rump tarantula
Guatemalan red veil tarantula
Mexican redrump tarantula
Painted red rump tarantula
Red rumped black velvet tarantula
Red rump tarantula
Red veil tarantula
Velvet red rump tarantula

Ceratogyrus bechuanicus (Purcell 1902)
Subfamily Harpactirinae
Curved horn baboon tarantula
Curvedhorn tarantula
Horned baboon tarantula
Starburst horned baboon tarantula

Ceratogyrus brachycephalus (Hewitt 1919)
Subfamily Harpactirinae
Greater horned baboon tarantula
Greaterhorned tarantula
Horned baboon tarantula
Horned monkey spider
Rhino horn baboon tarantula

Ceratogyrus darlingi (Pocock 1897)
Subfamily Harpactirinae
African horned tarantula
East African horned baboon tarantula
Horned baboon tarantula
Horned monkey spider
Long horned baboon tarantula
South African horned baboon

Ceratogyrus dolichocephalus (Hewitt 1919)
Subfamily Harpactirinae
Cranial horned baboon tarantula
Horned baboon tarantula
Horned monkey spider

Chaetopelma olivaceum (Koch 1842)
Subfamily Indeterminate
Middle East gold tarantula
Middle East olive gold tarantula

Chilobrachys andersoni (Pocock 1895)
Subfamily Selenocosmiinae
Burmese mustard tarantula
Kawkereet mustard tarantula
Mergui reddish brown tarantula

Chilobrachys sericeus (Thorell 1895)
Subfamily Selenocosmiinae
Asian mustard tarantula
Rangoon mustard tarantula
Mergui reddish brown tarantula

Chromatopelma (Eurypelma/Delopelma)
cyaneopubescens (Strand 1907)
Subfamily Theraphosinae

Greenbottle blue tarantula
Venezuelan green bottle-blue tarantula

Citharacanthus crinirufus (Valerio 1980)
Subfamily Theraphosinae
Costa Rican bluefront tarantula

Citharacanthus longipes (F.O.P.—
Cambridge 1897)
Subfamily Theraphosinae
Orangerump tarantula

Citharischius crawshayi (Pocock 1900)
Subfamily Eumenophorinae
Drumstick baboon tarantula
Kinani rusty-red baboon tarantula
King baboon tarantula

Coremiocnemis validus (Pocock 1895)
Subfamily Selenocosmiinae
Malaysian feather leg tarantula
Singapore brown tarantula
Singapore reddish brown tarantula

*Cyclosternum (Metriopelma/
Crypsidromus) fasciatum*
(F.O.P.—Cambridge 1902)
Subfamily Ischnocolinae
Costa Rican tiger abdomen tarantula
Costa Rican tiger rump döppel-ganger
tarantula
Costa Rican tigerrump tarantula
Costa Rican tiger tarantula
Döppel-ganger tarantula

Ephebopus murinus (Walckenaer 1837)
Subfamily Theraphosinae
Skeleton tarantula
Yellow flame knee tarantula

Eucratoscelus longiceps (Pocock
1898)
Subfamily Harpactirinae
African redrump tarantula
Feather leg baboon tarantula

Voi baboon tarantula
Voi red rump baboon tarantula

Eupalaestrus weijenberghi (Thorell
1894)
Subfamily Theraphosinae
Whitecollared tarantula

Hapalopus incei (F.O.P.—Cambridge
1898)
Subfamily Theraphosinae
Trinidad olive brown tarantula
Trinidad olive tarantula

Haplopelma (Melopoeus) albostriatum
(Simon 1886)
Subfamily Ornithoctoninae
Earth tiger tarantula
Edible birdeating tarantula
Lesser Thailand earth tiger tarantula
Lesser Thailand tiger tarantula
Thailand black tarantula
Thailand black velvet tarantula
Thailand earth tiger tarantula
Thailand edible tarantula
Thailand tiger tarantula
Thailand zebra tarantula
(In this complex of names, Siam,
Siamese, or Thai are sometimes used in
place of Thailand, making the potential
list four times as long!)

Haplopelma (Melopoeus) lividum (Smith
1996)
Subfamily Ornithoctoninae
Burmese blue bird spider
Cobalt blue tarantula

Haplopelma (Melopoeus) minax (Thorell
1897)
Subfamily Ornithoctoninae
Asian bird spider
Asian black tarantula
Asian zebra tarantula
Black velvet tarantula

Earth tiger tarantula
Lesser Thailand black birdeating
    tarantula
Thailand black tarantula
Thailand black velvet tarantula
Thailand earth tiger tarantula
Thailand tiger tarantula
Thailand zebra tarantula
Velvet tarantula
(As with *Haplopelma albostriatum* above,
Siam, Siamese, or Thai are sometimes
used in place of Thailand, making the
potential list even longer!)

Harpactira tigrina (Ausserer 1875)
Subfamily Harpactirinae
Golden baboon tarantula
Good hope yellow banded baboon
    tarantula

Heteroscodra maculata (Pocock
    1899)
Subfamily Eumenophorinae
Ornamental baboon tarantula
Togo starburst baboon tarantula
Togo starburst tarantula
Togo stout-hind legged starburst
    baboon tarantula

Hysterocrates crassipes (Pocock
    1897)
Subfamily Eumenophorinae
Cameroon brown tarantula
Cameroon mouse baboon tarantula

Hysterocrates ederi (Carpentier 1995)
Subfamily Eumenophorinae
Giant olive brown baboon tarantula

Hysterocrates gigas (Pocock 1897)
Subfamily Eumenophorinae
Cameroon red baboon tarantula
Cameroon red tarantula
Cameroon rusty baboon tarantula
Red baboon tarantula
Rusty baboon tarantula

Hysterocrates hercules (Pocock 1899)
Subfamily Eumenophorinae
African goliath tarantula
Giant olive brown baboon tarantula
Goliath baboon tarantula
Hercules baboon tarantula

Hysterocrates laticeps (Pocock 1897)
Subfamily Eumenophorinae
Cameroon rustred tarantula
Old calabar baboon tarantula

Iridopelma hirsuta (Pocock 1901)
Subfamily Aviculariinae
Fuzzy tree spider
Yellow banded birdeater
Yellow edged birdeater

Iridopelma zorodes (Mello-Leitão 1926)
Subfamily Aviculariinae
Bahia purple-red birdeater
Brazilian purple tarantula
Ecuadorian bird spider
Fuzzy bird spider

Ischnocolus hancocki (Smith 1990)
Subfamily Ischnocolinae
Larache gold tarantula

Lasiodora klugi (Koch 1842)
Subfamily Theraphosinae
Bahia scarlet birdeating tarantula
Bahia scarlet tarantula

Lasiodora parahybana (Mello-Leitão
    1917)
Subfamily Theraphosinae
Brazilian salmon tarantula
Campina Grande salmon pink bird
    spider
Salmon pink bird spider

Lasiodorides striatus (Schmidt and
    Antonelli 1996)
Subfamily Theraphosinae
Orange striped birdeater

Peruvian black birdeater
Peruvian striped birdeater
(This species, new to science, started out as *Pamphobeteus* "wallacei," an enthusiast- or dealer-generated pseudoscientific name. *Lasiodora* "wallacei" is another pseudoscientific name which is probably a synonym for this species. In 1996, the species was formally described and given the name *Pamphobeteus striatus* by Günter Schmidt. Shortly thereafter, it was again redescribed and placed in a new genus made specifically for it, *Lasiodorides,* again by Schmidt and Antonelli. As this book goes to press, the Committee on Common Names of Arachnids of the American Arachnological Society is considering an official common name for it.)

Megaphobema (Brachypelma/Euathlus)
  mesomelas (F.O.P.—Cambridge
  1902)
Subfamily Theraphosinae
Costa Rican orange knee
  tarantula
Costa Rican redleg tarantula

Metriopelma (Crypsidromus) zebrata
  (Banks 1909)
Subfamily Ischnocolinae
Bumble bee bum (i.e., "rump")
  tarantula
Costa Rican bumble bee tarantula
Costa Rican sun tiger abdomen
  tarantula
Costa Rican suntiger tarantula
Costa Rican tiger tarantula
Orange tiger abdomen tarantula

Mygalarachne (Sericopelma)
  rubronitens (Ausserer 1875)
Subfamily Theraphosinae
Giant red rump tarantula
Panama red rump tarantula

Ornithoctonus andersoni (Pocock 1892)
Subfamily Ornithoctoninae
Asian mahogany tarantula
Kawkereet mustard tarantula
Mergui reddish brown tarantula

Pamphobeteus antinous (Pocock
  1903)
Subfamily Theraphosinae
Bolivian bluelegged tarantula
Bolivian steely-blue legged bird spider

Pamphobeteus fortis (Ausserer 1875)
Subfamily Theraphosinae
Columbian brown tarantula
Columbian giant bird spider

Pamphobeteus insignis (Pocock 1903)
Subfamily Theraphosinae
Columbian purple bloom bird spider
Columbian purplebloom tarantula

Pamphobeteus melanocephalus
  (Mello-Leitão 1923)
Subfamily Theraphosinae
Brazilian striped bird spider
Paulo dark scarlet bird spider

Pamphobeteus ornatus (Pocock 1903)
Subfamily Theraphosinae
Columbian bird spider
Columbian pinkbloom tarantula
Columbian pinky-red bloom bird spider
Ornate bird spider

Pamphobeteus tetracanthus
  (Mello-Leitão 1923)
Subfamily Theraphosinae
Brazilian giant bird spider
São Paulo olive-brown bird spider

Paraphysa manicata (Simon 1892)
Subfamily Theraphosinae
Chilean copper tarantula
Chilean yellow rump tarantula
Dwarf rose tarantula

Phormictopus cancerides (Latreille
   1806)
Subfamily Theraphosinae
Haitian brown tarantula
Haitian curly hair tarantula
Haitian tarantula

Phormictopus nesiotes (Chamberlin
   1917)
Subfamily Theraphosinae
Cuban gold tarantula
Dominican Republic birdeater
Golden Cuban brown tarantula

Phrixotrichus (Grammostola) cala
   (Chamberlin 1917)
Subfamily Theraphosinae
Chilean beautiful tarantula
Chilean common tarantula
Chilean flame tarantula
Chilean pink tarantula
Chilean red back tarantula
Chilean rose tarantula
Flame tarantula
Rose tarantula
(*P. cala* is persistently confused with
P. spatulata by enthusiasts. *P. cala* is
rarely seen in the pet trade and the
hobby.)

Phrixotrichus (Grammostola) grandicola
   (Strand 1908)
Subfamily Theraphosinae
Common Negra gray tarantula

Phrixotrichus (Grammostola) grossa
   (Simon 1891)
Subfamily Theraphosinae
Pampas tawnyred tarantula

Phrixotrichus (Grammostola) iheringi
   (Keyserling 1891)
Subfamily Theraphosinae
Argentine black tarantula
Entre Rios tarantula

Phrixotrichus (Grammostola) pulchra
   (Mello-Leitão 1921)
Subfamily Theraphosinae
Brazilian black tarantula
Rio Grande do Sul black tarantula
Uruguay black tarantula

Phrixotrichus roseus (auratus)
   (Walckenaer 1837)
Subfamily Theraphosinae
Chilean rose tarantula
Chilean yellow rump tarantula
(*P. roseus* and *P. auratus* are probably
synonyms for the same species [Roewer
1942–1954]. Because *P. roseus* is the
senior name, it is used here.)

Phrixotrichus (Grammostola) spatulata
   (F.O.P.—Cambridge 1897)
Subfamily Theraphosinae
Beautiful Chile Tarantula
Chilean beautiful tarantula
Chilean common tarantula
Chilean flame tarantula
Chilean pink tarantula
Chilean red back tarantula
Chilean rose tarantula
Flame tarantula
Rose tarantula
(*P. cala* is persistently confused with *P.
spatulata* by enthusiasts. P. cala is rarely
seen in the pet trade and the hobby.)

Plesiopelma longisternale (Schiapelli
   and Gerschman 1942)
Subfamily Theraphosinae
Argentinean pygmy tarantula
Argentine pygmy pampas tarantula

Poecilotheria fasciata (Latreille
   1804)
Subfamily Selenocosmiinae
Sri Lankan ornamental black and white
   tree spider
Sri Lankan ornamental tarantula

Sri Lankan ornamental tree spider
Sri Lankan tree spider

Poecilotheria formosa (Pocock 1899)
Subfamily Selenocosmiinae
Ornamental tree spider
Salem ornamental tarantula

Poecilotheria metallica (Pocock 1899)
Subfamily Selenocosmiinae
Gooty ornamental tarantula
Ornamental Gooty plain leg tarantula

Poecilotheria ornata (Pocock 1899)
Subfamily Selenocosmiinae
Fringed ornamental tarantula
Ornate ornamental tree spider
Ornate tree spider
Sri Lankan ornate tree spider

Poecilotheria regalis (Pocock 1899)
Subfamily Selenocosmiinae
Indian ornamental black and white
    tarantula
Indian ornamental tarantula
Indian ornamental tree spider
Royal Indian tree spider
Royal ornamental tree spider

Poecilotheria smithi (Kirk)
Subfamily Selenocosmiinae
Ornamental tree spider
Yellow backed chocolate birdeater
Yellowbacked ornamental tarantula

Poecilotheria subfusca (Pocock 1895)
Subfamily Selenocosmiinae
Ivory ornamental tarantula
Sri Lankan ornamental ivory spot
    tarantula

Psalmopoeus cambridgei (Pocock
    1895)
Subfamily Selenocosmiinae
Chevron tarantula
Emerald tree spider

Orinoco tree spider
Trinidad chevron tarantula

Psalmopoeus irminia (Saager 1995)
Subfamily Selenocosmiinae
Chevron tarantula
Suntiger tarantula
Trinidad chevron tarantula
Venezuelan tiger tarantula

Pseudotheraphosa apophysis (Tinter
    1991)
False Brazilian goliath tarantula
False goliath tarantula
Goliath pinkfoot tarantula
Pink footed goliath tarantula

Pterinochilus affinis (Tullgren 1910)
Subfamily Harpactirinae
Highland baboon tarantula
Kilimanjaro sootblack tarantula
Kilimanjaro soot foot tarantula

Pterinochilus meridionalis (Hirst
    1907)
Subfamily Harpactirinae
Gray mustard baboon tarantula
Gray starburst baboon tarantula
Zambian baboon tarantula
Zambian gray baboon tarantula
Zambian gray tarantula
Zimbabwe grayish-yellow baboon
    spider
Zimbabwe gray tarantula

Pterinochilus murinus (Pocock 1897)
Subfamily Harpactirinae
Golden baboon tarantula
Golden monkey spider
Mombasa golden starburst baboon
    tarantula
**Mombasa golden starburst
    tarantula**
Mustard baboon tarantula
Starburst baboon tarantula
Sunburst baboon tarantula

Pterinochilus sjostedti (Tullgren 1910)
Subfamily Harpactirinae
Kilimanjaro baboon tarantula
Kilimanjaro mustard tarantula

Pterinochilus vorax (Gerstäcker 1873)
Subfamily Harpactirinae
East African lesser banded baboon
  spider
Lake Tanganyikan golden baboon
  tarantula
Lake Tanganyikan golden tarantula
(The authority is given as Pocock in one
work. The authors cannot confirm this.)

Selenocosmia javanensis (Walckenaer
  1837)
Subfamily Selenocosmiinae
Java yellow kneed tarantula
Javan yellowknee tarantula

Selenocosmia lanipes (Ausserer 1875)
Subfamily Selenocosmiinae
Mount Obie brown tarantula
Mount Obrie brown tarantula
New Guinea brown tarantula

Selenocosmia lyra (Strand 1913)
Subfamily Selenocosmiinae
Asian brown tarantula
Banda Kwala dark brown tarantula
New Guinea birdeater

Sphaerobothria hoffmanni (Karsch
  1879)
Subfamily Theraphosinae
Costa Rican horned tarantula
South American horned tarantula

Stromatopelma calceatum (Fabricius
  1793)
Subfamily Eumenophorinae
Feather leg baboon tarantula
Red featherleg tarantula
West African Feather Leg Baboon
  Tarantula

Tapenauchenius plumipes (Koch 1842)
Subfamily Aviculariinae
Olive tree spider
Trinidad mahogany brown tarantula
Trinidad mahogany tarantula

Theraphosa blondi (Latreille 1804)
Subfamily Theraphosinae
Brazilian goliath tarantula
Goliath birdeater tarantula
Goliath bird spider
(Colloquially, and even in many scientific
works, this tarantula is commonly called
Theraphosa leblondi; however, the "le"
part of the name is incorrect. When
Latreille first described the tarantula in
1804, his formal Latin description clearly
calls the tarantula *Mygale Blondii*. In a
subsequent informal description in
French, he called the tarantula *leblondi.*
[It was renamed to the genus *Theraphosa*
by Walckenaer in 1805.] By the rules of
priority, *blondi* is the official scientific
name with *leblondi* being a vernacular
pseudonym. [We extend our thanks to
Norman Platnick for his help with this.])

Vitalius roseus (Mello-Leitão 1923)
Subfamily Theraphosinae
Giant pink starburst bird spider
Giant pinkstarburst tarantula
Reddish bird spider

Xenesthis immanis (Ausserer 1875)
Subfamily Theraphosinae
Columbian lesserblack tarantula
Columbian purple bloom bird spider
Ecuadorian red-abdomen tarantula
Lesser black birdeating tarantula
Purple bloom bird spider

Xenesthis monstrosa (Pocock 1903)
Subfamily Theraphosinae
Columbian black birdeater
Columbian giantblack tarantula
Giant black birdeating tarantula

Appendix B
Bibliography

This is not an exhaustive list of all books and articles on tarantulas. The interested reader will find that most of these sources also contain bibliographies that will, in turn, point to still more references.

Many of the entries in this bibliography are not mentioned in the text. The reader is advised to peruse this bibliography carefully and refer to any articles, books, or periodicals that appear to hold the information sought. If the local library does not have the item that is required, it may be able to order it through an interlibrary loan program.

Nearly all of the periodicals mentioned here will continue to publish for many years to come. Those who are interested in keeping abreast of the field or are seeking more up-to-date information are advised to find current issues and the last several years' indexes.

Anderson, J. F. 1966. Excretia of spiders. *Comp. Biochem. Physiol.* 17: 973–982.

———. 1970. Metabolic rate of spiders. *Comp. Biochem. Physiol.* 33(1): 973–982.

Anderson, J. F., and K. N. Prestwich. 1975. The fluid pressure pumps of spiders (Chelicerata, Araneae). *Z. Morphol. Tiere.* 81:257–277.

———. 1982. Respiratory gas exchange in spiders. *Physiol. Zool.* 55:72–90.

———. 1985. The physiology of exercise at and above maximal aerobic capacity in theraphosid (tarantula) spiders, *Brachypelma smithi* (F. O. Pickard-Cambridge). *J. Comp. Physiol. B.* 155:529–539.

Apstein, C. 1889. Structure and function of spinning glands in Araneida. *J. Royal Microsc. Soc.* 1889:637–638.

Baerg, W. J. 1922. Regarding the habits of tarantulas and the effects of their poison. *Sci. Monthly.* 14:481–488.

———. 1925. The effects of the venom of some supposedly poisonous arthropods of the Canal Zone. *Animals Ent. Soc. Am.* 18:471–478.

———. 1926. Regeneration in the tarantula *Eurypelma californica* Auser. *Annals Ent. Soc. Am.* 19:512–513.

———. 1928. The life cycle and mating habits of the male tarantula. *Quart. Review Biol.* 3(1):109–116.

———. 1929. Some poisonous arthropods of North and Central America. *Trans. IV Int. Cong. Ent.* II:418–438.

———. 1938a. Tarantula studies. *Jour. N. Y. Ent. Soc.* 46:31–43.

———. 1938b. The poisons of scorpions and spiders—Their effect and treatment. *Nat. Hist. Mag.* June.

———. 1958. *The Tarantula.* Lawrence: University Kansas Press. (Father of tarantula books. Out of print and hard to find.)

_____. 1963. Tarantula life history records. *Jour. N. Y. Ent. Soc.* 71:223–238.

_____. 1970. A note on the longevity and molt cycle of two tropical theraphosids. *Bull. Brit. Arachnol. Soc.* 1:107–108.

Barnes, R. D. 1980. *Invertebrate Zoology*. Philadelphia, Pennsylvania: Saunders College/Holt Reinhart and Winston.

Bates, H. W. 1910. *Naturalist on the River Amazons*. London: John Murray Press.

Baxter, R. N. 1993. *Keeping and Breeding Tarantulas*. Ilford, Essex, England: Chudleigh Publishing. (Excellent photography. One of the better enthusiast books.)

Blackwelder, R. E. 1963. *Classification of the Animal Kingdom*. Carbondale: Southern Illinois Univ. Press.

Blaker, A. A. 1976. *Field Photography, Beginning and Advanced Techniques.* San Francisco: W. H. Freeman and Company.

Bonnet, P. 1930. La mue, l'autotomie et la régénération chez les Araignées, avec une étudè des Dolomèdes d'Europe. *Bull. Soc. Hist. Nat. Toulouse.* 59:237.

Bonnet, P. 1945–1961. *Bibliographia Araneorum*. 7 vols., Toulouse (Independent). (In French. Includes exhaustive listing of all scientific papers dealing with spiders through 1938 and most others through 1945. Includes one comprehensive classification system.)

Breene, R. G. 1995. *Common Names of Arachnids*. South Padre Island, Texas: American Tarantula Society. Subsequent printings list this as *Common Names of Arachnids, 1995.*

Breene, R. G., et al. 1996. *Tarantulas of Texas. Their Medical Importance, and World-wide Bibliography to the Thera-*phosidae (Araneae). Artesia, New Mexico: American Tarantula Society.

Brett, C. (producer) 1993. *Giant Spiders of the Lost World*. Survival Anglia, Summit Television. (Excellent photography.)

_____. 1994. *Giant Tarantulas*. Survival Anglia, Summit Television. Essentially identical to Brett 1993. Reissued by Time-Warner Communications.

Brignoli, P. M. 1983. *A Catalogue of the Araneae Described Between 1940 and 1981*. Dover, New Hampshire: Manchester University Press.

Brodie, D. B., Jr. 1989. *Venomous Animals*. Golden Press. Racine, Wisconsin: Western Publishing Company, Inc.

Browning, J. G. 1981. *Tarantulas*. Neptune City, New Jersey: T. F. H. Publications.

Bücherl, W., et al. 1968-1971. Spiders. *Venomous Animals and Their Venoms*. 3 vols. N.Y.: Academic Press. III:197–301.

Buchsbaum, R. 1948. *Animals Without Backbones*. Chicago: University of Chicago Press.

Buckley, S. B. 1962. The tarantula (*Mygale hentzi* Girard) and its destroyer (*Pompilus formosus* Say). *Proc. Ent. Soc. Phila.* 1:138–139.

Burdette, W. (editor). 1974. *Invertebrate Endocrinology and Hormonal Heterophylly*. N.Y.: Springer-Verlag.

Butler, W. H., and B. Y. Main. 1961. Predation on vertebrates by mygalomorph spiders. *West Australian Naturalist*, 7:52.

Butt, A. G., and H. H. Taylor. 1991. The function of spider coxal organs: Effects of feeding and salt-loading on *Porrhothele antipodiana* (Mygalomorpha: Dipluridae). *J. Exp. Biol.* 158: 439–461.

Caras, R. 1974. *Venomous Animals of the World*. Englewood Cliffs, N.J.: Prentice-Hall. (Interesting pictures.)

Carroll, G., D. Giler, and W. Hill (producers). 1979. *Alien*. Twentieth Century Fox Film Corporation. (This would be one of the best sci-fi horror films of all time except that it contains no tarantulas! See also Carroll et al., 1986, and Swerdlow et al., 1992.)

Carroll, G., D. Giler, and W. Hill (executive producers), Gale Ann Hurd (producer). 1986. *Aliens*. Twentieth Century Fox Film Corporation. (See also Carroll et al., 1979, and Swerdlow et al., 1992.)

Castro, F. F. M., M. A. Antila, and J. Croce. 1995. Occupational allergy caused by urticating hair of Brazilian spider. *J. Allergy Clin. Immunol.* 96(6):1282–1285.

Cazier, M. A., and M. A. Mortenson. 1964. Bionomical observations on the tarantula hawk wasps and their prey (Hymenoptera: Pompilidae: *Pepsis*). *Ann. Ent. Soc. Am.* 57:533–541.

Chang, P. C. T., H. K. Soong, and J. M. Barnett. 1991. Corneal penetration by tarantula hairs. *British Journal of Ophthalmology*. 75(4):253–254.

Charpentier, P. 1992. The Genus Avicularia. *Exothermae*. 1(1):1–52. Middlekerke, Belgium.

Cloudsley-Thompson, J. L. 1967. The water-relations of scorpions and tarantulas from the Sonoran Desert. *Entomologist's Monthly Magazine*. 103:216–220.

_____. 1968. *Spiders, Scorpions, Centipedes, and Mites*. London: Pergamon Press.

Comstock, H., and W. Gertsch. 1948. *The Spider Book*. Ithaca, NY: Cornell University.

Cook, J. A. L. 1972. Stinging hairs: a tarantula's defense. *Fauna, The Zoological Magazine*. 4:48.

Cook, J. A. L., V. D. R. Roth, and F. H. Miller. 1972. The urticating hairs of theraphosid spiders. *Am. Mus. Novitates*, #2498. (Very good article. Types of bristles vs. tarantula species. Some insights into habits and behavior.)

David, A. 1987. *Tarantulas: A Complete Introduction*. Neptune City, New Jersey: T. F. H. Publications.

de Vosjoli, P. 1991. *Arachnomania. The General Care and Maintenance of Tarantulas & Scorpions*. Lakeside, California: Advanced Aquarium Systems.

Den Otter, D. J. 1974. Setiform sensilla and prey detection in the bird spider *Sericopelma rubronitons* Ausserer (Araneae, Theraphosidae). *Neth. Jour. Zool.* 24(3):219–235.

Dodge, N. N. 1947. *Poisonous Dwellers of the Desert*. Gila Pueblo, Globe, Arizona: Southwest Parks and Monuments Association. (Many reprintings and new editions.)

Downes, M. F. 1987. A proposal for standardization of the terms used to describe the early development of spiders, based on a study of *Theridion rufipes* Lucas (Araneae: Theridiidae). *Bull. British Arachnol. Soc.* 7:187–193.

Eastman Kodak Company. 1969a. *Close-up Photography*. Rochester, NY. Publication number N-12A.

_____. 1969b. *Photomacrography*. Rochester, NY. Publication number N-12B.

_____. 1970a. *Photography Through the Microscope*. Rochester, NY. Publication number P-2.

_____. 1970b. *Basic Scientific Photography*. Rochester, NY. Publication number N-9.

Elliott, D. 1996. Hypoaspis *(Hypoaspis miles)*. Fungus gnat and thrips predatory mite. *Biological Control Manual*.

Applied Bio-nomics Ltd., 11074 West Saanich Rd., Sidney, British Columbia, Canada V8L 5P5.

Ellis, C. H. 1944. The mechanism of extension in the legs of spiders. *Biol. Bull.* 96:41.

Exline, H., and A. Petrunkevitch. 1939. List of species. Suborder Mygalomorphae. Catalogue of American spiders. Part One. *Trans. Conn. Acad. Art. Sci.* New Haven. 33:191–338.

Favre, D. S. 1989. *International Trade in Endangered Species*. Martinus Nijhoff Publ. Dordecht, The Netherlands.

Firstman, B. 1954. Central nervous system, musculature and segmentation of the cephalothorax of a tarantula *Eurypelma. Microentomology*. 19:14–40.

Foelix, R. F. 1979. *Biologie der Spinnen*. Georg Thieme Verlag. Stuttgart, Germany. (German edition.)

_____. 1982. *Biology of Spiders*. Cambridge, Massachusetts: Harvard University Press. (English edition.)

Gertsch, W. J. 1979. *American Spiders*. New York: Van Nostrand Reinholde Company.

Gertsch, W. J., and H. K. Wallace. 1936. Notes on new and rare American Mygalomorph spiders. *Am. Mus. Novitates*. 884:1–12.

Ghiretti-Magaldi, A., and G. Tamino. 1977. Evolutionary studies on hemocyanin. *Structure and Function of Haemocyanin*. J. W. Bannister, ed. Berlin: Springer-Verlag.

Gould, S. J. 1989. *Wonderful Life, the Burgess Shale and the Nature of History*. New York: W. W. Norton and Co., Inc.

Gurley, R. 1995. *A Color Guide to Tarantulas of the World,* books I and II. Ada, Oklahoma: Russ Gurley and Living Art.

Hadley, N. F. 1970. Micrometeorology and energy exchange in two desert arthropods. *Ecology*. 51(3):434–444.

Hancock, K., and J. Hancock. 1992. *Tarantulas: Keeping and Breeding Arachnids in Captivity*. Somerset, England: R & A Publishing, Limited.

Hemley, G. 1988. International wildlife trade. *Audubon Wildlife Report 1988/1989*. San Diego: Academic Press.

Hered, R. W., A. G. Spaulding, J. J. Sanitato, and A. H. Wander. 1988. Ophthalmia nodosa caused by tarantula hairs. *Ophthalmology*. 95(2):166–169.

Kaston, B. J., and E. Kaston. 1953. *How to Know the Spiders*. Dubuque, Iowa: Wm. C. Brown Company. (Very good, though rather technical, general book about spiders. Many reprintings.)

Levi, H. W., and L. R. Levi. 1968. *Spiders and Their Kin*. Racine, Wisconsin: Golden Press. Western Publishing Company, Inc. (Exceptionally good, general interest book about spiders. Many reprintings and copyright renewals.)

Lincoln, R. J., and G. A. Boxshall. 1987. *The Cambridge Illustrated Dictionary of Natural History*. Cambridge, England.

Linné, C. 1758. *Systemae Naturae . . .,* 10th ed., revised. Laurentii Salvii. Stockholm. (Linné published the first edition in 1735 and the twelfth and last edition in 1768. This tenth edition is the foundation for modern taxonomy.)

Linzen, B., et al. 1985. The structure of arthropod hemocyanin. *Science*. 229(4713):519–529.

Livingston, J. A. 1981. *The Fallacy of Wildlife Conservation*. McClelland and Stewart. Toronto. (Required reading for anyone propounding evangelistic ecologism.)

Loewe, R., R. Schmid, and B. Linzen. 1977. Subunit association and oxygen binding properties in spider hemocyanins. *Structure and Function of*

Haemocyanin. J. W. Bannister, ed. Berlin: Springer-Verlag.

Lund, D. 1977. *All About Tarantulas*. Neptune City, New Jersey: T. F. H. Publications.

Manton, S. M. 1958. Hydrostatic pressure and leg extension in arthropods with special reference to arachnids. *Ann. Mag. Natur. Hist.* 13(1):161–182.

Maratić, Z. 1967. Venom of an East African orthognath spider. *Animal Toxins*. F. E. Russel and P. R. Saunders, eds. New York: Pergamon Press.

Marples, B. J. 1967. The spinnerets and epiandrous glands of spiders. *J. Linn. Soc. (Zool.)*. 46(310):209–221, 1 plate.

Marshall, S. D. 1996. *Tarantulas and Other Arachnids*. Hauppauge, New York: Barron's Educational Series, Inc.

_____. 1997. Home is where the hole is. *Forum Magazine*. Artesia, New Mexico: American Tarantula Society.

McKee, A. W. 1984a. *Tarantula Observations, A Guide to Breeding. Vol. 1*. Kenmore, Washington: Tarantula Ranch Press.

_____. 1984b. *Tarantula Observations, A Guide to Breeding. Vol. 2*. Kenmore, Washington: Tarantula Ranch Press.

_____. 1986. *Tarantula Observations, A Guide to Breeding. Vol. 3. Breeders Digest*. Kenmore, Washington: Tarantula Ranch Press.

Meglitsch, P. A. 1972. *Invertebrate Zoology, Second Edition*. New York: Oxford University Press.

Melchers, M. 1964. Zur Biologie der Vogelspinnen (Fam. Aviculariidae). *Z. Morph. Ökel. Tiere*. 53:517.

Mello-Leitão, M. D. 1921. On the Genus *Grammostola,* Simon. *Ann. Mag. Natur. Hist.* Ser. 9, 7:293–305.

Mérian M. S. 1771. *Histoire générale des Insectes de Surinam et de toute l'Europe . . .* third edition. Paris. 1:18, plate xviii. [3 volumes]. (This is the last of several editions of this work.)

Meyers, N. 1979. *The Sinking Ark*. Oxford, England: Pergamon Press.

Minch, E. W. 1977. The behavioral biology of the tarantula *Aphonopelma chalcodes. Dissertation Abstracts International*. 78(2).

_____. 1978. Daily activity patterns in the tarantula *Aphonopelma chalcodes* Chamberlin. *Bull. Br. Arachnol. Soc.* 4(5):231–237.

_____. 1979a. Burrow plugging behavior in the tarantula *Aphonopelma chalcodes* Chamberlin (Araneae: Theraphosidae). *Bull. Br. Arachnol. Soc.* 4(9):414–415.

_____. 1979b. Reproductive behavior of the tarantula *Aphonopelma chalcodes* Chamberlin (Araneae: Theraphosidae). *Bull. Br. Arachnol. Soc.* 4(9):416–420.

O'Brien, M. R. 1997. Raising North American tarantula spiderlings. *Forum Magazine*. 6(1):20–22. Artesia, New Mexico: American Tarantula Society.

Palisot de Beauvois, A. M. F. J. *Insectes recuellis en Afrique et en Amérique dans les royaumes d'Oware et de Benin à Saint-Domingue et dans les Etats-Unis pendant les années 1786–1797*. Paris. Pp. 1–276, 91 plates. (Spiders, pp. 71, 72, 134, 135, plates I and III.)

Parrish, H. M. 1959. Deaths due to bites and stings of venomous animals and insects in the United States. *A. M. A. Archives on Internal Medicine*. Vol. 104, August.

Parry, D. A, and R. H. J. Brown. 1959. The hydraulic mechanism of the spider leg. *Jour. Exp. Biol.* 36(2):423–433.

Paul, R. J. 1992. Gas exchange, circulation, and energy metabolism in Arachnids. *Physiological Adaptions in Vertebrates. Respiration, Circulation,* and *Metabolism*. S. C. Wood, R. E. Weber, A. R. Hargens, and R. W. Millard, eds. New York, Basel, Hong Kong: Marcel Dekker, Inc.

Paul, R. J., T. Fincke, and B. Linzen. 1987. Respiration in the tarantula *Eurypelma californicum:* Evidence for diffusion lungs. *J. Comp. Physiol. B.* 157:209–217.

Perrero, L., and L. Perrero. 1979. *Tarantulas in Nature and as Pets*. Miami, Florida: Windward Publishing.

Petrunkevitch, A. 1911. Sense of sight, courtship, and mating in Dugesiella hentzi (Girard), a theraphosid spider from Texas. *Zoologische Jahrbücher* 31:355-376, plates 1–9.

_____. 1926. Tarantula versus tarantula-hawk: a study in instinct. *Jour. Exp. Biol.* 45(2):367–397.

_____. 1928. Systema aranearum. *Trans. Conn. Acad. Sci.* 29:1–270.

_____. 1952. The spider and the wasp. *Sci. Am.* 187:20–23.

Petrunkevitch, A., et al. 1939. Catalogue of American spiders. Part One. *Trans. Conn. Acad. Sci.* 33:133–338.

Platnick, N. 1971. The evolution of courtship behavior in spiders. *Bull. Br. Arachnol. Soc.* 2(3):40–47.

_____. 1989. *Advances in Spider Taxonomy 1981–1987*. Manchester, England and New York: Manchester Univeristy Press.

Pocock, R. I. 1900. The great Indian spiders. The Genus Poecilotheria: its habits, history and species. *Journal of the Bombay Natural History Society*. Bombay. 13:121–133, 1 plate.

Prestwich, K. N. 1983. Anaerobic metabolism in spiders. *Physiol. Zool.* 56:112–121.

Rao, K. P., and T. Gopalakrishnareddy. 1962. Nitrogen excretion in arachnids. *Comp. Biochem. Physiol.* 7:175–178.

Raven, R. J. 1985. The spider infraorder Mygalomorphae (Araneae): Cladistics and systematics. *Bull. Am. Mus. Nat. Hist.* 185(1):1–180.

_____. 1986. A cladistic reassessment of mygalomorph spider families (Araneae). *Proc. IX Internat. Cong. Arachnol., Panama 1983.* Smithsonian Institution Press. Pp. 223–227.

Roewer, C. F. 1942–1954. *Katalog der Araneae von 1758 bis 1940.* Kommissions-Verlag von "Natura." Bremen. (In German. Lists most synonyms for spiders' scientific names.)

_____. 1963. Araneina: Orthognatha, Labidognatha. *Insects of Micronesia*. Bernice P. Bishop Museum/Honolulu. 3(4):105–132.

Savory, T. H. 1928. *The Biology of Spiders*. London: Sidgewick and Jackson. (Out of date, but still informative.)

_____. 1964. *Arachnida*. New York: Academic Press. (Good overview of arachnids, but very little on tarantulas.)

_____. 1977. *Arachnida*. New York: Academic Press. (Revision of the 1964 edition. Both are listed here because of important changes.)

Schartau, W., and T. Leidescher. 1983. Composition of the hemolymph of the tarantula *Eurypelma californicum. J. Comp. Physiol. B.* 152:73–77.

Schmidt-Nielsen, K. 1975. *Animal Physiology*. New York: Cambridge University Press.

Schultz, S. A. 1984. *The Tarantula Keeper's Guide*. New York: Sterling Publishing. (The original edition of the present work.)

Schultz, S. A., and M. J. Schultz. 1997a. Of baby spiders & baby food jars. *Forum Magazine*. Artesia, New Mexico: American Tarantula Society.

_____. *The Mechanical Mom.* Artesia, New Mexico: American Tarantula Society (in preparation).

Schwartz, H. F. 1921. Spider myths of the American Indians. *Natural History, J. Am. Mus. Nat. Hist.* New York. 21:382-385.

Simon E. 1892. *Histoire naturelle des Araignées. Deuxième édition. Encyclopedique de Roret.* Paris. 1:1–256, 215 figures. (2 volumes in 8 books.)

_____. 1903. *Histoire naturelle des Araignées.* Paris. 2(4):669–1080, figures 793–1117. (2 volumes in 8 books.)

Slama, K., and C. M. Williams. 1965. The juvenile hormone v. sensitivity of the bug *Pyrrocoris apterus* to a hormonally active factor in American paper-pulp. *Biol. Bull.* 130:235–246.

Smith, A. M. 1985. *The Tarantula.* London, England: Fitzgerald Publishing.

_____. 1986. *How to Keep Tarantulas.* London, England: Fitzgerald Publishing.

_____. 1990. *Baboon Spiders. Tarantulas of Africa and the Middle East.* London, England: Fitzgerald Publishing.

_____. 1994. *Tarantulas of the USA and Mexico.* London, England: Fitzgerald Publishing.

Smith, C. P. 1908. A preliminary study of the Araneae Theraphosidae of California. *Ent. Soc. Am.* 1(4):207–249.

Snodgrass, R. E. 1952. *A Textbook of Arthropod Anatomy.* Ithaca, NY: Comstock. (At least one other edition was published in 1967.)

Stanhke, H. L., and B. D. Johnson. 1967. *Aphonopelma* tarantula venom. *Animal Toxins.* F. E. Russel and P. R. Saunders, eds. New York: Pergamon Press.

Stewart, D. M., and A. W. Martin. 1974. Blood pressure in the tarantula, *Dugesiella hentzi. J. Comp. Physiol.* 88:141–172.

Swerdlow, E. (executive producer), Carrol, G., D. Giler, and W. Hill (producers). 1992. *Alien[3].* Twentieth Century Fox Film Corporation. (See also Carroll et al., 1992, and Carroll et al., 1986.)

Turbang, P. 1993. *Guide de Mygales.* Delachaux et Niestlé. Lausanne, Switzerland.

Webb, A. 1992. *The Proper Care of Tarantulas.* Neptune City, New Jersey: T. F. H. Publications.

West, R. C. 1995. Mighty mites. *British Tarantula Society Journal.* 10(3):86–88.

Williams, F. X. 1956. Life history studies of *Pepsis* and *Hemipepsis* wasps in California (Hymenoptera: Pompilidae). *Ann. Ent. Soc. Am.* 49:447–466.

Wood, F. D. 1926. Autotomy in Arachnida. *Jour. Morph. Phys.* 42:143–195.

Wood-Mason J. 1875. [Stridulation of a theraphosid]. *Journal and Proceedings of the Asiatic Society of Bengal.* Calcutta. 1875:197.

World Wildlife Fund. 1986. *TRAFFIC (U.S.A.). Wildlife Trade Factsheets.* Washington, D. C.

Zoological Record. Zoological Society of London. London, England. (Exhaustive listing of all zoological taxonomic papers. Arranged by taxonomic group. Refer to the sections on Arachnids. Published annually.)

Index

284

This *Avicularia* species, probably *juruensis,* has also been sold in the pet industry as *A. magdalenae* with the common name of Brazilian yellowbanded tarantula.